Nixon Rebuilds

Nixon Rebuilds

From Defeat to the
White House, 1962–1968

JOHN DAVID BRILEY

McFarland & Company, Inc., Publishers
Jefferson, North Carolina

This book has undergone peer review.

LIBRARY OF CONGRESS CATALOGUING-IN-PUBLICATION DATA

Names: Briley, John David, 1955– author.
Title: Nixon rebuilds : from defeat to the White House 1962-1968 / John David Briley.
Other titles: From defeat to the White House 1962–1968
Description: Jefferson, North Carolina : McFarland & Company, Inc., Publishers, 2021 | Includes bibliographical references and index.
Identifiers: LCCN 2021016762 | ISBN 9781476683881 (paperback : acid free paper) ∞
ISBN 9781476643069 (ebook)
Subjects: LCSH: Nixon, Richard M. (Richard Milhous), 1913–1994. | Political campaigns—United States—History—20th century. | Political culture—United States—History—20th century. | United States—Politics and government—1961–1963. | United States—Politics and government—1963–1969. | Presidents—United States—Election—1968. | Presidents—United States—Biography. | BISAC: HISTORY / United States / 20th Century | POLITICAL SCIENCE / American Government / Executive Branch
Classification: LCC E856 .B725 2021 | DDC 973.924092—dc23
LC record available at https://lccn.loc.gov/2021016762

BRITISH LIBRARY CATALOGUING DATA ARE AVAILABLE

ISBN (print) 978-1-4766-8388-1
ISBN (ebook) 978-1-4766-4306-9

Front cover image: Nixon waves from his golf cart on August 12, 1968, the week after the 1968 Republican Convention in Mission Bay, California (Richard M. Nixon Foundation)

Printed in the United States of America

*McFarland & Company, Inc., Publishers
Box 611, Jefferson, North Carolina 28640
www.mcfarlandpub.com*

Table of Contents

Acknowledgments

I would have never completed this book without the help of a lot of individuals. I want to say up front if I left you out, it was not on purpose. At East Tennessee State University (ETSU), where I teach, there are several people who I want to thank. Both of my chairs in the political science department, Weixing Chen and Andy Battista, were solidly behind me in this research. Bert Bach, the recently retired provost of the university, was very generous in his support. Another colleague and friend, Joe Corso, who died in 2013, was extremely interested in my research on Richard Nixon. I want to give a particular thanks to Steve Fritz, one of the most prominent scholars on the German/Soviet battles of World War II. Steve has listened to my many Nixon stories over the past decade. He also has read over several chapters and suggested changes to make the manuscript better. I cannot thank him enough. Also, from our department, Jayme Davis helped me better organize the manuscript. I need to thank graduate students Will Richter, Jessi Stevens, and Amy Aubrey with help on various aspects of this research. I also need to give a shout-out to another former student, John Milstead, who looked at the George Romney papers for me while working on his doctorate at Michigan State. Two others not at ETSU helped me much in this project. Grete Scott, at Milligan College, did an excellent job of stylistic editing on the first draft. Earl (Butch) Tilford, a recently retired history professor, now living in Alabama, spent several hours marking up, reworking, and making recommendations on the manuscript. He did a superb job.

I initially wanted to write a book on the 1960 election. It was in the 2007–08 period. I did some preliminary research on what had been written and what I thought had been left out. I wanted to find out what had happened in the voting irregularities in Illinois and Texas during the election. I knew Earl Mazo had written several articles after the election, but Nixon told him to stop. I made some inquiries about Mazo's papers on the subject but got nowhere. In January 2010, I went to Southern California to attend the national college football championship. While there, I visited the Richard M. Nixon Museum and Library. It was my second visit to the museum, the first nearly twenty years earlier in 1991. I was introduced to Gregory Cumming, who supervised the archives there. He told me about a new collection of Nixon material that was going to be released in the summer of 2010 about the former president's wilderness period. Greg said that this was the one area of Nixon scholarship that no one had written. He sold me right then. I came back in August of that year for two weeks wading through the boxes and boxes of wilderness material. I came back to the Nixon Library three more times after that, collecting loads of primary documents. Each time, the staff was accommodating. I want to thank Greg, especially for all the things he has done to assist me in this endeavor. All the phone calls, emails, and introductions to famous "Nixon people" have immensely helped me.

I want to single out Ryan Pettigrew and Pamela Eisenberg at the Nixon Library for special thanks. Olivia Anastasiades, Carla Braswell, and Dorissa Martinez were also very eager to help me at the library. While at the Nixon Library, I met Paul Carter. Paul is a native California lawyer who created the "Nixon Map." He introduced me to the oral histories at California State Fullerton done by Nixon's contemporaries who grew up with the former president. I also want to thank Irwin (Irv) Gellman for special assistance in this project. Irv is probably the most knowledgeable Nixon expert in the United States. Any time I needed help on where to look for certain aspects of this project, he was very accommodating. Jason Schwartz of the Nixon Foundation was a great contributor to photographs.

The contributions of the Nixon alumni greatly enhanced this book. Pat Buchanan and Dwight Chapin are at the top of this distinguished list. During this period, Pat has written two books on the subject, and Dwight is busy at work on his remembrances of Nixon. Pat has been gracious and patient with my numerous emails and visits to his home in Northern Virginia. He also gave me access to all his memos from 1966 to 1968. His wife, Shelley, has also been very kind to me as well as a great information source on the former president. Her time with Nixon goes back to his days as vice president. Dwight has been very generous in his assistance and insight on Nixon. Geoff Shepard is another Nixon alumnus who has contributed a great deal to this project. He has also written two books on the Watergate investigation. John Whitaker, Bill Gavin, and Ray Price helped me a great deal before their untimely deaths during this period. All spoke with me for three hours and provided great insight on Nixon. Whitaker also gave me oral histories he had compiled of Nixon alumni. After talking to Price for nearly three hours, he even took me on the roof of his New York apartment building with a great view of the city. Ed Nixon, the younger brother of the former president, talked with me on three occasions on his remembrances. We lost Ed just last year. I also had a good conversation with John Sears in 2017 about his time with Nixon/Mudge, the 1968 campaign, and comparisons with Ronald Reagan. John died earlier this year. There were also interviews with Steve Bull, Neal Freeman, Tom Charles Huston, Craig Shirley, Kenneth Khachigan, Robert Odle, Aram Bakshian, Lee Huebner, Steve Hess, Sandy Quinn, and Bobbie Kilberg. I also need to thank Francis X. (Joe) Maloney for his assistance. Maloney was a lawyer from the John Mitchell firm that merged with Nixon/Mudge in 1967.

Finally, I need to thank all the people from the various archives and libraries that helped me. These include Barbara Cline of the Lyndon Johnson Library, Warren Finch of the George H.W. Bush Library, James Neel of the Gerald Ford Library, Chris Abraham and Chalsea Millner at the Dwight Eisenhower Library, Kurt Graham and Sam Rushay from the Harry Truman Library, Erica Fugger from the Center for Oral History at Columbia University, Monica Blank from the Rockefeller Archives, Kevin Leonard at Northwestern University, and Steve Davis at the Vanderbilt Television News Archives. I also need to thank James Rosen for giving me access to his research on John Mitchell, Nixon's former law partner and attorney general. James also gave me a new understanding of the Nixon/Mitchell relationship. Prominent Reagan author Craig Shirley shared his expertise about Nixon, Reagan, and the last seventy-five years of Republican Party politics. Craig was accommodating in all endeavors. At the end of this project, I exchanged several illuminating emails with outstanding Nixon scholar Luke Nichter. Luke has a biography on Henry Cabot Lodge coming out this fall.

Last, but certainly not least, I want to thank my wife, Susan, for her understanding and patience for listening to all things relating to Nixon. I could have never completed this without her.

Abstract

This book fills an important gap in the Nixon literature. This period is not merely filler between two major episodes of his life, but the essential backstory that explains his extraordinary comeback. This amounted to nothing less than a Lazarus-like achievement, for Nixon's winning the presidency in 1968 was, in its own way, as extraordinary and improbable as the triumph of Donald Trump in 2016. Then, as today, it took an unusual conjunction of circumstances for this unlikely event to occur. While most of the books written about Nixon focus on "big things," like the 1960 and 1968 presidential elections and Watergate, Nixon could never have been elected president in 1968 without his contributions to the mid-term elections of 1966. He emerged as the critical political figure that rebuilt the Republican Party after the disastrous 1964 presidential election, and was arguably the one person in the party who could appeal to all its political factions.

Through heavy reliance on primary sources and oral interviews as well as secondary sources like books and newspaper accounts, this book explores the process by which Nixon reinvented himself during the dark days of the mid–1960s as well as Nixon's insights into how America was changing. The period between 1962 and 1968 served as a laboratory for rebirth. Nixon's reemergence was a dynamic process, and that dynamism was one key to Nixon's political evolution. He realized some important things along the way: how to bridge the gap between Goldwater conservatives and moderate Republicans; how the temper, mood, and tenor of large sections of the American public were moving against the Democrats; and how one presidential candidate could take advantage of this. This is the unknown Nixon, a far more human Nixon than the Herblock caricature of a shady political figure who would do anything to win. Written in chronological fashion, covering Nixon's circling of the political arena from November 1962 to November 1968, the story begins with his last press conference after losing the California governor's election in 1962 and ends with his presidential victory in 1968. No political prognosticator in the country would have guessed that after "the last press conference" in 1962, Richard Nixon would be elected president of the United States. This book describes how Nixon accomplished the unimaginable.

Prologue

In what was purported to be his last press conference, on November 7, 1962, following his stunning loss in the California gubernatorial election, an embittered and disconsolate Richard Nixon lashed out at the press, which he blamed for his defeat, in his now well-known statement, "You don't have Nixon to kick around anymore, because, gentlemen, this is my last press conference."[1] While using the remark over the years as an example of what is typically seen as Nixon's "sore loser" nature, or as a derogatory observation on his later career, most commentators miss the key point: given the context of the time, it did indeed appear as if Richard Nixon's political career had ended. In fact, though, the contrary was true: the most salient events of his political life were yet to come.

In thinking about Richard M. Nixon, and attempting to cut through the fog of myth created by both historians and political scientists—the darkness and gloom of Nixon, for example, as against the brightness and charm of John F. Kennedy, his successful opponent in the contested 1960 election—visualize two images. The first could be represented by a pie chart of the 1960 election results. In the narrowest of election triumphs, Kennedy won 49.72 percent of the 68,832 votes cast, while Nixon secured 49.55 percent. This meant that Nixon had lost by an incredible .16 percent with his margin of defeat less than 1 percent in six states (Hawaii, Illinois, Missouri, California, New Mexico, and New Jersey) that totaled ninety-five electoral votes. In two of those states, Illinois and Missouri, along with Texas, where the losing margin was 2 percent, the Nixon campaign raised campaign allegations of widespread voter fraud, later largely unsubstantiated in the case of Illinois and Texas, that would have provided the necessary margin of victory in the Electoral College. And this, moreover, at a time when 20 percent more American voters self-identified as Democrats than as Republicans. Visualize, as well, a less public, more intimate view of the presidential election of 1960. Amazingly, just a week or so before the Democratic Party convention, both Democratic leaders of Congress, Speaker of the House Sam Rayburn and Senate Majority Leader Lyndon Johnson (who later served on the Democratic ticket with Kennedy), met with President Dwight Eisenhower and pleaded with him to do something to prevent Kennedy's nomination, since they considered him a "threat to the nation."[2] Admittedly, in Johnson's case, this might be seen as an example of a political rival seeking improper outside aid to secure the Democratic nomination as Johnson had not actively campaigned in the Democratic primaries, thus largely eliminating any possibility of his winning the nomination.

The second image would be the end of his life and would focus on the long lines of people—estimated by some sources as anywhere from 30,000 to 50,000

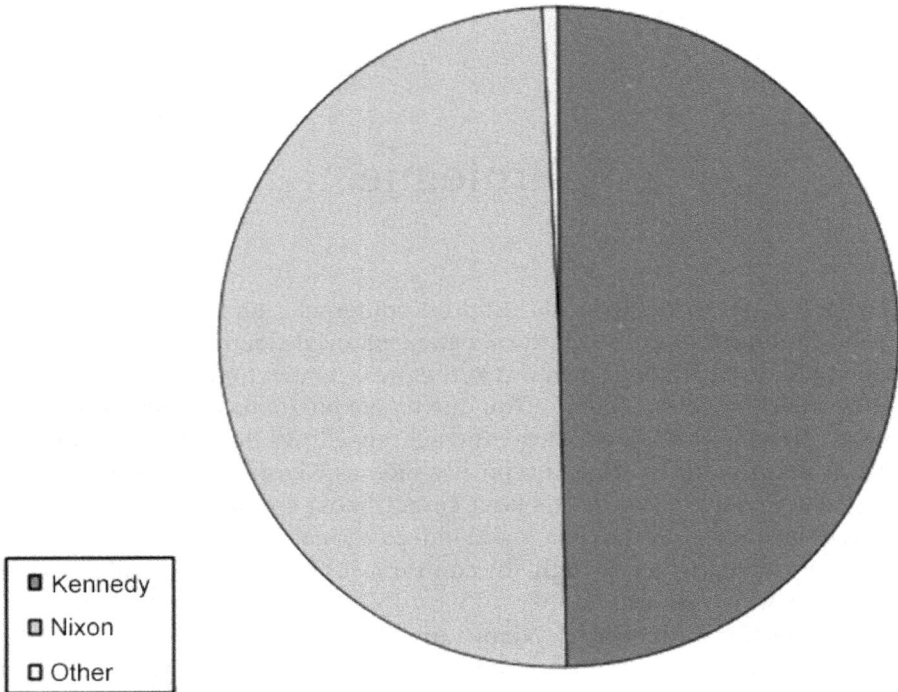

Pie chart of 1960 presidential election.

people—who in late April 1994 stood for hours in "a steady, drenching rain" to view his coffin. Just as the line began to inch forward, hail began to fall. Along the route of the funeral procession, thousands more people, on overpasses and front lawns, disregarded the downpour and responded to Nixon's last journey by giving the two-fingered "V for victory" signal. If he was indeed the unpopular, hated villain of the caricature, why were so many people standing in line to show their affection and respect for the former president? One possible answer came from Margaret Howard, who had cast her vote for the Eisenhower-Nixon ticket and waited with her daughter and granddaughter to view the former president. "I thought he was an honest man," she stated simply, "and I didn't like the raw deal he got in Watergate."[3]

There are other examples such as these, numerous but largely unknown, of his lasting impact on the people around him. One would be the generosity that Nixon showed to the "little people" that he encountered on the road, with all that it revealed about his character.[4] Stephen Hess, who worked with Nixon on several writing projects throughout the sixties, insisted that Nixon was the most giving person he had ever collaborated with.[5] The engaging side of Nixon, in fact, often made a surprising impression on people, even with different political loyalties, who met him for the first time. After joining the Mudge Rose law firm in New York, Leonard Garment, one of the firm's chief litigators, threw a party for his friends in the legal community who were almost all Democrats. Nixon was unfazed by dealing with an audience composed of supporters of the opposite political party. Garment's friends were amazed by what they saw and heard from Nixon, not only in his intellectual qualities, but also how different he was from the brooding, public image that much of the media had

Top and above: Mourners lining up on the day before Nixon's funeral in Yorba Linda, California, on April 26, 1994 (Richard M. Nixon Foundation).

created around him.[6] One final example typified the private Nixon; after he became president, Nixon heard that one of his military aides who happened to be Black was getting ready to take his family on a vacation. This was at a time when Blacks were just beginning to work in important positions in Washington. Nixon asked the aide if he had decided where they were going. When the president got an undecided response, Nixon suggested that the aide take his wife and two kids to the presidential retreat at Camp David for a week. No one except the president ever went to the rural Maryland hideaway, which contained everything necessary for relaxation and recreation in one place. The aide accepted and thought it was among the most generous things that had ever done for him in his entire life, both then and afterward. The former brigadier general, Vernon C. Coffey, died in 2019.[7]

Amazingly, Richard Nixon is the only major political candidate besides Franklin Roosevelt who was on the winning side in four of five presidential elections. He is the most widely written about president in the post–World War II period. However, in all the books devoted to him, few have more than a chapter about his wilderness period from 1962 to 1968. For instance, *A Companion to Richard M. Nixon*, published in 2011, claims to be the "essential guide to the historical, political, cultural, and psychological analyses of the 37th president of the United States." Part of the Blackwell Companions to American History series, it covers the evolution and current state of Nixon scholarship up to 2010, boasting twenty-nine chapters about different aspects of Nixon's life and presidency. Each of the chapters was written by an expert in that field. Seven chapters detail the pre-presidential years, but, remarkably, not one highlights the most neglected and unexplored area of Nixon scholarship: the critical wilderness period.[8]

This book fills an important gap in the Nixon literature. This period is not merely filler between two major episodes of his life, as it is often dismissively viewed, but the essential backstory that explains his extraordinary comeback. This amounted to nothing less than a Lazarus-like achievement, for Nixon's winning the presidency in 1968 was, in its own way, as extraordinary and improbable as the triumph of Donald Trump in 2016. Then, as today, it took an unusual conjunction of circumstances for this unlikely event to occur. As late as 1967, in fact, hardly anyone would have predicted that in November 1968, the newly elected president of the United States would be Richard Nixon. While most of the books written about Nixon focus on "big things," like the 1960 presidential election, the 1968 presidential election, and Watergate, Nixon could have never been elected president in 1968 without his contributions to the mid-term elections of 1966. He emerged as the critical political figure who rebuilt the Republican Party after the disastrous 1964 presidential election, and arguably the one person in the party who could appeal to all its political factions.

This book explores the process by which Nixon reinvented himself during the dark days of the mid–1960s as well as Nixon's insights into how America was changing. The period between 1962 and 1968 served as a laboratory for rebirth. In a real sense, it mirrored his initial meteoric rise to prominence between 1946 and 1952, when he had gone from an obscure congressman to Dwight Eisenhower's vice presidential nominee. It was Nixon who single-handedly had the courage to continue the investigation of Alger Hiss after the Democrats took back the House of Representatives after the 1948 elections.[9] When confronted with the "fund crisis" and friends of Eisenhower urging the general to drop him from the ticket in 1952, a young senator from California addressed the problem head-on with the "Checkers" speech. Many in the national media dismissed the speech as pedestrian, but people listening at home had a different perception. Thousands of calls, letters, and telegrams came in after the speech with Nixon having a 350 to 1 positive response rate.[10] Then, as in the later period, his rise had been fueled by a series of sharp political assessments and crucial decisions.

Nixon's reemergence was a dynamic process, and that dynamism was one key to his political evolution. In the process of traveling the country and meeting myriad average Americans in the period from 1962 to 1968, he realized some important things: how to bridge the gap between Goldwater conservatives and moderate Republicans; how the temper, mood, and tenor of large sections of the American public were moving against the Democrats; and how one presidential candidate could take advantage of this. It was Nixon who was told when he moved to New York that he did not have a base on which to mount a national campaign because the Republicans in that state favored Nelson Rockefeller, but he shrugged that off because he knew that he had a national following. Nixon knew he was the one candidate within the Republican Party that could appeal to both Rockefeller liberals and Goldwater conservatives even though he was neither. He occupied the center of the party then and remained in the political center again in the presidential campaign against Hubert Humphrey and George Wallace in 1968.

This is the unknown Nixon, a far more human Nixon than the Herblock caricature of a shady political figure who would do anything to win. It by no means suggests that he was an angel, but he was flawed like the rest of mankind. It is precisely because of some of his flaws that he was able to connect with wide swaths of the electorate. Nixon came across as real because he was just that. A long-time critic who covered Nixon throughout his political career said he was just "one of us."[11] The book is written in chronological fashion, covering Nixon's circling of the political arena from November 1962 to November 1968. The story begins with his last press conference after losing the California governor's election in 1962 and ends with his presidential victory in 1968. No political prognosticator in the country would have guessed that after "the last press conference" in 1962, Richard Nixon would be elected president of the United States. This book describes how Nixon accomplished the unimaginable. His future as president certainly was not pre-ordained.

1

Obituary or Rebirth?

The day after the fated news conference, after answering a few phone calls, Richard Nixon decided he needed an extended rest in the Florida Keys and the Bahamas. John Davies and Charles Gregory ("Bebe") Rebozo accompanied him on vacation. Davies had been the director of communications in the campaign, while Rebozo, a Miami businessman, was fast becoming Nixon's best friend. Pat and the girls joined them after their schedules were settled.[1] Doing his best to relax and recover, Nixon wondered whether he was writing his political obituary or christening his political rebirth.

One of the people also impacted by the loss in the governor's election was a young college student from the University of Southern California (USC) named Dwight Chapin. He worked as a fieldman in charge of three counties outside of Los Angeles for the Nixon campaign. Chapin's introduction into politics came two years earlier in the presidential campaign when two of his fraternity brothers were recruiting people to hear Robert Finch speak on campus for Nixon. He worked later that summer as a gofer for CBS during the Democratic Convention that was held at the sports arena on the USC campus. Several of the old pros from the Nixon campaign told Dwight that their candidate was going to lose, but he refused to believe it. He was there the next morning when Nixon said it "was his last press conference." Dwight was crushed emotionally. He left the hotel, borrowed his mother's convertible, and drove around Los Angeles, trying to process just what happened. Dwight knew he had worked his butt off for the best candidate and still that candidate lost. Was his life in politics over? Was Richard Nixon's too?[2]

Two years after that distressing night, Dwight had graduated from college. He was working as H.R. (Bob) Haldeman's junior assistant at the J. Walter Thompson Company in Los Angeles, one of the country's most successful advertising and marketing companies. One day, Haldeman told Dwight that they were going to the Republican Convention in San Francisco for the entire week. He did not tell him why. It was there that Dwight's life again intersected with the former vice president. This time Nixon was not running for office but was a partner in a large New York law firm.[3] Dwight did not know it yet, but their political careers did not seem to be over.

At the same time, unbeknownst to the former vice president, something was brewing in the broader political and media environment that would affect Nixon and his political future. The first step toward the answer came in the form of a television documentary by one of the country's most prominent and well-respected journalists.

Who Was Howard K. Smith?

Howard K. Smith was one year younger than Richard Nixon. He was a native of Ferriday, Louisiana. It is located across the Mississippi River from Natchez, Mississippi. Other notable people from that small Louisiana town include Jerry Lee Lewis, Mickey Gilley, and Jimmy Swaggart.[4] In 1962, Lewis would be the only recognized celebrity from Ferriday besides Smith. Smith captained the Tulane University team before he became a Rhodes Scholar at Oxford University. He then spent his formative years as a reporter covering the rise of Hitler and World War II.[5] He wrote first for United Press and second with the Columbia Broadcasting System (CBS) as one of "Murrow's Boys," named after the famous radio and television journalist Edward R. Murrow.[6] Smith spent the next twenty years as a highly successful journalist at CBS. Later, he left the Tiffany network after a dispute with management over his editorializing at the end of one of his news documentaries on racial problems in Birmingham, Alabama, in the fall of 1961.[7] Smith next signed with the American Broadcasting Company (ABC) in 1962 to do a prime-time news show entitled *Howard K. Smith News and Comment* that began on February 14.[8] The format allowed much more freedom than Smith had with CBS. The Nationwide Insurance Companies sponsored the program. The company was headed by Murray Lincoln, who regularly sent his insurance agents on tours of the United Nations. Lincoln believed Smith's worldview and approach to the program would be similar to those of the agents and policyholders. Half of Nationwide's advertising budget supported this venture.[9]

Everything went fine until late September when Smith featured Cuba and Fidel Castro. By then, Castro had dropped all claims he was anything other than a Marxist. At the end of this broadcast, Smith opined that it might be necessary to invade Cuba to keep the Soviets from setting up bases in this hemisphere. Smith, who had been in London during the Munich agreement in September 1938, was highly critical of that policy, which ignored the threat that the Germans posed for the rest of the world. Smith was now incensed that the Kennedy administration seemed to be doing the same thing. Murray Lincoln was horrified by Smith's conclusions. He had his vice president for public relations call the journalist after the show to complain that the program was no more than Yankee imperialism.[10] A month later, Smith told his viewers that his next show, called "The American Fighting Man," was to coincide with Veterans Day. The gubernatorial election in California changed Smith's mind after Nixon lost. He switched his topic in the middle of the week to "The Political Obituary of Richard Nixon."[11] Smith never anticipated the firestorm that would follow this decision.

Who Is the Winner Now?

Howard K. Smith had always operated under time and deadline constraints as a journalist. By changing the topic in mid-week, he lost half of the time that it usually took to do a program of this type. He started by coming up with a list of 10 people associated with Richard Nixon's occupation as a national political figure. In the end, Smith got four interviews. The pro–Nixon interviewees were Gerald Ford and Murray Chotiner. Ford was a former football player at the University of Michigan and a Republican member of the U.S. House of Representatives. Chotiner was a lawyer and political consultant who worked with Nixon in some earlier political campaigns. The anti–Nixon people for the show were Jerry Voorhis and Alger Hiss. Hiss had just recently been released from prison on his perjury charge. Walter Cronkite of CBS News had interviewed him earlier in the week. Hiss initially refused to do the interview but called back the day before the program was scheduled, agreeing to the meeting. Hiss wanted to proclaim his innocence in the discussion, but Smith wanted the focus on Richard Nixon.[12]

A couple of days before the show aired, word leaked that Hiss would appear; two prominent sponsors (Kemper Insurance and Schick) wanted to pull their advertising from the network. ABC allowed the insurance company to withdraw but held Schick to their contract. Schick indicated that after this contract expired, they would not be doing any future advertising with ABC. Four of the 80 affiliates with the network refused to run the show.[13] Hawaiian Punch pulled its December advertising.[14] Interestingly, the day before the show broadcast, Jerry Voorhis called and requested that Smith eliminate his interview. Smith refused.[15]

Former President Eisenhower even got involved the morning that the telecast was scheduled to air. He called his former press secretary, James (Jim) C. Hagerty, now the head of ABC News, to inquire about a rumor that Alger Hiss was getting thirty minutes on a program to denounce Richard Nixon. Hagerty assured his former boss that this was not the case and that Hiss was only a small part of the program. Reports in the media indicated that Ike had tried to block the show from appearing, but the confusion was addressed a couple of days after the program aired. Eisenhower adamantly stated that he "was astonished Mr. Hiss was on the program. I expressed amazement, but never in my life have I asked anybody not to report a story after they got it fully."[16]

The show began with Smith introducing his guests. After that, he got right to the heart of the matter by saying, "If I had to draw up a list of the most interesting political figures of the present time, it would include Khrushchev, DeGaulle, Mao Tse Tung, John Kennedy ... and the one who has just left politics, Richard Nixon. The basic thing to say about Mr. Nixon is a truism—nobody is neutral about him. In his one race for the presidency ... he missed by only one-tenth of one percent. If 4,000 voters in Texas and 28,000 in Illinois had changed their minds and voted the other way—that is not enough people to fill half the football stadium on a Saturday afternoon—Nixon, not Kennedy would be President today."[17]

Jerry Voorhis was up next in the questioning about the former vice president's career. In 1946, Nixon had defeated the former five-term congressman in his re-election campaign. Voorhis recalled, "In this campaign, I was confronted with a clever sort of innuendo and more than that too, really, which was a little bit astonishing. I mean here I was represented as being a hand-picked candidate of certain organizations which, incidentally never did endorse me, and their philosophy was being red-tinged, and they're being Red-infiltrated ... the philosophy which guided Mr. Nixon's politics was a general philosophy that the way to win is to tear down one's opponent in every way one can."[18]

After comments by Murray Chotiner disputing Voorhis's claims, Hiss appeared on the program. He was only on the show for about two minutes. Hiss believed that Nixon was motivated politically and not by the facts. Hiss did not seem angry or bitter in his assessment of the former vice president. After these brief comments, he never appeared again. The former State Department official and convicted perjurer stated, "If it hadn't been Mr. Nixon, perhaps someone else would have tried to jump into the same [political] situation and benefit by it."[19]

Gerald Ford next countered Hiss's claims, saying, "The American people owe a great deal to Dick Nixon for his dedication to finding out all of the possible facts that the committee could find out about the Alger Hiss case and its ramifications." The Michigan congressman believed Nixon's "sole purpose was to find out what happened and why Mr. Hiss did this or that we as Americans owe a great debt of gratitude for his energy in seeing that the committee did what the committee's responsibility was supposed to be."[20]

Smith spent the next quarter of the program recounting Nixon's career from the Hiss case, from when he was named as Eisenhower's running mate to the present time. Soon after that, the secret fund was discovered. It was then that Nixon encountered his second crisis, Smith explained, referring to the best-selling 1962 memoir *Six Crises* written by Richard Nixon. He recalled how Tom Dewey, former Republican presidential candidate and New York governor, had recommended Nixon for the job and then told him that he needed to resign. He recounted how a courageous and determined Nixon "went on national television to defend himself in one of the most remarkable incidents in modern American politics—the Checkers speech … corny or not, the Checkers speech on T.V. saved Nixon's life and made him Vice President of the United States." Smith told viewers how a relaxed and calm Richard Nixon had served Ike and was most likely "the most active and influential Vice President ever." Finally, Smith explained how after a bitter Nixon's near-miss for the presidency and the last loss for the governor of California, "the master tactician threw tact to the winds with those words" in his last press conference.[21]

Before Smith's concluding remarks, Chotiner and Ford weighed in on Smith's analysis. Chotiner thought that Nixon's assessment of how the press covered the '62 campaign was factually accurate, and unless the political winds changed, "Mr. Nixon will not run for an elected public office at any time." On the other hand, Chotiner stated, "[Nixon's] advice, his counsel, his ability, his experience, certainly would be lost to the country if we were just simply to say well from now on Mr. Nixon is not going to be used for the benefit of the United States. From that standpoint, I do not think he is through."[22] Gerald Ford followed, arguing that the public sometimes misunderstood Nixon's actions. Ford strongly believed that Nixon sometimes had problems showing people that he was not cold and uncaring but was a warm and gracious person.[23]

The program concluded with Smith's closing remarks on how this may be Richard's life and how he would most likely take a spot in the private sector, make lots of money, and be able to spend more quality time with his family. His final comments were, "There is no doubt that Mr. Nixon performed great services in his investigation of Communism and in his tours of the world for America. But, his achievements have to be weighed against those tactics. I suspect that is what the voters did."[24]

Media and the Public Weigh In

The controversy grew after the program. In the following week, Jim Hagerty offered Richard Nixon airtime to respond to Hiss on the next week's program, but he declined through an aide, Robert H. Finch. Finch was a close friend and confidante who ran Nixon's 1960 presidential campaign. Finch was outraged at the offer of free airtime, noting that the offer came after the network received thousands of calls from outraged viewers. He contended, "I find it incredible that this national network would allow its facilities to be used by an Alger Hiss to pass judgment on a distinguished American and then fall back on such an atrocious, pathetic gesture as this offer."[25] Another Nixon aide weighed in on his displeasure with the program's half-truths. Herb Klein, press secretary during the 1960 and 1962 campaigns, believed that the show attempted to "distort the life of a great American 'set a new low in undistinguished reporting' by substituting innuendo for facts."[26]

Much of the country agreed with Finch and Klein. The *Los Angeles Herald-Examiner* called the program a "witch-burning."[27] The *Chicago American* stated, "Hiss' appearance was an affront to American justice because of its implication that—aside from luck—there is no difference between the convicted criminal and his prosecutor."[28] The *Omaha World-Herald* compared the program to allowing avowed enemies of the United States equal time with patriotic Americans. It suggested getting "Colonel Abel back for a guest appearance to describe the hardships of the Communist spy business."[29] Even the liberal *Nashville Tennessean*, who was no friend of Richard Nixon, agreed that the ABC program had gone over the line. Their editorial stated, "To name an ex-convict a pallbearer for the former vice-president, then provide him with a shovel full of dirt to pour over the grave and permit him to deliver part of the eulogy makes as much sense as having ABC declare Benedict Arnold, the father of our country."[30]

The outrage over the airing of the show was not limited to Republicans. Thomas Dodd, Democratic senator of Connecticut, was equally appalled by ABC's decision to put Alger Hiss on the program. Dodd sent a protest telegram to ABC and the Federal Communications Commission (FCC) stating his "personal disgust" and asking the regulatory agency to "investigate this entire incident." The Connecticut senator was no supporter of Richard Nixon but believed that "what is involved here has nothing to do with politics."[31]

Jim Hagerty issued a quasi-apology on the following week's program, defending the presence of Alger Hiss on the show after clarifying his position: "I'm against Hiss and everything that he stands for.... But that doesn't alter the fact that he did play an important part in the political career of Richard Nixon."[32] In his memoirs, some thirty-plus years later, Howard K. Smith said that the network got over 60,000 pieces of correspondence on the show.[33] In Nixon's autobiography, 15 years later, he estimated the number at 80,000.[34] In either case, most of it was negative.

Beset by all the negative publicity, Nationwide commissioned ARB Surveys, a New York–based marketing firm, to conduct a nationwide survey of its viewers focused on the impact of Hiss's appearance. Nationwide came to a somewhat different conclusion based on the response. Their findings agreed that the show was highly controversial and took strong editorial stands, but they did not believe that Smith was alienating his audience. They did acknowledge that the Hiss affair had its share of cynical viewers, but a larger group was pleased with the veteran journalist's "objectivity, frankness, and honesty." The authors went on to say, "On balance, while there are those who have been alienated by Smith's editorial policy, more people are pleased with it than displeased."[35]

In summary, the fallout of "The Political Obituary of Richard Nixon" indicated that Nixon was not politically dead, and large numbers of interested Americans were sympathetic to him. Howard K. Smith may have inadvertently awakened a sleeping giant. While it may have been the intent of the show to depict Nixon as politically moribund, it demonstrated the opposite. It was the first step back toward the political arena for Nixon. How long the comeback would take and in what venue was uncertain.

What Next?

Nixon spent the days fishing, reading, and swimming. There were some small dinner parties but nothing significant. His wife and daughters joined him before Thanksgiving. Jack Paar, the host of the *Jack Paar Show* (the forerunner to the long-running and highly successful *Tonight Show*) and a friend of the family from his vice presidential years, also visited the Nixons in the Bahamas. Paar's daughter Randi was good friends with the Nixon girls. The veteran talk show host announced that Richard Nixon would be a guest of the show after the first of the year.[36] Another friend who joined Nixon while in the Bahamas was Elmer H. Bobst. He was the chairman of the board of Warner-Lambert Pharmaceuticals. Bobst encouraged Nixon to move back to New York for a more stimulating public and private life as well as many more business opportunities. Nixon was still unsure.[37]

Nixon returned to California refreshed before heading to New York in the middle of the month for some business meetings. There he met with old political and personal friends concerning his future, who agreed to a future meeting after the first of the year. Stephen Hess accompanied Nixon to this meeting at the Waldorf Astoria in early January of 1963. The group included Robert C. Hill, Paul Keyes, Bunny Lasker, Tom Duggan, Peter Flanigan, and a few others. Hill was a former ambassador in the Eisenhower administration and a significant political player in New Hampshire, the home of the first presidential primary. Keyes was an old California friend with great wit who wrote and produced for Jack Paar, among others in Hollywood. Lasker was head of the New York Stock Exchange. Duggan was a newscaster from Los Angeles, and Flanigan was a prominent New York investment banker and Nixon fund-raiser from the 1960 campaign.[38]

The discussions ranged from Nixon staying in politics to leaving altogether to become a lawyer in the private sector. His wife loved their new home in Los Angeles, but the governor's race had burned her out. Nixon thought that she would be glad to leave California. He wanted to be closer to the center of political action, and it was not on the west coast. Nixon felt as if he had outgrown the Golden State, or maybe the state had left him behind. Nixon had a lot to think about in the next few weeks. Before he made any big decisions, Nixon headed back to Los Angeles.

On January 8, the Nixons held a large dinner party at their house for the American Football Coaches Association (AFCA) and their Kodak sponsors. While Nixon had not been much of an athlete, he enjoyed the stimulating and competitive aspect of sports and was a big football fan. The following indicated this. The college coaches included Bud Wilkinson of Oklahoma, Woody Hayes of Ohio State, Duffy Daugherty of Michigan State, Paul Dietzel of Army, Bowden Wyatt of Tennessee, Jess Neely of Rice, John McKay of Southern California, and Nixon's old coach from Whittier, "Chief" Newman. The Los Angeles Rams head coach Harlan Svare and several of his players attended, including the McKeever twins, Marlin and Mike. Their owner, Bob Reynolds, and his general manager, Fred Haney, represented the Los Angeles Angels baseball team. Johnny Weissmuller, the former swimming great and *Tarzan* actor, as well as former Heisman Trophy winner Glenn Davis were among Nixon's other famous guests.[39]

Nixon had been invited to speak at the coaches' convention but had prior commitments. However, he did have a long conversation at the dinner party with Gerald B. Zornow, vice president for marketing, and Joe Allendorf, director of sales for Kodak, about the importance of sports in the development of young men in America and its relevance to the overall spirit of competitiveness to the country. Allendorf recalled the former vice president's views, reflecting on this nexus: "He expounded a firm feeling that once we allow competitive spirit to deteriorate, our country will start downhill." He also expressed a fear that if athletics were to be too competitive, society might stop holding children to higher standards lest they be hurt by competition.[40]

Meanwhile, Paar scheduled Nixon for March 8. The show mixed discussion of personal and political issues coupled with the host's sarcastic humor. Before Nixon appeared on the show, he discussed with Stephen Hess the types of problems he anticipated and the best way to handle these. Most of these issues had to with national security and foreign affairs.[41]

The show started with a discussion of what was next for Richard Nixon. The non-committal Nixon admitted, "Some of my friends felt very strongly that I ought to at that particular time in my life concentrate entirely on frankly making some money, and I have received some very attractive offers in that respect." Nixon also said that he was free to express his view on his party or politics as he views it.[42]

Much of the remainder of the program had to do with public issues, most notably what to do in Cuba. Nixon strongly supported President Kennedy in the missile crisis but thought the United States could be doing more to rid the Americas of communism. This approach would not be risk-free. He compared Cuba to cancer, stating that the tumor needed removing lest it become fatal.[43]

The most exciting part of the show dealt with Nixon's recent trip to the Bahamas. Paar told his audience how he felt sorry for Nixon's daughters and imagined they would be taking his last loss in California too hard. He and his daughter thought a night on the town in Nassau would cheer them up. One of the places they went to was an open-air nightclub called "Over the Hill," which had over a thousand people there. There was a twisting/limbo contest in progress when they walked in. One of the musicians recognized Paar and convinced Nixon's daughter, whom he believed to be Paar's daughter, to do the twist and limbo. She did an animated version of the popular dances. He announced her as the winner, crowning her "twist-limbo queen of the Bahamas." All the while, he thought he was talking to Randi Paar. He then asked the newly crowned winner her name, and she said, "Trish Nixon." The host looked curiously back at Paar, who nodded. His eyes widened, and he asked Trish if she were the daughter of the former vice president. She nodded. The crowd went wild with applause. Paar ended the funny story with his guest, "To tell you the truth, Mr. Nixon, if she had done that in Mississippi in '60, you'd be the President by now."[44]

After a brief discussion of world events, a piano was rolled onto the stage. Nixon did not know that this was coming. Paar explained that Mr. Nixon played the piano and had recently composed a selection for his wife. The former vice president handled the surprise request gracefully, playing his composition on the piano for the audience. He earned a rousing reception from the studio audience as the show ended.[45]

This television event showed a different side of Richard Nixon, a complex and likable man far from the angry politician feeling sorry for himself. Eighty-five percent of letters and phone calls Paar received favored Nixon. The most frequent comments were that he looked good, witty, and knowledgeable.[46] For Nixon, things were looking up.

Nixon had one more major public event before he made up his mind. He had been invited to address the American Society of Newspaper Editors (ASNE) in Washington, D.C., in April. He accepted the invitation. Nixon got there a day early and worked around the clock with John C. Whitaker on his address. Whitaker was a great admirer of Nixon and had worked as an advance man in the 1960 campaign despite his lack of political background. After meeting Nixon in 1959, Whitaker thought he might be interested in working in his upcoming presidential campaign. Whitaker knew that Nixon was genuine after listening to him describe to a journalist in great detail the science surrounding the testing of nuclear weapons. Very few people in the world understood the technical aspects of nuclear testing, especially a politician with a non-science background. John Whitaker made his mind up right then that Nixon was not another phony politician but a political force to be reckoned with.[47]

The hugely successful speech went a long way toward making Nixon the leader of the loyal opposition, even if he had neither a political future nor a geographical, political base of his own. Nixon hit hard on the theme of taking on Cuba and communism. One prominent newspaper editorial titled "A Premature Obituary?" suggested a rejuvenated Richard Nixon, one stronger than the one in the 1960 presidential campaign. The editors commented on this new development and what it portended for Nixon's political fortunes: "We cannot escape the observation that, had Mr. Nixon spoken with the same candor in 1960, the presidential contest might well have had another outcome."[48]

A new Nixon was emerging, one in his political sense that he answered to no one but himself and his judgment. Maybe the two and a half years since his presidential defeat and five months after his gubernatorial loss signaled the beginning of a new Nixon. Only time would tell, but he needed to make one big decision on the direction of his career.

The Big Apple Awaits

On May 2, Richard Nixon announced he was leaving California for a new position in New York. It was an easy sell to Pat. His old friend Elmer Bobst, who had encouraged the possibility of moving to New York while Nixon was vacationing, remembers being paged on the golf course for a long-distance phone call from California. Nixon told Bobst he decided to move back east and rebuilt his political base while providing for his family as he enhanced his public persona.[49]

A couple of days later, Bobst was discussing some legal matters with Milton Rose, who was his company's attorney. Rose was a senior partner with Mudge, Stern,

Baldwin, and Todd, a mid-level Wall Street firm. Bobst told Rose that his firm was in "need of some new blood." Rose seemed put off by the comment and asked him to clarify. Bobst explained that it was not younger blood that was needed, but "new blood at the top." Bobst recommended Richard Nixon as a titular leader of the firm. The wily attorney said, "Yes! Right away." Most of the other partners readily agreed.[50] However, there was one partner, John Alexander, who needed some additional clarification about Nixon's intentions. During a round of golf at the Baltusrol Country Club in New Jersey, the partner questioned Nixon's commitment to legal work at the firm. Alexander told Nixon that his earlier job with Earl Adams' firm in Los Angeles involved him running for governor and writing *Six Crises*. Nixon explained to him that he had an agreement with Adams concerning his political and writing activities. Also, Nixon let him know, "A politician does not change his base." If the former vice president still wanted to be a politician, why would he move entirely across the country in a state where his most prominent political rival was the governor. Alexander seemed comfortable with the response.[51] Until Nixon officially joined the firm on June 1, he would serve as a consultant for six months before formally being admitted to the New York bar. After that, the firm would be renamed. Before all of this took place, Nixon turned to finding a place to live and taking a summer vacation with his family.[52]

A New Home and a European Trip

The Nixons put their home in California on the market as they prepared to move to the "Big Apple." Pat's cousin, Ned Sullivan, took them with a real estate broker to explore Westchester County and the Upper West Side, before moving to a ten-room cooperative apartment right in the heart of the city at 62st Street and Fifth Avenue, overlooking Central Park. The other apartment dwellers approved them the next day. Even though the apartment needed paint and remodeling, Nixon seemed extremely happy with their selection, commenting, "Pat can make anything look good." One of the tenants of the building was the governor of New York, Nelson Rockefeller, and a Republican with presidential aspirations of his own.[53]

In 1947, during his first term as a member of the House of Representatives, Richard Nixon had promised his wife a European vacation after he toured the war-ravaged areas with the Herter Commission. Sixteen years later, he finally made good on that promise. Jack and Helene Drown and their daughter, Maureen, accompanied the Nixon family. Maureen was 20 years old at the time. Helene was Pat's closest friend from her single days when teaching in Whittier. The Nixon girls (ages 15 and 17) were in high school. Julie recalled, over twenty years later, how their father had a bit of a learning curve with two teenage girls. The younger Nixon daughter wrote, "On my birthday in Florence, the Drowns teasingly had given me several Italian movie magazines.... I walked into the sitting room and found Daddy scowling and reading a movie magazine. He read one-half of it."[54]

It was no typical family tourist holiday. The vacation was coupled with work and some politics for the former United States vice president. Nixon was greeted as if he were still vice president or possibly, soon-to-be president. He met with Charles de Gaulle in France, Francisco Franco in Madrid, Konrad Adenauer in Bonn, and

Gamal Abdel Nasser in Cairo. While in West Berlin, Nixon visited the newly erected wall that separated the two sides of the former German capital. Nixon also saw East Berlin, where hecklers, who had been sent there by their communist government, surrounded him. He went back later that night for an unannounced visit and had "a very moving experience." Nixon later recounted this story in November at an annual meeting of the Grocery Manufacturers of America:

> That evening I went back alone. The Communists didn't know that I was coming; the Communist police didn't know that I was in the city for the first two hours. As we were walking, my wife and I and two others along a dark street, a man darted out from an alley. He came up and said, speaking English, "Mr. Nixon, I am awfully glad you came back after your visit this afternoon. We couldn't say anything then because the police were around." But, he said, "I want to tell you the Americans are our only hope." A policeman came up on the corner, and he went back into the alley. He was right, I believe. The Americans are his only hope, and freedom is America's only hope.[55]

Although Nixon was considered a "private citizen," he was not treated as such and held press conferences along the way, speaking out on foreign affairs. While in Rome, he got a phone call from President Kennedy, who was also in the Italian capital on a state visit. Richard considered this trip for the Nixons as "one of the happiest times of our lives (and) what made it special was that it gave us a chance to be together as a family."[56]

Who Was "Mudge Rose"?

"Mudge Rose" was the shortened version of the Mudge, Stern, Baldwin, and Todd law firm, named after a former partner and a current senior partner, Milton Rose. This firm had over 70 lawyers with 24 senior partners. The address was 20 Broad Street, adjacent to the New York Stock Exchange. Sixteen of the 24 top partners came from Harvard, Yale, or Columbia law schools. The offices occupied three floors in their New York location. The firm also had offices in Washington and Paris.[57]

The firm had a colorful history dating back to 1869. It reached its high point in 1930 as Rushmore, Bisbee, and Stern, one of the four most significant New York law firms. It was firmly implanted in the city's legal establishment, serving as counsel to customers such as Chase National Bank, Chase Securities, Bank of Manhattan, and the BMT Subway system. One of the senior partners was Charles Rushmore. He had made a fortune in South Dakota mining operations, and the local mountain of the four presidents was named after him. During the Great Depression, most of the firm's business was with Chase and the Bank of Manhattan, who took a big financial hit in the thirties.[58]

Mudge Rose had a bit of a comeback from 1950 to 1963 as a result of a small group of young partners led by Randolph Hobson "Bob" Guthrie, a native of South Carolina. One of the senior partners of the firm described him as having "a shrewd legal mind and endless commercial cunning" with a manner of a "good-ole-boy small-town insurance executive, not *Harvard Law Review*, as was the fact." The firm's largest clients included Warner-Lambert, PepsiCo, General Cigar, Stone and Webster Engineering Corporation, Studebaker-Worthington, Continental Baking, and El Paso Natural Gas.[59] This upper-middle bracket firm served clients that encompassed corporations, banks, railroads, brokerage and underwriting houses, trusts, foundations, and insurance companies, along with some commercial and industrial concerns.[60]

Back to Work

Richard Nixon returned from his summer vacation remarkably refreshed and ready for his new job. Nixon arrived at seven in the morning and rarely left until six in the evening. He was a magnet for new business while reconnecting with many old political and business associates. He would sometimes eat lunch twice a week at The Recess, an exclusive private club close to his office in the business district. Thomas Dewey, Herbert Brownell, and William P. Rogers, Eisenhower's attorneys general, along with Maurice Stans, former budget director under Ike, were among the members with whom Nixon conversed and dined. Nixon would usually get the choice table at a corner with two picture windows and a great view of the East River.[61]

The former vice president had total discretion over his schedule and, with that, engaged in a certain amount of speech-making, usually to business or professional groups that enhanced his firm's bottom line and reputation. While supposedly out of politics and in Nelson Rockefeller's backyard, this did not keep Nixon from speaking out on issues when it suited his purposes. On September 23, Richard Nixon delivered the keynote address at the annual convention of the Mutual Agents of New York in Syracuse. More than 800 people packed into the crowded ballroom in Hotel Syracuse to hear him address the shortcomings of the nuclear test ban treaty being debated in the Senate. He told the audience, "Approval of the test ban treaty will be marked by a new stepped-up Soviet offensive to extend communism, without war, in the free world." After the speech, he received a sustained standing ovation before the crowd closed in to speak with him or get his autograph.[62] The ovation was not precisely the kind of response that one would expect for a two-time political loser.

October was a busy month for the new senior partner of Mudge Rose. On October 2, Dick and Pat were guests of Herbert Brownell at Yankee Stadium for the first game of the World Series.[63] On October 12, Nixon was among the 700 prominent guests honoring former President Eisenhower in Hershey, Pennsylvania, upon the eve of his 73rd birthday. Lewis Strauss, former chairman of the Atomic Energy Commission, said the party would have "no political significance." Nelson (Rocky) Rockefeller and his three brothers were slated to attend, while the front-runner for the Republican nomination for president in 1964, Barry Goldwater, was not invited. Governor Rockefeller was expected to challenge Goldwater for the GOP nomination.[64] In fairness, this event was related to ties from Eisenhower administration, of which Rockefeller was a member, and Goldwater was not.[65] In between these two events, Nixon was the keynote speaker at the National Metal Trades Association as well as the America Coca Trades dinner.[66]

Before leaving on a week-long business trip to Paris in the middle of the month, there was a reception for Nixon at the apartment of John Alexander, one of the senior partners at Mudge Rose. Here, he was introduced to the firm's partners in a relaxed atmosphere. It was also the first time Leonard (Len) Garment, one of the senior partners and chief litigator, met Nixon. It was the beginning of what would become a lifelong friendship. He remembered that Nixon was bigger and taller than he had seemed on television or in the newspapers, and he had a big smile.[67]

A few weeks later, Garment was able to talk a bit more to the former vice-president at a catered lunch at the office. After the lunch, he asked Rose Mary Woods if he could speak briefly to Nixon. She told him to knock and enter his office. After some small talk, the conversation became quite personal. Garment told Nixon that he was a Democrat, that he had voted against him in 1960, and that he had hosted a fund-raiser for Bobby Kennedy in his home. Nixon replied that none of that mattered. He had plenty of Republican friends and was eager to work with others who saw the world differently than he did. The new senior partner told Garment that he could boost the firm's business but that he was not going to "whore around" by lobbying Congress on behalf of his clients. Also, Nixon told Garment he wanted the firm to hire lawyers who were willing to work hard and were not born with silver spoons in their mouths. He called these people "scrappers."[68]

Garment was a celebrated jazz clarinetist who had played with Woody Herman in the 1940s. He was a graduate of Brooklyn Law School, not exactly the Ivy League, and had made his way into the world by outworking others, much in the way that Nixon had done. The most accomplished partner from Nixon's point of view was Bob Guthrie, who did not run his mouth telling the world how smart he was and what he had done, but showed himself through his actions. Nixon liked fighters and risk-takers like Garment and himself.[69] In an interview with Jonathan Aitken, nearly thirty years later, Garment recalled the bond between the two lawyers: "Our driving force was that we so much wanted to succeed. We both had ambivalent attitudes towards the Establishment, toward the world we had left, and to the world we aspired to. Instinctively we knew that we could be instruments for each other's purposes."[70]

Shock in Dallas

The first three weeks of November were business as usual, with Nixon speaking to three different business and professional associations while getting all his paperwork turned into the New York Bar Association. On November 21, he attended a Pepsico board meeting in Dallas. After the meeting, he talked with reporters. He hoped the people of Dallas would have a warm welcome for President Kennedy and Vice President Johnson, who would be touring the city the next day. In contrast, earlier that fall, Adlai Stevenson, the U.S. representative to the United Nations, was heckled and pelted with eggs by right-wing demonstrators. Nixon flew back to New York the next morning, unaware of what was happening in Dallas as he flew home.[71]

After arriving at the airport, Nixon took a cab to his apartment, where he was supposed to meet with Stephen Hess about a book project on the upcoming 1964 election. On the way there, his cab driver was conversing with a man at a stoplight about the shooting of the president in Dallas. When Nixon reached his apartment, Hess was there waiting for him. Hess had been a speechwriter for Ike during his last two years and had worked with Nixon on some projects after the failed 1960 campaign. Hess said that Nixon looked shell-shocked as he entered his apartment. It seemed to Hess that Nixon thought if he had won in 1960, Nixon would now be dead. Nixon showed Hess the paper, saying that he had just come from Dallas and had implored the public to give Kennedy a courteous reception. He hoped that it was not a right-winger. Nixon phoned Eisenhower, who was at the Waldorf Astoria, to talk about the assassination. Colonel Schultz, his aide, told the former vice president that Ike was taking a nap and could not be disturbed. He then called J. Edgar Hoover, the director of the FBI, to find out what he knew. Hoover told Nixon the assassin was a communist named Lee Harvey Oswald, who had earlier lived in the Soviet Union. This somewhat relieved Nixon. The assassination changed the political future of the country. The book project was abandoned, though Hess would continue to collaborate on other works with the former vice president.[72] As it turned out in the subsequent investigation of the assassination of the president, Oswald's wife told the police that he initially had set out to kill Nixon on November 21, but she had talked him out of it.[73]

Although not close to Jack Kennedy, Nixon had been a friend, and the two were more than acquaintances before the 1960 election. During the campaign, his opinion changed for the worse concerning the former Massachusetts senator. After the election, there had been "no love lost" between the two. Nixon had been publicly critical of the Kennedy administration, but he admired "his ambition and his competitiveness."[74] Nixon wondered how the tragedy would affect the president's family. Nixon remembered losing his brothers Arthur and Harold, and he wanted to show his sympathy to the Kennedy family. He stayed up late in the night, composing a letter to Jacqueline. It was heartfelt and personal.

> Dear Jackie, November 23
>
> In this tragic hour, Pat and I want you to know that our thoughts and prayers are with you. While the hand of fate made Jack and me political opponents, I always cherished the fact that we were personal friends from the time we came to Congress together in 1947. That friendship evidenced itself in many ways including the invitation we received to attend your wedding.
>
> Nothing I could say now could add to the splendid tributes which have come throughout the world to him.
>
> But I want you to know that the nation will also be forever grateful for your service as the First Lady. You brought to the White House charm, beauty and elegance as the official hostess for America, and the mystique of the young at heart which was uniquely yours made an indelible impression on the American consciousness.
>
> If in the days ahead, we could be helpful in any way we shall be honored to be at your command.
>
> Sincerely,
> Dick Nixon[75]

Mr. Nixon's personal and business calendar was altered for the next few weeks. He and Pat attended the funeral in Washington on the 25th. The country virtually shut down over the weekend of Kennedy's death. The three television networks covered the event almost exclusively. For those living in the United States at the time, they would never forget this colossal event. Ask anyone who was around at that time, and they will tell you what they were doing when they heard about the assassination. The Nixon family was no different. A couple of weeks after the death, Mrs. Kennedy sent a poignant hand-written letter back to Richard Nixon that reflected their shared past and perhaps his future.

Dear Mr. Vice President,

I do thank you for your most thoughtful letter—

You two young men—colleagues in Congress, adversaries in 1960—and now look what has happened—Whoever thought such a hideous thing could happen in this country—

I know that you must feel—so long on the path—so closely missing the greatest prize- and now for you, all the question comes up again—and you must commit all you and your family's hopes and efforts again—Just one thing I would say to you—if it does not work out as you have hoped for so long—please be consoled by what you have already—your life and your family—

We never value life enough when we have it—and I would not have had Jack live his life any other way—though I know his death could have been prevented, and I will never cease to torture myself with that—

But if you do not win—please think of all that you have—With my appreciation and my regards to your family. I hope your daughters love Chapin School as much as I did.

Sincerely
Jacqueline Kennedy[76]

Most of his scheduled events were canceled or postponed for December, but there was some good news. The bar of New York had accepted Nixon. His essay for admission to the bar was described to a veteran court official as the finest that he had read in 28 years. The question that he wrote on was, "What do you believe the principles underlying the form of government of the United States to be?" The court generally seals bar admission papers, but Lowell C. Wadmond, chairman of the Appellate Division's Committee on Character and Fitness, obtained permission from Justice Bernard Botein to make Nixon's response public.[77] Nixon was not going to stand in the way of this positive development. The glowing assessment of an overseer of the legal community could only enhance his reputation as a lawyer and add another feather in his cap as a thoughtful contender for a future public official of the highest sort.

2

All the Way with LBJ?

When Richard Nixon joined the Mudge Rose firm in June, he intended to focus on legal work with politics on the side, thinking it would be almost impossible to defeat Jack Kennedy in 1964. Had what happened in Dallas in November changed that? Perhaps it was time for a reassessment. He initially thought that Lyndon Baines Johnson (LBJ) would be easier for the Republicans to defeat, but watching LBJ rising to the occasion, Nixon was thinking much differently. In early January, the former vice president rented a suite at the Waldorf Astoria to meet again with his brainstorming crew to discuss the presidential political possibilities of 1964. This crew included Bob Finch, Bob Haldeman, Fred Seaton, John Whitaker, Steve Hess, Bunny Lasker, and several others.[1] Goldwater formally announced on January 3, and Nelson (Rocky) Rockefeller was already in the running. These two represented the conservative and liberal wings of the Republican party. In every presidential election going back to 1940, the northeastern and liberal wing of the party had held sway in intraparty matters. Goldwater and the conservatives sought to change this. Nixon thought that Goldwater was the favorite but not by much.[2]

A couple of days later, on January 9, the Associated Press interviewed Nixon in his law office. He would not say that he would accept the nomination if drafted but stated he would "make any sacrifice" to see his party nominate the strongest candidate. Nixon told the reporters that he was willing to lead the party without being the candidate or nominee. He certainly wanted to play a role in the

Nixon on a park bench with his dog Checkers in New York in 1964 (Richard M. Nixon Foundation).

campaign by speaking on the issues relevant to the American people. Nixon used a sports metaphor in describing his role as a team player in this process. He would come into the game "not on the sidelines, but in the thick of the battle—a blocking back."[3]

Is Nixon Running?

Nixon, now the veteran team player, continued to speak out on the issues. He was the guest of honor speaker for the Printing Week awards dinner in Philadelphia on January 16, where he focused on the weakness of the Kennedy-Johnson foreign policy. Nixon also made it clear that while he did not intend to enter any of the upcoming presidential primaries, he thought Republican presidential candidates Goldwater and Rockefeller were "hardworking" and well-funded. Also, he stated that the party needed new faces like Governor George Romney of Michigan and Pennsylvania Governor William Scranton.[4]

Two weeks later, Nixon spoke along with six others at a significant Republican fundraiser in New York broadcast nationally on closed-circuit television. The other speakers included the four possible candidates, along with former President Eisenhower and Senator Thruston Morton of Kentucky. Nixon told reporters after his speech that he would remain uninvolved in the upcoming New Hampshire primaries and discouraged any write-ins on his behalf. David S. Broder of the *Washington Star*, who covered the event, said Nixon sounded "like a man who wants another try for the presidency throwing the door wide open for a write-in campaign on his behalf in the New Hampshire primary."[5]

Candidate or not, Nixon had asked William Safire, who headed his consulting public relations firm, to provide him an honest appraisal of all the speakers at the telethon. He had worked for Nixon off and on since they met in Moscow in 1959. Nixon did not want "spin" from a yes man but an honest and direct opinion. Indeed, this request suggests Nixon was seriously considering running for president. Safire relayed his specific observations to Nixon in a letter the next day. In this assessment, he went through all of those who spoke one by one. Rockefeller was sincere. Scranton was inconsistent and did not even measure up to Adlai Stevenson. Romney looked the best but oversold himself. Goldwater looked tired and had no fire. Morton was bright and professional, but minor league. Eisenhower was dull and uninspiring. Nixon looked buoyant and at home in the limelight with a few technical issues.[6]

Nixon kept the same political pace in February by speaking at events around the country. At a Lincoln Day dinner in Cincinnati, Nixon acknowledged he would accept a draft if the convention deadlocked. Addressing the current civil rights bill in Congress, he believed "responsible civil rights leaders to take over from the extremists" for the law to have a positive effect on race relations. Nixon had favored the 1957 and 1960 civil rights bills and supported the one discussed in the Congress. He said that a "significant bipartisan" civil rights bill would pass, but extremists might also hinder its effectiveness for future positive change.[7]

On March 5, Nixon traveled to Washington to testify before the Senate subcommittee on presidential succession and disability. Since the death of John Kennedy, the country had been operating without a vice president. The Senate was trying to fix this problem. Nixon, who had filled in for Eisenhower during his heart attack and stroke scares during the 1950s, was easily one of the most knowledgeable persons that the Senate could have called on the subject. His opening words loosened up the subcommittee: "This is the first time I've been present in this room or on this side of the table. I'm glad I'm here voluntarily, and not under subpoena."[8] On a more serious note, Mr. Nixon said that he thought the president should appoint a vice president and have the Electoral College approve it.[9] Russell Baker of the *New York Times* described Nixon's excellent presentation: "Without a paper before him, Mr. Nixon talked extemporaneously for nearly 30 minutes. His sentences were crisp and direct, his syntax orderly and his argument systematically organized. It was a measured performance of the constitutional lawyer who has mastered his brief, and at the end, there were few loose ends for Mr. Bayh to question him about."[10]

The question of non-candidacy and the role of the vice president got even messier when Nixon appeared on the *Today Show* the weekend before the New Hampshire primary. Hugh Downs asked him whether he would accept the vice presidential nomination. Nixon responded: "And as far as I am concerned, I'm making it clear I'm not a candidate for President or a candidate for Vice-President, but I will do whatever my party asks me to do, and I feel everybody else should too."[11]

The New Hampshire primary's results were as surprising as ever. The independent-minded voters of the first presidential primary were not kind to front-runners Goldwater and Rockefeller. The unexpected winner was Henry Cabot Lodge, Jr., who was from neighboring Massachusetts. Lodge, Nixon's former running mate in 1960, received 33,400 votes to Goldwater's 21,700, Rockefeller's 19,500, and Nixon's 15,700.[12] Nixon's results were impressive for a non-candidate who had not campaigned in the state. Lodge's success was a stroke of good luck since he had not declared for the nomination. Nixon would soon talk to Lodge, whom Kennedy had named as ambassador to South Vietnam during his three-and-a-half-week business trip to Asia.

It was Lodge in 1952 who first pitched the idea of being vice president to Nixon. Lodge was the chairman of the nascent Eisenhower for President campaign. He had name recognition (his grandfather being a prominent politician) and was a senator from Massachusetts. While Thomas Dewey and Lucius Clay (general and friend of Eisenhower) were running the campaign behind the scenes, it was Lodge who was the face of it.[13] He was essentially Eisenhower before the general returned from Europe. Lodge even "formulated his political and policy positions without Eisenhower's consent or knowledge."[14] Lodge helped Ike win the New Hampshire primary and had the first-hand experience of uniting the Eisenhower moderates with the Taft conservatives at the convention.

The Asian Pepsi Tour

On March 22, 1964, Nixon departed New York for a trip through Lebanon, Pakistan, and on to Asia. He took with him a handful of business executives and was joined by his good friend Donald M. Kendall, the president of the Pepsi Cola Company in Manila, for the remainder of the trip.[15] There he met with seven heads of state, the governor of Hong Kong, and other government officials on the trip. These meetings were built around Pepsi receptions and luncheons. The Nixon party generally spent about two days in each destination except for Japan, where they stayed four and a half days. Japan had become the most critical ally in the region and the largest trading partner, boasting more business potential than all the other countries in the area. There Nixon met with the prime minister and foreign minister along with business clients on golfing outings. He helped open a Pepsi bottling plant in Hiroshima.[16]

Everywhere Nixon went, he heard foreign leaders express their doubts about amateur leadership and concerns with Washington's Vietnam policy.[17] Nixon said both American and South Vietnamese military leaders thought Washington was out of touch with the war. These leaders believed that they needed to bomb North Vietnam and conduct ground operations into Laos, where arms and supplies were coming into South Vietnam.[18] Reporters asked Nixon in Saigon whether he thought that Vietnam would become an issue during the campaign. He replied, "I hope that it doesn't; it will only become an issue if the policy of weaknesses worthy of criticism if it is plagued with inconsistency, improvisation, and uncertainty. That has been the case in the past…. There is no substitute for victory in South Vietnam."[19] In the last part of that quotation, Nixon was paraphrasing General Douglas MacArthur's comment on Korea.

Nixon had a long dinner conversation with Ambassador Lodge about American policy. Lodge was basking in his surprise write-in victory in New Hampshire and strongly considering resigning his present position to campaign for president. Much of the meeting had to do with politics. Probably the first item had to do with the relationship between the two. There had been some bad blood between them after the 1960 election. After "burying the hatchet," they discussed the primaries, the state of the Republican Party, and the 1964 elections.[20]

While in Taipei, the former vice president stayed as a house guest of General Chiang Kai-shek, the president of Taiwan. He told Nixon that MacArthur, who had just died, had been a friend and reliable backer of Chiang during the Chinese civil war and afterward. The leader of the island nation agreed heartily with Nixon that the only way that South Vietnam would win this war would be by the military. Nixon recalled this in his memoirs: "He said that we could never win without invading North Vietnam, and he laughed at the Strategic Hamlet Program being pursued. 'It is the familiar fallacy that economic development will defeat the Communists,' he said. He leaned closer to me and almost whispered, 'but only bullets will really defeat them!'"[21]

Back to the USA

Barely back in the country, Richard Nixon was the featured speaker at two events in New York. At one, he hammered away at the indecisive Johnson administration's foreign policy in Asia. He stated, "The United States has gone too far in catering to neutrals. Neutralism, where the communists are concerned, is only surrender on the installment plan."[22] Nixon returned to the nation's capital, where he had been a year before to speak to the American Society of Newspaper Editors. He highlighted what he had heard from Asian leaders about American leadership in Asia sinking to "its lowest point since Pearl Harbor." He worked against a "Yalu River concept in South Vietnam … the rules of the game must be changed."[23] Nixon believed that the only way for South Vietnam (and the United States) to win this war was to take the battle to the enemy and not feel restrained by borders that the enemy did not recognize.

Mr. Nixon took a lighter tone a week later when he appeared at the annual Gridiron Dinner in D.C., at which the national media looked at politics in a satirical manner. He referred to his retirement from politics and his less than positive relationship with former President Harry S. Truman: "I hope a man can lose his temper once in sixteen years and be forgiven for it.... If this [Gridiron] party is supposed to be dedicated to love, what better evidence is there for Harry Truman to take a drink from Dick Nixon without asking someone else to taste it first?" Mr. Truman smiled and raised his glass with the gesture.[24]

A week earlier, a story by Peter Kihss on the front page of the *New York Times* titled "GOP Nomination Still Wide Open, Publishers Feel" did not hurt Nixon's chances for the nomination, even though he continued to argue that he was not a candidate. Most of those publishers polled on the nomination acknowledged that Senator Goldwater had a slight lead but believed that Nixon would be the eventual winner of the contest. The author pointed to the comments by John S. Knight, head of the Knight Newspaper group in Akron, Miami, Detroit, and Charlotte, as representative of the publisher's association. Knight believed that the historical analogy of the 1951 battle for the Republican nomination would repeat itself: "Some Goldwater support will slip away as it did with Taft. I think that Nixon will be the man they most easily can agree on as not being too far on one side or another."[25]

Richard Nixon believed the three presidential primaries in the next seven weeks would clear things up. The first one would be on May 12 in Nebraska. There Nixon already had an inside operation of sorts headed by good friend and former interior secretary and newspaperman Fred Seaton, who had been organizing a behind-the-scenes write-in campaign. Five days before the primary, Nixon was the main speaker at the National Conference of Christians and Jews' annual meeting in Omaha, Nebraska. The speech was heralded as non-political but may have had some effect on the primary. The state had long been considered an easy win for Goldwater, so Rockefeller did not campaign there. Goldwater won with 49.5 percent, a little less than half of the votes, but Nixon got 31.5 percent of the votes as a write-in. Lodge, Rockefeller, and others split the final twenty percent of the vote. Seaton dubbed this as "the beginning of the Nixon surge." It was not.[26]

Seaton was not the only part of the Nixon team cheering on the sidelines after the Nebraska victory. John Whitaker wrote a letter the next day to Rose Mary Woods, Nixon's secretary since 1951, on what he thought the win in the Cornhusker state meant:

> Nebraska was wonderful and I assume that we are playing under the domino theory, i.e., knock over Nebraska, Oregon, and ultimately leading to a Rockefeller victory in California. Maybe it is just wishful thinking, but I am starting to get the feeling from the papers that Rocky just might pull through in California, and Sam Lubell [pollster] seems to think that Rocky could catch Lodge in Oregon. Should all of these things happen, I would say that RN looks like a good bet on the second session of balloting.[27]

The Oregon primary occurred three days later, where he had won in 1960. A write-in group had added him to the Oregon ballot several months earlier. He had not campaigned there, but he also did not remove his name. Goldwater and Lodge were not on the ballot. Rockefeller won with 93,000 votes to Lodge's 78,000, followed by

50,000 for Goldwater and 48,000 for Nixon.[28] The "surge" that Seaton had predicted and that Whitaker wished for was turning out to be a tingle.

Nixon believed that the June 2 California primary was the one primary that should determine the winner of the Republican nomination. He watched from the sidelines, leaving it to Rockefeller and Goldwater, knowing the winner would likely be nominated. A week out, Gallup estimated Nelson Rockefeller up 49–40 over Senator Goldwater. Much of Rockefeller's staff packed up and went home to New York several days early because they thought they had won the race. In the end, Barry Goldwater pulled out a squeaker with a little over 51 percent. The candidate himself had gone back to New York to be with his wife, who was expecting a baby. The baby was born on the weekend before Tuesday's contest. This baby reminded the conservative voters of California that this was the second marriage for both, that the new wife was over twenty years younger, and that she already had three kids from her first marriage of whom her husband had custody. On the night of the primary, the wire services had called Rockefeller the winner, and CBS News predicted a Goldwater win. The final tally was 1,120,403 votes to 1,052,053, with a turnout of 72 percent. The next day, Rockefeller pulled out of the race. It was seemingly over, and Barry Goldwater would be the nominee.[29]

Goldwater Is the Winner, Isn't He?

While the Goldwater bandwagon rumbled toward the nomination, a series of events occurred that may have muddied the victory waters for the Arizona senator. Nixon, Romney, and Scranton met at the Republican Governors Conference in Cleveland, Ohio. Nixon had earlier agreed to do a three-city speaking and fund-raising tour in Michigan starting on June 8. The short tour had been scheduled from at least as far back as April 20. On June 3, the day after the California primary, Sherman Unger got a call from an administrative assistant of Governor James Rhodes of Ohio stating, "It is imperative" that the former vice president attend the Republican Governors Conference in Cleveland on June 6–8. Unger was an Ohio attorney who was doing some work for Nixon. Nixon's people replied that it was impossible to do so because of their commitments in Michigan. They relented after the Host Committee for the conference agreed to charter a plane to Muskegon to pick up Nixon after his fund-raising event on June 8. It was the last stop on the three-city Michigan tour. The first stop was in Detroit, where he spoke to the Economic Club. Earlier that morning, Nixon had breakfast with Governor Romney and Max Fisher at the Sheraton-Cadillac Hotel. During this conversation, the governor talked about "Republican principles and the need to maintain a moderate posture of the Party." There was never any mention of him running for president, but only reminders that he was prepared to fight for these moderate principles.[30]

Governor Romney returned to the Cleveland conference and attended the dinner headlined by former President Eisenhower, with whom he met privately afterward. Eisenhower encouraged Romney but maintained that publicly he remained neutral. The Nixon party flew to the conference later that night and, upon arrival, received a message from Governor Romney requesting to meet before breakfast the next morning. They met, and Romney indicated that he was ready to challenge Goldwater with

the support of most of the Republican governors. This meeting lasted about 15 minutes. At breakfast, Romney sat next to William Scranton, the governor from Pennsylvania, who agreed to organize support. As the breakfast ended and Nixon was
preparing for an interview, Romney told Nixon what Scranton had told him. At this
press conference, Nixon announced that it appeared that one of the governors was
ready to be a candidate. Afterward, Rhodes and Romney met in Nixon's suite. Nixon
told them he would remain neutral if one of the governors opposed Goldwater.[31]

Nixon reminded Governor Romney that he had committed to serving the people of Michigan throughout his term and, therefore, should wait three or four days to
decide otherwise. The governor told Nixon he would ask Herb Brownell, Len Hall, or
Ray Bliss to run his campaign. Afterward, Romney left the Nixon suite and claimed
"several Republican governors" had urged him to challenge Goldwater. Scranton next
met with Nixon to say that he intended to support Romney but would not do until
Romney came out publicly. After the meeting, when Romney asked Brownell, Hall,
and Bliss to manage his campaign; all three declined. Then, Romney's press secretary
put out a statement that the Michigan governor would not be running for president
in 1964. A detailed memorandum of these occurrences in the Nixon files state, "At no
time during this entire trip did Nixon attempt to initiate any candidacy by Governor
Romney or anyone else. He simply discussed in a general fashion the situation as it
then existed. No specific suggestions or requests were made."[32]

All the parties attended the next day's breakfast. Nixon told the governors that
he had no prepared comments but would freely answer any questions. He fielded a
few procedural questions about the convention and how he thought the party would
fare in the general elections in November, but nothing about the meeting and his
non-candidacy. As he left the conference, Nixon told reporters that there was "a very
live interest in a stop Goldwater option." Goldwater responded that the former vice
president was "looking more like Harold Stassen every day."[33] The Stassen reference
had to do with the former Minnesota governor running for president numerous times
without a chance of winning. It was not something that Nixon wanted to hear as he
was flying to Baltimore for a fundraiser before he went to London on a business trip.

If there were an effort to stop Goldwater, Nixon would not be a part of it, but
there would be one last try for the northeastern liberal wing of the party. It would lie
in the hands of William Scranton. The Pennsylvania governor, mulling this about for
several months, had been encouraged to run by former President Eisenhower in Get-
tysburg, who lived just down the road from the capital in Harrisburg. Ike's encour-
agement did not mean endorsement, as he wished to be neutral. After the chaotic
governors' conference in Cleveland, coupled with Goldwater voting against the Civil
Rights Act a day later, Scranton had had enough and decided to run. Before he phoned
Nixon in London with his decision, Nixon told him that he had better watch out for
Eisenhower, who had earlier encouraged Romney in the same way. After Scranton's
announcement, Nixon said that he would not endorse anyone else before the July
convention.[34]

Scranton made a last-minute effort to derail the Goldwater train as it headed to
San Francisco. He campaigned hard over the next month but was not able to make
much headway with convention delegates before the convention. Scranton continued
to take his fight to the convention, but the better organized Goldwater forces had the
votes and won on the first ballot. Rockefeller spoke at the convention but did not get

a good reception. The New York governor was booed over and over again by the supporters of the Arizona senator.[35]

Nixon introduced the new Republican presidential nominee graciously. Goldwater had publicly supported him. He returned the favor. An aroused crowd in the Cow Palace cheered and clapped as Barry Goldwater came to the podium, shaking Nixon's hand while the band played "The Battle Hymn of the Republic" in the background. It was a joyous moment for Goldwater. He did not dissatisfy his supporters and was unapologetic in what he believed. It was not a unifying speech like Nixon had just given: "Those who do not care for our cause we do not expect to enter our ranks in any case. I would remind you that extremism in the defense of liberty—is—no vice! And let me remind you also—that moderation in the pursuit of justice is no virtue!"[36] Mainstream Republicans, moderate and apprehensive, remained unapologetic.

Goldwater-Miller Is the Ticket

Barry Goldwater chose William E. Miller as his vice presidential running mate Miller was a conservative member of the House of Representatives from New York. It was not a choice of ideological balance. Because of all of the seeming disunity coming out of the Republican Convention, Nixon convinced Goldwater to meet on August 12 in Hershey, Pennsylvania. Goldwater would meet with some of the Republican governors and General Eisenhower to clarify some of his remarks. Rockefeller, Scranton, Romney, and Rhodes were among those present. After the meeting that Ike coined a "love feast," all seemed to agree that they were all Republicans who could disagree and still come together. Nixon acknowledged this, claiming the party allowed for regional and personal differences on some issues: "I want all Republicans to win; I am just as strong for a liberal Republican in New York as I am for a conservative Republican in Texas, and I can just as enthusiastically campaign for both because we need conservatives and liberals to have a majority."[37]

There were apparent disagreements between Goldwater and some of those present, particularly Rockefeller and Romney. Rockefeller complained that Goldwater would not reject the support of some groups that he thought were extremist and, by not doing so, mostly accepted their positions. Goldwater wanted the help of all people, and just because he did not explicitly come out against a group's opinion did not mean that he accepted it. Romney wanted clarification on whether a President Goldwater would be able to implement the recently passed civil rights bill that he had not voted in favor of. Goldwater said that he would be able to follow the law.[38] The two liberal governors seemed somewhat pacified after the meeting but would not state in clear and definitive terms that they were endorsing Goldwater.

Earlier in the month, the USS *Maddox* was fired upon by North Vietnam while patrolling off the coast. President Johnson called Goldwater, who was vacationing in Newport Beach, about the incident and asked for his support before he went public on the issue. He easily got it. Senator Goldwater was a former pilot and a major general in the Air Force Reserves. Later in the week, the president asked for and got a near-unanimous motion from Congress on the incident off the Gulf of Tonkin. This resolution gave him a nearly free hand on military actions. This occurrence mostly took the issue of Vietnam out of the campaign.[39]

Meanwhile, in August, Nixon returned to his law office to take a few weeks' break from campaigning. He was able to get in a round of golf with professional football Hall of Famer Otto Graham and John Pont, the head coach of Indiana. Graham also gave Nixon an autographed football from the College All-Star Game earlier that month.[40] At the end of the month, the Democrats met in Atlantic City, New Jersey, to nominate Lyndon Johnson for president and Hubert H. Humphrey, a senator from Minnesota, for vice president.

After Labor Day, Richard Nixon had a few speaking engagements before going out full-throttle on the campaign trail for the Goldwater-Miller ticket. He also had to register to vote in New York, which he did with his wife and two aides from his law office.[41] The most notable event for Nixon took place in September in Detroit at the Michigan State Republican Convention, where he asked everyone to put aside their differences with Senator Goldwater since these differences were small compared with Lyndon Johnson. Nixon said that each candidate should decide "how he can win the most votes," and if that means running a campaign separate from the national candidate, then they should do so. The convention endorsed the Goldwater ticket, but Governor Romney would not do so personally.[42]

On September 29, there were twin news releases about Richard Nixon's campaign plans for the next five weeks. The news release from his law office indicated that he would be campaigning over 25,000 miles and 150 appearances on behalf of Republican candidates. There were hundreds of requests for his appearances from all 50 states.[43] In the Republican National Committee's (RNC) news release, they made most of the same points as the Nixon office with quotes from Barry Goldwater and William E. Miller. Goldwater said, "Dick is a man most highly regarded throughout the nation by people from all walks of life and has tremendous popular appeal. His stirring speech during the convention is only a sample. I'm sure of the impact Dick Nixon will bring into the campaign." Miller added that Mr. Nixon is "one of the truly distinguished men of our day and will bring the message of the Republican party to grassroots America."[44] It was indeed a great introduction to a difficult campaign.

The three themes Nixon brought to the Goldwater campaign centered on strengths of the local Republican candidate, Goldwater, as being "reasonable"; criticisms of the Kennedy-Johnson years, primarily in the foreign policy arena; and questioning of Lyndon Johnson's character and integrity. Nixon wondered, which LBJ would we get on domestic issues? The New Deal? The southern Democrat? The Great Society man?[45]

Richard Nixon traveled with a small party. Dale Grubb, a former FBI agent, was his aide. Executive aides Rose Mary Woods and Shelley Scarney, from his New York office, made all of the trips. Woods had been with Nixon since 1952, and Scarney intermittingly since 1959. The last member of the traveling party was Lee W. Huebner, a Ph.D. student from Harvard and an editor of "The Ripon Society," a reform-oriented research and policy group not formally related to the Republican Party. Ideologically, the group was moderate to liberal.[46] Nick Ruwe handled liaison work out of the New York office with the RNC. Ruwe had done advance work for Nixon since the 1960 campaign. There also were a few old Nixon hands who were working part-time and filling in the gaps when necessary. These included John Whitaker and Charlie McWhorter.[47]

Wherever he went, Nixon emphasized Republican unity. He was trying to make up for Goldwater's extreme statements to mollify the more liberal parts of the party. Historian Mary C. Brennan summed up this dilemma: "Nixon hoped to persuade Republicans not to desert the party ... and to bring 'back into the fold' those Republicans who had already left." Nixon worried that a post–Goldwater debacle coupled with massive defeats would cause Republicans to want to end the GOP. It nearly happened.[48]

No matter what the Goldwater campaign did, it seemed that they could never get their message through to the American voters. Conversely, President Johnson could seemingly do no wrong. One exciting event happened late in the campaign. Patrick J. Buchanan, the editorial writer of the *St. Louis Globe-Democrat*, related how the Walter Jenkins affair should have tarnished LBJ's reputation and given the Goldwater campaign a much-needed boost. Jenkins was a close personal assistant to the president and been with him for several years. Jenkins, found having sex with another man in the basement of the Washington YMCA, was arrested a week later. The story went public three weeks before the election. Buchanan recollected how "Goldwater and the conservatives would finally get their chance, but the news cycle killed them. On our front page was the St. Louis Cardinals winning the World Series with a 7–5 victory over the New York Yankees, Khrushchev being ousted by the Kremlin,

Nixon campaigning for Goldwater in Rochester, New York, on October 5, 1964 (Richard M. Nixon Foundation).

and the Red Chinese detonating their first nuclear bomb. So much for the Goldwater comeback."[49]

Richard Nixon campaigned as a man possessed. The only break in these 31 days was to take off a day and a half to attend Herbert Hoover's wake and funeral in New York and Washington on October 23 and 24. It was to no avail. LBJ won in a landslide, with 45 states and 61 percent of the popular vote. The Democrats gained 40 seats in the House, giving them a 2–1 majority and increased their lead by two in the Senate to 62–38. Nixon remembered the incredible obstacles in this campaign in his memoirs: "It was especially heartbreaking because Republican voters seemed to be interested in the campaign that year; everywhere I went, I found the audiences big and enthusiastic. But time after time, the senatorial or congressional candidate on whose behalf I was to speak begged me to avoid associating his candidacy with Goldwater."[50]

Lyndon Johnson became president after the assassination of John F. Kennedy. Johnson was the immediate political beneficiary of a country in mourning after Kennedy's death. He came into the office with approval ratings above 70 percent. Johnson was also an accomplished politician who knew how to get things done in Congress. He had been his party's leader in the Senate during the Eisenhower years. All he did before the general election campaign was to get a tax cut bill through Congress and sign the most comprehensive civil rights bill since Reconstruction. In short, Johnson was riding high going into the fall election of 1964.

On the other hand, the Republicans were in the process of deciding what kind of political party they were going to be. The moderate/progressive northeastern wing of the party had primarily been in control nationally since the election of William McKinley in 1896. In 1964, however, the Republicans chose to break with the establishment and go the other way in nominating a staunch conservative in Barry Goldwater, which effectively sundered the party. The party's most visible moderate leaders in Rockefeller and Romney did not support Goldwater, nor did they campaign for the Republican nominee, virtually guaranteeing an electoral disaster. It was Richard Nixon, until now identified with the more moderate wing of the party, who gave the nominating speech at the convention for Goldwater and then campaigned harder than the candidate himself during the general election. The magnitude of the electoral calamity could not be disguised, though, and following the debacle, the Republican Party was on the edge of oblivion. Party leaders had a lot of work ahead if they did not want the Republican Party to go the way of the Whigs in the 1850s.

Even though Goldwater and the conservatives had suffered a humiliating loss, they were not going away. Still, despite the dire circumstances, the two-time loser Nixon undertook the task of studying the election to try to understand what had gone wrong. In the process, he also began to rebuild his brand, as well as that of the nearly broken Republican Party. For the Republicans, the only direction was up, but resurrecting the party would take hard work, insight, and skill to reunite the fragmented organization.

Even though it was a massive loss for the Republicans, all was not lost for Nixon. He had done more than his share of hard work for the party. Others refused to campaign for the doomed Goldwater campaign. There would be another day in the future when the memories of the 1964 presidential campaign would loom large in the minds of Republican voters. It was also another step in the right direction for the comeback of Nixon.

3

Picking Up the Pieces

The bloodletting began a day after the Republican disaster. Nelson Rockefeller issued a statement pushing Goldwater and his supporters out of the Party.[1] One of those supporters was Richard Nixon, and he was not about to let Rockefeller's comments remain unchallenged. He called a press conference the next day to accuse Rockefeller of being a "spoilsport" and a "petty divider" who sat on the sidelines by refusing to campaign for Goldwater. Nixon said Rockefeller's resistance cost the party some strong candidates, many of whom were more moderate than Goldwater. The press conference received national coverage, with two stories about Nixon appearing on the front page of the *New York Times*.[2]

A week later, Nixon was off to Asia on another business trip. This time Bob Guthrie and Nick Ruwe accompanied Nixon along with Henry Kearns, who had traveled with the Nixon party earlier in the year. This time he visited Taiwan and Japan. Again in Taipei, Nixon was a house guest of Chiang Kai-shek, and while there, he attended political, business, and ceremonial functions with his host. At one of the functions, William Rusher, the editor of *National Review*, was also attending and tried to set up an interview with Nixon. The two agreed to talk back in the states.[3]

Nixon's frequent air travel caught up with him in Tokyo, where he experienced rather severe leg pain accompanied by swelling in the lower part of his legs due to the lack of movement on airplanes, impeding circulation and threatening deadly blood clots. Rest and a couple of medications reduced the swelling and pain in his legs. He still met with the prime minister and several high governmental officials while in Japan. Nixon also attended the second annual "Turkey Bowl," a goodwill football game between the American high school U.S. Air Force team and the Kanto High All-Stars.[4]

Republicans Fight It Out

The Republicans were looking forward after the disastrous election, which left the Democrats with a 68–32 margin in the Senate and a 295–140 advantage in the House. A week before the election, Eisenhower had suggested that the party form an advisory council after the election to suggest ways to reunite its members. The primary objective would be to define mainstream Republican values in everyday language for the general public.[5] Nixon's post-election press conference made it clear the party needed to move to a more centrist position.

At the Republican Governors Conference in Denver the first week of December, the bloodletting over the Goldwater disaster continued. George Romney and Mark Hatfield told Ike that Dean Burch should resign as head of the Republican National Committee. They wanted to dispose of Goldwater and chose the closest person to him, his former aide. William Scranton accused the former presidential candidate as practicing "non-exclusion" and agreed that the party needed a new chair that was more broadly representative of Republicans. Burch refused to resign, and the party still seemed to be in disarray.[6]

At the end of the conference, Senator Goldwater wrote a three-page single-spaced letter on U.S. Senate letterhead responding to Romney's claims, inquiring as to what Republican principles he had violated during the campaign. He also sent Richard Nixon and Dean Burch a copy of the letter. Goldwater stated that he had urged all Republicans to support Nixon in 1960. He reminded Romney that he did not support the recent Republican ticket and that it had been he and Rockefeller who were not inclusive.[7]

Romney responded before Christmas with a twelve-page, single-spaced, meticulously written letter about their differences. It contained so much rambling detail that the Arizona senator probably never read it. Romney made it clear that he tried to get a private meeting with Goldwater to hash out the differences on the role of the federal government, civil rights, urban issues, and what constituted an "extremist." Romney believed an extremist was "one who advocates the overthrow of our government through violent or peaceful means, one who uses threats or violence or unlawful or immoral means to achieve political ends ... regardless of the effect on others. Such political extremism destroys liberty and is a vice." It was a marked contrast to what Goldwater said in his acceptance speech. There were several times when they were supposed to meet privately, but something came up on Goldwater's end. Romney felt that he was being shunted aside and not taken seriously by the Republican presidential candidate.[8] By the time the general election campaign was in full swing, it was too late to meet. While Romney supported Republican candidates in Michigan and elsewhere, he did not personally endorse Goldwater because of their differences.

Three days after Christmas, the Michigan governor wrote to Eisenhower about the Goldwater/Burch situation. Romney explained to the former president that he had talked to Burch and that Burch responded he would resign at the Republican National Committee's request. Romney's impressions from his meeting with Burch were that the former Goldwater aide acknowledged "that he lacks the background and understanding required to bring people together rather than to continue a program that tends to drive people apart." Romney was feeling Ike out on the best way to go about this, hoping maybe the general would speak directly to Burch about changing his mind before the national committee meeting in the third week of January 1965.[9]

Dean Burch talked to the National Press Club on January 8 and adamantly denied he was resigning. However, four days later, on January 12, he appeared with Goldwater to announce that he was leaving his party chairmanship. Mary S. Brennan described the strange about-face in *Turning Right in the Sixties*: "The mysterious circumstances surrounding Burch's resignation provides insight into the structure of the Republican Party, the conservatives' position within the organization, and the growing maturity of the conservatives as political activists.... Burch and Goldwater agreed that Burch would step down and be replaced by Ohio state chair Ray Bliss." They did so for the unity of the party.[10]

At about the same time, alarm arose over the publication of a chapter excerpted in *Esquire* magazine from a forthcoming book written by Rowland Evans and Robert Novak that put Richard Nixon in a negative light. The authors accused him of lying about the incident with Governor Romney at the Governors Conference earlier that year in Cleveland. Romney maintained Nixon told him he should run for president against Goldwater. There were several related stories in the national press about the incident, coupled with an Evans and Novak column. Sherman Unger also wrote a letter on the matter to J.F. terHorst of the North American Newspaper Alliance. TerHorst had authored one of the stories freely using the Evans and Novak column. Unger, who had been with Nixon in the meeting with Romney, pointed out numerous factual errors, including a "Romney confidante" being present, along with an omission that Unger and John McElroy, an administrative assistant of Governor Rhodes, were present. Unger sent a copy of the letter to Nixon. The former vice president made no comments on the subject, and the press went away.[11]

The New Republican Leader?

A month after Johnson's inauguration, the National Republican Party was still trying to sort things out. They had a new party chairman in Ray Bliss, but a certain amount of uncertainty on who would be the titular leader of the party after the November debacle. With former President Eisenhower still very popular but seen as too old and mostly retired, and Senator Goldwater discredited by the 1964 blowout, there appeared to be only one person with the potential to bridge party divisions: Richard Nixon. The problem with Nixon was that he did not currently hold a political position. Nixon would still comment on national issues but also wished to concentrate on his hectic legal schedule. When speaking out, he did so on his terms. Nixon was in demand on the speaking circuit; for every public appearance that he accepted, there were many others he turned down. In addition to the several national boards on which he served, Nixon had been elected chairman of the Boys Club of America in December 1964.[12] Former President Herbert Hoover had previously held this post.

In early April, Richard Nixon traveled to Helsinki, Finland, with Newfoundland Premier Joseph Smallwood and business associate John Shaheen to finalize a $50 million pulp project. Nixon was acting on Shaheen's behalf as his legal counsel on this international project. Shaheen's company, Octane Oil, was a major investor in the Newfoundland Pulp and Chemical Company, which were teaming with United Paper Mills, a Finnish concern, to build a paper mill in Newfoundland. The new plant would employ 550 people and indirectly provide work for approximately 4,000 woodchoppers.[13]

As it turned out, it only took a day to finalize the agreement. They had allowed for three days in Finland before heading back to the United States. Nixon talked his associates into taking a day sightseeing trip to Moscow, 20 hours away on a train. With his political connections, the former vice president was able to get visas for his whole party in less than three hours. While there, they visited Moscow State University. It did not take long for Nixon to enter into a spirited discussion with the deputy rector of the university, Nicolai Beleyesov. The Moscow official was pestering Nixon about the Ku Klux Klan, John Birch Society, and other extremist groups, wondering how a so-called freedom-loving country could allow their president to be shot and killed. Nixon countered that no country was perfect and wanted to know, "What happened to Beria?" who was Stalin's head of internal security. "Why was he killed? Trotsky [former war minister who fled to Mexico in one of Stalin's purges], what happened to him?"[14] Beleyesov replied to Nixon by saying, "Trotsky was killed on American [actually Mexican] territory."[15] In response, the former vice president coolly stated, "If you want to talk about force, then we should talk about Soviet action against the Freedom Fighters in Hungary. As for the Ku Klux Klan, you can tell your students we are trying to remove all vestiges of prejudice and hatred, as evidenced by the Ku Klux Klan. We are trying to remove inequity and poverty in the United States."[16]

Before leaving Moscow, Nixon made a surprise visit to the apartment of Nikita Khrushchev, the former premier. Khrushchev was not at home. The story got big play back home and was on page one of the *New York Times*, comparing this visit with the famous "kitchen debate" six years earlier in 1959. Nixon held an impromptu news conference before flying to London and, in it, contrasted the conditions in the Soviet Union with the last time that he was there. He thought that the campus was more open to political discussions. It surprised him that Vietnam was brought up during the visit, and he said that he had supported the president's "strong stand" in the past. Nixon said that in the 1966 congressional elections, Republicans should adopt strong positions on both foreign and domestic policy.[17]

Two weeks after his trip to Finland and the Soviet Union, a generally favorable profile of Richard Nixon appeared in the Sunday edition of the *New York Times Magazine*, written by prominent Washington journalist Robert J. Donovan. Donovan described Nixon's place in Republican and national political circles as that of an "elder statesman" and key fundraiser, a person filling the leadership gap vacated by Goldwater.[18]

Nixon spent the next month concentrating on his legal business in New York. The one exception was a trip to Nashville, Tennessee, on May 2 for the dedication of a new Boys Club facility. Nixon was welcomed at the airport by Governor Frank Clement and Nashville Mayor Beverly Briley. He held a brief press conference where he told reporters he was not here for a partisan political event but acknowledged, "Tennessee had always been good to me." Nixon remembered how he had carried the state in the 1960 presidential election as well as the two previous presidential campaigns with Eisenhower.[19] He went on to say that he was very supportive of President Johnson's dispatching of American troops to the Dominican Republic to quell unrest there. Nixon emphatically stated that the United States did not need another Cuba on its doorstep. He believed that the United States should employ a "little preventive medicine" on Castro for stirring up turmoil in the Caribbean because the "real danger" was the spread of international communism.[20] Also, Nixon called on the United States to renew efforts for missile site inspections and Russian forces in Cuba. He explained that the "only way to prevent the spread of international communism is to keep the aggressor from gaining."[21]

After a luncheon at the nearby Colemere Club, Nixon addressed the crowd of 250, heralding the accomplishments of the private voluntary organization to enable all young boys to reach their full potential as productive and responsible American citizens. Nixon compared the group with the "pioneer camps" of the Soviet Union, where he recently had visited. He said, "There wasn't much difference as far as the boys—in physical appearance ... but the atmosphere was vastly different because our Boy Scout camps the youngsters got personal attention."[22] He next extolled the virtues of giving in a free society and the importance of individual contributions to private organizations because it empowers those who give as well as those who receive it, in this case, the young boys in the Boy Scouts.[23]

Nixon accepted an invitation on June 9 to be one of the principal speakers for a state-wide Ohio "Salute to Ray Bliss." It aired live in prime-time television in eight Ohio cities. Former President Eisenhower was the headline speaker. The other speakers were Romney, actor George Murphy, Charles Percy, William Scranton, Thruston Morton, Gerald Ford, Ronald Reagan, and Nixon. Murphy was a former actor and now a Senator from California. All of the speakers except Eisenhower and Nixon had only five minutes to speak. The event would showcase the broad ideological range of the Republican Party to raise one million dollars. The featured topics and assigned speakers were Nixon—foreign policy; Scranton—human welfare; Murphy—limited government; Percy—job opportunities; Ford—fiscal responsibility; Morton—education; and Reagan—free enterprise.[24]

Although a big success to the Ohio and national Republican parties, the telethon got negative press because Barry Goldwater was not among the invitees. The organizers of the event received several letters expressing their displeasure over the snubbing of the former presidential nominee. Nixon echoed this in a letter to Governor Rhodes a few days later, stating he was "delighted that the Ohio finance dinners were such a resounding success. The only flap that developed was with regard to Goldwater not being present, but I think that the overall national publicity was a plus because of the extraordinary high financial returns."[25] Given the context that Bliss was now national chairman, it was not surprising that the former Arizona senator was not invited to the Ohio affair.

Nixon keynoted an event in Milwaukee the following day sponsored by the Republican Finance Committee of Wisconsin. Over 2,000 people paid $100 a plate to attend. The ticket sales were up over ten percent from the previous year. Nixon was invited as the speaker. Just eight months after the '64 landslide losses, Nixon was emerging as a force. Ever the pragmatist, Nixon said unless the party made big gains in the 1966 elections, "We are not going to have a launching platform high enough or solid enough" to mount a successful presidential campaign in 1968.[26] An editorial written in the *Milwaukee Sentinel* titled "Nixon Realistic" hailed Nixon as "both an optimist and a realist" and opined that if Republicans made a comeback in the 1966 midterms, "Nixon will have a power base that will make him a force to be reckoned with in 1968."[27]

After the Wisconsin fund-raiser, Richard Nixon returned "home" for the weekend to Whittier, California. There on June 11, he delivered the principal address of the new $1.25 million Bonnie Bell Wardman Library at Whittier College. On stage with Nixon was Paul Smith, president of the college. Smith had been Nixon's mentor while he was a student at Whittier. He had taken six courses in history and political science from Smith and received straight A's. Smith had not been surprised at how successful his prize student had been. He recalled later in an oral history Nixon's tenacity and brilliance as a student when he assigned the ten-volume (over 5,000 pages) Abraham Lincoln biography by John Hay and John Nicolay: "I distinctly recall my conversations with him when I examined his papers. He had gone assiduously through the longest and most exhaustive biography of that American martyr and was deeply, personally involved in what he was reading. Good education strives to make the student forget the process of learning and arouse his interest in the substance of the assignment."[28]

Nixon visited his mother, awarded honorary doctorates at the commencement ceremonies, taped a television show for KNBC in Los Angeles with Bob Hope and Senator Margaret Chase Smith, played golf with Hope, and reunited with other friends and relatives. Nixon also made a guest appearance at a Republican women's luncheon. He awarded a scholarship bearing his name to a top student at Whittier College. The honor student's name was Geoff Shepard, and he was going into his final year at the Quaker college. Shepard got even better news two days after the event when he got a phone call from the sponsor saying that Nixon had matched the scholarship's amount with a personal check.[29]

Richard Nixon believed that it was essential to have a goal and a plan toward the advancement of that goal. While he had not advanced to an earlier goal of becoming president, that did not stop him from striving upward. Successful people know what to do when knocked down: they get up. The people in the audience for the library dedication at Whittier College knew that they were looking at one of their own, a man who had come from humble beginnings to become vice president and nearly president. After losing the governorship just two and a half years earlier, Nixon was not only succeeding in his legal business but helping to bring his political party back from humiliation. Before taking a trip nine days later with Pat and his family to Mexico City to celebrate their twenty-fifth wedding anniversary, he traveled back to New York to speak to the American Foundation of Religion and Psychiatry.[30] He also hosted a tribute for Karl Mundt in South Dakota.[31]

Refreshed from the family trip to Mexico City and the July 4 holiday, Nixon spent the weekend back in Los Angeles to speak at the Lions Club International Convention. He was one of three principal speakers that included Governor Brown and Randolph Churchill, the son of Winston Churchill. To the 8,000 convention delegates in the sports arena, Nixon spoke of the excellent service the Lions rendered globally. He also addressed the war in Vietnam and how "important it was for America to speak with one voice when the security of America is involved." He urged LBJ to reject calls from leading Senate Democrats, Mike Mansfield and J. William Fulbright, urging more concessions from the United States. Nixon said that "…kind of talk encourages our enemies, discourages our friends, prolongs the war, and weakens our position at the bargaining table."[32] Meanwhile, Nixon told his secretaries to limit his speaking engagements so he could catch up on his writing.[33]

At the end of July Nixon attended a GOP fundraiser in Potomac, Maryland, at the home of Louise Gore, a Goldwater delegate at the 1964 convention. He also got in eighteen holes at the Burning Tree Country Club before the social gathering. A *Washington Post* story said that Nixon looked tanned and fit.[34] Another story, written by Evans and Novak, argued that in addition to exposing Nixon "to the richest taproots of the Party, these excursions also give him a powerful argument to cash in on the goodwill of Republicans elected to Congress next year."[35] In their August 11 column, the two writers, no great friends to the former vice president, made it clear they thought he was running for president again but were unclear how successful or unifying he might be to the Party. They wrote, "One influential Eastern Republican snaps: 'If Nixon was the nominee of the Republicans in 1968, the Republican party would meet the Whigs in the hereafter within six months.' … 'Lacking both funds and staff, Nixon relies on the Goldwater effect—and the Goldwater movement. Considering the domination of the Party's convention by conservatives, it just might work."[36]

Nixon made only one more major appearance in August before another two-week trip to Asia. This one was in West Branch, Iowa, at the Herbert Hoover Presidential Library. A new postage stamp had been released in 1964, a year after Hoover's death, to celebrate his 91st birthday. Former President Eisenhower was there and made a few brief remarks before introducing his former vice president as the main speaker. The speech drew high praise as well as commentators who attended from around the country. Senator Jack Miller from Iowa complimented the address for "its timeliness, its complete bipartisanship and its importance with respect to the war in Vietnam."[37] Miller had the entire speech put into the Congressional Record of the 89th Congress.

Back to Asia

Nixon's next trip to Asia was from August 25 to September 10, when he visited Japan, Hong Kong, Taiwan, Malaysia, South Vietnam, and Australia. Pat Hillings met Nixon in Tokyo and accompanied him the rest of the way. Two days before he was to leave, his office got an urgent call from the Australia desk of the State Department, inquiring about a September 9 visit with Prime Minister Robert Menizes. They wanted to know what the visit was about, if it was a business trip, and what kind of business he would be discussing. His office replied that he saw Menzies as a personal friend, and he was going to Australia on business for a client. They did not disclose who the client was.[38]

Nixon held press conferences in all the countries he visited. After his Taiwan visit with Chiang Kai-shek, he stated the Nationalists would attack across the Formosa Strait if Communist China entered the war in Vietnam. He spent three days in South Vietnam and visited the countryside, touring areas of fighting. In Saigon, Nixon said that President Johnson should not mention the word "negotiations." Talking about negotiating would only prolong the war. He thought that the war would continue for three to four years and that more American men on the ground and a sustained bombing attack and naval blockade on North Vietnam were necessary.[39]

Pat Hillings had known Richard Nixon since 1948 when he was a law student at the University of Southern California. He had worked in every Nixon campaign since then. Hillings won Nixon's old congressional seat after Nixon went to the Senate in 1950. Hillings held that seat for four terms before returning to Arcadia, California, in 1959. Since then, Hillings had practiced law and owned a travel agency. One of his larger clients was Ford Motor Company, which allowed him to travel liberally in ten western states. Also, one of the benefits of being on the board of directors for West Coast Airlines was free flights. All of this served him well for helping out Nixon with his travels, both domestic and foreign. Nixon was happy for the help because Mudge Rose did not offer him any personal staff outside the law firm. Hillings would often perform several tasks on the road like scheduling, advance work, and media relations.[40]

After getting back, Nixon spent seventeen hours in Los Angeles before flying to

Washington for a September 12 live appearance on *Meet the Press*. Most of the discussion explored American foreign policy. Nixon said the Johnson administration should tell China to keep their "hands off" all Asian wars, including Vietnam, as well as the India-Pakistan conflict. His comments on Vietnam were similar to the ones delivered a week earlier in Saigon. He also stated he opposed any United Nations mediation efforts in Vietnam and that it was impossible for the United States to accept "a settlement imposed on neutrals." Nixon believed any reasonable settlement must include the "defeat of the aggression and punishment of the aggressors."[41] Afterward, Rosemary Woods talked with Earl Mazo, one of the panelists on the show, about his honest opinion of how Nixon performed. Mazo told her, "He was not only good but magnificent. He was so concise, so pointed, and so damn right." Also, Mazo told Woods he had received a call from a good friend of his wife who loved Romney. Both the friend and his wife agreed, "It would be wonderful if Romney had Nixon's brains."[42]

More Politics and Business

Later that week, Nixon traveled to Shakopee, Minnesota, to speak to a group honoring Maurice Stans in the honoree's hometown. Stans was a prominent accountant and investment banker who served as director of the Bureau of the Budget during the final three years of the Eisenhower administration, and was now working on Wall Street. The dinner event attracted a capacity crowd of 700 in the small Minneapolis suburb. Stans was delighted, and Nixon described him before his hometown friends and family as "a man of character and a nationally outstanding citizen and public servant."[43]

The next weekend, the Nixons were invited by the Stanses and a few others to attend the World's Fair on Long Island. The itinerary involved visiting several exhibits followed by a dinner. After seeing the first event at the Johnson Wax building, Nixon was greeted by several hundred well-wishers. Stans was amazed by the number of people who seemed to come out of nowhere to get a picture or autograph. This utterly spontaneous event lasted several hours, causing the Stans party to miss the other exhibits and arrive an hour late for their dinner reservation.[44] All of this was amid extremely high public approval ratings for Lyndon Johnson. The Republican Party might not be dead after all.

On September 22, Nixon spoke to an overflow crowd in Alliance, Ohio, honoring long-time Congressman Frank T. Bow, who had been a member of the House of Representatives since 1950 from the same district that launched the career of President William McKinley. Nixon addressed the virtues of the two-party system and areas of agreement and disagreement with President Johnson. An editorial in *The Alliance Review* compared the former vice president's speech with another famous Ohioan from another time. It said, "Mr. Nixon's masterful presentation, lasting nearly an hour and given without a single note and one second's hesitation, was highly reminiscent of how Ohio's late beloved Senator, Robert A. Taft, performed at the podium."[45] Taft, who was the oldest son of another Ohio president, William Howard Taft, was often referred to by the media as "Mr. Republican." Not a bad comparison for a man attempting to bring his political party together after a disastrous defeat a year earlier.

Trying to further the theme of Republican unity, Nixon traveled back to the West Coast to honor and support his former presidential campaign director, Robert Finch, who was running for lieutenant governor. He addressed a crowd of 1,000 at the Hollywood Palladium. Speaking against the context of some several highly publicized splits in the California Republican Party, Nixon said, "Unless we Republicans can make one party among ourselves, there is going to be only one party in the nation, and it isn't going to be ours."[46]

There were two governor's elections in 1965 that captured Richard Nixon's attention, in Virginia and New Jersey. He worked several campaign appearances in the two states sandwiched between recruiting trips for his firm at Harvard, Yale, Indiana, and Michigan law schools. In Virginia, Linwood Holton was trying to become the first Republican governor since Reconstruction. Nixon and Holton traveled 1,100 miles across the state to large crowds in Norfolk, Harrisonburg, Lynchburg, Roanoke, and Big Stone Gap, where the former vice president called for "a major political upset in the making."[47]

Richard Nixon had agreed in September to campaign for state senator Wayne Dumont, Jr., in the governor's race in New Jersey. Little did he know then that what would become a major controversy in this election was about to happen. In a statewide televised debate on October 18, Dumont challenged the incumbent governor, Richard J. Hughes, to fire one of the history professors at Rutgers University. The last two minutes of the debate centered on Dr. Eugene Genovese's comments to a teach-in the previous April in which Genovese welcomed a Vietcong victory in Vietnam. Hughes did not agree with Genovese's comments but would not try to fire him, citing academic freedom.[48]

In an October 24 campaign appearance, Nixon seemed to agree with Dumont's perspective. He also made particular distinctions and qualifications on why he had come to this conclusion concerning Genovese. Nixon claimed, "The question is very simple: whether the taxpayers should continue to pay the salaries of one who has used his position to give aid and comfort to the enemy during wartime. When it comes to a choice between American boys defending the freedom of speech and Prof. Genovese using that freedom, I am for American boys every time."[49] These comments shook up what had been a rather conventional and boring race. All the so-called Republican contenders like Rockefeller, Scranton, and Romney had been in New Jersey campaigning but generally stayed clear of the issue or leaned toward a near-absolutist position of the freedom of speech section of the first amendment, but not Richard Nixon. He knew that he had a problem with setting himself apart, and one with which a sizeable part of the American public would agree. Why should state-supported universities employ people who want to root for the other side when they are involved in a shooting war and ultimately destroying this country? Perhaps Nixon had stumbled on the silent majority.

Most of the national media, in a rush to judgment, were highly critical of any mention of the abridgment of free speech. However, there were others in the fourth estate like Arthur Krock who supported Nixon's statements, grasping the distinctions involved. Krock was the Washington bureau chief of the *New York Times* and a three-time Pulitzer Prize winner. His colleagues often referred to him as the "Dean of Washington Newsmen." Krock sent a letter to Nixon and said that he was "surprised that the press critics of your New Jersey speeches ignore your point ... but

I am disturbed by those with influence and great responsibility in our affairs who blandly ignore it."[50] Krock's newspaper was quite contrary in their editorial toward Nixon's comments but published his clarifications in an October 29 letter to the editor. In this, Nixon used a couple of historical examples two Democratic presidents had used: "I say as long as the demonstrators and those participating in an individual capacity, no action should be taken to curtail their activities. But any individual employed by the state should not be allowed to use his position for the purpose to aid and comfort to the enemies of the state."[51] Former President Eisenhower, who was usually quite reticent in these circumstances, wrote his ex-understudy congratulating him and stating that he agreed "emphatically with the views that you express and would be more than delighted to endorse them."[52]

The weekend after the November elections was the last major political event for Richard Nixon. He traveled to Albuquerque, New Mexico, for the annual Western States Republican Conference. Nixon and Barry Goldwater were the major speakers at the conference, with the former vice president speaking at night and his Arizona counterpart speaking during the day. In his speech, Nixon called Republicans to take care of their own by dealing with the radical right (John Birch Society) but thought that the extreme left in the Democratic Party was much more dangerous to the country. Nixon also believed the party would gain thirty seats or more in next year's congressional elections, and it was incumbent on the Republicans to do well in these elections if they had any chance of reclaiming the presidency.[53]

Nearly three weeks after the '65 elections, Nixon appeared on CBS's *Face the Nation*. He predicted the Vietnam War would be a significant issue in both the 1966 congressional elections and the subsequent 1968 presidential contest. Nixon re-iterated many of the same criticisms that had been made earlier in the year while in Asia. On the one hand, he was trying to be supportive of President Johnson's actions but felt that he could go much further in taking the war to North Vietnam. Nixon did not want to see the United States get bogged down in another ground war in Asia. When questioners asked about his '68 presidential aspirations, Nixon stated that he "was a political realist" and "the candidates for 1968 will come onto the scene after the election of 1966."[54] He was essentially re-stating what he had said earlier in the month in Albuquerque. What more could he say?

Richard Nixon agreed to do only a few more public events before the Christmas holidays. The day after his *Face the Nation* appearance, he was the keynote speaker at the Chicago Boys Club "Night of Inspiration." Nixon was introduced to a crowd of nearly 1,000 by Chicago Boys Club president and prominent businessman W. Clement Stone, and Mayor Richard Daley, certainly no friend to the former vice president.[55] It was the kind of event he liked because it aligned with his views on the role of a vibrant private sector in a democratic society. They should help develop in those young men who came from difficult circumstances leadership skills that would help them to be better citizens and contributors to society.

On December 3, Nixon agreed to speak at the luncheon of the 70th Congress of American Industry put on by the National Association of Manufacturers. This event, much closer to home, was held at the Waldorf Astoria in New York City. Nixon had been scheduled for the same event two years earlier but canceled at the last minute because of the Kennedy assassination. Nixon addressed the overflow crowd of over 1,000, stating the nation's economy was on a "collision course for inflation for inflation" and "unless strong corrective action is taken, the American people face higher prices, higher taxes, and wage and price controls within the next two years."[56] He stepped up his criticism of the Johnson administration's Vietnam policy, a place he had visited three months earlier. Nixon declared, "We have reached what Churchill might have called the end of the beginning. Secretary McNamara said this week that we have 'stopped losing the war.' This is the first time that any administration official has cut through the rosy communiques—including particularly his own—to admit the inadequacy of our efforts up to now."[57]

Full-Time Help on the Political Side?

One of the last events of the year Nixon agreed to attend was a last-minute fill-in performance for an ailing Senate minority leader in Belleville, Illinois, across the river from St. Louis. After the event, a reception was held in his honor at the home of Don Hesse, a cartoonist from the *St. Louis Globe-Democrat*. One of the guests at the reception came up to Nixon and introduced himself. He told Nixon that he knew that he was going to run for president in 1968, and he would like to work for him. The guest was an editorial writer for the paper by the name of Patrick (Pat) J. Buchanan. The former vice president continued to talk to his new acquaintance and asked several questions about his background and what he did at the *Globe-Democrat*. Buchanan told him what he did on his job, where he was from, where he went to school, and the like. Next, Buchanan told Nixon that he had met him several years earlier in 1959 when he caddied for him at the Burning Tree Country Club in Washington, D.C. Nixon often got comments like this from people that he was talking to and decided to see if his new acquaintance was telling the truth. He asked Buchanan who the golf pro was at the country club and who Nixon was playing with. Buchanan answered correctly and even identified the color of his golf bag. After some more small talk, Nixon told Buchanan that he could not even think of running for president as a Republican in 1968 unless the party made significant gains in the congressional elections of 1966. Buchanan realized that he had said enough. He did not want to monopolize Nixon's time and let him talk to the other guests at the reception, but he was hopeful of a call back from the former vice president.[58]

The next day Hesse drove Nixon to the St. Louis airport from Belleville, some forty-five minutes away, to catch his flight back to New York. After some casual conversation, Nixon asked the cartoonist some specific questions about Pat Buchanan. When Hesse returned to work, he told Buchanan that he must have made a positive impression on Nixon because he was all that they discussed. Certainly, Buchanan was glad to hear that and hoped to hear from Nixon soon, even though the Christmas holidays were coming up. A couple of days before Christmas, Buchanan got a phone call from Nixon, who told him that he wanted him to come to New York and talk about further employment opportunities. Right after the first of the year, Buchanan would fly to New York for the interview. It was a sit-down lunch alone with Nixon that lasted three hours. There were several probing questions about what he thought about several political issues and what he thought Nixon should do about these if he were president. Also, Buchanan was asked how his hiring could help Nixon. He told him that he was an excellent researcher and writer and would help with whatever he needed.[59] The end of the interview came down to a question about Buchanan's ideology. Buchanan relayed what came next:

> "You're not as conservative as Bill Buckley, are you?" he pressed. I had written a *Globe-Democrat* endorsement of Buckley for mayor of New York but felt a noncommittal answer might be best: "I have great respect for Bill Buckley." At meeting's end Nixon said that he wanted to hire me—for one year. The pay would be $13,500—a rate of $12,000 for the first six months and $15,000 for the last six.... My assignments would be to handle his growing volume of mail, help produce a monthly column for the North American Newspaper Alliance, and assist him in the off year elections in 1966. I accepted, but told him that he should call the publisher. Nixon did.[60]

When Buchanan went to work for Nixon as a special assistant, he found that outside of Rose Mary Woods, he was the only full-time person helping the former vice president with political affairs. Pat Nixon worked part-time, helping with the large volumes of mail. Nixon had some help from one of the partners, Len Garment, and two of the new associates, Tom Evans and John Sears, but given their legal obligations to the firm, it was only from time-to-time. To pay for the new employee and costs associated with campaigning, Nixon needed pledges of extra money for the new financial commitment. He had already obtained a significant one from Congressman Bob Wilson of California, chairman of the Republican congressional campaign committee, to target districts and have Nixon campaign there in the fall election. He also had support from a group of Republican contributors headed by Peter Flanigan, an investment banker with Dillon, Read & Company who was a major fundraiser in the 1960 presidential campaign, and Maurice Stans, former commerce secretary in the Eisenhower administration. The Flanigan-Stans group agreed to invest in this new venture called "The Committee for the Loyal Opposition." This collection of men and women had contributed to conservatives' causes in the past. They included Elmer Bobst, Henry Salvatori, Gordon Reed, John G. Pew, Jeremiah Millbank, Dewitt and Linda Wallace, and Walter Harnischfeger.[61] While Nixon would continue to do work for the firm, he had put together a working team for the political sweepstakes ahead.

On the political side, Nixon spoke at some Lincoln Day dinners and helped Republican candidates in the fall 1965 local and state elections. While some Republicans may have waited on the sidelines at this low point of the party, Nixon saw an opportunity by doing the grunt political work that needed to be done and, at the same time, helping rebuild his brand. He was in the process of trying to rebuild a fractured party. On the business side, Nixon made two more trips to Asia and one to Europe. This was also at a time when LBJ was busy at work on the "Great Society," passing large pieces of legislation with a Democratic Congress. At the same time, Johnson was escalating the United States' military presence in Vietnam. Even at the height of Johnson's popularity, though, Nixon was requested to speak to almost every major business or civic club in the country. For every event he accepted, Nixon turned down fifteen to twenty more. While it might not have been evident then, it looked like Nixon was on his way to a political comeback.

4

Rebuilding the Coalition

Richard Nixon knew that 1966 would be crucial to the Republican Party and his chances of a successful run for the president. While publicly playing down the notion of being a candidate in 1968, he was laying the groundwork for such a campaign if certain things fell into place. In the first six months of the year, he split his time nearly equally between business/professional responsibilities and political ones. Nixon made sixty-one official appearances during this period, with thirty-six devoted to politics and twenty-five dedicated to business. Amidst these appearances, Nixon devoted at least four weeks to a prominent legal case that he was arguing before the United States Supreme Court. He had scheduled a four-week tour of the world in July while allowing for five to six weeks for the congressional campaign that followed in August through November, coupled with his busy legal and professional business. There would not be much time for leisure in this crowded calendar.

One of the first appearances he made in the new year was a birthday celebration for Everett Dirksen, who was turning 70. The party was held in Washington, D.C., at the Mayflower Hotel, a favorite resting place for Nixon while in the nation's capital. He seemed to be in good spirits and smiled when asked if he was running for president, replying, "Of what organization?"[1] This gathering was well attended by many prominent politicians, particularly those of the Republican Party who were paying tribute to the long-time member of Congress. Dirksen first came to the House of Representatives in 1933 and the Senate in 1950.

After attending a fund-raiser for the Republicans in Ohio, Nixon spoke to the Compressed Gas Association as a favor to Harsco, an industrial metals company on whose Board of Directors Nixon served. He also met with the officers of the Von's Grocery Company, who were attending a meeting in New York. Von's was a southern California-based grocery chain whose owners had backed him in nearly all past political campaigns.[2] Nixon traveled back to D.C. on January 22 to be one of the speakers to the Alfalfa Club, along with Vice President Humphrey. This club was a social association made up of prominent business people and politicians who met once a year. The Alfalfa Club included approximately 200 members, essentially a Who's-Who of American industry and politics. Its members also included former Presidents Dwight Eisenhower and Harry Truman, along with President Lyndon Johnson. The club takes its name from the alfalfa plant, which is willing to do anything to get a drink. The honorary president of the group was a former secretary of state, Supreme Court justice, governor, senator, and house member from the state of South Carolina, James F. Byrnes. Nixon took with him three guests: Robert Abplanalp, long-time friend, Roger Hull, President of Mutual Life Insurance of New York, and Hobart Lewis, president of *Reader's Digest*, an influential news magazine that had featured several Nixon-authored articles in the past.[3]

Nixon came back to D.C. for a luncheon in which he was the keynote speaker for the National Institute of Rug Cleaners. He was there as a favor to one of his cousins from California, Merle West, who had his own rug cleaning business in Whittier. He wrote a personal letter to Nixon two weeks after the occasion; his heartfelt thank-you that ended with, "When you are a President in Washington, which you will be, I hope I may have an invitation to come by and see you some afternoon. Many, many thanks, Dick, and my best regards for you and your family."[4] Maybe West knew something that the rest of the country did not yet know.

Cold and snow blanketed the East Coast on the last weekend in January. On Saturday, Nixon spoke to the Women's National Republican Club at a Waldorf-Astoria gala luncheon honoring Frances P. Bolton, a member of the House of Representatives from Ohio. After the luncheon, he flew to Washington, where he was scheduled to be the guest on *Issues and Answers*, ABC weekly news program. Five days before the program, Nixon received a memo from former aide Agnes Waldron, who was now working for the American Enterprise Institute. It urged him to use "the opportunity to point out the [Johnson] administration is not to be trusted ... and his support is wide enough but I suspect has little depth. So far as being a master politician may be concerned people are now discovering that he really is a petty bully with no convictions whatever. The heat of the kitchen is just beginning to reach him and thus far his reaction indicates that he can't take it."[5] Nixon did that and more.

The format of the program was one in which the interviewer, Bill Lawrence, would ask in the beginning what issues were to be discussed and the interviewee Nixon would follow in answering the questions surrounding these issues. Lawrence started it out listing the issues: "Do you support the Johnson Administration policy in the Vietnam War? Will a resumption of bombing and an escalation of the war help or hurt the president politically? What issues will win for the GOP in 1966?"[6] Nixon started by addressing the final issue first. After he went through the past twenty years of presidential/congressional politics, Nixon stated he thought that the "[Republicans] are going to field the best group of congressional candidates that we have had since the year twenty years ago when I first ran for office in 1946." He next was asked about his campaigning for other candidates over the past two decades and whether Nixon thought he had a power base in his adopted home state of New York, given that Rockefeller and Lindsay had said that they were not interested in running for president in 1968. In typical straight-ahead fashion, Nixon replied he would not: "Any power that I have politically resides on a national basis. The fact that all over this country in states in which I have campaigned for others through the years, that I have a number of friends who recognize the service to the Party and who believe that I could serve the Party in the future."[7]

The middle portion of the program dealt with what Nixon's role might be in this campaign and what it suggested for the future, particularly the 1968 presidential contest. Nixon saw his role as being one for the party trying to regain its footing after the '64 disaster and to be a competitive political party again. He did not rule out running for president but thought it was highly unlikely that he again would be a candidate. Nixon commented that for the moment, he did not see himself as a future presidential candidate.[8]

The final segment dealt with Vietnam. Nixon was very precise when he stated that he supported President Johnson in three major areas of the war and wanted to give him wide latitude as commander in chief. The three areas he agreed with included that he wanted to "save the independence of South Vietnam, to stop communist aggression, and ... the peace offensive. I support it in the sense that he at least must try to negotiate a peace if we can negotiate it with honor." Nixon argued the administration should bomb all viable military targets in North Vietnam. He also believed that LBJ's support problem was not from the Republicans but the Democrats. He said, "Over half the Democratic senators, according to a *Newsweek* magazine poll a few months ago, either publicly or privately questioned the president's policy. That gives the impression, when it is read abroad, that America isn't backing the president." Nixon went on to say, "It will become an issue only if President Johnson fails to toe the line which preserves peace by rewarding aggression. If he takes that strong line, he will have Republican support. But Vietnam will be a real issue in congressional districts and in Senatorial contests between Republicans against those Democrats who do not support the strong line."[9]

Stephen Hess had been asked by Nixon earlier in November of the previous year to see if he could locate a plane so that Nixon could make several Lincoln Day dinners in February. He was able to convince officials of the Lockheed Corporation to let Nixon rent a nine-passenger Lear Jetstar company plane for the tour. Hess knew the company had allowed Vice President Humphrey to fly in it earlier that year; perhaps Nixon could do the same. This plane had been used the year before in the famous James Bond thriller, *Goldfinger*. It was playfully known as the "Pussy Galore plane," named after the villainess who headed a crime gang and flew the plane in the movie. After this, Nixon had asked Hess if he could come to work for him full-time in New York. Hess turned him down due to previous commitments including a book contract about the Republicans and two young children. However, he would be available from time-to-time to help with some short-term future assignments.[10]

John Whitaker was another among Nixon's wide group situated all over the country who could assist him without a great deal of notice. Whitaker grew up in the D.C. area, went to Georgetown University, and had a Ph.D. in geology. He worked for the Aeroservice Corporation doing aerial photography looking for the best places for mining, oil and gas drilling, and whatever someone needed in the way of aerial photographs. One of their biggest customers was the U.S. Geological Survey. Whitaker met Nixon in 1959 and worked as an advance man for him in 1960. He traveled with Nixon on weekends, working his regular job the first four days of the week. This February would be a bit different. He took off work for ten days to make several thousand-mile journeys across the country, though most of it was concentrated in the South.[11]

The trip started with a two-day tour to one of Nixon's favorite cities in the South, Nashville. He had been here just nine months ago, dedicating a new Boys Club facility. After arriving at the Hermitage Hotel, Nixon held a 30-minute press conference before speaking at Vanderbilt University, sponsored by the Vanderbilt Forum and the Young Republican club. The topic was "America's Role in the Vietnam War." The occasion was taped by one of the Nashville television stations to be shown locally the next day. After a couple of hours' free time at the hotel, Nixon journeyed to the Capitol Park Inn for a GOP fundraiser where he was the keynote speaker. After that, he went to the Grand Ole Opry and did a 15-minute live radio interview before going to another reception at the home of Guilford Dudley, a prominent Nashville businessman.[12]

Nixon had a much more open second day. After breakfast he met for coffee with Tennessee's Black leaders, who were looking for ways to broaden the party's appeal among minority voters. After a luncheon honoring Sinclair Weeks at the home of Weeks' stepdaughter, he met with Congressman Bill Brock and his administrative assistant, Bill Timmons, to thank them for their help with the Nashville visit. Brock was hoping for a brokered GOP primary fight over the Senate contest between Howard Baker and Ken Roberts, of which the party would turn to Brock as the compromise candidate. Nixon told him he would not take a position on it and hoped that the Republicans could avoid a nasty intraparty squabble. Timmons asked Nixon to speak to the Young Republicans at their summer conference the next year. Timmons was an essential player in the group, dominated by conservatives. Nixon ended his day in Nashville with a quiet dinner with the publisher of the *Nashville Banner*, James Stahlman, before flying back to New York.[13]

Nixon flew to Seattle for the next two days before returning to New York to work on legal business in the middle of the week. The Lincoln Day dinner was attended by a standing-room-only crowd of 3,500 at Exhibition Hall, but the event the next day may have even overshadowed the dinner. Over 2,500 teenagers from Seattle and King County high schools gave Nixon a standing ovation after he engaged in a lively question and answer session. One of the questions dealt with the Republican primary contest between George Christopher and Ronald Reagan for the governorship of California. Nixon hedged a bit, arguing, "Either Reagan or former Mayor George Christopher would be better than Governor Brown." On the broader questions of how well the party would do in the mid-term elections, he was much more definitive, predicting 30 to 40 seats gained in the House and 4 to 5 in the Senate.[14]

David S. Broder, the national political correspondent of the *New York Times*, was also working on a book about the Republican Party. Broder accompanied the Nixon entourage for the trip to Seattle. On the way back to New York, Broder interviewed Nixon, asking what he had scheduled for the future. He quoted Nixon in his *Times* February 10 piece: "There is a special aura about a presidential candidate, even one who has lost. It lends weight to his words.... I think I do better in adversity than when I am living off the fat of the land."[15]

After spending Wednesday at his office in New York, Nixon traveled back to the capital for another Lincoln Day dinner. Most of his speech centered on Vietnam, arguing the military should have a freer hand. He also said that the harbors should be mined and airstrikes increased. Nixon was bolder than in his comments in Seattle when he predicted the exact numbers of Republican gains in seats. He received some criticism for the president's economic policy when he said, "This Texas six-shooter is going to go off and blast a hole in the family budget."[16]

He returned to the South for the weekend. On Friday, Nixon went to Atlanta to speak there and had hoped to meet with Howard "Bo" Callaway, the only Republican from Georgia in the House of Representatives. However, Calloway had another commitment and could not make the fundraiser. He was coming under a lot of pressure from Republicans in Georgia to run for governor in the fall. In a letter to Calloway, the former vice president wrote that he understood the stress of being pushed into a position. On the other hand, Nixon was upbeat when he stated, "Based on my brief visit to Atlanta and discussions with scores of your friends at the dinner, I would say that your political stock is at [an] all-time high and is an excellent investment looking toward the future.... In the meantime, keep up the good work, your star is shining brighter."[17]

Nixon concluded his short whirlwind Lincoln Day tour with a capacity Saturday night crowd at the Convention Center in Louisville. The speech centered on many of the themes mentioned earlier in the tour: creating a united party as the loyal opposition, drawing a firm line against aggression, and combating the North Vietnamese. The speech was overshadowed by a shorter one he gave earlier in the day after laying a wreath on the grave of Abraham Lincoln's grandfather. This address was bipartisan, and it concerned two former presidents who presided over this country in times of war with a nod toward the current president. Nixon stated that Lincoln waged war to preserve the union; Truman waged war to defend freedom. "If the communists are victorious in Vietnam, there will be a bigger war later. If the United States stood up to aggression, more wars might be prevented."[18]

Nixon made two trips to Washington in March. The first was for a March 3 luncheon with the Bull Elephants, Republican House members. He returned to the nation's capital on March 12 for the annual Gridiron Dinner, where Vice President Humphrey headed up the Democrats' skit, and Senator Dirksen led the Republican one. President Johnson was not slated to be there but made a surprise visit to the delight of the over 500 guests of this political satire affair. Nixon was teased about his recent political losses by Dirksen when he said, "Every time that he throws his hat into the ring, it turns out to be a towel." Nixon responded with a gibe of his own at his friend, Senator George Murphy of California, by saying, "I used to know a George Murphy in Hollywood. He was the author of Murphy's Law: If anything can go wrong, the Republicans will nominate it."[19] Perhaps one of the funniest skits of the night was given by Bill Moyers, an aide to Lyndon Johnson, when he sang the famous gospel hymn, "In the Garden":

> I came to the garden with Lyndon
> While the dew is still on the Roses
> And the voice I hear falling on my ear
> Has the twang of a Texas Moses
> And he walks with me and he talks with me
> And tells me I am his own
> And the news we share as we tarry there
> May never, never be known[20]

President Johnson briefly visited the Gridiron Dinner after the end of the skits and made some passing comments. As he was leaving the podium, the president asked Nixon if he would have coffee with him the next morning at the White House.[21]

Upon arriving, Nixon was taken to the second floor, where the first family lived. It seemed a bit odd going to the living quarters at this time in the morning to talk to the president, but Nixon followed. A butler escorted him to the president's bedroom, where Johnson was sitting in his bed in his pajamas. LBJ discussed the situation in Vietnam with him, saying he could mainly bomb the hell out of them, but it might not be enough given that China was right behind them. In the middle of this critical foreign policy conversation, Mrs. Johnson came into the bedroom in her dressing gown and got into the bed beside her husband. She was very kind to the former vice president and greeted him warmly before she lay down. The conversation continued with Lady Bird joining in. Toward the end of their discussion, Johnson seemed to be looking into the future about what might become of him, the war in Southeast Asia, and the political future. Nixon recalled this meeting a little more than a decade later:

> "When I leave this office, Bobby, Hubert, or you will have the problem of China on your hands." I urged a diplomatic communication with China as soon as possible.... Johnson did not respond, but I sensed that he agreed with me. I said that since it was an election year, I would be out campaigning and making speeches for Republican candidates just he had done for Democrats in 1954 and 1958 when the Republicans were in office. "I know you will understand and not take any criticism I make on issues as being directed personally at you," I said. "I know Dick," he replied. "We politicians are just like lawyers who get together for a drink after fighting each other like hell in the courtroom." Johnson got up and walked to his dressing room closet, where he chose a pair of presidential cufflinks from the jewelry box and gave them to me. We shook hands and I said goodbye.[22]

In between the two visits, Nixon made a note to himself that the next time that he came to D.C., he wanted to make sure that he met with Bill Brock, a Tennessee member of the House of Representatives. Nixon wanted input from Brock on which congressional districts in the South to include in his fall campaign. Nixon wanted to meet with the 22 freshman Republican congressional members and make sure that John Duncan, the new member from the Knoxville area, was included in the meeting.[23]

Nixon only made two more political appearances that month: one in Montana during their annual state convention and the other in Arizona for a Republican fundraiser. He did not want to spread himself too thin as he began to prepare a case before the Supreme Court. In both appearances, he hit the Johnson administration hard on foreign policy with criticisms concerning Cuba and Vietnam. However, the most memorable aspect of these appearances came from a memo to Nixon from his new aide, Pat Buchanan, on the state of the Montana conservatives and the so-called divides of the Republican Party. Buchanan wrote:

> From what I have read, the Montana conservatives are a pretty ornery bunch, playing something of the rule-or-ruin game. But most conservatives of this type still look to Barry Goldwater as Southerners look upon Robert E. Lee, the Great Leader of the Lost Cause.... The Republican Party is now and has been large enough for both the views and membership of John Lindsay and William F. Buckley. But a rash of third parties around the nation, conservative parties would mean permanent minority status for both conservatives and the Republican Party.[24]

Two Other Major March Developments

While Nixon was crisscrossing the country for the Republican Party, two major developments occurred. The first dealt with a problem in the conservative rank and file community, at least in William Rusher's mind. In response to an earlier Evans and Novak column, *National Review* publisher William Rusher wrote a short note to Nixon to explain the recent supposed comment written by the columnists: "In a recent conversation with newspaper reporters, Nixon described the Buckleyites as a threat even more menacing than the Birchers." *National Review* and *Human Events* were the two most widely read magazines on conservative opinion. If one of these publications had problems with Richard Nixon, then most likely so would several of their readers. On November 2, Rusher fired off another letter to Nixon: "Quite frankly, I cannot believe that you uttered those words. But it is critically important to many conservative Republicans to know whether, in fact, you did or did not—only you can tell us that." Rusher tried again for a response on January 10, 1966, but to no avail. In the March 8, 1966, issue, Rusher attempted to call out the former vice president for an answer when he stated, "If Richard Nixon in fact believes this viewpoint represents 'a threat to the Republican party even more menacing than the Birchers,' there are a lot of people who would like to know about it. If he doesn't then he has been seriously misrepresented, and he should say so."[25]

Without knowing the mindset of Richard Nixon at the time, one certainly can speculate as to why he did not respond to Rusher. First, it is unclear whether he said this. Second, Nixon had a history of problems with the John Birch Society, the most recent being in his 1962 gubernatorial election in California. Third, he had learned from his past that sometimes issues were not worthy of being addressed. Fourth, while Nixon was the most well-known of all the Republicans, he had only recently hired a full-time political aide. Finally, while he had a high opinion of William Buckley, Nixon had a lesser view of Rusher. Also, it is a bit puzzling that the *National Review* "Focus on Washington" piece, written in the same period by "Cato" (presumably Rusher or Buckley) in the October 19, 1965, issue, was highly positive about Nixon on the same subject. In response to Senator Thomas Kuchel's comment on those on the right politically of him (Kuchel) being a "fanatical, neo-fascist, political cult overcome by a strange mixture of corrosive hatred and sickening fear, recklessly determined to control our party or destroy it," the author wrote:

> Senator Kuchel was answered effectively by Richard Nixon who told Republicans of his state: "The radicals of the Left pose a far greater threat to the Democratic Party in California than do the radicals of the Right in the Republican Party. The left-wing radicals are part of the very fabric of the Democratic Party in California…. As titular leader, [Governor Brown] should call on the Democratic Party of California to purge itself of the left-wing extremists who control the California Democratic Council and the California Young Democrats." Mr. Nixon was practicing what most Republicans seem to have forgotten—that you win elections by attacking the opposition, not your own Party.[26]

It appeared Nixon thought the uproar in *National Review* must have been a "tempest in a teapot," but that was not what his new political aide thought. Pat Buchanan told Nixon he felt they needed to respond forcefully to Rusher's question. In the April 5, 1966, issue, Buchanan wrote to clarify what Nixon said and meant. In his letter, the aide wrote, "Last Fall, while campaigning for Republican candidates in California, Virginia, and elsewhere, Mr. Nixon was on several occasions asked in press conferences for comment on Mr. Buckley's candidacy [for Mayor of New York City], and the John Birch Society. Mr. Nixon invariably replied that Mr. Buckley, by his repudiation of the Birch Society in his column, had thereby made himself a stronger candidate and threat to the Republican candidate, Representative Lindsay."[27]

Buchanan's letter seems to smooth things over a bit, but not entirely. Cato wrote, "It is just this sort of calculating caution that has often characterized Richard Nixon's public style, leaving even those who agreed with his stated views a bit uneasy about the man himself." However, in his last paragraph of "Mr. Nixon's Reply," the author wrote, "So all's well that ends well. And if Richard Nixon is willing to give personal leadership to Republican conservatives, he will find them ready to follow him."[28]

The other significant March development involved results of a poll taken by *Esquire* magazine that was sent out to Republican senators, congressmen, state officials, national committee members, state chairs, contributors, organizers of various sorts, writers, and publishers. The questionnaire was mailed the day after the November elections in 1965 to determine, "Who was the leading contender for the Republican presidential nomination in 1968." Republicans all over the country were the recipients of over 160 questionnaires. The results were summarized in an article entitled "The Best Republican for '68," written by Steven V. Roberts. Richard Nixon was the overwhelming winner, with 72 (forty-six percent) votes. He was followed in a distant second by George Romney with 14 (nine percent) and William Scranton with 10 (six percent). The final 12 responses were split between Mark Hatfield, John Lindsay, Nelson Rockefeller, and Ronald Reagan. Fifty-four responders declined to name any candidate.[29] It was undoubtedly good news for Nixon.

In this survey, the people's names were listed, as well as why they thought the way that they did. The primary reason that the respondents named was for party unity and that Nixon was the only candidate that could bridge all sides of the Republican Party. The conservatives were the dominant force in the party and the most active in the state and local party delegations. They also were the most vocal in the Young Republicans (YR) and the Young Americans for Freedom (YAF). Both groups were active in the Goldwater candidacy and were considered bellwethers for the future. One of the most exciting bits of analysis in Roberts' article came from the National Chairman of the YAF, Tom Charles Huston. Huston's reasoning went like this: "It seems to me that the most important criterion at this time is general acceptability by all wings of the Republican Party. Only Richard Nixon meets this criterion.... Nixon seems to occupy the highly desirable middle ground from whence the Party is likely to pluck the next presidential candidate."[30]

There were several other reasons listed in the survey cited for Nixon being the ideal candidate among the Republicans, but two stood out. The first dealt with the political leaders on the ground for the party and what they thought of a Nixon candidacy. Robert R. Barry, a former member of Congress from Westchester County, New York, explained this when he said, "Whereas the average voter is not insistent upon party loyalty, the seasoned politician never forgets, and since conventions are usually controlled by political leaders rather than popular movements, they feel safer with Nixon." The second involved the qualifications and experience of the candidate. Harry C. Carbaugh was a National Committeeman from Tennessee. He wrote that Nixon "knows more about government and foreign affairs than any other living American and if elected will make a great President." The former secretary of commerce from the Eisenhower administration put it even more succinctly when he stated, "Richard M. Nixon is the most qualified man to be President of the United States."[31]

A Lot of Law in April

After the Arizona fundraiser on March 28, Nixon allowed two days away from his important legal business. In April, he flew to New Orleans on a Friday afternoon to attend a Republican rally in Kenner, right outside of New Orleans. The next day he attended a Republican Convention in New Orleans. Nixon spoke of the party rebounding from 1964 and called on President Johnson to step up the war against the North Vietnamese and not give in to those arguing for "peace at any price." In between the two events, he also appeared at Tulane University, where he proclaimed that the race issue was dead for Republicans. Nixon stressed he had supported three civil rights bills over the past three administrations and that he would not campaign or back any Republican who advocated segregation.[32]

Nixon took his wife and two daughters to New Orleans. Nixon's last appearance in the "Crescent City" had been during the 1956 presidential campaign. The Nixon women walked around New Orleans and took a plantation tour. It was the first time Tricia and Julie had ever been to New Orleans. Mrs. Nixon talked of old memories from their last visit during the war and contrasted it with the current one. She seemed almost wistful in her description: "We were here about 25 years ago. We both worked hard that year, saved our money and drove here. We went on one of those banana boats. I think it was, to the Caribbean. We were in New Orleans about two days.... Antoine's [famous New Orleans restaurant where the Nixons had eaten on their earlier visit] hasn't changed a bit. The first time that we were just tourists."[33]

Nixon traveled to Durham, North Carolina, at the end of the month on April 30. This event had nothing to do with politics. He was taking part in a special ceremony at Duke University's Annual Law Day event that was honoring Justin Miller, a former dean at the school where Nixon was a student over thirty years before. Miller had left the University of Southern California School of Law, where he was dean, to take the same position at the budding North Carolina law school. Miller had been there at the beginning of what would become one of the top law schools in the country. Nixon was very thankful for the opportunity that Dean Miller provided him over three decades ago and the special place in his heart that Miller and Duke University occupied. The former vice president was quite eloquent in his tribute of Justin Miller for inspiring him to pursue a law degree.[34]

On April 27, Nixon was scheduled to appear before the United States Supreme Court to argue an appeal on behalf of the James Hill family versus *Life* magazine. This rather complicated right of privacy case had been brought to the Mudge Rose firm by Mr. Hill, a classmate of Bob Guthrie, one of the firm's partners. Leonard Garment was the litigator assigned to the case who had argued the case in New York state court and had won a lucrative settlement of $175,000 in compensatory and punitive damages for the Hill family. On the appeal of the case to the state court, the settlement was affirmed. Next, *Life* magazine filed an appeal to the U.S. Supreme Court.[35]

Garment approached Nixon in the summer of 1965 after the verdict about the possibility of Nixon arguing the case before the U.S. Supreme Court. Garment agreed to be the co-counsel on the matter. He believed this was a perfect opportunity for the former vice president to show another side to his public image. Nixon would be arguing for the rights of individuals against an overarching press with no respect for the right of privacy. Garment convinced him to take the case. Nixon had not tried a case in court since returning to his legal practice. It was unusual for senior partners, whose primary duties were to bring in new business and make overall policy for the firm.[36]

The facts of the case went back to September 9, 1952, when three convicts escaped from prison in Lewisburg, Pennsylvania. Three days later, they broke into the home of James and Elizabeth Hill in suburban Philadelphia. They held the Hills, along with their five children, hostage for nineteen hours. The convicts left without physically harming the family. Several days later, they were caught in New York and returned to prison. There was a lot of publicity generated because the home invasion caused a great deal of mental anguish for the family, particularly Elizabeth. A few months later, it got so bad for the family that they decided to sell the house and move to Connecticut. In 1953, Joseph Hayes wrote a novel, *The Desperate Hours*, based in large part on the Hills' tragedy. The novel was made into a Broadway play the next year, followed by a movie in 1956. In its February 28, 1955, issue, *Life* published a behind-the-scenes account of how the movie had developed. In the article titled "True Crime Inspires Tense Play," the magazine photographed the play during its Philadelphia tryout and took several of the actors from the cast to the actual Hill house to re-enact scenes at the site of the crime. Six separate photographs showed the actors at the home in various scenes of crimes against the Hill family.[37] In both the play and the following movie, there was a good deal of torture and violence associated with the break-in at the Hills' home. In reality that had not occurred. The Hills asked for a public apology from the magazine but got none. The additional publicity from the magazine article and the movie created a great deal of anxiety for Elizabeth. She had been fine until the magazine article came out. After that, Mrs. Hill had horrible nightmares, which led her to seek a psychiatrist's help. The therapy that she received included thirty electroconvulsive shock treatments. Her doctors testified that the mental anguish resulting from the publicity had caused long-lasting psychological damage. *Life*'s attorneys countered that Elizabeth Hill's mental problems were a result of malingering and menopause.[38]

Nixon relentlessly prepared the case. It harkened back to his days of "Old Iron Butt" when a young, aspiring Duke Law school student spent countless hours studying for classes and exams. Garment was amazed by the degree of preparation and thoroughness Nixon employed. In *Crazy Rhythm*, the veteran litigator wrote, "He worked particularly hard grinding his points down to their essentials. His preparation was almost obsessive; he left nothing to chance. His behavior was a sign not only of professional pride but of his determination not to let recent defeats drive him from the public arena."[39]

When the time came to argue the case before the Court, he was ready. Pat and her daughters were among those sitting in the audience. Former Justice Stanley Reed was also in the chamber. They witnessed a different Nixon than the one in the political world. He was arguing that the right of privacy that the Court had first put forth a year earlier in the *Griswold v. Connecticut* case was just as important as the freedom of the press argument *Life* was arguing. Nixon made legal distinctions between the right of privacy and that of libel and defamation. He stated he thought *Life* magazine generally was accurate in their stories and that it was "the most popular picture magazine in America." However, in their portrayal of this story, they had gone too far by commercially exploiting the Hill family in a false and fictitious manner. In the notes of Justice Abe Fortas taken the day after the argument, Fortas said that Nixon had made "one of the best arguments that he had heard since he had been on the Court and that he could be one of the great advocates of our time."[40]

After the case, Nixon and Garment flew back to New York that night. As usual, Nixon was back at work, making detailed notes on his yellow legal pad. Garment left him alone, read a novel, and got home near midnight. The next morning when he returned to work, Garment was greeted by five-page single-spaced memoranda from Nixon that were a self-examination of what he did and did not do in his argument before the Court. Garment thought it was the most instructive example of "discipline and tenacity" that he had ever seen.[41] Nixon was always prepared and expecting the unexpected. A decision by the court was expected in late summer.

The Republican Road Back

One might think that after the intense last month preparing for the *Hill* case, there might be a break or at least a pause in Richard Nixon's schedule. However, the next three months were hectic, with Nixon functioning on four to five hours of sleep per day. He would make some business and community appearances, but he spent most of his time spent on political endeavors to help the Republican Party on its comeback trail. Nixon knew that 1966 was critical to reversing the losses that it suffered two years earlier. There was no one better than Nixon to bring out the crowds and generate publicity for the potential candidates.

The journey started in Concord, New Hampshire, on May 2, where Nixon spoke to the New Hampshire Federation of Republican Women's Clubs to an overflow crowd of over 1,000. He advised his party to declare war on the "appeasement wing" of the Johnson administration and stand united in this election cycle against the divided Democrats. Nixon said the tables would be turned this time around, with the Republicans united against their split counterparts. William Fulbright and Bobby Kennedy were leading the appeasement wing. Nixon said their Vietnam policy would lead to disaster in Asia, and this Republican Party would back President Johnson to stand against further aggression by the North Vietnamese Communists.[42]

The three-month tour continued halfway across the country to Houston, Texas. Nixon spoke there to the Harris County Republicans at a Testimonial Dinner for Senator John Tower. Tower was the only Republican member of the United States Senate from the South, meaning the 11 states from the old Confederacy. Tower had won the open seat in 1962 that was vacated when Lyndon Johnson moved into the vice president's position. The first issue was the role of the John Birch Society within the Republican Party, a question troubling Richard Nixon. On September 30 of the previous year, the Republican Joint Senate-House Leadership made their position clear when Senator Dirksen said, "The John Birch Society is NOT part of the Republican Party."[43] Two months later, Ray Bliss, speaking for the Republican National Committee, agreed with this and took it even further with his comments on extremism: "I ask all Republicans to reject absolutely and without reservation any resort to slanderous irresponsibility. I ask all Republicans to reject membership in any radical organization which attempts to use the Republican Party for its own ends."[44]

Even though the national party had spoken clearly about groups like the John Birch Society, some local party organizations still grappled with the issue. The Birchers were attempting to take over the party in the most populated county in the state. George H.W. Bush was the chairman of the Harris County party and was running for one of the congressional seats in the district. Bush, who was the son of former Connecticut Senator Prescott Bush, had run two years earlier for the Texas Senate seat and lost to Ralph Yarborough, the incumbent Democrat. Bush was opposed to the Birchers. However, he believed that some of these folks could be channeled into the party with their stanch anti-communist stands. The other major issue dealt with the illegal registration of over 500 people. Nixon experienced this on even a larger scale in the 1960 presidential election in south Texas.[45]

After landing in Houston, Nixon held a brief press conference before meeting with a group of Young Republicans who were campaigning for George Bush at the Hotel America. Nixon had met Bush two years earlier and was impressed with the Texas businessman. After his initial meeting, Nixon told John Whitaker that the young Bush was "good vice-presidential material."[46] That night Nixon spoke to Harris County Republicans at the Shamrock Hilton at a $100-a-plate fundraising dinner testimonial to Senator Tower. He reiterated his claim that the Republicans would earn 40 or more seats in the House, five governors, and "even more important," at least 600 state legislative seats across the country. Nixon said that the congressional seats were "the backbone of the party." It would more than reverse the 500 seats lost in the 1964 election.[47]

Sending a Clear Message in the South

He went back to New York for only one day before hitting the road again. While he was in his home city, Nixon presided over "A Salute to Our American Heritage" at the annual convention dinner of the Boys Club of America.[48] Nixon flew to Jackson, Mississippi, the next day for a fundraising dinner at Millsaps College in Jackson. One might think of this visit to be of little importance, but it was important given the history of almost no Republican party in the state and problems that had to be addressed before he got there. The only Republican congressman in Mississippi was Prentiss Walker, a segregationist elected in 1964. Agnes Waldron had called Nixon to give him a heads up on potential problems in the state and particularly with Walker. She was passing on to her former boss what she had heard about him. Her sources indicated NBC had pictures of Walker meeting with the Klan and that Robert Novak knew about it. They also noted that most people thought, "Walker is considered pretty much of a nut."[49] Nixon wanted to make sure that when he visited Mississippi, Black Republicans would be able to hear his address. He wanted to make sure that they were not in the back of the audience. It was accomplished. Walker had his picture taken with Nixon and other Mississippi party officials at the airport. Nixon never specifically mentioned Walker at the press conference or in his address at the college, but it was quite clear in what he thought about Walker's public positions on race.

His important speech in Mississippi was about how the Republicans could build their party in the South to be part of a real two-party system in the region. There was a great deal of substance and symbolism in his address. Professor John Quincy Adams (not the former president) of the political science department introduced Nixon. Adams had come to Millsaps from a teaching position at Southwest Texas State College, where Lyndon Johnson went to school.[50]

Nixon began his speech by talking about his background growing up in California, and how his religion intertwined with his career path. He spoke about his Quaker heritage resulting from his mother's family and how his father had grown up as a Methodist but converted after his marriage. Nixon noted he graduated from Whittier

College, a Quaker institution. After that, Nixon told them he went to Duke University School of Law, a southern college founded by Methodists and Quakers. Nixon next transitioned into a discussion about the South and how it had been primarily a one-party region despite producing some of the great leaders of our nation's past. Nine of our first twelve presidents came from the South, three of which Nixon called among our greatest: Washington, Jefferson, and Jackson. Nevertheless, since the Civil War, the country had gone a little over a hundred years without electing a president from the South except for Woodrow Wilson, who grew up in the South before moving to New Jersey, where his career took off. Nixon believed that it was now the time for more strong leaders, this time from the Republican Party. He showed how sensitive he was to people from one region of the country, trying to understand their values and solutions to problems. Many people in the South felt that Washington and the North, while spewing negative publicity about their civil rights issues, felt compelled to tell the South how to put its house in order. Nixon readily acknowledged that there were racial problems in the country, but they were not limited to the South, or Mississippi in particular. He also pointed out that he had supported three civil rights bills in the last ten years. Nixon did not believe that the Republican Party could grow as the Democrats had in the past if they continued to support segregation. He wanted the party to progress in the region, but it should not do so by dividing the races. Nixon stated, "There is no future in the race issue," and that he would not campaign for any Republican candidate who used it.[51]

After the speech, he answered questions submitted by students. One of these dealt explicitly with the race/party issue and how that the Mississippi Republican Party in the 1964 campaign had projected itself as a segregation party. Nixon was reflective in his response and took it head-on, making specific distinctions between the two parties, stating that the Democratic Party in the South had a history of racism. The Republicans were offering a new way.[52]

Clarke Reed, chairman of the Republican Party in Mississippi, sent Nixon a thank-you letter and a collection of news clippings from Mississippi newspapers about the visit. Reed let the former vice president know that both Jackson newspapers had recently run negative stories on the Republicans. Both publications were "owned by the same family and will stop at nothing in an attempt to cloud the differences between the two parties." Reed added that they had both gone all out for Senator Eastland (D–Mississippi), a vaunted segregationist, and several of the articles written in the Jackson papers were by George Tolliver. The latter was a paid publicist on Eastland's staff.[53]

News about the Jackson visit and subsequent speech were now getting national coverage. *The Plain Dealer*, a Cleveland, Ohio, paper, picked up a story from the *New York Times Service* about the event and what it signified for the Republicans' future. Nixon was described as "the standard-bearer of our party today"[54] and had far more support than any other Republican mentioned for president in 1968. Much was made in the national press about Nixon not having a political base after his loss in California, combined with his move to New York, where Nelson Rockefeller reigned supreme in the hearts of the Republicans. It was beginning to look like he had substantial support in the South, the only region of the country where Goldwater did well in 1964. The article pointed out that the 11 states of the old Confederacy had forty percent of the delegates needed for nomination in the last presidential campaign. That number would increase given that the only electoral votes that Goldwater won outside of Arizona were from the region. It also made note that there were a half-dozen Black Republicans at the dinner, which was a first for either political party. It was done at Nixon's behest.[55]

Return to a Former Home

Nixon spent the next four days back in his native California. It would be full of political events and a Mother's Day visit to Hannah Nixon in Whittier. It was a significant political year for the state, as they would be electing a governor and lieutenant governor. En route to Los Angeles, Nixon stopped in Dallas, where Buffalo Bills quarterback Jack Kemp joined him. Kemp, who hailed from the L.A. area, would accompany Nixon to events, particularly those involving Robert Finch, who was running for lieutenant governor of California. Kemp had met Finch several years earlier when he was a student and football star at Occidental College. The two stayed in touch and became friends over the years. Kemp was looking at political possibilities when his football days were over. Finch had worked for Nixon first as an aide in 1958 and was campaign manager for Nixon in his presidential run in 1960 as well as George Murphy's 1964 Senate contest.[56]

Finch met the two at the airport. In less than ninety minutes, Nixon arrived at the studios of KNXT-TV in Hollywood to tape *Newsmakers*, scheduled to air the next day, a Sunday afternoon. Nixon spent Saturday night and Sunday with his family in Orange County. The following two days, he campaigned for Bob Finch. The two flew to Monterey on Monday morning for a fundraising breakfast, followed by a luncheon event in Santa Barbara. Nixon and Finch arrived in San Diego at 3:30 in the afternoon, trailed by two more fundraisers, one at the Bahia Resort Hotel and another at Sea World.[57]

Nixon was the featured speaker the next day at the San Diego Kiwanis Club "Pillars of Freedom" luncheon. Over 1,700 attended the address. The subject of his speech concerned the American policy in Vietnam. Herb Klein, an old friend and aide, now the editor of the *San Diego Union*, introduced Nixon. Nixon shared a couple of funny stories about Klein and himself. One of these involved Nixon's handling of the press and who was to blame: "I have known him during the years that he served with me and I just can pay tribute to him in a very few words. As all of you know, I am an expert when it comes to handling the press. Everything I learned about handling the press I learned from Herb Klein."[58]

The speech itself detailed how the United States got involved in Vietnam. It also included the war's origins and the status of the conflict. Nixon was applauded three times during his address. The first came when he stated, "We should use more air and sea power against all military installations." The second occurred when he said, "Senator Fulbright has never been to Vietnam. I, for one, would be willing to start a little fund to send him there," with the final one being that he "would suggest that [Fulbright] talk to a marine."[59] Fulbright had broken with President Johnson on the war and was becoming a thorn in the side of the Texan. He had commented earlier in the year that Saigon, the capital of South Vietnam, was nothing more than a brothel for American troops.

Into the Heart of America

Nixon spent the next two weeks in America's heartland holding two fundraisers in Kansas: one in Wichita and another in Kansas City. The two themes continued to be to take the fight to the North Vietnam communists and what the creeping problem of inflation signaled for the future economy. Nixon was still able to keep up his excellent sense of humor amid this grueling pace that had him working 70 hours a week. When asked in Kansas City about Lyndon Johnson and his supposed drop in the polls, he said, "I don't think that he comes over too well on television, and believe me, I know what television can do to you." It was an obvious takeoff on his appearance in the first televised debate against John F. Kennedy. Also, he was making light of LBJ's recent brushes with the fourth estate when he stated, "He's having trouble with the press. Well, I'm an expert on that too."[60] He also teased himself at the famous 1962 news conference where he said they would not have Richard Nixon to kick around anymore.

His next stop was in Decatur, Illinois, where Nixon attended a fundraising dinner for the local congressman, William Stringer. This area of rural, southern Illinois was where the GOP had a lot of strength. Republicans Les Arends and Robert Michel manned the two congressional districts. Pat Buchanan outlined some talking points about the trip in a memo sent to Nixon while he was on the road. He pointed out, "Decatur, Illinois is the soybean capital of the world (outside of Manchuria). ... The only issue that we should skirt is the domestic communist one. Open season on all others.... This is their political event of the year."[61]

Nixon did not disappoint the 600 attending the event as he railed away at the war policy: "We run the risk of World War III by following the present course in Vietnam.... It is not in our interests to have a long war or a ground war.... The communists want to bleed us white." He discussed several other enticing political issues before ending with the future of the Democratic Party. Nixon said, "The Democratic Party is deeply divided because of the Vietnam issue and the fight for the heir apparency between Vice President Hubert Humphrey and Robert Kennedy."[62] Staying united would be a must for the Republicans to take advantage of the Democratic split. Richard Nixon would continue to make this case everywhere that he went into this election cycle.

His next stop in Cleveland, Ohio, the annual Junior Achievement award dinner at the Hotel Sheraton with an overflow crowd of 3,000, had a "good citizenship" theme. Junior Achievement is a group comprised of young people learning the virtues and principles of the free enterprise system. Nixon began by noting all the prominent business and industry leaders in the audience of mostly teenagers, saying, "I'm the only man here who never made a president." He next turned to the young crowd, acknowledging their idealism and place in society, but challenging them "to always shoot higher than you think that you can reach." Nixon knew from his own experience what it meant to shoot higher, even amidst failure. He continued, "Unless you do, you won't give to America as much as you can. Losing is not defeat: defeat is when you quit. You learn from losing."[63] No one, not even Democrats, could call Richard Nixon a quitter.

In his busy Cleveland schedule, Nixon found time to tape a public service film titled "Building Political Leadership," made by Republic Steel Corporation, to distribute to students in the greater Cleveland area. Next, he held a brief press conference where he addressed the current political scene. Nixon also made time to present the Boys Club of Cleveland "Boy of the Year" to a young Stanley Chudzinski.[64]

Pittsburgh, Pennsylvania, was the last stop on this heartland tour. In the steel capital of America, nearly 1,600 people paid $100-a-plate for the opportunity to hear him extol the virtues of the Republicans while never missing a chance to criticize the Democrats. The title of the fundraiser was "Republican a Go-Go." The program cover showed a female elephant dancing inside a hanging cage, an allusion to the popular television music show "Hullabaloo."[65] It was an attempt to break out of the straitlaced image that many had of Republicans. Escorting Nixon to the speaker's platform was a group of go-go girls. One official who helped put the event together said, "We wanted to show there's a little life, a little excitement in the Republican Party." The former vice president said that he had never attended a dinner that was more fun. In addition to the go-go girls dancing to loud rock music, there was even a two-year-old elephant that performed tricks on the stage.[66]

Back in Familiar Territory

After three weeks on the road, Nixon needed to catch up on his legal business. He spent the first three days of the week in New York before heading out on Memorial Day weekend. The first stop was a luncheon on Thursday for the Republican Women of Capitol Hill in Washington. That night, he gave a major speech to the National War College that transcended partisan politics. In addition to his usual topics of discussion, Nixon added some new specifics to the United States' position in Vietnam. When asked what he thought the result would be if the war were ended at the negotiating table at this moment, Nixon said that South Vietnam and its 15 million people would come under Communist control destroying credibility in Asia and Europe. He concluded that America should end the war by not appeasing the Communists.[67]

After a one-day visit to Kansas City, Missouri, where he spoke to the Association of American Editorial Cartoonists, Nixon returned to New York. Four days later, he went to the most western part of the state in Jamestown to attend a fundraiser for Congressman Charles E. Goodell, a three-term member of the House running for re-election in the state's 38th district.[68] Nixon got a big welcome from the 500 Republicans attending the dinner at the Hotel Jamestown. He got an even stronger editorial endorsement from John A. Hall, editor of the *Jamestown Post-Journal*, who called Nixon "the leading statesmen of the era," noting his experience in foreign policy.[69]

Back home, Nixon traveled to Westchester County to speak at the annual dinner put together by top businessmen in the area in the Westchester County Association. The group, which had a strong economic development focus, chose between Bobby Kennedy and Richard Nixon, with Nixon emerging as the overwhelming favorite.[70]

When President W. Allen Wallis of the University of Rochester invited Richard Nixon to speak at its 1966 annual spring commencement, he did not envision the controversy surrounding the invitation. In the thirteen-month interval, Nixon thrust himself into the issue over a state university firing a professor who advocated a Vietcong victory. Nixon's stand on the issue cemented his conservative credentials within his party but worried some in his camp that perhaps he had gone too far, inserting himself into the issue of academic freedom. Len Garment and Bill Safire thought Nixon should soften his stand and make him more palatable to the academic elite.[71]

Two months before the June commencement, the university announced Nixon would be speaking and would receive the customary honorary doctorate. Usually, the commencement speaker is awarded an honorary degree. A faculty group led by Professors Joseph Frank and Christopher Lindley presented a resolution opposing the honorary degree due to his position on academic freedom. Of the 250 faculty, some 175 signed the declaration. Also, 215 of 512 senior students approved another resolution against the Nixon invitation. The university confirmed that Nixon would give the commencement address but did not mention the honorary degree.[72]

Prominent Washington attorney and former president of the American Bar Association, Charles S. Rhyne, wrote a spirited letter to the *New York Times* in defense of Nixon. He had successfully argued for congressional redistricting in the famous *Baker v. Carr* case before the United States Supreme Court in 1962. Rhyne, who met Nixon while a student at Duke University, reminded the readers of the hypocrisy and the historical ignorance of the faculty surrounding the controversy: "This is a rather startling exercise of intolerance. ... The purpose of 'academic freedom,' like the constitutional provision protecting freedom of speech, is to stimulate that progress which flows from the unfettered expression of divergent and controversial views.... The Rochester faculty, in effect, denies that Mr. Nixon has such rights."[73]

As it turned out, Nixon spoke at the commencement but did not wear the cap and gown. He told Wallis that he did not need the honorary doctorate, despite the Rochester president's attempted insistence. The speech received some excellent reviews, as evidenced by the letters to the editor of Rochester's paper, *The Times-Union,* who endorsed the address in an editorial titled "Nixon Sets Proper Limit to Academic Freedom." "Nixon set his limit beyond criticism of the conduct of the war or even the war itself. But he declared that 'any teacher who uses the forum of a university to say that he welcomes victory for the enemy in a shooting war crosses the line' of intolerable abuse of academic freedom."[74] In addition to the widespread publicity of the commencement address, it was included in a college textbook edited by Glenn R. Capp, a prominent professor of communications at Baylor University, which came out later in the year. The book was titled *Speaking on the Great Society.*[75]

Two days later, Nixon was back in Washington speaking to the GOP's annual congressional gala where he predicted significant victories in November: "With God's help, Gerald Ford will be speaker of the House next year." Ford was given a Steuben crystal elephant for his work as House minority leader. Nearly all Republican members were at this affair, along with other party officials. Former GOP chairman and 1960 Nixon co-campaign manager Len Hall was also there. Barry Goldwater had met with several members at a private reception before the event but did not attend the gala itself. He had a prior engagement across town.[76]

The Barnstorming Continues

Nixon returned to the Midwest for a series of fundraisers in Chicago, Indianapolis, and Minneapolis. In Chicago, he spoke at the 75th annual General Federation of Women's Clubs with law and order as his major theme. He only briefly criticized the president for his handling of France's withdrawal from NATO and the administration's Vietnam policies. Nixon called a recent shotgun attack on James Meredith, the first Black student at the University of Mississippi, "the latest symptom" of lawlessness in the country, which he declared in decline. Nixon finished his address, calling "for a national crusade to restore respect for the rule of law." This crusade, Nixon claimed, must begin in the homes and continue in the schools, for there can be no lasting progress and no Great Society without the rule of law.[77]

Indiana was the home state of Hannah Nixon, and it had almost been almost a second home for Richard since he had been here over 25 times since 1952 and won the state easily in 1960. Nixon spoke at the state's GOP slate at the "Republicans-A-Go-Go," following the same theme as an earlier party dinner in Pennsylvania. Over 3,000 people attended the event.[78]

After a brief stop in Minneapolis where Nixon spoke at a fundraiser for Congressman Clark MacGregor, he was back the next day in New York attending a party for the associates in his firm. In returning to the campaign trail, his first stop was to keynote a Congressional Boosters Club luncheon in Philadelphia, followed by a meeting with Walter Annenberg, the prominent Philly businessman. Nixon then headed back to California, stopping in Nevada for another fundraiser, this time for Lieutenant Governor Paul Laxalt, who was then running for governor.[79]

Nixon made a return call to his home state, spending several hours in Whittier and Orange County visiting his mother and family before heading back to Los Angeles to celebrate Republican primary victors. Nixon also directed a fundraising gala at the sports arena for Ronald Reagan and Robert Finch. Reagan won his primary with a 2–1 margin over George Christopher, while Robert Finch won by an even more significant margin. Nixon gave a rousing speech to the nearly 20,000 Republicans. Some of the most notable lines had a clear California ring when he talked about extremism in the Democratic Party and the California Democratic Council. Nixon said, "This is the outfit which harbors draft card burners, troop train blockers, beatniks who brought the greatest university in the United States to its knees. This is the outfit which advocates appeasement against Hanoi, Havana, and Peking." The benefit raised over $300,000.[80]

The Nixon blitz began the following day with a fundraising breakfast for Bob Finch. After a brief press conference, he attended a fundraiser luncheon at the Pacific Mutual Building. That afternoon, it was off to San Pedro to address a Republican Candidate's School, and then he rushed to a Pacific Palisades dinner at the home of Ronald and Nancy Reagan.[81] Nixon would give the former actor advice on what was ahead in the general election campaign. An excellent example of this was in a letter that Nixon wrote right after Reagan's primary victory stating he should be ready for the media attacks.[82]

Nixon would then head back to the Midwest. Two days spent in Chicago had him appearing at the American Medical Association meeting and a fundraising picnic for Nixon's upcoming congressional campaign. Old hands Peter Flanigan and Maurice Stans headed up this group of about two dozen, calling themselves the "Birdwatchers of '66." Nixon told the group that he would need about $100,000 to cover expenses. Another group from the House, the Republican Congressional Campaign Committee, was kicking in some money, and Nixon hoped the Republican National Committee would also provide an airplane for transportation. However, Ray Bliss refused to say he would not show favoritism to potential presidential candidates without noting no other major Republican had offered to do the kind of cross-country touring that Nixon had promised. They were able to get around the airplane problem when the group got a commitment from William Lear to use the Pussy Galore Learjet again.[83]

He next headed to Detroit, where, along with Governor Romney, Nixon spoke to the U.S. Junior Chamber of Commerce. For the next week, Buchanan and Hillings accompanied Nixon on trips to Birmingham, Tulsa, and Roanoke. Jules Witcover, a columnist for the *Baltimore Sun,* traveled with the Nixon entourage group during this next swing. Witcover was impressed with the Nixon tenacity and self-control and "campaigned like an athlete in training."[84]

The last leg of this trip was from Roanoke to Washington, where Witcover was able to get an interview with Nixon. Nixon spoke about his campaigns in the past and where he was going politically. He talked about men of ideas versus men of action, harkening back to his studies of Theodore Roosevelt and Woodrow Wilson at Whittier College. Nixon looked at himself as sort of an "egghead" like Adlai Stevenson but acknowledged that he did not write as well as the Democrat from Illinois. Nixon said he wished he had more time to think and write, but he was too busy. He even sometimes thought about leading the contemplative life of an intellectual. Finally, Nixon explained he knew that he would have to battle the press and but that it was all part of the battle of ideas.[85]

Nixon headed into the July 4 holiday for a ten-day vacation with his family in Florida. He had scheduled a couple of minor events for the rest of the month before leaving for a four-week foreign trip that would take him to Europe, the Middle East, and Asia before heading full speed into the autumn congressional campaign.

5

Had Enuff?

On this foreign trip, Richard Nixon wanted to determine how America's friends around the world viewed Johnson administration foreign policy. The trip was both professional and personal. Pat and his daughters accompanied him on the first half excursions to London, Dublin, Paris, Rome, and Israel. The family split up in Rome when Nixon headed for Asia. The Nixon women spent three more weeks abroad, touring in Israel, Lebanon, and Turkey. They were walking through the major thoroughfares of the Old and New Testaments at such places as Bethlehem, Jerusalem, Jericho, Ephesus, Troy, Istanbul, and the Dead Sea.[1]

Bebe Rebozo accompanied the former vice president for the entire trip. John Shaheen, a friend and client of the law firm, and his wife joined the Nixons for the first leg of the journey. Shaheen was scouting out business possibilities in the United Kingdom. Albin Smith, another Nixon client, was also on the England/Ireland portion of the journey looking for investment opportunities.[2]

Before the Nixons went to France, they had lunch and spent part of the day with J. Paul Getty at his estate outside of London. Getty was thought to be the richest man in the world at the time, having made his first million in the oil business before he was twenty-five years old. Also, Getty owned the most extensive private art collection in the world. Nixon told an interesting story about his host and their tour of his palatial property that put happiness and material wealth in a broader perspective: "We were served on gold plates, gold silverware—ware—it wasn't just gold-covered—gold—solid gold silverware and gold goblets.... So I look up at the head of the table, and here sat J. Paul Getty, the richest man in the world. You know what he had? Graham crackers and milk. And so I realized that there are other things than being rich."[3]

While in Paris, the Nixons were house guests of Paul Louis Weiller at his estate. Weiller was a prominent industrialist who had been a French war hero in the First World War. They were also dinner guests of the Duke and Duchess of Windsor during their short stay in France. They next flew to Rome, where the former vice president met with the Pope. The family stayed on in Rome to do more sightseeing before going to the Holy Land while Richard went on to Israel. In his two-day visit there, Nixon met with the prime minister and embassy officials. He also met with the former prime minister and one of the founders of modern Israel, David Ben Gurion.

En route to Asia, Nixon flew to Pakistan and met with President Khan, where they discussed Indian-Pakistani relations along with those of the United States.[4]

The most important part of the trip was a two-day stay in South Vietnam. Nixon outlined his intentions in a letter to Ambassador Lodge two and a half weeks earlier on July 21. He made it clear to his former running mate he had no interest in publicizing his visit to the war-torn country and would not comment until he returned to the United States on August 20. The ambassador was very accommodating and was able to set Nixon up with a two-hour luncheon meeting with Brigadier General Edward Lansdale, an old hand in Asia and a special aide to the ambassador. Lansdale had worked with the French in Indochina during the 1950s. He was the creator of the successful counterinsurgency strategy that the Philippine army employed against communist guerrillas in the period after World War II. It was the strategy the United States was currently using in the war. Nixon next met with William Westmoreland, head of American forces in Vietnam, for a briefing on the war.[5]

Nixon then spent a day in the Philippines, where he met with President Ferdinand Marcos and Carlos Romulo. Marcos had been involved in Filipino politics for three decades and was elected president in 1965.[6] General Romulo had been a prominent figure in the Philippines going back to the MacArthur period of the 1930s and had served the Filipino people as both president and prime minister. He had served as head of the military, president, and leader of the United Nations General Assembly.[7]

During his two-day stay in Hong Kong, Nixon met with several government officials and business clients like Harold Lee and Linden Johnson. He next traveled to Tokyo, then Seoul, and back to Tokyo for four days.[8] In Japan and South Korea, the former vice president met with the president, prime minister, and foreign minister. In Japan, he also called on several business clients, including Pepsi, Mitsui & Company, and Pan American Airlines. Nixon had dinners sponsored by the Japanese government and Mitsui & Company. Nixon left Tokyo on August 15 and traveled to Hawaii for three days of political campaigning.[9]

It was certainly not the first time Richard Nixon had been to the island state of Hawaii. He campaigned there in 1960 and lost by only 115 votes, less than one-tenth of one percent of the electorate in a state where Democrats outnumbered Republicans nearly two to one. Nixon visited all five islands on behalf of the GOP candidates for Governor Randolph Crossley and Lieutenant Governor George Mills. The most significant event was on Oahu, where 1,000 attended a $50-a-plate dinner at the Hawaiian Hilton Village.[10]

Back in the U.S.A.

Back in New York City less than twenty-four hours, Nixon spoke to a Cities Executive Luncheon. Two days later, he was the principal speaker at the 67th Annual National Convention of the Veterans of Foreign Wars (VFW). Other prominent speakers included Secretary of State Dean Rusk and Secretary of Defense Robert McNamara. In a telephone conversation with Rose Mary Woods earlier in the year, past VFW Commander Joseph L. Lombardo told the Nixon aide, "He's our first choice—the greatest friend we have ever had." Lombardo said that they were expecting 2,000 members, including some prominent Senators and members of Congress, as well as the national media for the principal address. Significantly, that this critical group chose Nixon as their most distinguished guest is worth noting, especially given the large Democratic majorities in Congress and a Democratic president leading the current war in Vietnam.[11]

The VFW's annual convention was one with which he was familiar, having spoken there seven times during his stint as vice president, the last being in 1960. The VFW had represented veterans from the Spanish-American to Vietnam wars. Its symbol was the Cross of Malta, the emblem of courage. The eight-pointed cross is formed by four arrowheads at the points. Each of the points represents one of the eight Beatitudes (Blessed are the...) that Jesus spoke on the Sermon on the Mount as written in Matthew's gospel.[12] Nixon did not disappoint his audience and received several standing ovations during his speech.

Even though the fall congressional campaign would not start for two and a half weeks, Nixon would be extremely busy leading up to its start. The next big event that Nixon would undertake was on August 23 in Washington. He spent half a day talking with Republican leadership in Congress along with the Policy Committee and the Republican interns. The most important appointment, however, was at the Shoreham Hotel from 5:30 to 7:00 with several heavy hitters from the conservative movement. These included leaders from interest groups representing conservative causes such as the National Right to Work Committee, Americans for Constitutional Action, American Conservative Union and the Free Society Associations, the Young Republicans and the Young Americans for Freedom, as well as prominent conservative columnists such as William Rusher, James K. Kilpatrick, and Ralph de Toledano.[13] This meeting came on the heels of a similar meeting between Barry Goldwater and the conservative movement leaders at his D.C. apartment twelve days earlier.[14]

Pat Buchanan did all the advance and background work for the meeting. While Nixon was in Asia, the aide was busy doing intelligence work for the fall campaign. Buchanan had been the jack of all trades for Nixon since being hired in January. One of the many tasks he handled was shoring up support within the conservative movement, where he was a comparative novice. Buchanan sent Nixon a lengthy memorandum on August 5 about a long luncheon with William Rusher from the influential conservative magazine *National Review*. The memo offered some interesting insights that Buchanan gleaned from the luncheon, what some others from the right thought of Rusher, and what the conservative opinion writer believed about Nixon. Buchanan wrote, "Not only thought of as an amateur but is also thought of something of a weasel."[15]

The meeting between Nixon and the conservative leaders went well. He knew several of the columnists first hand, but he had not met some of the activists in the room. Nixon discussed his most recent trip to Asia and what he thought about American foreign policy. He explained which political issues would be necessary for Republicans in the fall campaign. Nixon reiterated how the party needed to do well in this election in terms of the upcoming presidential race in 1968.[16]

When Nixon returned to New York, he prepared for a dinner meeting with several other members of the firm and their largest account, Pepsico. The principal officers of the large soft drink company were there.[17] The next day, Nixon appeared on the *Today Show* with Hugh Downs. Nixon believed that President Johnson had resigned himself to a long war in Vietnam. He said, "We need new tactics, new leadership, and new methods to shorten the war and bring it to a conclusion without appeasement of the enemy." It was nothing new, but what was a bit different was what he said about LBJ and his chief Democratic rival. Nixon stated that Senator Robert F. Kennedy "has attacked the President and gained much support, including that from the hard-core left." He then said, "Political realities in 1968, President Johnson may have to seek a stronger running mate, and that would be Senator Kennedy."[18]

At the end of the month, Nixon traveled back to Washington to speak at the 48th Annual National Convention of the American Legion. He stressed many of the same themes that he had earlier stated in his address to the VFW, but with more specifics. Two weeks after the event, Nixon received a "personal and private" letter from Secretary of State Dean Rusk, pointing out supposed inaccuracies from his speech to the American Legion. While Rusk acknowledged he had not seen the full text, he pointed to statements attributed to him that were published in the *Washington Post* in an early September 1 piece. The article stated that Nixon said, "Ninety-five percent of North Vietnam's oil supply is delivered in ships owned by U.S. allies." Rusk corrected this by writing, "All the bulk is brought in by Soviet tankers, while package products, such as oils and greases, are usually carried by Soviet dry cargo ships. Concerning cargo other than POL, free-world shipping to North Vietnam in 1966 dropped to its lowest level in many years. Six ships per month arrived in March, April, and May, and the number dropped to five in June and two in July."[19]

Nixon responded to Rusk, thanking him for bringing this to his attention. After checking the transcript, Nixon wrote that the *Post* did not accurately report what he said. It had never been his intention to state that 95 percent of the oil entering North Vietnam came in on Western vessels, but that it mostly came in by sea. Nixon, quoting from his speech, wrote, "Coming in North Vietnam, however by sea at the present time are tankers. Ninety-five percent of all the oil comes in by sea…. Some are theirs; many are under the subterfuge of charters to Eastern Communist countries." After making this correction, Nixon got in a little jab of his own. He wrote, "Incidentally, as has probably been reported to you by your missions abroad—despite the disagreements as to means between us—I was kept very busy in press conferences in London, Paris, Rome, Tel Aviv, Karachi, Bangkok, Saigon, Manila, Tokyo, and Seoul defending the American effort in Vietnam against the criticisms of Democratic Senators and Congressman who have in effect been calling for peace at any price."[20] One can only imagine what Dean Rusk's response was to this 100 percent accurate statement from Nixon. It possibly involved some combination of four-letter words that the secretary of state did not utter in public.

Official Campaign Begins

Richard Nixon began in earnest a 35-state campaign over the next eight weeks for a Republican Congress on September 11. Pat Hillings, Rose Mary Woods, Charlie McWhorter, and John Davies accompanied him for the entire trip. Hillings handled the local media and politicians while Woods did administrative work. Charlie McWhorter worked alongside Hillings, while Davies was Nixon's aide or "body man." Davies fended off others for Nixon on the plane or at events to give him room to work. Nixon kicked off this journey by appearing on CBS's *Face the Nation* on Sunday morning, followed by a fund-raiser in Staten Island.[21] The same day, he authored a *Los Angeles Times* opinion piece picked up by various other Sunday newspapers. Nixon argued that the Johnson administration, after months of dragging their feet on several foreign and domestic issues, will "over-react on both fronts with too much, too soon." He believed that the conduct of the war in Vietnam would be the most important issue facing the country at this time. He would try to be supportive of the president taking the fight to the enemy, and as long as he did so, Lyndon Johnson could count on Nixon's support and the support of most of the Republican Party.

With this in mind, Nixon offered five initiatives to shorten the war in Vietnam without appeasing the enemy or leading to another war. The efforts are the following:

1. Spell out actual aims more clearly and be frank about the sacrifices that are needed.
2. Step up the air and ground war.
3. Affect [*sic*] an effective economic quarantine of North Vietnam.
4. Help Saigon help build their social, political, and economic institutions.
5. Support Saigon diplomatically.[22]

Nixon next stopped three times in Ohio and once in northern Kentucky, where he spoke of Republican unity and the necessity of a viable two-party structure to the American political system. Nixon believed that if the Republicans did not do well in this election, "The two-party system will have suffered a blow from which it might not recover."[23]

Before heading to the West Coast, Nixon visited Davenport, Denver, and Salt Lake City. In Davenport, Nixon criticized particular domestic programs like the Job Corps and Head Start as he campaigned for Fred Schwengel, a five-term congressman defeated in 1964.[24] In Denver, he told supporters this was an excellent opportunity for a Republican comeback, and President Johnson was "playing politics with prosperity."[25] It was against the backdrop of a national economy, which was growing at a four percent clip with virtually full employment. Nixon believed expanding the welfare state with the war in Vietnam would lead to higher inflation and an additional tax increase. In Salt Lake City, he addressed a lunchtime crowd with similar themes. When questioned by a reporter there about his upcoming visit to California to campaign for Ronald Reagan and other Republicans, the issue of the "Birchers" emerged. Nixon stated he would not "lay down a code of conduct for other candidates. I believe that Mr. Reagan has made clear the Birch members must accept his views, not theirs."[26]

Meanwhile, the *New York Times* published the results of an Associated Press poll of 48 Republican state chairmen and national committeemen, indicating three-quarters (36) of respondents thought that Richard Nixon would be their nominee in 1968. George Romney came in second, with four respondents hedging their replies as either Nixon or Romney or maybe Ronald Reagan if he could win the governor's race in California. Robert J. Corbert Jr., the Virginia state chairman, summed up Nixon supporters when he said, "I believe that Mr. Nixon is going to be our nominee. Mr. Nixon is also my preference at this time because he's done the best job of keeping his name before the public."[27] Nixon refused to comment on the poll but was happy. He wanted to talk about the opposition and Democratic infidelity. This Democratic conflict was between friends and supporters of the president, Bobby Kennedy, and Hubert Humphrey. Nixon said, "Those birds are really flying out of Washington these days Lyndon is flying all around the country trying to elect his congress. Bobby is flying around the country trying to elect delegates for 1968. Hubert is just flying around."[28] Of course, the Democrats probably thought something similar about Nixon in his quest to make the Republican Party more competitive.

Nixon was in familiar territory as he spent Friday and parts of Saturday in southern California on campaign swings through Van Nuys, Burbank, and Los Angeles. He stressed Republican unity and believed that there was a "Johnson drag on Democratic candidates." He noted, "Many Democratic candidates who ran with him in 1964 are now running away from him."[29] Also, Nixon thought Ronald Reagan would defeat Pat Brown for governor by a wide margin. The political environment in California was much different than his quest four years earlier. He said, "The Democrats are divided now after a bitter primary whereas they were united in 1962."[30]

The theme of Republican unity and Nixon's pledge to campaign for any Republican that wanted his support—except members of the John Birch Society and segregationists—created conflict on his visit to Fairbanks, Alaska. Nixon had made the seven-plus hour flight from Los Angeles to campaign there for congressional candidate Howard Pollock and gubernatorial candidate Walter Hickel. In a news conference before the convention banquet at the University of Alaska, Nixon repeated his promise not to support an avowed member of the John Birch Society. At the dinner afterward, he endorsed both Pollock and Hickel but did not mention Lee McKinley, who was the Republican candidate for Senate. Nixon made sure that McKinley, an avowed Bircher, was not seated close to him so that his opponents could not say that he was supporting such a candidate. After Nixon's speech, McKinley left the dinner with no comment to reporters.[31] Two days later, Nixon told Pat Buchanan, who had been doing the advance work back in New York, that he felt terrible for having to spurn McKinley. He thought McKinley was probably a decent guy, and that he took the non-endorsement with class. Buchanan knew that Republicans had criticized Nixon himself in the past.[32] Nixon had twenty years of experience in politics, and it had toughened him up. Nixon did not enjoy all aspects of the political game but knew that they were necessary.

As the Nixon party left Alaska for the lower forty-eight states, Gallup published its latest presidential popularity poll. After one week of the congressional campaign, Lyndon Johnson had sunk below fifty percent for the first time in his presidency at a 48 percent approval rating. His disapproval rating was 42 percent. Experts suggest adding and subtracting three percentage points for accuracy, so these numbers are mostly the same. Ninety percent of the people were divided down the middle on whether or not they approved of the president. The final ten percent were undecided, probably indicating that they were not clued into what the president was doing or had little interest in national politics. When Johnson came into office, his approval approached 80 percent and stayed in the 70s for most of 1964.[33] A rating below 50 percent was a good sign for the Republicans and Richard Nixon.

After arriving back in Los Angeles, Nixon took a day off to recover from this intense first week of campaigning. The next stops involved a swing through the Wisconsin cities of Milwaukee, Kenosha, and Sheboygan. While there was no great news on the outside during these events, the real news was on the inside. Nixon had Pat Buchanan join the small staff traveling with him. Buchanan had done the political advance work back in New York during the first week of this campaign. Advance work is something most political observers know little or nothing about, but it is integral to a candidate's success. Buchanan talked to the candidates or their campaign managers to find out the significant issues in their district: what subjects to avoid, local tidbits like the college and its nickname, and local hangouts. He summarized this for Nixon, who, on the road, got all he needed to know. Nixon would commit most of the information to memory. When he gave speeches, Nixon would never use papers. With Buchanan now on the road with Nixon, John Sears handled the advance work from New York. Buchanan wrote speech inserts that complemented the advance material. He rarely attended the events themselves but worked back at the hotel with his portable typewriter. This process freed up some additional time for Nixon to think and write in longhand what he was planning to discuss at the next event.[34]

The campaign continued west with large crowds in relatively small cities. An estimated crowd of 3,000 attended a luncheon in the municipal auditorium in Minot, North Dakota, some fifty miles south of Canada. Nixon appeared on behalf of Thomas S. Kleppe, the former mayor of Bismarck running for Congress against Rolland Redlin, who came to the House on LBJ's coattails in 1964. Nixon was predicting a 40-seat gain for the Republicans in the House and said Kleppe would be one of them.[35] The next night another large crowd greeted Nixon in Casper, Wyoming, before he headed to Oklahoma and Nebraska. In Bartlesville, home of Phillips 66, he was greeted by a cheering crowd of over 7,000 as "Mr. Republican." In response, Nixon made light of the slogan "All the Way with LBJ" that the president used in the 1964 election. He quipped, "All the way with LBJ means higher taxes, tighter money, and inflation at home and a five-year ground war in Asia with higher casualties than Korea."[36] Nixon ended the day as the main speaker at a $50-a-plate fund-raiser entitled "Operation Success 1966" in Omaha, Nebraska.

Nixon started the next day with a morning breakfast rally in Council Bluffs, where he criticized the Johnson administration's farm policy and poked fun at LBJ's vice president. He said, "The administration is trying to make farmers the patsy for Johnson inflation, but that's a bum rap. How can you blame the farmer for rising prices when parity is at 78 percent, five points lower than it averaged in the eight years of the Eisenhower administration?" Nixon also told one of his favorite Hubert Humphrey jokes. He said, "At a recent rally in Ohio, he had erroneously been called the Vice-President of the United States. 'Now I'm not particularly sensitive. I've been called almost everything, but please don't call me Hubert.'"[37]

Upon leaving Iowa, he returned to New York to speak to a crowd of 600 in Tarrytown for Frederick J. Martin, Jr. The latter was running against the incumbent Democratic Representative Richard Ottinger.[38] After recharging his batteries over the weekend in New York, Nixon prepared for a three-day, four-state swing into the South, where the Republicans hoped to make major inroads in the once impregnable Democratic strongholds.

One of the few bright spots from the 1964 elections for Barry Goldwater and the Republicans was in the Deep South. Five of the six states—the other being Arizona—that the Republican nominee for president won were southern states: Alabama, Georgia, Mississippi, Louisiana, and South Carolina. All the states except Georgia were states that Strom Thurmond, a Democrat who became a Republican in 1964, won as a third-party candidate in 1948. Arguably, some of the Goldwater votes had a white backlash component to them. The Democratic Party had dominated the South since the end of the Civil War. There had only been three Republican governors elected from the eleven states of the old Confederacy since that time. The Republican Party that Richard Nixon was hoping to build in the South was one based on solid party principles such as free enterprise, smaller government, and a robust military. It did not include overt segregationists who exploited racial issues. When he toured several southern states earlier in the year, Nixon made it abundantly clear that this Republican Party was the party of Lincoln. He respected states' rights but did not see them as a hindrance to better race relations.

Over the next three days, the former vice president would make campaign stops in four southern states, starting with two events in Tennessee. These two appearances were in Democratic western Tennessee: Memphis and Jackson. Nixon made it clear in Memphis to a crowd of 3,000 in Ellis Auditorium that the Johnson administration's handling of the war in Vietnam and excessive domestic spending were the most significant issues of the campaign. All three Republican congressional candidates, the United States Senate candidate (Howard Baker, son-in-law of Senate Minority Leader Everett Dirksen), several state legislative candidates, and a former Miss America, Barbara Walker Hummel, were in attendance. Nixon said, "This year will be the greatest defection of Democratic voters from a Democratic administration since 1946. Thousands of Democrats in Tennessee and millions across the nation will vote for Republican candidates for the House and Senate—not because they have deserted their party but because their party has deserted them."[39] In Jackson, a massive thunderstorm forced the event inside the New Southern Hotel. Nixon received loud applause after power accidentally cut off the microphone into which he had just said, "I think that fellow should be content with turning out the lights in the White House." He got an even louder ovation when speaking about cutting off foreign aid to any country trading with the enemy in Vietnam: "We want to help the needy, but we believe that the lives of the American men come first. Any nation that trades with Hanoi should not receive foreign aid from the U.S."[40]

The next day was filled with events in Asheboro, North Carolina, and Columbia, South Carolina. After flying into Greensboro, Nixon spoke briefly with reporters before driving to Asheboro in the middle of the state. In a statement made available to reporters beforehand, he made some of his strongest criticisms of President Johnson's handling of the war. Nixon had made some earlier statements about the upcoming October conference in Manila, but never in such stark terms as stating the president should withdraw his offer of negotiations in Geneva and not consider a bombing halt absent a commitment by Hanoi to negotiate.[41]

The theme of the Republican event in Columbia was "Had Enuff?" which focused on problems with the expanded welfare programs of the Great Society. This theme was a colloquial takeoff from the 1946 Republican congressional campaign of "Had Enough." There were signs all around the convention room at the hotel, stating, "Great Society—New Leech on Life."[42] At his appearance at the Wade Hampton Hotel in Columbia, Nixon laid down what he thought would be the cornerstone of a new Republican Party in the South. He said, "In building the party of the South, one of the foundation stones will be a new concept of states' rights. The old concept belonged to the past."[43] Not once did he appeal to racial techniques used by others when campaigning in the South. Pat Buchanan witnessed the Columbia event and thought that an earlier closed room smaller group was, without a doubt, the most memorable of the entire 1966 campaign. Nearly a half-century later, the Nixon aide wrote about the two speakers, Strom Thurmond and Albert Watson. It had an energy that he had not seen before in this campaign and he knew that this is where the strength of the Republican Party was and would be in the future.[44]

The final stops on this southern swing were in Fort Lauderdale and Miami, Florida. At a press conference before his final event, he reminded reporters that he had supported civil rights bills during the Eisenhower presidency—the Brown decision in 1954, the Civil Rights Bill of 1964, and the Voters Rights Act of 1965—but made a distinction in how far he wanted to push the issue. Nixon said he did not condone riots, violence in the streets, or the "mob rule" that some non–Southern cities had experienced.[45] Later, he got a good laugh from the large gathering inside a Fort Lauderdale auditorium when he said, "I don't know what this means, but the sign outside says, 'Nixon Tonight—Wrestling Next Week.' I'd suggest coming back. It'll be Bobby versus Lyndon."[46]

Nixon flew home after his successful tour through the South. He had one more campaign appearance before a break to prepare for a critical legal case. At a fund-raiser in Wilmington, Delaware, he accused the president of perpetually playing politics with the country's future. Nixon said in response to a question about the upcoming peace conference that Johnson "has put politics ahead of the policy so many times that the leaders on Capitol Hill are publicly asking whether he is going to the Far East—he is even playing politics with world peace.... Based on three weeks of campaigning in 17 states and 30 congressional districts, it is apparent that there is one all-embracing issue in this election ... the issue is Lyndon Johnson."[47]

Break from the Campaign Trail?

Richard Nixon took a temporary break from the congressional campaign to prepare for his second appearance before the United States Supreme Court in the *Time v. Hill* case. He spent the better part of the next weeks in preparation for the October 18 pleading. Nixon still managed time for a couple of events in Chicago. In between those events, he taped an interview, along with Vice President Humphrey, for a program on CBS titled "Party Prospects."[48]

At the same time, there was a front-page story in the *Washington Post*, strongly suggesting that what Nixon had been saying was grossly inaccurate. This survey of political correspondents across the country was coming one month before Election Day. The *Post's* National Correspondents concluded this after going over the data: "A month before Election Day—despite the bear market and the backlash, despite Vietnam and Lyndon Johnson's sliding popularity quotient—a 50 state political survey shows little promise of a big GOP breakthrough this year in Congress."[49]

Nixon was also the headline speaker for the 22nd annual Al Smith Dinner in New York on October 13. The other speakers for this major social occasion were Nelson Rockefeller and John Lindsay. It was always customary to have the governor of the state and the mayor of the city address the annual occurrence. This event was presided over by the senior Catholic official in New York, Cardinal Francis Spellman. In 1960, Nixon had shared the headline speaker position with his opponent John F. Kennedy. Six years later, he praised Kennedy's "grace and charm" and lamented, "Kennedy did not live to see his dreams realized." The slain president's brother, Bobby, had been asked to speak but was not offered the headline. Bobby Kennedy turned down the offer, saying that he had other plans. The *Washington Post* noted that Kennedy spent the night at home in McLean, Virginia.[50] How ironic that the state's top Democratic politician turned down this event honoring the former New York governor and Democratic presidential nominee in 1928, and that in the end, all the principal speakers were Republicans.

Meanwhile, President Johnson campaigned for Democratic candidates before he left for Asia on October 18. In Wilmington, Delaware, Johnson said a vote for Republicans could cause the country to "falter and fall back and fail" in Vietnam.[51] At the same time, a detailed article on the significant issues of the day, written by Richard Nixon, appeared in hundreds of American newspapers and was entitled "Quest for Peace or Quest for Votes?" The former vice president laid out a detailed plan for a Pacific Charter similar to the one that Roosevelt and Churchill spelled out in the Atlantic Charter before World War II. This charter, like the one in 1941, was issued before the United States' entry into the war. It detailed the principles for which each country stood.[52] Nixon responded to the president's criticism of Republicans in a statement that compared LBJ's comment to Woodrow Wilson's 1918 attempt to spell out the terms of World War I before the Peace Conference: "These crass attacks upon the loyal opposition today are reminiscent of the tragic blunder of Woodrow Wilson in the election campaign of 1918. President Wilson attacked the Republican members of the Congress who had stood with him in the war effort. President Wilson's attack backfired, and he eventually left for the Paris Peace Conference with far less support from home than he might have had."[53]

Two days later, Nixon reargued his case in front of the Supreme Court for the Hill family against *Life* magazine, a rare occurrence for the Court since the justices could not agree on the legality of the New York right to privacy law. They wondered whether it conflicted with the Court's ruling on the same issue in *New York Times v. Sullivan* in 1964. At the trial court level, a $30,000 judgment was awarded to the Hills. In his spring argument, Nixon was generally complimentary of the magazine yet said that they got some things wrong in the article "The Desperate Hours." In this second argument, the former vice president was much less constrained in his critique of the liability of the Luce publication. He said that the court in the New York case had held that "*Life* lied and knew it lied."[54] His fellow litigator, Len Garment, thought Nixon did much better than in the spring. The problem, Garment thought, was that something had changed in the questioning from the majority of the court, but he was not sure why. He felt that while the majority had been with them in the spring, only Warren and Fortas seemed to be supporting them now.[55] On a lighter note, one of the questions that Nixon received from the justices came from William J. Brennan, Jr. (whom Eisenhower had called his second biggest mistake in court namings). The justice told Nixon the court case came "from your state." Obviously, he was referring to California, forgetting Nixon had moved to New York three years earlier. Finally, Brennan noticed his error and tried to correct himself. He was interrupted by Nixon amidst general laughter in the courtroom. Nixon announced, "It was my state. I'm proud of it."[56] In another ironic twist to this case, this same magazine had endorsed Richard Nixon for president in 1960. After this hearing, Nixon would resume his campaigning for Republican congressional candidates across the country for the final three-week push.

No. 22.

IN THE

Supreme Court of the United States

OCTOBER TERM, 1966

TIME, INC.,

Appellant,

against

JAMES J. HILL,

Appellee.

ON APPEAL FROM THE COURT OF APPEALS
OF THE STATE OF NEW YORK.

BRIEF FOR APPELLEE ON REARGUMENT

RICHARD M. NIXON,
20 Broad Street,
New York, New York 10005,
Attorney for Appellee.

GOLDTHWAITE H. DORR,
LEONARD GARMENT,
DONALD J. ZOELLER,
DOUGLAS M. PARKER,
NIXON, MUDGE, ROSE, GUTHRIE & ALEXANDER,
20 Broad Street,
New York, New York 10005,
Of Counsel.

September 24, 1966.

Nixon brief for Supreme Court case of *Time v. Hill*, October 1966 (Richard M. Nixon Library).

Full Speed Ahead

As soon as he finished arguing, Nixon flew to San Francisco to begin a full day of campaigning. As soon as he got off the plane, he answered several questions from all three television station crews who were waiting to meet him. He then went to his hotel, to another press conference, and a brief lunch before riding over the bay to Oakland. There, Nixon spoke for nearly an hour before going on to Palo Alto. He discussed the next couple of days of campaigning with Bob Finch before going to bed for three hours following 21 hours and 3,000 miles of travel. Three hours later, Nixon woke up for a television interview and a breakfast with Finch. The day was just beginning as he flew to Bakersfield for another press conference and fund-raiser for former Olympic champion Bob Mathias, who was running for Congress.[57] At this event, Nixon called on President Johnson to repudiate racist Democratic candidates. He said, "It is the Democratic party—the party of Maddux, Mahoney, and Wallace that has the backlash problem." Nixon was referring to the Democratic gubernatorial candidates in Georgia, Maryland, and Alabama. All of these candidates (including James Johnson in Arkansas, whom he had left out) had campaigned on the backlash issue. It got a front-page story in the *Washington Post* the next day.[58]

Nixon then flew to Ontario, California, for a fund-raiser supporting congressional candidate Jerry Pettis. While in Ontario, he saw Roy Day, the publisher who was one of the "Committee of 100" members who sought out a candidate to run against Jerry Voorhis in 1946. Chatting with Day, his first campaign manager in that congressional election, was like an "old home day." At the rally at Chaffey High School, Nixon called the 89th Congress "the toothless old lapdog of President Johnson and the first in history which the president has considered his property. Lyndon Johnson's arrogant claim to ownership indicates how far up the road we have come from the day when Congress was a separate co-equal and respected branch of government."[59]

The California trip was a big success, with one exception that the press failed to notice. The Ontario event was slated to have several hundred or more in attendance, but only about eighty people showed up to greet the former vice president. Typically, all of his activities on this campaign had been at capacity crowds, so this one was an outlier. Pat Buchanan witnessed firsthand what happened when Nixon returned to the hotel and called a meeting of everyone who was with his campaign, where the boss "called in the advance men and chewed them out." Buchanan was perplexed at first, "but every advance man knew that 1966 was the dress rehearsal for 1968."[60]

David Broder of the *Washington Post* was with the Nixon team as they toured the West Coast. While in California, he also witnessed Robert Kennedy campaigning. Broder made some interesting observations about the two veteran politicians using baseball analogies. The Baltimore Orioles had recently swept the Los Angeles Dodgers in the 1966 World Series. Broder compared Nixon's speeches to a "shortstop with a .276 average, who gives you a good performance day in and day out but doesn't win many ball games—dependable but terribly predictable." On the other hand, he thought Kennedy was like a "hot-hitting rookie right fielder, who drops too many fly balls but is a threat every time he comes to bat—unpredictable and therefore very exciting."[61] The experienced national political correspondent made some additional comparisons and concluded that he thought in the end, Nixon would emerge as the winner in this campaign and the near future. Broder said Nixon was the old pro, and

Bobby was just a rookie. Kennedy was looking for a shot at the presidency in 1972 and not 1968: "The rookie of the year still tends to swing at a bad pitch."[62]

After returning to New York early Saturday morning, Richard Nixon had one more scheduled event in New London, Connecticut, that night before appearing on *Meet the Press* on Sunday. Two weeks before the elections, he stated again that the Republicans would gain at least 40 seats in the House and three in the Senate. Nixon also predicted his party would win six governorships and nearly 600 state legislators.[63] In the last thirty years, the midterm election average losses of the president's party had been ten. If Nixon were right in his predictions, then forty-plus seats would undoubtedly be seen as significant.

In marked contrast to the headline the next day, page one of the *Washington Post* read "Heavy Ticket Splitting Seen Reducing GOP Gains in Congressional Races." It was based on the most recent polling data compiled by Louis Harris. Harris predicted, "The mood of the country is shifting in a way that indicates a reduction in the Democratic losses forecast in Congress, but a buildup in Republican gains in governorships." On the question of which party was the best suited for the following three questions, the answers were a bit different than the headline suggested. On foreign policy and settling the war in Vietnam, the public favored the Democrats 52–48. On the two domestic issues of "controlling the cost of living" and "cutting down riots and racial violence," the country sided with Republicans 54–46.[64] As to the integrity of this particular pollster, we must remember, "Louis Harris was John Kennedy's pollster in 1960." Harris predicted a nine-point Kennedy win in the popular vote with the large states of California and Ohio in JFK's column. The popular vote in 1960 was a tie, with California and Ohio going to Nixon.[65]

At the same time, Gallup released its poll on the war in Vietnam, showing the public growing weary of the way the war was being conducted but still believing that the United States was doing right in sending troops to Southeast Asia. Three things came away from this poll with President Johnson and the Republicans claiming the upper hand with the American people: "On the peace proposal being floated by the Johnson Administration, nearly three out of four support the general proposition of mutual de-escalation or favor it with some reservations; A majority of Americans agree with what Nixon and the Republicans have been advocating, an escalation of the war, and there is widespread approval for the South Vietnamese taking up a larger share of the fighting of the war." Finally, this survey indicated that despite the pessimism toward the war, a majority of Americans believe that sending troops was not a mistake.[66] The next two weeks would certainly be exciting.

Richard Nixon knew the last two weeks of the congressional campaign were a make-or-break situation for the Republicans generally and for his comeback specifically. Unlike Nixon, much of the major national media predicted some modest gains for the party. *The Washington Post*'s William S. White, a long-time Johnson friend, stated that because Nixon had tied himself inexorably to the campaign, he had the most to win or to lose. There was no middle ground.[67]

The first stop on this push was a swing through the state of Michigan at the invitation of House Minority Leader Gerald Ford. Ford felt Nixon would have more impact in his home state than any other Republican, even Governor George Romney, a reported front-runner for the 1968 presidential race. Romney was cruising along to re-election when Nixon barnstormed across the state with stops in Detroit,

Kalamazoo, and Grand Rapids. After accusing Congress of being a lap dog of Johnson, he lightened up the crowd with these remarks: "Ford has acquired a new name—Thunderbird. Hubert Humphrey has become Mockingbird and Bobby Kennedy has been called everything."[68]

Despite all the national media posturing about Nixon and Romney on the same stage, the headlines coming out of Michigan quoted the former vice president accusing Robert Kennedy of undercutting President Johnson while he was touring Asia. Kennedy had said a couple of days earlier in California, "The people of South Vietnam should have the right to decide their destiny." He referred to South Vietnam's then leader, General Nguyen Cao Ky, but added, "it is clear they don't want the communists either."[69] Nixon was highly critical of the New York senator's criticisms of the president while he was out of the country meeting with a crucial ally during a war. He stated, "Until the people of Vietnam have a chance to indicate whom they want, it is not for Senator Kennedy or any American to say they do not want the man they have."[70]

Nixon spent the next two days campaigning in Oregon and Washington. He heard several reports from his contacts in California, Oregon, and Washington that LBJ would visit there over the last weekend of the campaign before finishing out with appearances in the Midwest and the East Coast. While in Spokane, he warned Western Republicans that a "last minute blitz" could slow down the "great Republican tide" sweeping the country.[71]

As the Nixon campaign headed back east, the former vice president stopped briefly in Albuquerque, New Mexico, and Boise, Idaho, before going to Mississippi and Arkansas. Fred LaRue joined the campaign in Mississippi and assured Nixon of support there and elsewhere in the South. In Fort Smith, Arkansas, Pat Buchanan recalled two events that initially looked bad but turned out fine in the end. First was the mispronunciation of a Republican candidate's last name, John Hammerschmidt, at a press conference, but Nixon caught the second time he said it. The latter had to do with Nixon instructing Buchanan not to let anyone disturb him in the afternoon because he wanted to rest: "After about a half an hour, I saw a large man striding across the yards, headed straight for Nixon's room. I must have been 75 yards away and started running. Too late. The guy was pounding on Nixon's door, yelling, 'Hey Dick! Hey Dick!' I got there as Nixon was opening the door. I was aghast that I had let this clown get to him. But Nixon was suddenly all smiles. 'Pat,' he said, 'meet Win Rockefeller!'"[72] Winthrop Rockefeller was Nelson's younger brother and was running for governor in Arkansas against a Democratic segregationist by the name of Jim Johnson. Everything turned out right for Buchanan as the two had been close friends for several years.

On Saturday, the campaign headed to Indiana for stops in Evansville, Terre Haute, and Columbus. In Evansville, Nixon used his knowledge of baseball to respond to Postmaster General Lawrence F. O'Brien's evaluation of the current Congress. O'Brien said they had a "fabulous" .905 batting average in supporting the president. The former vice president corrected him: the 89th Congress had "no hits, no runs, and a lot of errors."[73] Continuing with the baseball theme in Terre Haute, Nixon claimed the Johnson Congress had "struck out" on vital issues from foreign policy to crime. Before a crowd of 5,000 at Columbus High School, he criticized climbing inflation by proposing tax deductions as the cure.[74]

While at a press conference in Evansville, Nixon pointed Buchanan toward a man, saying, "That is the enemy."[75] The particular enemy that the Nixon aide saw was none other than Robert Novak, half of the famous (or infamous in Nixon's assessment) Evans and Novak column. While Novak seemed to delight in aggravating the former vice president, the pair admitted in a nationwide column the day before that Republicans throughout the nation were warming to Nixon despite George Romney's attempt to ingratiate himself to the party after his 1964 performance. They wrote, "Romney's operation coattails are defensive in nature. If successful, it can snuff out old charges that Romney is a loner uninterested in the Party. But it cannot suddenly displace Nixon in the affection of the county chairman across the country."[76]

On Sunday, Nixon authored a column carried by the North American Newspaper Alliance (NANA) titled "Democrats Gamble on Racism, in South." In this piece, he repeated a claim made on the campaign trail that "below the Mason-Dixon line, the party of Jefferson and Wilson has become the party of Maddux, Mahoney, and Wallace." Nixon was critical of the double standard that the national media used in linking members of the John Birch Society to the Republican Party. However, when segregationists like Maddox and Wallace spoke, almost no one asked the Democrats to denounce them. He wrote, "Lyndon Johnson, Robert Kennedy, and Hubert Humphrey have not lifted a finger or invested an ounce of their political prestige to prevent the seizure of their party by the lineal descendants of 'Pitchfork Ben' Tillman and Theodore Bilbo. They allowed it to become a political party in which Bull Connor is completely at home."[77] Tillman, Bilbo, and Connor were avowed racists and segregationists who had belonged to the Democratic Party in the South.[78]

Counting Down the Days

In the heart of Humphrey country, early in his address to a large crowd in Bloomington, Nixon quoted another well-known Democrat, Jim Farley, who had helped orchestrate the successful campaigns of Franklin Roosevelt. Farley said, "A man is judged by his own ability to carry his own precinct." Nixon was applying this political maxim to Vice President Humphrey, who would be campaigning on behalf of Democratic candidates in his home state later in the week. The incumbent Democratic governor, Karl F. Rolvaag, was trailing his Republican challenger Harold LeVander going into the last week of the election. President Johnson was also thought to be coming to his vice president's home state the day before the election. Nixon further goaded Humphrey by saying if he did not pull his state this year, then LBJ would probably think twice about keeping him on the ticket. Also, Nixon withheld any "assessment" of President Johnson's Asian trip until the president returned and reported to the nation.[79] Nixon made it clear he did not intend to criticize the president when he was out of the country, unlike Senator Kennedy.

While Nixon was campaigning in Minnesota, there was behind-the-scenes maneuvering among New York Republicans. Bill Safire, whom Nixon considered a friend, supporter, and public relations confidante, had been called to see if he was interested in meeting with Jack Wells and William Pfeiffer of the Nelson Rockefeller re-election campaign in New York City. Safire had been doing some public relations work for the Rockefeller campaign when he was approached by Wells, who wanted Nixon to put in some kind words for the governor while campaigning in Syracuse.

Rockefeller's people knew Safire was a Nixon supporter who could help them. Since Nixon had moved to New York nearly three years earlier, New York Republicans tied to the governor and who ran the party's politics had frozen Nixon out. Besides, Rockefeller made it clear he did not need anyone campaigning on his behalf, certainly not his Republican rival. After a poll appeared in the *New York Daily News* a week before the election showing Rockefeller behind Democrat Frank O'Connor 42 to 38 in his re-election campaign, aides finally decided they needed Nixon's help. Rockefeller had never been influential with the upstate New York Republicans, and his top campaign people thought it would help if Nixon endorsed him.[80]

Jacob Javits was a senator from New York and Rockefeller supporter. Javits said, "The strong use of Nixon in the last days of the campaign would focus too much attention on Nixon and away from Rockefeller, causing a controversy that could lose more votes than it would gain." After the Javits comment with which Rocky agreed, they wanted Nixon to do it but insisted that he was doing it on his own as a plug for the entire Republican ticket in the state. Nixon told Safire, "Don't tell them what I am going to do, but you can tell them I will do the right thing." Ultimately, Safire worked out the logistics with Nixon, who insisted that if he did, Rockefeller, Javits, and the other New York Republicans would welcome the news as if it surprised them and be highly complimentary of Nixon. Nixon also insisted that Rockefeller back a Republican Party event in Iowa during the last week of the campaign. The New York governor never agreed to the Iowa condition, but hoped Nixon would indeed do "the right thing."[81]

Buchanan talked earlier with the former vice president about the issue and thought it was wrong to endorse Rockefeller after his behavior in the 1964 campaign. Nixon assured him that they would be able to get something back from Rockefeller in the future.[82] In Syracuse, he urged the upstate Republicans to get behind the governor. The Nixon endorsement made New York papers, but what got national attention was his remarks on the war. Nixon called for an "economic offensive" to help end the Vietnam War. Nixon made four significant points showing how this could be accomplished: "First, there should no American foreign aid sent to any nation trading with or aiding the Vietnam communists. No loans or grants extended to Eastern Europe communist regimes trading with Hanoi and Havana. No exporting strategic materials to the Soviet Union while Moscow provided military support to Hanoi. Foreign companies trading with Havana and Hanoi should be denied the right to trade with the United States."[83] Earlier that day, Nixon argued Johnson's Far Eastern trip was useful because it provided an opportunity to talk with regional partners. Nevertheless, Nixon did not think that any progress had been made toward bringing North Vietnam to the peace table.[84]

"Chilling winds and freezing temperatures" greeted Richard Nixon the next day as his plane landed at the Tri-Cities Airport in northeast Tennessee. In this Republican stronghold of Tennessee, which had only one two-year term by a Democrat since Reconstruction, he was introduced by Representative James H. (Jimmy) Quillen, who declared if Nixon wanted the presidency, he could win it. Nixon graciously accepted the introduction and then spoke to an overflow crowd of 4,000 at a hangar stumping for Howard Baker in his race for the Senate seat against Democrat Ross Bass. Nixon predicted that the "race in Tennessee is one of the tightest in the country," and that the tide was turning for Republicans in California, Illinois, Michigan, Ohio.[85]

Before leaving New York for the Tennessee event, the former vice president made his first comment on President Johnson's 17-day tour of Asia, observing little progress toward a peaceful settlement had resulted from the seven-nation conference. Nixon reiterated his apprehensions about developing long-term American involvement in Vietnam. He said it was time for open debate on the war since the administration "has presented no formula for defeating aggression" and predicted losing could mean "World War III can soon be on us."[86]

Nixon had been working feverishly that morning on a final draft of his analysis of the president's Asian trip. Buchanan and Safire were assisting the former vice president on this effort. Buchanan had alerted the New York media that Nixon would have a comprehensive assessment of the administration's efforts and its effects on U.S. national security and the allies in the region. The two aides waited until Nixon flew back from Tennessee late in the afternoon to review the analysis one last time. They quickly passed out copies to the crowd of newsmen waiting at the law firm's office. Safire called his friend, Harrison Salisbury of the *New York Times*, to make sure the paper made the 9:00 p.m. deadline to appear in the morning edition. It made the first-page upper right corner with the headline, "Nixon Criticizes Manila Result." The full text was also printed on page 18.[87]

Last Weekend's Bombshell

As the former vice president, Nixon knew that President Johnson would likely respond to his criticisms of the Asian trip but was unsure exactly how his Democratic opponent would play it. On Friday morning at LaGuardia before flying out to Maine and New Hampshire, CBS's Mike Wallace interviewed Nixon. Meanwhile, Pat Buchanan monitored LBJ's news conference in Washington. Nixon wanted to discuss the president's response with Buchanan on the flight to Waterville, Maine.[88]

One of the first questions Johnson received concerned his press office's announcement the day before that he would have minor surgery requiring a week-and-a-half rest. The president quizzed the reporters by saying, "We don't have any plans, so when you don't have plans, you don't cancel plans." LBJ was just getting warmed up: "We have no plans for any political speeches between now and the election. I have had a very active year, and I would hope I could spend a relatively quiet weekend and go and vote on Tuesday morning."[89]

His final response inspired more challenging questions. Most knew the president planned to campaign for Democratic candidates on this final weekend. There were detailed accounts of such plans in papers like the *New York Times* and *The Evening Star* that told of specific campaign event cancellations by the president in at least 11 states.[90] On top of Nixon's criticisms, Garrett S. Horner of *The Evening Star* then asked the president to comment on Nixon's assessment of his Manila meeting.[91] Johnson nearly lost his composure with what Jules Witcover described as "sarcasm dripping from every phrase" when he responded, "I do not want to get into a debate on a foreign policy meeting in Manila with a chronic campaigner like Mr. Nixon." Johnson lambasted Nixon as an opportunist waiting for his political competitors to stumble so he could step in for another run at the presidency. He concluded, "Mr. Nixon doesn't serve his country well by trying to leave that kind of impression in the hope that he can pick up a precinct or two, or a ward or two."[92]

Garrett Horner could not believe his ears when Johnson made the "chronic campaigner" comment. He recounted this in the next day's account of the news conference in *The Evening Star*. Horner wrote, "Mrs. Johnson could not hide her astonishment when she heard her husband say that the Republican 'chronic campaigner' never had realized what was going on even when he was vice-president.... Suddenly both her feet hit the floor. With her lips forming an 'oh' or 'oh no' of astonishment, she appeared to be about to rise out of her chair."[93]

On the plane ride to Waterville, Pat Buchanan recounted how Johnson blasted his old Republican opponent and seemed to take the former vice president's analysis of his foreign trip personally. In effect, on the last weekend of this campaign, the president of the United States had just handed the supposed leader of the opposition party an almost equal place in the national spotlight.[94] Richard Nixon enhanced the opportunity by saying the "shocking attack on him at a news conference had broken the bipartisan line on Vietnam policy." He added, bipartisanship "does not mean abject approval of whatever policy the President may announce." He went on to say that he hoped that both sides could discuss the matter "like gentlemen."[95]

On the next campaign stop in Manchester, New Hampshire, Nixon sounded like an elder statesman and not a chronic campaigner as Johnson described him: "I regret that the President had chosen to reduce this debate to personal levels, and I will not travel that road with him." A question came back at Nixon concerning how the "old Nixon" would have responded. He smiled and said, "I'm the only expert on the old and new Nixon." He later added that it was he, not members of his own party, who had stood up for the president for his Vietnam policy: "Let the record show that all over the world I have defended the administration's announced goal of no surrender to aggression."[96]

Former President Eisenhower, stunned by Johnson's comments, issued a vigorous response defending Nixon. Ike said the former vice president "was constantly informed of the major problems of the United States during my administration. Any suggestion to the contrary or any inference that I, at any time, held Dick Nixon in anything less than the highest regard and esteem is erroneous."[97] George C. Christian, the press secretary to President Johnson, tried to calm the raging political waters by stating their own as the president spent the weekend in Texas. Christian said, "For those of you who were there, I don't think the President showed any temper or personal attack toward Nixon. I think that the President is in as good a humor as he has ever been in his life. I know for a fact that he rather likes Mr. Nixon personally."[98]

To be sure, the Sunday political shows had a lot to discuss. Nixon appeared on ABC's "Issues and Answers" and on NBC, where he presented the party's response to the top political issues of the day. Nixon criticized Secretary of Defense McNamara for using "political fakery" while holding up the headline from Saturday's *World Herald-Journal*, "LBJ Election Eve Move: Cutback in Viet Draft." Nixon said this was a charade by the Johnson administration, instead of predicting "we'll have over 500,000 men in Vietnam next year." Nixon also called McNamara "Lyndon Johnson's Charlie McCarthy, his political stooge," referring to a comedian's dummy.[99] Finally, the program host Bill Lawrence asked Nixon about his immediate plans after the campaign. Nixon replied, "After this election, I am going to take a holiday from politics for at least six months."[100]

On the NBC show, Ray Bliss selected Nixon as the party's chief spokesman, replacing the film *What Goes on Here?* The Republican National Committee had shown the film earlier to several prominent journalists and politicos who thought it was too graphic for national television. Bliss finally realized the former vice president was the right person to speak for the party.[101] Nixon began by saying that Johnson's attack was "one of the most savage personal assaults ever leveled by the President of the United States against one of his political opponents. I shall answer it not for myself but because of a great principle that is at stake. It is the principle of the right to disagree." Nixon ended the program by stating he respected the president.[102]

Most of the national press, usually no fans of Nixon, were now defending him. Mary McGrory of *The Evening Star* was among them: "[Nixon] is no longer a has-been. He is a man to be reckoned with at the White House, and his party cannot ignore this new claim.... By his own lights, as a result of the presidential cuffing, Nixon is where a week ago, he said Bobby Kennedy was—'sitting in the catbird seat.'"[103]

Although Nixon was confident he was on the way back, many in the national press still called him a "has-been" or a "loser." On the last leg of his two-month, 35-state campaign tour, Nixon believed more than ever that the tide was turning as he approached his last stop. Nixon appeared with 10 of the 11 congressional candidates, predicting the greatest Republican victory in 20 years. Before flying home to New York, in a voice made raspy from the daily speechmaking, Richard Nixon said that he was "glad to finish the campaign in the state that gave me my fighting spirit, my mother's home state of Indiana."[104] Hannah Nixon had indeed instilled in her son a determination never to give in. He would know the results of his efforts in less than 24 hours.

Election Day Results

Nixon voted and then returned to his office to catch up on daily correspondence. In responding to a thank-you note from Governor Rockefeller for his efforts in Syracuse, Nixon wrote a personal and heartfelt reply with a view on both of their political futures and how they could work together after stating that apart from their differences, "I hope that sometime during the months ahead we can sit down and have a good talk about foreign policy" and noted, "When the history of this campaign is written, it will be recorded that win, lose, or draw you fought a most gallant battle."[105]

That night, the Nixon entourage, including the traveling and office team along with several advance men, met at a suite reserved for them at the Drake Hotel. The room felt happy as the returns came in. The Republicans did what Nixon predicted and more.[106] A record turnout of 56 million voters (48 percent of voting age population) showed substantial gains for the party, winning 47 seats in the House and three seats in the Senate, in addition to eight new governors, and gaining control of half of the state legislatures. In the end, they won some 700 seats, more than making up for the 529 seat loss in 1964. Over half of the one-term Democratic members of the House lost their seats. The Republicans controlled the governor's office in five of the seven most populous states in America. Only Illinois and Texas elected Democratic governors. The country's two most populous states, California and New York, had governors soon considered presidential contenders. There were winners

from across the ideological spectrum for the GOP, the most notable being conservative Ronald Reagan in California, along with moderates Charles Percy of Illinois and
George Romney from Michigan, and liberals such as Nelson Rockefeller, Mark Hatfield in Oregon, and Massachusetts's Edmund Brooke. In the South, the Republicans
won the governorship in Arkansas (Winthrop Rockefeller) and Florida (Claude Kirk),
with Howard Baker winning the Senate seat (Tennessee), all for the first time in history. These victories would make the Republican Party much more competitive and
restore balance to the two-party system.[107]

Richard Nixon worked the suite, congratulating those whom he had campaigned for and others. It was a memorable night for the former vice president whom
many thought dead politically, and it was the best night that the Republicans had
had since 1946, the year Richard Nixon won his first campaign. Sometime after 1:00
a.m., Nixon left with Nick Ruwe and John Davies for a celebratory spaghetti dinner
at the El Morocco while Buchanan and Sears stayed in the suite going over election
returns and having a little party between themselves. Nixon returned home at 2:30
that morning and called back to the Drake one more time to see if he had missed any
developments. He had Sears recount the highlights one more time and told the young
political aide, "We've beaten the hell out of them, and we are going to kill them in
1968."[108]

A day after the election, Richard Nixon stayed at his law office commenting on
his view of the mid-term results, saying, "The resurgence of the Republican Party is
being analyzed right now in the capitals of the world. So that there will be no chance
for miscalculation, let it be absolutely clear to Hanoi and Peking that the new House
of Representatives will be much stronger than its predecessor as a bulwark of support
for a United States policy of 'no reward for aggression.'"[109]

Before a vacation in Florida, Richard and Pat Nixon invited several members of
his staff, including Buchanan, Sears, and Rose Mary Woods, for a celebratory dinner at the El Morocco. There Nixon recalled the highs and lows of earlier campaigns
and how much he appreciated their service over the past two months. They were all
inducted into "The Birdwatchers of 1966." They received a silver coin with an image of
Winston Churchill and the words that he spoke after the Munich appeasement: "The
belief that security can be obtained by throwing a small state to the wolves is a fatal
delusion."[110] Again, it was Nixon who defied the conventional wisdom of the political
pundits. While many of the so-called experts were forecasting Democratic losses in
the House in the 20s, Nixon was predicting double that. Nineteen sixty-six had been a
good year for the Republicans and Nixon. His incredible hard work paid off in the end
and put the Republican Party back on the map. For the next several months, Nixon
would avoid politics and let others sort out the significance of the 1966 election.

6

Let 'Em Chew on Him
for a Little While

On the Sunday before the election, Richard Nixon had told Bill Lawrence of *ABC News* that he was going to take a federal holiday for at least six months. Even though he meant what he said as it related to public appearances, Nixon would not shy away from politics entirely. Pat Buchanan was shocked. He did not know how they would run a presidential campaign during a six-month break. Buchanan, himself, had taken a leave from his job in St. Louis and wondered if he needed to return there. Nixon reassured his political aide of his job security and the reason for the decision. He believed there are times in a politician's life to back off and get out of the headlines. Nixon thought it best to let the national press write about someone else, like George Romney, who was getting a lot of attention as a potential Republican nominee. He told Buchanan to "let 'em chew on him for a little while" and see how he likes it. Buchanan understood and got to work. With Nixon's approval, the office stated on his behalf what the recent elections had meant.[1] The statement that was built reflected things he had been saying throughout the recent congressional campaign:

> [The election] is the sharpest rebuke of a President in a generation and a rebuke of the President's lack of credibility and lack of direction abroad.... The President now has a mandate to open his mind to new solutions, to accept constructive criticism, and to reinstitute a tradition of bipartisan policy.... I had predicted throughout the campaign that a gain of 40 House seats, three Senate seats, and six governorships would mean the resurgence of the Loyal Opposition ... one that should be consulted and should participate far more in the decisions that we are called on to support.... The final result was even better than I anticipated.[2]

A couple of days after the elections, Warren Weaver, Jr., of the *New York Times*, compiled statistics from *Congressional Quarterly* (CQ) on the House candidates whom Richard Nixon, Robert and Ted Kennedy, Lyndon Johnson, and Hubert Humphrey actively campaigned for in the 1966 elections. *CQ* only counted appearances outside the home state of the politician. In Nixon's case, they considered him "stateless," as the former Californian was now living in New York. The writer, staying with the baseball analogy even though the season had ended a month before, wrote, "The political equivalent of the batting championship for the 1966 campaign went to Former Vice-President Richard M. Nixon hands down." He was the clear runaway winner with an average of .667. Johnson was second, with an average of .519, followed by Humphrey with a .500 clip. The Kennedy brothers rounded out the top five with below .500 batting averages: Ted at .397 and Bobby at .391. Also, Weaver pointed out that out of the 319 Republican candidates for the House of Representatives who did not receive Nixon's blessing, only 143 of them won for a .448 average. Of all the candidates that Nixon campaigned for, the percentage was even higher at .686.[3]

In the days and weeks after the election, it came as no surprise to the small staff at 20 Broad Street in New York that almost all major newspapers, television, and radio networks agreed on who the clear winners of this election were, with a couple of exceptions. The exceptions were the two largest weekly news magazines in the country, *Time* and *Newsweek*. Both magazines had the same six Republicans on their post-election covers: Rockefeller, Reagan, Romney, Brooke, Percy, and Hatfield, but no Nixon. In fairness, once you got into the article itself, they readily acknowledged Nixon as the clear winner.[4] In response, Pat Buchanan wrote a 2,000-word analysis of the incredible Nixon effort on behalf of Republican candidates, countering his "loser" image. He sent it to his former boss, Richard Amberg, the publisher of the *St. Louis Globe-Democrat*, who subsequently reprinted it under his byline on page one of the Features section in a weekend edition. It got a tremendous response, and the firm ordered thousands of reprints to send all over the country. In "Nixon: GOP's Big Winner in '66," Buchanan wrote, "The only man who could stake out an honest claim to the national victory was the old Republican War Horse himself, Richard M. Nixon.... It was ironic that just two years later, beaming from the covers of the nation's newsweeklies would be several of the same faces had last been seen grinning from their lifeboats in 1964.... It was the fighting spirit of the GOP that Nixon restored and fueled during the great comeback."[5]

After the success of the Nixon letter, Buchanan modified the earlier work and drafted two new messages. The first letter was to be signed by Fred Seaton, former secretary of the interior under Eisenhower. Seaton was a newspaperman in Nebraska who worked with Nixon in the latter few weeks of the '66 campaign and had tried to put together a presidential run for him in 1964. The Seaton letter made all of the significant points and said Nixon was the man the country needed in 1968. The letter was sent after the first of the year to all Republican members of Congress, state chairs, and a hundred members of the Republican National Committee. Buchanan flew to the small town of Hastings, Nebraska, in the first week of 1967 to meet with Seaton and had the letter mailed from there to look authentic.[6]

The second letter was shorter in length but included the same evidence of the true winner of 1966. It was signed by John Davis Lodge, former ambassador, congressman, and governor of Connecticut, who also had been a movie star in the 1930s. He was the brother of Henry Cabot Lodge, Jr., and grandson of the famous Senator Henry Cabot Lodge, Sr., from the World War I period. The typed letter left space on the bottom for Lodge to personalize it to his many friends in the media, entertainment, and political worlds. This letter was a big success and got a great response from its readers, who were added to the Nixon mailing lists.[7]

The Three R's

While Richard Nixon enjoyed his vacation in Florida and self-imposed holiday from politics, analysts tried to sort out what had just occurred in the midterms. Besides Nixon, many of them focused on the three R's: Rockefeller, Romney, and

Reagan. On the day after the election, Nelson Rockefeller repeated "unequivocally" after winning a third term as governor that he would not be running for president in 1968. The New York governor stressed while he was not actively seeking the Republican nomination, he was in the party's mainstream. Political experts interpreted this to refer to the moderate/liberal wing of the Republican Party. He said he thought that George Romney was in the race but sidestepped questions about the political future of Ronald Reagan. Those analysts who knew the background of the 1964 Republican contest for president believed the New York governor was backing Romney.[8]

The Republican Party's chances in 1968 were the topic of discussion on Sunday political television shows for the next two weeks. George Romney appeared on NBC's *Meet the Press* on November 13, while Barry Goldwater was on ABC's *Issues and Answers* the same day.[9] The following week, on November 20, California governor-elect Ronald Reagan visited *Issues and Answers*. Romney was all smiles on the NBC telecast after his convincing victory of over half a million votes and was introduced as a leading contender for the Republican nomination. While the Michigan governor would not commit to candidacy, he certainly talked like a candidate. Romney said he thought the Republicans had "a very large number of people who could beat Mr. Johnson," when asked by the panel whether he or Richard Nixon could defeat the incumbent. He referred to a "credibility gap" on the administration's handling of Vietnam, but Romney did not say what he would do instead.[10]

In his ABC Sunday show appearance, Barry Goldwater spoke plainly on where he stood. He said that he was still bitter over Romney's refusal to back him in 1964, and he was supporting Nixon in 1968. Goldwater did not want to "belittle" the Michigan governor's re-election and was not "against" him but said that he wanted to know a good deal more on where he stood on several issues. He stated that he was "urging him to get out and clarify his position so it will give many people, not just me, a chance to know him and to come to a decision." Goldwater said he thought "President Johnson would have been beaten this year had he run." Acknowledging that he was a "Nixon backer," the former Arizona senator was quite adamant on what he thought was the former vice president's biggest asset: "I happen to think that Dick Nixon is the most knowledgeable man we have in politics on American foreign policy and particularly Asia."[11]

On an identical ABC telecast the following Sunday, Ronald Reagan echoed many of the same themes. One of the reporters asked Reagan whether the Republican Party could nominate someone who did not support the ticket in 1964. Without explicitly mentioning Romney's name, the former actor was clear in his response: "A lot of that would deal with whether that individual repented or not." He went onto say he did not "think that a convention would probably support someone, let's say, who stayed aloof or who actually opposed the will of the party and then was completely unregenerate about this said, 'I was right, and the party was wrong.'" While Reagan was referring specifically to Romney in the above quotation, this would also apply to any other Republican who had not supported the ticket in 1964 like Rockefeller. Reagan denied any presidential ambitions for 1968 and explained he "had a four-year contract with the people of California."[12]

Unbeknownst to the Nixon staff, three days before Reagan appeared on *Issues and Answers*, Tom Reed met with the governor-elect. He outlined a delegate strategy to obtain the Republican nomination in 1968. Reed, who had successfully managed Reagan's gubernatorial campaign, met with the Reagans at their Pacific Palisades home to discuss plans. They were joined by one of the partners of the Spencer-Roberts firm, who handled had public relations for Reagan in 1966. Reagan went along with the project. The same day that Reagan was on the ABC telecast, Reed flew to New York to meet with Clifton White, the political strategist. The latter constructed the conservative coalition that nominated Goldwater in 1964. White indicated he had already been contacted by Romney to see if he would work for him but did not commit. With that, Reed asked White if he would join the Reagan campaign. White said yes. He flew back to California the next day and met with Reagan to give him the good news. Ten days later, White flew to California to meet with the new governor and Reed to finalize the agreement. Though he had not yet made a public statement, Ronald Reagan was a candidate for president in 1968.[13]

In a November 10 memo to Nixon, Buchanan noted Clifton White was not committed to anyone for 1968. Tom Charles Huston, who met earlier with White, communicated this information to him. White indicated to Huston he would not decide until at least March 1967.[14] Had the Nixon campaign known about White's agreement with Reagan, they might have proceeded differently toward him in the future.

At the same time that Reagan appeared on *Issues and Answers*, moderate to liberal Republican governors were meeting in the West Indies. Reagan admitted to his ABC audience he was not invited to the meeting but would be attending the Republican Governors Conference the following month in Colorado Springs. George Romney did participate in the meeting in the West Indies, where he had lunch with Nelson Rockefeller. Romney, a devout Mormon, said he "never talked politics on Sunday." It did not stop him from answering a question from reporters about Rockefeller's statement on "consensus" from the Republican governors. They were moving away from a dogmatic ideology that had doomed them in the last presidential election. Romney said, "That's Governor Rockefeller's word. I associate that with someone who has not fared so well with consensus. I think that we need leadership."[15] After his luncheon with Rockefeller, the former American Motor's chairman softened his tone, announcing he was in complete agreement with Rockefeller. Romney backpedaled, explaining he had objected to the word "consensus" because he associated it so much with President Johnson. He said the two were on the same page and that he would be happy to substitute the word "agreement."[16]

On the final Sunday in November, the *New York Times* ran a positive feature on the 1968 Republican presidential hopefuls. They included two of the three R's, Romney and Reagan, along with Nixon and Charles Percy, the senator-elect from Illinois. The author, Warren Weaver, Jr., took Nelson Rockefeller at his word in his piece titled "Four Hearties of the Good Ship GOP." While stating the pros and cons of each prospective candidate, Weaver wrote, "Nixon had essentially no political power base at all after leaving California and wasn't all that welcome by East Coast Republicans like Rockefeller, Javits, and Lindsey. Nevertheless, Nixon has emerged once more as a full-fledged Presidential candidate."[17]

True to his word, Richard Nixon put aside any talk of politics as he presided over the dedication of a memorial hall to the late President Herbert Hoover at the national headquarters of the Boys Club of America, an organization which he served as chairman. The president's son, Allan, accompanied Nixon at the ceremony. Nixon told the audience, "I make it a practice never to mix politics and activities of the Boys Club of America. It was Mr. Hoover's policy, and it is mine."[18]

At the same time as the dedication, there were several national polls that had Romney leading Nixon as the 1968 Republican candidate. Gallup had Romney leading Nixon among Republicans 39–31 and independents 34–22. The Harris Poll had Romney beating LBJ 54–46 and Nixon, along with Rockefeller, Percy, and Reagan, losing to the incumbent.[19]

Nixon went back to work at the law firm and participated in three more events before returning to Florida for a Christmas vacation. He hosted a luncheon at the Links Club in New York for Robert Finch to introduce the new lieutenant governor-elect of California to the East Coast establishment.[20] After that, Nixon keynoted at the annual meeting of the American Farm Bureau Federation in Las Vegas,[21] and then flew to San Francisco for the state's annual Chamber of Commerce meeting. Keeping true to his "no politics" pledge, he turned down Casper Weinberger's invitation to speak on a panel discussion on Vietnam in the Bay area.[22] He would leave that to his prospective Republican opponents.

There would be two remaining opportunities in 1966 for the three R's. At the Colorado Springs meeting, much of the focus was on Romney and Reagan. While Romney was a veteran at this kind of event, it was the first for Reagan. Romney and Reagan had a good meeting. The Michigan governor told the press that he would be traveling around the country shortly and would decide in six months whether he was going to be a candidate. He also said he would have to educate himself on the issues, especially Vietnam. Romney also met with Rockefeller and got a $300,000 commitment from the New York governor. A week later, at the National Governors Conference in White Sulfur Springs, West Virginia, Romney met with other moderate/liberal Republican governors. He told them that while he planned to run for the presidency, should he decide to withdraw, he would do so in time for another ideologically similar candidate to jump into the race.[23]

Along with polls generous to George Romney, many political pundits were starting to support him. However, they were also beginning to look more closely at the Michigan governor's record and background. If he were going to run for president, Romney would have to deal with the national press, something entirely new to him. What happened next took up much of the political discussion for the last month of 1966.

The Letter

A few weeks after the 1964 presidential election, George Romney had written a 12-page letter to Barry Goldwater explaining why he had not endorsed him during the campaign. Nixon, along with several media pundits, received the letter. Then the letter surfaced. It all occurred less than a month after both Goldwater and Reagan went on national television questioning why the Republican Party would nominate someone in 1968 who had not supported the nominee in 1964. At the same time, *Human Events*, a conservative weekly newspaper, published a poll among 1964 delegates that showed over one-quarter of those delegates would not support a candidate who had not supported the 1964 nominee. This poll also showed that the delegates favored Nixon over Romney, right after two major national polls had shown Romney leading the Republican pack.[24]

The substance of the convoluted letter was that Goldwater had run a national campaign geared to southern segregationists. The reason that Romney did not endorse Goldwater was he had not spoken with him on civil rights and extremism. It went back to a series of events in the summer of 1964 when Goldwater voted against the Civil Rights Act because he believed it was unconstitutional and violated a state's rights. Goldwater explained at least four times to Romney his reasons for doing this, disavowing any racist overtones to his decision.[25]

Romney, like several liberal Democrats, equated states' rights with racism. Goldwater told Romney if he were elected, he would enforce laws with which he disagreed. Besides, Romney tried during the Republican convention to add more robust language to the party's civil rights plank, but the amendment failed. The Michigan governor also said he had tried for nine months to talk to Goldwater.[26] When Nixon got Goldwater to meet with the other primary party members at Eisenhower's house a few weeks after the convention, everyone, including Romney, seemed to agree Goldwater had clarified his positions on several issues, including civil rights. Romney's version of the Hershey meeting was that he met the night before with William Miller, Goldwater's running mate. He gave him specific language that should be included in Goldwater's position on civil rights: "The rights of some must not be enjoyed by denying the rights of others. Neither can we permit states' rights at the expense of human rights." Romney said that Miller had no problem with it and said that he would give it to his running mate. The fact that Goldwater did not mention it during the Hershey meeting or in his remarks after the meeting made Romney think he did not support civil rights; therefore, the Michigan governor could not endorse him.[27] Goldwater did not see it like this at all. He felt he had addressed the issue numerous times and that Romney seemed to believe what he was saying. Additionally, Goldwater probably thought that as the nominee of the Republican Party, he, not Romney, would speak for himself and the party.

When the letter was published in its entirety in the *New York Times* on November 29, a lot of criticism followed. It was criticized not only for the substance and its accuracy but the reasoning behind the rambling tirade. Much of the criticism came from the conservative community. Dean Burch, the former Republican Chairman, called the charge that the campaign was appealing to southern segregationists "baloney." Burch accused the Michigan governor of "starting 1964 all over again." It would not help the Republican cause in the future, nor would it help Goldwater. The former Republican presidential nominee was gearing up for a 1968 run for the Arizona Senate seat that had been held by Carl Hayden since 1927.[28] Goldwater received several hundred letters from people all over the country, agreeing with him and confused by Romney.[29] The most eloquent response among conservatives came from William Buckley. In his nationally syndicated column, Buckley wrote in defense of Goldwater:

> The featured excuse of Governor Romney was that Senator Goldwater forged a campaign designed to appeal to southern segregationists. In making that claim, the governor underwrote the exasperating point that to favor states' rights is to favor segregation. If one wishes to play at that sort of game, one could remark that to favor Mormonism which Governor Romney does, is to favor the doctrine of the congenital and perpetual inferiority of the

black race, a little dogmatic problem within Governor Romney's church which he is overdue in reconciling with his political faith.[30]

On the other hand, Romney also had people in the national media who agreed with him and felt the problem was with Goldwater and not the Michigan governor. In their prominent, nationally syndicated *Inside Report*, Evans and Novak defended Romney and thought that the letter would serve him and the party well in the future. They also believed that someone in the conservative camp, not Romney, leaked the letter. The pair wrote in their December 16 opinion piece, "As Republicans now face another two years of possible blood-letting, they should be asking not why Romney refused to endorse Goldwater but why Goldwater could not sign an innocuous civil rights statement in the summer of 1964 that would have done much to unify the party."[31]

Romney met with several influential associates at an all-day meeting at the Waldorf Astoria in New York at the end of December. Two former Nixon supporters, Leonard Hall, who had been Nixon's campaign manager in 1960, and Clifford Folger, who was Nixon's finance chairman, attended this meeting. The other individuals noted in the *New York Times* piece included Walter DeVries, Max Fisher, Robert J. McIntosh, Richard Van Deusen, and William Seidman. All of these men had Michigan connections to Romney. DeVries was a political scientist who had been active in his earlier gubernatorial campaigns, while Fisher had been a vital fund-raiser for Romney. Fisher had also done things for Nixon in the past. McIntosh had been a department head in the Romney administration, while Van Deusen had been his legal adviser. Seidman was the head of a prominent accounting firm in Detroit. While Romney was publicly saying that he would not decide his intentions for another six months, it was clear to most political observers at the time that he was in the race for president.[32]

New Faces

Two days before the end of 1966, Richard and Pat Nixon attended the 12th annual International Debutante Ball at the Waldorf Astoria hotel. They were there to see Julie's formal debut into the social scene of New York. David Eisenhower, the grandson of the former president, escorted the Nixons' youngest daughter. The two had been dating for the past couple of months while in their first years of college, Julie at Smith and David at Amherst. Before that, they had not seen each other since a White House function in 1957. Pat was the honorary chair of the ball for this celebration. The Nixon house was full of joy as the New Year approached.[33]

The year 1967 certainly brought new changes to the law firm. The firm of Caldwell, Trimble, and Mitchell merged with the firm of Nixon, Mudge, Rose, Guthrie, and Alexander. John Mitchell was made a partner of the newly merged firm, and his name added to the masthead after Alexander's. The eight-man firm was a leader in the municipal bond legal business. It was a niche area of the law that none of the other major Wall Street firms had entered. Mitchell had gained a national reputation in the field with business all over the country.[34] Bob "Kingfish" Guthrie had worked on several cases that year with Mitchell involving the bond business. Kingfish had enlisted Nixon to convince Mitchell to join their firm. The two met for lunch a few times about a proposed merger. Mitchell claimed to have met Nixon numerous times since the 1950s, but the former vice president did not remember meeting him until their

NIXON MUDGE ROSE GUTHRIE ALEXANDER & MITCHELL

JOHN H. ALEXANDER
BLISS ANSNES
PETER W. ASHER
ARTHUR M. BECKER
MILTON BLACK
JOHN F. BROSNAN
GEORGE E. BUCHANAN
WILLIAM H. CANNON
GOLDTHWAITE H. DORR
THOMAS W. EVANS
RICHARD B. FARROW
JAMES G. FRANCOS
LEONARD GARMENT
GERRIT GILLIS
RANDOLPH H. GUTHRIE
MATTHEW G. HEROLD, JR.
JOSEPH V. KLINE
WILLIAM B. LANDIS
JOHN LARSON
FRANKLIN B. LINCOLN, JR.
WILLIAM A. MADISON
JOHN N. MITCHELL
RICHARD M. NIXON
RICHARD S. RITZEL
MILTON C. ROSE
NORMAN M. SEGAL
HARRY G. SILLECK, JR.
HENRY ROOT STERN, JR.
JAMES P. TANNIAN
ROBERT E. WALSH
GEORGE W. WHITTAKER
DONALD J. ZOELLER
GERALD B. GREENWALD
(D. C. BAR ONLY)

20 BROAD STREET

NEW YORK, N.Y. 10005

212 HAnover 2-6767

JOHN T. TRIMBLE
COUNSEL

CABLE ADDRESS:
"BALTUCHINS—NEW YORK"

1701 PENNSYLVANIA AVE., N.W.
WASHINGTON, D. C.
202-298-5970
CABLE ADDRESS:
"BALTUCHINS—WASHINGTON"

12, RUE DE LA PAIX
PARIS 2E, FRANCE
742 05.99
CABLE ADDRESS:
"BALTUCHINS—PARIS"

New letterhead after the merging of John Mitchell's firm with Nixon Mudge Rose in January 1967 (Richard M. Nixon Library).

luncheons the year before.[35] The two would become much more acquainted later in the year after Nixon's six-month public moratorium from politics. In the meantime, the small Nixon staff would be privately hard at work getting their message out about who was best posed to lead the Republicans in 1968.

Another new face joined the Nixon staff in January, even though she was not new to Nixon. Her name was Shelley Scarney. Scarney's association with the "Boss" went back to 1959. After graduating from the University of Michigan with a degree in political science that spring, Scarney got a job offer from a company in New York. She jumped at the opportunity because it had been a dream of hers to live there. On her way to the Big Apple, Shelley stopped in Washington, D.C., to visit several girlfriends from Michigan. While there, she saw a job opening with the vice president of the United States. Even though she had already accepted a job offer in New York, Shelley decided to apply for the position. As it turned out, she got the job that summer. Scarney worked with Nixon through the rest of his vice presidency, including the grueling 1960 campaign. In 1961, she went to work with General Dynamics in San Diego and took a sabbatical from that job to work with H.R. "Bob" Haldeman, who managed Nixon's 1962 California governor's campaign. She later moved to New York to take a position with McDonnell and Werner. Scarney joined the Nixon team campaigning for Goldwater in 1964 and then went back to her New York job. Her desk was now the receptionist position outside the office of Rose Mary Woods.[36]

More Political Rumblings

On January 3, seven southern state chairs and other prominent Republicans met privately in Key Biscayne to explore how best to address the threat of George Wallace as a Democrat or a third-party candidate. The former Alabama governor had made a national name for himself with his stand against the civil rights movement. When Wallace could not succeed himself as governor in 1966, he had his wife, Lurleen, run as a stand-in while he worked behind the scenes. If he ran against Johnson as a Democrat, the Republicans were not so worried; it was the threat of a third-party run that concerned them, especially in light of their recent gains in the 1966 elections. William P. Murfin, chairman of the Florida delegation, saw this a problem: "If he runs, we're in trouble. Right now, this is the one thing that could put [President Johnson] back in office." Peter O'Donnell, the Texas chairman, seemed less concerned, saying it was an open question as to whether Republicans or Democrats would be hurt more. While Richard Nixon remained the top choice of southern Republican leaders, Ronald Reagan was emerging as the second choice after his win in 1966.[37]

Four days later, Nixon convened a two-day meeting of seven prominent politicos at the Waldorf Astoria, Herbert Hoover's home in his later years. Symbolically, the location meant a great deal for Nixon. Four of the seven had worked with him before: Peter Flanigan, Bob Finch, Tom Evans, and William Safire. Safire, the last to arrive, was not familiar with three of the new faces. One was a Wall Street financier of the Goldwater campaign, Jerry Millbank. The other two were Republican state chairmen who had been at the Key Biscayne meeting earlier in the week. They were Peter O'Donnell and Fred LaRue of Mississippi. O'Donnell also served as the head of the Southern Association of Republican States. At the same time, LaRue had worked with Nixon on some events in the South in the previous congressional elections. Safire wrote of the importance of this meeting eight years later:

> "The purpose of this group," Nixon began, "is to begin planning now to win the nomination. It is important that we keep the existence of this group quiet, not only because of the press but because we don't want to hurt the feelings of anybody we've left out." This added to a warm organizational feeling; we were the "inner circle" of one of the few men could actually make it, and Nixon wanted us to know it....[38]

Bob Finch emphasized the importance of convincing delegates that Nixon could win, erasing the "loser" image. The easiest way to do that, Finch believed, was to beat Romney, perceived as the leading competitor and the best-financed, in the key primaries. There would be 12 primaries, but favorite son candidates would most likely head eight of these. That left at least four primaries with true head-to-head competition. The states, in chronological order, were New Hampshire, Wisconsin, Nebraska, and Oregon. If Nixon could win those primaries, other states leaning toward Nixon might become even stronger.[39] The former vice president told them next what must be done: "If I were to do nothing, Romney would be nominated.... Whoever is running has to start running now."[40] Nixon appointed this group to work behind the scenes to get the word out that he was running. They also began hunting for delegates in the states.

Richard Nixon held to his six-month moratorium even though the group wanted him out front. He explained it was essential to stick to his plan and "let Romney take the point," knowing from experience the degree of scrutiny Romney would receive and thinking the Michigan governor could not take it. Nixon's position was reinforced the day before the meeting in a memorandum from Pat Buchanan. The subject matter involved Buchanan reaching out to an AP reporter named Stan Johnson, who had covered Romney. Buchanan wrote that Johnson, who traveled with Romney, deemed George's press relations atrocious, and he felt Romney was "one of the dumbest individuals that he had ever met."[41]

Toward the end of the two-day meeting, Finch argued for a national chairman. He thought that Gaylord "Parky" Parkinson, the California doctor who was the chairman of the California Republicans, would be a good choice. Nixon agreed and asked Finch to have Herb Klein run the idea by Parkinson. Finally, Nixon went through a state-by-state delegate count and estimated that he had 603, 64 short of the 667 needed. Safire surveyed the room to see if others determined if their position was much more reliable than Nixon believed, but the major challenge was to convince others that Nixon was a winner.[42]

Two days after the critical New York meetings, Nixon went to Washington's Mayflower Hotel for Senator Dirksen's birthday party.[43] Later in the month, he held fund-raisers for the Boys Club in Minneapolis with World War II famed General Mark Clark[44] and in Fort Lauderdale with General Wilton Persons, a military veteran of both world wars, who for six years was Ike's special assistant at NATO.[45] Sandwiched between these two fund-raisers was an appearance at the University of Florida's Accent Symposium. The other co-headliner was Ralph Nader, a consumer advocate from New York. There were several other notable speakers at the Gainesville event, including Tom Wicker, William Rusher, and James Farmer. The topic was "Responsibility of Dissent."[46]

At the end of the month, political news shifted to New Orleans, where the Republicans convened their national meeting of state chairs. The four-day conference was well attended with the Romney staff very visible. Law firm partner Tom Evans went to the event as an observer, along with Charlie McWhorter and Sherman Unger, who, unlike the Romney team, were not chasing delegates. It was announced there that the Wisconsin primary would be open, with no favorite son candidate, as Nixon had earlier anticipated. A poll was also taken at the event among party leaders on who they thought should win the Republican nomination. Nixon took 27 first-place votes to Romney's 19, while 36 leaders were uncommitted.[47] The Seaton letter was also starting to draw dividends, as several responses came back to 20 Broad, saying that they backed Nixon in 1968. John Sears was putting these responses into a political file for next year's primaries.[48]

The day after the New Orleans conference, a front-page story written by David Broder titled "Nixon Begins Building His Staff for 1968" appeared in *The Washington Post*. Broder wrote that Gaylord Parkinson had met with Peter O'Donnell, Fred LaRue, and Tom Evans at the conference to discuss the possibility of joining a "Nixon for President" staff. The California obstetrician, who had stewarded Ronald Reagan and the Republicans in 1966, had a famous dictum named after him called "Parkinson's Law" or the "11th Commandment." Parkinson's Law stated Republicans should not speak ill of others in their party, especially during a campaign. Parkinson acknowledged he did meet with the three Nixon men and also had a similar offer from the Romney campaign. After the meetings in New Orleans, Parkinson and his associate, Robert Walker, flew to New York for a dinner engagement with Nixon. LaRue and O'Donnell met with him the next day. O'Donnell indicated Texas would support Senator John T. Tower as its favorite son candidate and expected other southern states to follow suit. Broder also mentioned the Seaton letter. Broder quoted Seaton, saying he received an encouraging response. The former secretary of the interior stated that he had received about 125 letters and half a dozen phone calls, most of them favorable. He also said Nixon had not been consulted in the letter-writing project.[49] It was good news for the Nixon team heading into February.

Dr. Parkinson accepted the chairman position for "Nixon for President" soon after his dinner with the former vice president, bringing along Ron Walker as his assistant. Walker also worked in Republican politics in California. Nixon did not publicly announce the hiring of the two political campaign professionals, wanting to keep it out of the news, but the Romney team would not let him. They were irked that Parkinson had turned them down and leaked the story to the press, pointing out the inconsistency of the moratorium on politics.[50]

With the Parkinson and Walker hiring, Nixon spent most of February preparing for the first of four major foreign trips. With the Harris survey showing Romney leading with Republicans and Independents 41–28 over Nixon, with a 10-point advantage in a contest with LBJ, the Michigan governor toured Alaska and several Western states.[51] All of the good press he had received for the past few months, however, was starting to change. Even Evans and Novak, who for several months had been singing the praises of Romney, questioned his campaign's organization. The veteran reporters, in the February 13 "Inside Report" column, wrote, "Romney is under pressure to make a superlative showing on his weeklong Western tour beginning Friday. But that tour, a series of disconnected trips to thinly populated Western states arranged helter-skelter by the Governor himself, is itself a sign of the Romney disorganization."[52]

At each of the stops, Governor Romney held press conferences where most the questioning dealt with Vietnam. His responses were inconsistent until he finally refused to take any more questions about Vietnam, claiming he would take a "fresh look" at the war. Even so, Romney continued to offer contradictory statements on the war. At one stop, he talked about hitting the North Vietnamese harder; at another, he suggested more peacemaking gestures.[53]

More New Additions to Nixon Staff

While Romney campaigned through February, Nixon told Pat Buchanan to find a good man in New York to balance his conservative views. Buchanan had only been in New York a little over a year and did not know many people. He enlisted the help of Neal B. Freeman, a prominent writer at the *National Review*, who provided eight possible candidates. In a February 20 memo, Buchanan sent Nixon the short list with some brief comments about each. The top two candidates were Raymond "Ray" Price and Jack Saloma. Price was a prominent writer who had worked for several magazines like *Colliers* and *Life,* as well as editing the recently closed *New York Herald Tribune,* the newspaper of the northeastern liberal Republican establishment since Horace Greeley. Saloma had a Harvard Ph.D. and was an assistant professor of political science at Massachusetts Institute of Technology (MIT) and president of the Ripon Society, a group of Boston-based academics and students who espoused liberal Republican principles. The group made many headlines in 1964 at the San Francisco convention, where it backed William Scranton. Saloma had also heartily denounced

Barry Goldwater as a traitor to Republican principles and refused to support him in the election.[54]

Buchanan gave Nixon the pros and cons of the candidates. He thought that Saloma's high profile actions in 1964 would probably be divisive among party regulars and especially to conservatives. Choosing the MIT professor might undo the core conservative support where Buchanan and Nixon believed all the dominant energy of the party was located. On the other hand, if they chose Ray Price, they might have another problem because his newspaper had endorsed Lyndon Johnson for in 1964. Price wrote the editorial. Nixon told Buchanan this should not be a problem. What the young aide did in 1964, Nixon commented, did not matter and "once he signed on and got bloodied in a few battles, he would be with us."[55]

Nixon called Walter Thayer, former head of the *Tribune* and current president of Whitney Communications, who also owned *Parade* and *Interior Design* magazines, Corinthian Broadcasting, and several smaller media concerns. Nixon told Thayer he was looking for Ray Price and wanted to talk to him about a job. He had met Thayer when he worked for Eisenhower and had a good relationship with him. Thayer called his former employee, who was at home in his New York apartment nursing a bad hangover. Price had worked for Charles Percy one year before in the last month of his Senate campaign in Illinois and was currently working on a novel. Thayer relayed Nixon's remarks and told Price that he would be glad to talk to him. Price had worked on the fringes of Republican politics since 1948 when he was a student at Yale. He had been a friend there to William Buckley, the godfather of the conservative movement. Even though Price's politics were left of Buckley's, he was in the mainstream of northeastern Republican politics. Price had always been associated with Rockefeller Republicans. However, he barely knew the man and never had the animus toward Nixon that many in that part of the country had.[56]

After speaking with Thayer, Price had just taken some milk, coffee, and aspirin to soothe his aching head when, within 15 minutes, Nixon called to invite him to his apartment for lunch in two hours. Price pulled himself together enough for the informal luncheon, which was a relaxed affair with TV trays that lasted three hours. Price was fabulously amazed and impressed with Nixon as he peppered him with questions about all types of political subjects and his view of the world. He said, "Nixon was much more impressive in person" and "had a first-rate analytical mind."[57] At the end of the interview, Nixon offered him a job. Price expressed interest and promised to get back to him within a week. During the next seven days, Price read articles and books on Nixon. With all that research completed, Price called Nixon back seven days later and agreed to come work for him as a personal aide in his law office. Price reported to work on March 1. After coming to the office on 20 Broad, he met others on Nixon's staff.[58]

The first day of Price's new job proved to be a whirlwind of activity. Nixon, incredibly busy preparing for his Europe trip, put Price to work alongside Pat Buchanan. Dwight Chapin was also starting his first day after Nixon offered him the job in late January. He was still working in advertising and marketing at J. Walter Thompson and had been working for Bob Haldeman, another Nixon man. Chapin, of course, had worked for Nixon in the 1962 governor's race, at the Republican convention in San Francisco in 1964, and as an advance man in 1966.[59]

Also joining the team was Robert "Bob" Ellsworth, a former member of Congress from Kansas. He first met Nixon during the 1960 election when the two campaigned together in his home state. They ran into each other over the next few years. During the 1966 campaign, they were on the same plane leaving Washington, D.C. The former vice president had just completed his oral arguments in the *Hill* case and was flying to California through Chicago, and Ellsworth was on his way to Kansas City. The former vice president told Ellsworth to see him in January after the elections at his office in New York. At their meeting, Ellsworth told Nixon precisely what he thought of Romney and the former vice president. Ellsworth said, "Romney doesn't have it. Let him have his six months. I think that they've made a big mistake putting all of their chips on him. I hope you'll go for it. Johnson, with all his troubles, will be easy to beat." Nixon did not respond individually, but Ellsworth could tell that he was listening.[60] Ellsworth was then working in Washington in private practice as an attorney on K Street. While he had been in Congress, Ellsworth was known as a policy wonk on foreign affairs, mainly Europe and NATO. He did not formally join the Nixon team until later in the year but would accompany him on his upcoming three-week trip to Europe in March.[61]

7

The World Tour

On February 13, a memo was sent to major media outlets on Nixon's four upcoming fact-finding trips. Each trip would take about three weeks, with 3–7 days in between each trip. The State Department briefed Nixon before he left on the first trip. One other person, usually an old friend, would accompany Nixon on each trip. At each stop, he called on the United States ambassador, the head of the host government, the foreign minister, the leader of the opposition (if possible), other significant political figures, and local citizens. The first trip would be to Europe. The purpose of this trip was to assess the status of NATO, develop a proposal for expanding trade relations with Eastern Europe, and explore the latest developments in the nuclear arms race. Robert Ellsworth, a former congressman from Kansas and current attorney in Washington, D.C., accompanied Nixon. No press conferences or public appearances were scheduled because Nixon would not speak on these subjects until he was in the United States.[1]

On March 3, two days before the trip was to begin, Nixon received word he was unable to get a visa to visit Poland, which he had visited as vice president in 1959. The press speculated Poland was moving to a harder Soviet line regarding the United States. Nixon stated that he regretted the perceived harder line of the Polish government.[2]

It was the first time that Nixon had been to Western Europe since 1963. He believed that he needed to "bring his impression up to date" about what was going in the world and how the rest of the world perceived America. Nixon wrote later in his memoirs, "By undertaking these trips, I was building on my political strong suit." He wanted to make sure that if he was indeed going to run for president again, he understood the current international environment and how this environment impacted the United States and its foreign policy.[3] The first two legs of the trip were to visit old friends in England and France. Nixon met with the top government officials of both countries and discussed how to strengthen the current relationship between the two countries. While in England, he met with Prime Minister Harold Wilson, Foreign Minister George Brown, and the leaders of the opposition, Ted Heath and Alec Douglas-Home. One of the most exciting parts of the England trip was all the buzz about Soviet Premier Alexi Kosygin's visit the week before. All of the significant figures whom Nixon and Ellsworth spoke with were saying that the Soviet leader's stay was a public relations coup. In summary, after the trip, Ellsworth wrote that Kosygin was "genuinely anxious about the problem."[4]

In France, Nixon met with de Gaulle, George Pompidou, and Foreign Minister Couve de Murville. In addition to Ellsworth, Charles "Chip" Bohlen, the U.S.

ambassador to France, assisted Nixon. Bohlen, an old diplomatic hand, served as Franklin Roosevelt's interpreter at Tehran and Yalta as well as ambassador to both the Soviet Union and the Philippines before his current post in Paris. De Gaulle told Nixon that the United States should try to end the war in Vietnam on the best possible terms: the sooner, the better. He also believed this would improve their relationship with the Soviet Union. De Gaulle had told Nixon four years earlier that it was better for the United States to recognize Communist China before it became too powerful.[5]

Before leaving France, Nixon spoke briefly to the press, answering several questions about the Atlantic Alliance, American troops leaving France, and France abandoning the military agreement of the alliance. He said, "The departure of American troops does not constitute in any way the ending of the Atlantic Alliance; or its weakening." Nixon also said he would actively participate in the forthcoming American elections but would not say in what capacity. Finally, he stated the majority of Americans agreed with President Johnson's policy in Vietnam and that he thought that the war could be a factor of "political irritation" in the upcoming presidential election.[6]

The next stop was in Bonn, West Germany, where after meeting the chancellor, vice-chancellor, and finance minister, Nixon's meeting with the 91-year-old builder of West Germany, Konrad Adenauer, was the highlight of the entire trip. Adenauer told him the United States was taking Europe for granted and was perhaps too vested in Asia to recognize this. Nixon would write of this moving experience in his memoirs over a decade later:

> He predicted that when de Gaulle left the scene, the Communist Party in France, and then in Italy, would gain strength. He completely discounted the Soviet Union's alleged interest in hastening peace in Vietnam, and the popular speculation that the Soviets would turn to the West out of fear of China. "Make no mistake about it," he said, "they want the world. The whole world. Most of all they want Europe, and to get Europe they know they must destroy Germany."[7]

Italy was their next stop, where they met with Premier Aldo Moro, President Giuseppe Saragat, Pope Paul VI, and the Secretary-General of NATO, Manlio Brosio. Everyone except the Pope expressed the same concern about communist sympathies: that the United States was too caught up with Asia and Vietnam to worry about Europe's problems. The Italian media were drawing comparisons between Nixon's concise diplomatic comments in support of the Johnson administration's position in Vietnam and Robert Kennedy's unsettling statement on the American stance while in Rome two weeks before.[8]

Different View from Eastern Europe?

Nixon then spent five days in the Soviet Union. Nixon had wanted to meet with Alexi Kosygin and Leonid Brezhnev, but they refused to meet with him. He wondered if LBJ was still mad at him over his Manila communiqué comments and had pressed the Soviet leaders to deny meeting with him. Nixon was even refused a CIA briefing before the trip, the first time that this had occurred since he left the vice presidency in 1961. Despite all of this, Nixon spent a couple of days in Moscow, most of it with Ambassador Lewellyn Thompson. Nixon had known Thompson for many years as the ambassador to Austria and later, to the Soviet Union during the Eisenhower years. Thompson began serving his second tour there in January. The two drove about the city, with Nixon commenting on the number of changes since he visited two years earlier.[9]

One of the most unusual events of the trip occurred at the U.S. Industrial Design Exhibit in Sokolniki Park in Moscow. Nixon engaged in a rather lengthy conversation with a Soviet construction engineer by the name of Vladimir Panov. Panov knew that Nixon was a political figure who had been to his country before. He asked if Nixon remembered giving Khrushchev a lesson about "horse manure" in the famous 1959 Moscow Kitchen Debate. They discussed how Nixon and Khrushchev had political differences but were still friends, so much so that Khrushchev gave Nixon a shotgun. Nixon told Panov that he did not hunt, but if Panov came to the United States, Nixon would let him shoot his Russian rifle. Panov told Nixon about hunting and his soldier days in World War II. The construction engineer went on to say he had met several American soldiers in the war and described what they did when they liberated Chemnitz: "We drank whiskey rather well with your boys, and they drank vodka." Toward the end of their dialogue, Panov stressed to Nixon that the two great countries should find a way to live in peace. The conversation ended with Nixon's idea that the two countries should go to the moon together. Panov said he was very sorry that the American astronauts had recently died.[10]

After being shunned by the Soviet officials, Nixon next headed to Bucharest, Romania. It was one of the Soviet allies increasingly making signals that they wanted a good deal more autonomy from Moscow. Nixon was well aware of Romania's position, being a small country in the heart of Europe whose fate recently had been controlled first by Nazi Germany and then by the Soviet Union. He had two long foreign policy conversations with the two most influential leaders in the country.

The first conversation, the shorter of the two, was with Foreign Minister Corneliu Menuscu. The meeting took place at the American Embassy in Bucharest. This dialogue was different than those earlier conducted earlier in the capitals of London, Paris, Bonn, and Rome. Those four countries were allies of the United States and felt comfortable discussing problems between themselves. After exchanging pleasantries and acknowledging Nixon was not a member of the United States government but instead, a "notable American and a representative of the American people," Menuscu asked why the Soviet leaders had not talked to Nixon when he was in their country. Menuscu explained that the Soviet Union was a large and powerful country close to them, and they needed to be concerned with its wishes. While they wanted better relations with the U.S., they had to take into account the Soviet views. Romania could not make foreign policy in a vacuum. Nixon assured Menuscu that it was in both countries' interest to have better relations. After this exchange, Nixon spoke briefly to the deputy foreign minister of trade about improving economic ties.[11]

The longer and more substantive conversation Nixon had in Bucharest was with Secretary-General Nicolae Ceausescu. This wide-ranging dialogue revolved around four major problem areas: European security, inter-bloc relations, the Non-Proliferation Treaty, and Communist China. Ceausescu believed that European security could be achieved without the problem of German unification being solved. He thought this was more of an issue for the United States and less so for the European countries. The Romanian leader also believed both East and West

Germany would have to be involved in solving the problem of European security. Ceausescu agreed with Nixon that Germany could not remain indefinitely divided. He also thought that the same principle applied to Korea and Vietnam, but reunification would have to be done peacefully. Nixon complimented the Romanian leader for his independence and his "understanding attitude." He thought that other Eastern European countries should limit their verbal attacks on the West German government. Nixon told Ceausescu, "It was good to hear at least one Eastern European voice express a reasonable opinion."[12]

Ceausescu again addressed the general question of overall European security, arguing the answer must rely on the recognition of the independence and national sovereignty of each country as well as a policy of non-interference in their domestic affairs. It was routine diplomatic speak, but what he said next was not. Ceausescu said, "Romania opposed the presence of troops of one country on the territory of another. The achievement of European security should not be considered as directed against anyone or another country. The presence of foreign troops in other countries hindered the development of real security. In other countries, the leaders may be reserved on this question, but in Romania's contacts with these leaders, they all say they want to get rid of foreign troops as soon as possible."[13]

The Romanian leader said his country had a good relationship with the Soviet Union. In Nixon's copy of this conversation, he underlined this passage and wrote "tongue in cheek," realizing that Ceausescu "knew what he said would get back to the Soviets." Ceausescu stated the differences in the socialist countries were analogous to family disputes, and they should not hamper overall good relationships. Nixon wondered if Eastern European countries would continue making independent decisions rather than be part of the Soviet-controlled block. Nixon conceded there was a certain amount of independence in NATO and mentioned de Gaulle, Wilson, and Kissinger. Nixon agreed it was important for the two countries to have mutual exchanges that could lead to a better understanding. He also noted the Soviet Union had strong views on many of these issues. Nixon wanted to make sure that he understood Ceausescu was implying socialist countries tended to see problems in the same way because of their similar socio-political systems. He assumed that there would not be any problems in the future if Romania advocated a course of action unapproved by the Soviets. Ceausescu replied with a resounding, "Yes." Nixon ended this segment of the discussion with a problem that he had with the Soviet leadership: their future relationship with China. He said, "After all, China had some 700 million people and was inevitably an important factor in the world. Today it represented no great military problem, but 20 years hence could represent a threat to the peace of the world if it is still isolated."[14]

Before returning to China, Ceausescu wanted to discuss the Nuclear Non-Proliferation Treaty currently being negotiated. He noted adjustments needed to assure the peaceful use of atomic energy, smaller powers being left behind from a security perspective, and the production of weapons. Nixon responded that nothing could be done about the manufacture and stockpiling of these weapons by the two powers until the China question was addressed. He was doubtful the United States could have normal relations with China until the Vietnam War was settled. The Romanian leader reminded Nixon that the former vice president had been there in 1964 and agreed with him that China was a great country but generally misunderstood.

He did not think China could continue in isolation. Ceausescu said it was unrealistic to believe that 50 years from now, China would be a secondary power. He cited the 19th-century example of England and France as great powers and the U.S. as a minor power. Ceausescu added he could not understand why America still supported Chiang Kai-shek since Taiwan could not be part of China. Nixon reiterated his point about normalizing relations with the communist giant after the Vietnam War was resolved. He also wondered how the Soviet Union would respond to détente between China and the United States and whether difficulties between the two communist powers were a family quarrel that was too problematic to settle.[15]

Finally, the two sides disagreed on what should be done about Vietnam. Ceausescu could not understand why the U.S. continued to bomb North Vietnam and did not think negotiation could take place until the bombing stopped. Nixon made it clear that he was a member of the opposition party in the United States. Still, he strongly supported President Johnson's policies in Vietnam. He would be visiting South Vietnam within the next month and would re-examine his position after the visit. Nixon concluded with the possibility of an eventual rapprochement between the U.S.S.R and China. He believed that it would have an essential bearing on atomic weapon policy. Nixon felt that either the Soviet Union or the U.S. needed to have some kind of commitment from the Chinese if any real progress toward nuclear disarmament would take place.[16]

Nixon spent the last two days of the Europe trip in Czechoslovakia, where he toured Prague, Lidice, and Malnik. In Prague, Nixon visited the old Jewish cemetery and synagogue. In Lidice, Nixon saw a rebuilt city that had been decimated by bombs in World War II. The Nazis leveled Lidice in retaliation for Heydrich's assassination.[17] Back in Prague, he was the guest of honor at a reception sponsored by the Society of International Relations and held at the famous Waldstein Castle. At the dinner, Nixon spoke to many influential people, including the deputy foreign minister, the chairman of the foreign relations committee in the National Assembly, and other members of the Czech political elite. He also spoke to the Institute for International Politics and Economics, a prominent think-tank and research facility in Prague.[18]

Going into the trip, Bob Ellsworth had thought that foreign policy was Nixon's strong point. This belief was reinforced after the European tour. The former congressman was continually amazed at the former vice president's insights on this journey and how his opinions were evolving. Ellsworth recalled his thoughts to a Nixon biographer nearly 25 years later when he said, "Accompanying Nixon to appointments like these, I began to realize that here was a quite extraordinary mind at work. He saw international politics as the highest stakes game in the world.... He was often thinking two or three moves, sometimes even a generation ahead." Ellsworth understood Nixon realized the European order had become rigid, sterile, and bipolar, and that America must change that.[19]

Brief Re-Loading Back Home

Nixon returned home at the end of the month, insisting that he have at least four days in the office before returning to his worldwide tour. While he was away, there had been good news and bad news. The good news was Gallup's mid–March poll showed him in a clear lead over George Romney. The pollsters attributed that to four separate measurements:

    1. The top choice of Republican voters for the 1968 nomination among all leading candidates {39–30},

    2. The candidate they thought would make the best run in 1968 {39–34},

    3. The preferred candidate by a wide margin, in a "show-down" race against Romney {53–41}, and

    4. The candidate who generated the greatest enthusiasm among Republican voters.[20]

The bad news was the news leaks out of the Washington office where Parkinson and Walker were just settling in. Nixon told his new hires they needed to keep a low profile and not communicate every new campaign development. Evans and Novak had earlier claimed, after David Broder broke the news, that Romney had leaked the information to the press. Broder called Pat Buchanan a day later and asked for his comment. Taken aback, he refused to comment. The political team at Nixon, Mudge, Rose, and Mitchell was beginning to think differently as to the leak's origin.[21]

In the run-up to an important meeting with the Washington team and others before Nixon went to Asia, Buchanan stated in a March 28 memo to Nixon, "Parkinson has dismally handled a major interview, and his aides have released vital data they were specifically told to withhold; they have sent letters to newsmen inviting them to join the committee, which betrays an ominous stupidity; they have let an incredibly stupid form of letter go to General Eisenhower; and Parkinson has gone directly against instructions by naming Walker Executive Director." Furthermore, in the memo, Buchanan pointed out that if they fired them, they might take other vital people like O'Donnell and LaRue with them. Buchanan wrote that they needed to make clear to Parkinson and Walker that the executive director's appointment would not hold if the leaks did not stop. Finally, he noted that no one in their office trusted the two new appointees. Buchanan specifically mentioned himself, John Sears, Tom Evans, Rose Mary Woods, and Len Garment. In concluding the memo, the political aide wrote, "Unless Parkinson can make some show of loyalty and competence, there is going to be a continued adverse reaction to him, a reluctance to turn over data to him, and a decided inclination to work our own fields, to bypass him, to parallel his efforts and not infrequently work against him."[22] Nixon had a lot to ponder as he headed to Asia in his second fact-finding trip around the world.

As he got off the plane from his three-week tour of Europe, Richard Nixon spoke briefly to reporters outlining his initial assessment of how American foreign policy was perceived. Sticking to his political moratorium, he did not criticize the president or any other Republican candidates. However, every European leader told Nixon that reducing American troops would increase the risk of Soviet aggression. Nixon believed Moscow wanted to Finlandize Europe. Coming on the heels of aiming a medium-range ballistic missile system at Western Europe, the Soviets were diplomatically pushing a security agreement that excluded the United States, thus rendering NATO harmless. Nixon said he hoped President Johnson would schedule a trip to Europe within the year and see first-hand what Nixon had just witnessed.[23]

Back to Asia

After spending a few days in his New York office, he took a quick trip to Key Biscayne, Florida, where he had just purchased property near his good friend Bebe Rebozo. Then he began his sixth trip to Asia in four years. Nixon flew to Los Angeles on April 1, arriving a little after seven at night. Tom Evans and John Davies met him at the airport before he departed for a two-night stay at the Ambassador Hotel. Ray Price flew from New York the next day to meet Nixon for the Asian trip. The following day was a busy one. Nixon left the hotel for a two-and-a-half-hour meeting with Bob Haldeman. He next went back to Whittier and, with his brother Don, visited their ailing mother in a nursing home. After that, Nixon flew to Palm Desert for a nearly two-hour visit with General Eisenhower, then on to Los Angeles. That night at the hotel, he had a private dinner with Bob Finch before leaving for Hawaii the next morning.[24]

While Nixon was dining with Finch, Ray Price went to dinner with John Davies, an old Nixon friend from California who briefed the new aide on what to expect on the oncoming trip. He told Price that on the airplane flights, he would take the aisle seat while Nixon got the window. Because he worked while in the air, this seating arrangement provided Nixon a buffer from anyone on the plane wanting to meet him. Usually, Nixon would be writing notes on his yellow legal pad and would let Davies know when he wanted to talk. Once they arrived at their destination, their schedules were usually pretty tight, but occasionally there was free time for sightseeing.[25] Price's head must have been spinning. Five weeks ago, he was unemployed, writing a novel, and had never met Richard Nixon. Now he was flying with Nixon on a three-week trip to 11 different Asian countries. There were only four instances when Nixon met alone with foreign officials: in Tehran with the Shah of Iran, in Bangkok with the king of Thailand, in Pakistan with President Ayub Khan, and in Taipei with Chiang Kai-shek. Otherwise, Price attended every meeting on the trip.[26]

Price would bring along research materials from New York. His job was to be handy with whatever Nixon needed. Usually, Nixon wanted to know who they were going to see, pertinent facts about the destination, talking points on bilateral relations, and political implications. Nixon already knew a lot about Asia and had met with most of its leaders on previous trips.[27]

After a five and half hour flight from Los Angeles, the first stop was in Honolulu. It was most likely the only part of the trip where they had free time. Twenty-four hours later, they departed for the eight-hour trip to Tokyo. Japan was the United States' largest trading partner in Asia and second only to Canada in total bilateral trade in 1967. A little over two decades after the end of World War II, Japan had the fourth-largest economy in the world.[28] Nixon had been here more than ten times. Price noticed a dramatic change in the country since 1954 when he was in Japan while serving in the Navy.[29]

The three-day visit in Japan involved a whirlwind of activity. They stayed at the official residence of the American embassy with Ambassador U. Alexis Johnson. The embassy was previously occupied by General Douglas MacArthur when he ruled over the country for seven years after the allied victory in the war. After lunch and dinner engagements with many notable people while in Japan, Nixon met separately with Prime Minister Eiasaku Sato, Foreign Minister Takeo Miki, and former Prime

Minister Nobosuke Kishi. The meetings with Kishi, the minister of commerce and industry of the Japanese government during World War II, and the brother of the current Japanese prime minister, were his longest. Later, Nixon also had individual meetings with party leaders of both the Liberal Democratic and Socialist parties before departing for Hong Kong.[30]

As he was leaving Japan, Nixon talked with reporters. He contrasted what he had heard in Europe about Americans being too entangled in Asia with his recent impressions from Asia: "If the credibility of the United States is destroyed in Vietnam, it will be destroyed in Europe as well. The Europeans may not know it now, but they will damn well know it then. Asia is changing faster than any other part of the world.... The Asians feel that here is where the action is.... Free Asia is more united than Western Europe."[31]

The next two visits to Hong Kong and Taiwan were one day each. Nixon had visited both countries several times as the vice president and an attorney. While in Hong Kong, he met with Consular General Edward E. Rice and Governor Sir David Trench. He also saw old acquaintances Harold Lee and Linden Johnson while in the British colony.[32] It only took an hour and a half to fly to Taipei from Hong Kong. The two Americans were there for less than 24 hours but did have time to be briefed by the American Embassy and to attend a meeting with Chiang Kai-shek. Chiang was a longtime friend of Nixon, and there was a great deal of mutual admiration. Nixon wrote of this meeting ten years later: "Chiang still dreamed of returning to the mainland, and once again, he urged that America support such an effort. His burning desire to return to the mainland was understandable and admirable. But it was totally unrealistic in view of the massive power of the Communists had developed."[33]

There were two more visits, the Philippines and Thailand, before Nixon landed in South Vietnam for a more extended stay. In Manila, Nixon visited with President Marcos and Vice President Fernando Lopez. He also saw old friend Carlos Romulo, who had served in a host of high government positions and was now the president of the University of the Philippines. Ray Price commented the country was looking for an identity amidst a mix of cultural heritages—some Asian, some Spanish, and some American, but few Filipino. Price wrote Nixon was intrigued by the contrast between the magnificent presidential palace, and Vice President Fernando Lopez's office—"a tacky warren of plain wooden tables and Woolworth-modern furnishings, and a gaggle of secretaries."[34] In Thailand, Nixon met privately with the king while Price enjoyed walking around Bangkok. Bob Ellsworth had some business there and would join the pair on their next stop in Saigon for the rest of the Asia trip.[35]

Three Days in South Vietnam

The most important part of the trip was Nixon's fifth visit to South Vietnam since 1963. The now three-person Nixon team stayed three days. The fact that Bob Ellsworth was accompanying Nixon and Price for the rest of the Asian journey was significant because it signaled he was gaining in stature. Nixon stayed at the official residence with Ambassador Lodge while Price and Ellsworth checked in at the nearby Park Hotel. Before going to the embassy, Nixon called for American opponents of the war to join him in his moratorium on criticism. He said, "I would hope that the leading Democratic critics would see that the way to get peace is to have a morato-rium on the kind of criticism which gives aid and comfort to the enemy."[36] The first night, the embassy hosted an official dinner with their senior political and economic officials along with Edward Lansdale and General William C. Westmoreland.[37]

The next day was a busy one. After breakfast, Nixon met with Lodge to discuss the overall political situation in South Vietnam, followed by another meeting with JUSPAO, the Joint United States Public Affairs Office, charged with disseminating information. After this, Nixon talked with Prime Minister Nguyen Ky, the second most powerful man in the country besides President Nguyen Thieu. After a work-ing lunch with Lansdale and briefings on pacification, Nixon met for three hours with General Westmoreland about the military situation in the war. A working dinner with prominent South Vietnamese officials capped off Nixon's day.[38]

The second day was another busy one. They would travel in-country viewing American military installations and operations in Da Nang on the coast, Pleiku, and Ban Me Thuot in the central highlands before returning to Saigon. In between the dif-ferent cities, there were various briefings about different political and military aspects of the region. They were advised to dress casually with open shirts, trousers, hats, and sunglasses as the average daytime temperature would be in the mid-eighties. The day ended with another working dinner with Barry Zorithian, the head of JUSPAO, at his residence.[39]

The final day in South Vietnam started with a tour of the port facilities around Saigon, followed by a visit to the Tan Son Nhut airbase outside the capital city. Nixon met with reporters before catching a flight to Jakarta, Indonesia. While avoiding crit-icism of the Johnson administration's efforts, Nixon was quite animated in what he thought was needed to end this war. He believed the war was winnable but it would take more troops, and the political leaders opposing the war were giving aid and com-fort to the enemy. Nixon also thought the American Communist Party was support-ing the antiwar movement. He identified Martin Luther King, Jr., as undermining the war effort.[40]

Five More Countries to Go

After leaving South Vietnam, Nixon headed for the newly independent countries of Indonesia and Singapore. Indonesia was a multi-island former Dutch colony occu-pied by the Japanese during World War II. The Dutch tried to regain control after the war and were unsuccessful. Indonesia won its independence in 1949. Sukarno, the country's president and founding father, had survived a communist coup attempt in 1965. While Nixon did not see Sukarno, his second in command, Mohammed Hatta, Foreign Minister Adam Malik, and a few other prominent Indonesians attended a dinner honoring Nixon at the American embassy.[41]

It was only a two-hour flight from Jakarta to Bali, Singapore. The former Brit-ish colony was another Asian country occupied by Japan during the war. After that, the British regained the territory only to cede its independence in 1963. Singapore is a small island state in southern Malaysia. It briefly merged with the country for two years before separating in 1965. Lee Kwan Yew was the prime minister of the fledg-ling city-state. Nixon had a 50-minute visit with Kwan Yew and S. Rajaratnam, the foreign minister.[42] He also attended a luncheon at the embassy residence with the foreign minister, press liaison officer, deputy editor of the largest newspaper, head of the largest bank, and director of operations of the executive service corps. That night, a cocktail party was a "Who's Who" of American multinational executives who came to meet Nixon representing Kodak, Ford, General Motors, Firestone, Bank of America, American Express, and Mobil Oil.[43]

The next three days in India and Pakistan were probably the most tense and exciting of the entire Asian trip. The two South Asian countries were feuding over Kashmir and did not have diplomatic relations with each other. Nixon's Party had to fly into India first to get to Pakistan. From New Delhi, the three boarded a small private plane that took them to Lahore, Pakistan, right over the Indian border. Once there, they took a connecting flight to Rawalpindi. However, they had to get to Lahore first, and this was quite an adventure. The plane was supposed to cross the border a little after 4:00 p.m. local time. They had clearance for that short period. If the aircraft crossed after 5:00 p.m., it would be shot down by the Pakistanis. They barely made it in time. When they got to the small airport in Lahore, they were met by a mob of demonstrators with signs saying "Down with the U.S." and "Nixon Go Home." Three cars were waiting for them at the airport. Nixon and Ellsworth went in the first car while Price waited behind to go over the itinerary for the return flight the next day. As Price got into his waiting car, the mob advanced toward him, and one young boy tried to fling himself onto the vehicle. Price's driver swerved and missed killing the boy by an inch or two. They were later told by the consul general that the local authorities had assured him that the requested police escorts for the cars would be there. The police escort arrived too late and missed the Nixon entourage. This scare brought back memories of the near-tragedy in Caracas in 1958 for the former vice president.[44]

The Nixon team was in Lahore for about four hours, during which they met with U Thant, the secretary-general for the United Nations, for tea for an hour before flying to the capital. Once they arrived, things settled down. After an American embassy briefing, Nixon left for a private luncheon with President Mohammed Ayub Kahn that lasted for two hours. After an informal dinner, they headed back to India.[45]

The adventure continued with more excitement on the next day in New Delhi, India. They were met at the American embassy by Ambassador Chester Bowles, a former Democratic governor of Connecticut. He conducted a short briefing outlining the tense situation between India and Pakistan. Bowles convinced Nixon he needed to have a press conference primarily made up of Indian reporters later in the day to explain the United States' position. While Nixon was hesitant, Bowles assured him that he had clearance at the highest level for him to do this, even though he was not part of the official government. After visits with various government officials and Prime Minister Indira Gandhi, Nixon met with the press to try to clear up some misperceptions of the American government vis-à-vis the Indian-Pakistani conflict. The conflict was also seen within the context of the Cold War. Pakistan was being supplied with weapons from the United States, while India got its armaments from the Soviet Union. The U.S. weapons were supposed to be defensive and not used against India, but some had been. Nixon did an admirable job in the press conference, and at least some of the tension in the world's largest democracy had decreased.[46]

Ray Price left India with an extraordinary amount of respect for how Nixon handled the situation, but he was troubled by something else while in India. He was present at the meeting with Indira Gandhi and saw another side of her that the public was not seeing. While Gandhi touted the Soviet anti–American line on foreign policy, she made it clear to Nixon that the United States needed to stay in Asia, especially in Vietnam, if Washington did not want the whole region to go communist. Gandhi confided she accepted the domino theory, a position opposite from her public stance. While Price lost a lot of respect for the Indian prime minister after the visit, Nixon was not surprised.[47]

It was the last stop on the Asian tour. Initially, the trip was going to include Israel and Greece, but political and military events in the two countries caused a postponement until later in the year. The Nixon party arrived in Tehran at 3:00 a.m. and were driven straight to their guest quarters at the embassy. They were briefed at 11:30 in the morning by several members of the ambassador's staff and other United States government officials. Nixon had a two-hour luncheon meeting with the Shah at the Imperial Palace. Price and Ellsworth attended an embassy luncheon in their honor at the same time. The two aides had most of the afternoon free until a 6:00 P.M. reception, followed by a dinner in Nixon's celebration at the official residence. While the pair was sightseeing around Tehran, Nixon had an hour meeting with the foreign minister. The dinner that night was attended by influential Iranians. The guest list included all of the Shah's cabinet and other prominent members of the government, including the president, speaker of the Iranian legislature, various senators, the president of its largest university, chief of the internal police (Savak), and eight Iranian ambassadors to other countries. The guest list was six pages long. This dinner surpassed even the large event in South Vietnam, also including several essential members of the business community from companies like Northrup, Pan-American Airlines, Pepsi, B.F. Goodrich, and Pfizer. Another prominent American noted at the dinner was Kermit Roosevelt, Jr., the grandson of Theodore Roosevelt. Roosevelt had played an important role in restoring the Shah to power in Iran in 1953.[48]

Back Home and Political News

After a short stop in Geneva, the Nixon team returned to New York. Nixon made a few general remarks at the airport, some specifically about Vietnam. Most of the questions were follow-ups to General Westmoreland's questions the day before at the annual meeting of the Associated Press. The former vice president agreed with the American commander, saying, "The defeat of Communist aggression is now without question inevitable."[49] It was several months before Westmoreland's "victory" tour at the end of the year. The former vice president further urged President Johnson not to give in to the numerous peace offers that Hanoi was making, which several members of his party seemed to favor. Nixon was adamant that the president should "make it clear what are the minimum conditions and insist on them." He ended his comments by saying, "There is this monstrous myth abroad, created and believed in Hanoi, that the United States is so divided that they [Hanoi] can win in Washington and the United States the victory they cannot win on the battlefield."[50]

While in Asia, Gallup did mid–April polling that showed a strong preference for Richard Nixon at the top of the ticket. The first question asked, "As of today, which one of these men do you personally prefer as the Republican candidate for president in 1968?" It was Nixon more than three to one over Romney, 1227–341. Ronald Reagan was third in the poll with 233 votes, with the rest scattered among Percy, Rockefeller, and a few others. The second question asked, "If the choice in the convention in 1968 narrows down to Richard Nixon and George Romney, which one would you prefer to have the convention select?" This question ended with the same result: Nixon defeated Romney 1562–523. The last question assumed Nixon was the clear front-runner. Gallup wanted to know who their second choice would be. Reagan won, with 429 votes over Romney's 249 votes.[51] It was becoming more evident that despite Ronald Reagan's claims to the contrary, he was running for the nation's highest office, and that he was well-liked.

The other major Republican who had consistently denied candidacy for president was continually in the news. Nelson Rockefeller made available to the press a letter written on April 11 by Governor Tom McCall of Oregon imploring the New York governor to reassess his earlier decision to stay out of the presidential race. The round-robin letter asked other Republican governors to hold off endorsing anyone for the nomination until they could agree together as a group. Rockefeller responded that although he was "delighted" if moderates wanted to win, the best chance was with George Romney. He consistently ran 10 points ahead of Lyndon Johnson in the polls.[52] Indeed, Romney was glad to hear the positive comments from his principal benefactor, but the Republicans nationally did not feel the same way.

In the middle of the month, Romney made his first of three appearances in the South, generally considered to be strong Nixon country. His first stop was in Williamsburg, Virginia. The Michigan governor's strong civil rights message got a good reception from the crowd of 300 at the Williamsburg Lodge. However, in a political reception before the event, the atmosphere was different. Nixon was escorted to the event by I. Lee Potter, the National Virginia Committeeman, and Linwood Holton, the 1965 Republican candidate for governor in Virginia. Both were longtime Nixon men, and Holton had been on the "Nixon for President" committee.[53] At the reception, Romney was rebuked by the party faithful for not backing Goldwater in 1964. Evans and Novak said that he "was viciously attacked in a closed-door huddle" by the Virginian Republicans.[54]

Two days before Nixon left for his trip to Latin America, newly-elected Maryland Governor Spiro Agnew traveled to New York to convince Nelson Rockefeller to reconsider the presidential race. After a one and half hour meeting, Agnew spoke to reporters: "I am disappointed. I feel a tremendous sense of need to have a candidate of the Rockefeller type." Agnew was generally considered an ideological moderate to liberal and was later reminded that he had spoken highly of Governor Reagan, a conservative, just a few days before. Agnew stated he thought Reagan was drifting toward a more moderate stance.[55]

The day before the trip, the former vice president spent most of the day in Pittsburgh presiding over the annual convention dinner of the Boys Club of America. He was accompanied by Dwight Chapin, Bebe Rebozo, and Al Cole of *Reader's Digest*. In between the luncheon and dinner, Nixon hosted a Latin American briefing in his suite for ambassadors William Pawley and Max Bishop. At the dinner, Nixon presented the Herbert Hoover Memorial Award to his old California friend and actor Bob Hope. The Nixon party flew back to New York after the event.[56]

Latin American Journey

During Richard Nixon's 1967 journey into Latin America, the shortest of his four trips, he visited five countries in 11 days to include Peru, Argentina, Chile, Brazil, and Mexico. Bebe Rebozo accompanied him throughout the journey. It would not be the first time that he had been to the area. Nixon had visited Brazil, Mexico, Central America, and the Caribbean countries during his first term as vice president. In 1958, Nixon went on a grueling eight-country tour over three weeks. Overall, the trip had been considered a success, but there had been significant demonstrations in Peru and Venezuela. In Lima, he was spat on and nearly killed by a mob of leftist protestors in Caracas. During the Venezuela melee, Eisenhower could not get any information about what was going on and put American forces on high alert. Ike strongly considered a military response in the Latin American country but was talked out of it when he finally got in touch with Nixon after the near-death experience.[57] Nixon hoped this trip would be much better.

In the nine years since Nixon had visited South America, several changes had occurred. First, the 1958 trip was taken to assure the countries below the equator in the western hemisphere that the United States was not taking them for granted, despite all of the attention the U.S. had been giving the Soviet Union and China. The trip earned Nixon a great deal of respect from the American people. When his plane arrived back in Washington, he was greeted on the tarmac by 15,000 people, along with the president and several members of his cabinet. Afterward, another 85,000 people lined the streets to greet Nixon as he rode in an open convertible back to White House to meet with President Eisenhower and Secretary of State Dulles. The Eisenhower Administration was in the process of putting together an economic package together for the region based upon a common market, including the creation of an inter-American bank and study groups on the price of commodities from South America. Then the Cuban Revolution erupted in January 1959, with Castro the next year declaring his alliance with the Soviet Union.[58] In 1961, the Kennedy administration announced their Alliance for Progress, a ten-year plan with both economic and military components, aimed at avoiding another Cuba. In 1965, LBJ sent American troops to the Dominican Republic to restore order. It was against this backdrop that Nixon made his trip to Latin America.

The first stop was in Lima, Peru. It was much different from his last trip, during which 2,000 protestors had confronted him at San Marcos University. In 1958, the crowd was so wild that he only made a few brief comments about free speech to the mob before his security team whisked him out of there and canceled his scheduled talk to the students. Nixon had headed to his hotel, where he was greeted by more protestors, including a demonstrator who spat on him right before he entered the hotel lobby.[59]

This time, after arriving in Lima near dinner time on Friday night, he went to the embassy and ate an informal and happily uneventful dinner. The next day was packed with events. Nixon spent Saturday meeting several government officials, including the president, foreign minister, Senate president, and two possible presidential candidates for the 1969 elections. On Sunday afternoon, Nixon visited two self-help, U.S.-funded construction projects. That night, there was a large dinner held at the embassy residence and attended by some American business leaders who worked in Peru.[60]

A place Nixon had never visited, Chile, was next. It had nearly a hundred and fifty-year history of parliamentary democracy, which was unusual in this part of the world. After a nearly five-hour flight from Lima to Santiago, Nixon arrived at 11:20 in the morning for a luncheon briefing at the embassy. In the afternoon, he toured projects administered by the Peace Corps and the United Nations Education, Scientific, and Cultural Organization (UNESCO). That night, several Chilean members of the cabinet, other political leaders, and major publishers attended a dinner in Nixon's honor. The next day, he visited an industrial plant partly funded by the United States before a noonday meeting with the president and foreign minister. He had wanted to meet with some university students. Still, in a briefing letter from Bob Ellsworth, who had done the background work for the trip, Nixon was cautioned against the meeting by business leaders and embassy officials.[61]

Nixon and Rebozo departed Chile at 6:15 p.m., landing in Buenos Aires, Argentina, a little over two hours later. They would be staying at the American Embassy for their two-day visit. Argentina was a country which, at the turn of the 20th century, had one of the world's ten largest economies and a capital that would rival many European countries. However, both world wars and incredibly poor political leadership by Juan and Eva Peron, and others, had led to an economy that depended upon exports and commodity prices. Argentina had become so increasingly unstable that a military coup deposed the president in 1966 and still ruled the country. The routine there was similar to what had occurred in Peru and Chile. Nixon met with many high-ranking military and political officials, including an excellent one-hour meeting with President Juan Carlos Ongania. He visited another self-help project in San Martin funded by the State Department's Agency for International Development (AID). The military turned political leader Ongania impressed Nixon as "a man of complete honesty and integrity ... who respects free institutions."[62]

The next two and a half days were spent in Brazil, South America's largest country. The former Portuguese colony had formerly been a democracy, just like Argentina, but a military coup took over the country in 1964. After flying into Rio de Janeiro late on a Thursday night, Nixon had an informal press conference at the airport before reaching the embassy residence a little before midnight. He had to leave the home six hours later for a two-hour flight to the capital city, Brasilia. After a brief stop at the embassy, Nixon had a thirty-minute meeting with President Marshal Artur da Costa e Silva and then headed back to the airport for a return visit to Rio. When Nixon returned to Brazil's largest city, he had another meeting with the foreign minister. The following day was a little less hectic. Nixon spent the morning talking to prominent people in the area, followed by a luncheon at the embassy. The afternoon he toured a slum in Rio and visited some university students.[63] During his visit to the slum area of Praia do Pinto, Nixon had some exciting conversations with Brazil's poor. One conversation was with a toothless pregnant woman with three children. Nixon asked her, "What do you need to improve your life?" She replied, "Money." He next asked, "What does your husband do for a living?" She did not know what to say, given that she did not have a husband. Nixon thanked her and went to another person in the slum. As he was leaving, the woman said, "May things go well." The woman was asked by a reporter following the exchange if she knew who he was. Her response was, "I think that he is connected to the movies."[64]

The last night that he was in Brazil, there was a two-hour reception in Nixon's honor at the embassy. It was the most well-attended event of the entire trip. The list of people took up nine and a half pages in his official papers of the visit.[65] The next morning, Nixon left for a 13-plus hour trip to Mexico City, his last stop in Latin America. Before he boarded the plane, Nixon spoke to the press about his initial assessment of his foray: "United States–style democracy won't work here, I wish it could. If I were to pick a system, it would be a DeGaulle-style democracy with strong leadership at the top and democracy at the bottom."[66]

The last two days of the trip were uneventful. Mexico was the country with which Nixon was probably the most familiar, having grown up in California. Nixon spent his honeymoon in Mexico and since had been on several trips there both formally and informally. He was asked on his last night in the country about whether or not George Romney was eligible to be president, even though he was born in Mexico. Nixon did not believe that it was a problem because his parents' United States citizenship would carry over to him. Nixon was echoing comments that Romney made earlier in the day when asked the same.[67]

Busy Break Before the Last Trip

While Nixon was in Latin America, he got some more good news on a *Newsweek* poll showing him as the first choice of 28 Republican states, with a delegate total of 622 votes. Ronald Reagan was second with 300 votes. The winner would need 667 delegates.[68] There were two other polls, which also showed Nixon's popularity rising and Romney's declining. Harris had Nixon increasing his April "first choice preference" by three points, 31 to 34, while the Michigan governor lost two points, 34–32.[69] Gallup saw much of the same trend for two hypothetical Republican candidates with the former vice president extending his lead to double digits over his closest opponent. Nixon was up four points in May, 39 to 43, and Romney was down two from the same period, 30 to 28. Gallup also saw Nixon leading for the first time over Romney among independent voters, 28 to 23. In one month, Romney had lost 10 points among independents. It was certainly significant.[70]

Nixon spent a week working before going on the last of his world tour trips. He did some legal work, but most of the week was spent making appearances and preparing for the trip to the Middle East and Africa. Nixon was the keynote speaker at the American Feed Manufacturers Association annual meeting in Chicago[71] and the Empire Club of Toronto.[72] He shared with a crowd of 2,000 what he had discovered on his recent tour of Latin America. Jules Witcover of the *Baltimore Sun* covered the event: "Nixon held the attention of about 2,000 farm-feed manufacturers with a brilliantly presented if somewhat oversimplified analysis of the continent's woes, a subject not ordinarily of interest to this audience. But the man's sense of organization and his self-assurance were nothing short of awesome as he performed without a single note, reeling off statistics on production, population growth, educational levels, and gross national products."[73] He did much of the same in Toronto, where he took his guests on a metaphoric tour of the world, explaining what he thought was needed. It was the first time he had given a speech in Canada, even though he had done business there for the law firm.[74] It was a classic Richard Nixon moment. He studied long and hard, memorized pertinent facts, and put these facts in a logical progression in the situational context. It was nothing new. Even when he had large numbers of people who did not like him or his politics, they could never doubt his ability or competence.

Nixon attended a testimonial to Congressman Delbert Latta in Bowling Green, Ohio, titled "Nixon Day Banquet." He was pressured by the Ohio organizers to criticize the Johnson administration but limited his remarks to a few jokes. Technically, his six-month moratorium was over, but he waited until he got back from his world tour to present his findings. Three thousand people attended the banquet at Bowling Green State University. ABC filmed part of the event for a special on Nixon.[75]

Nixon made two more public appearances close to home before leaving for Africa. He spoke at a luncheon for World Affairs Council,[76] followed by a dinner speech at the Bobst Institute Hahnemann Medical College.[77] Both of these events were in Philadelphia. At the luncheon, he gave Pennsylvania a preliminary assessment of his foreign trips and where he was going next. On the plane ride, Nixon had discussed the current tension in the Middle East with Pat Buchanan, since Egypt, Syria, and Jordan were mobilizing their forces for what looked like an invasion of Israel. At the behest of Egypt's President Adbul Nasser, the United Nations peacekeeping forces had been pulled out of Sinai to the Israeli border. Nasser was threatening Israel by sending troops across Sinai and down to the entrance to the Gulf of Aqaba, cutting off access to the Red Sea. If they controlled this narrow strait and cut off the oil coming in from Iran, Egypt could bring Israel's economy to a standstill. They temporarily shut down shipping lanes into southern Israel in the Gulf. Nixon had predicted at the luncheon that the Middle East parties did not have the capacity or will to engage in a war.[78]

Africa and the Middle East

The final leg of the global fact-finding tour would go through Europe to Africa, to the Middle East, and back to Europe. Pat Buchanan accompanied him on this three-week journey to 14 countries and his first trip to Africa since 1957.[79] The first stop was in Rabat, Morocco, where the pair arrived after an overnight stay in Paris. As they got off the plane, they were greeted by Ambassador Henry Tasca's news about the war that had broken out in the Middle East. Nixon modified his earlier prediction, saying that he did "not believe that either side had the capability without massive assistance from a foreign power, of winning a quick victory."[80] He missed this one.

The stay in Morocco was a hectic one given the situation. All of the Arab countries, including Morocco, pledged solidarity with Egypt. When they met with the foreign minister, he assured them that they still considered themselves good friends of the U.S. However, they were also closely tied to their Arab brothers and would be sending troops to help them. For Nixon and Buchanan, it looked like their whole trip would be canceled. Indeed, the next week was out. They were supposed to visit Egypt, Tunisia, Algeria, Lebanon, and Saudi Arabia. The two Americans stayed an extra day in Morocco, trying to sort out what they were going to do.[81]

They returned to Paris while the United Nations attempted to put together a cease-fire. Nixon had been here only two months ago. This time, they stayed at the Crillon Hotel. Almost as soon as the pair arrived in France, Nixon was summoned by de Gaulle to meet at the Élysée Palace, a couple of blocks away. He wanted to discuss the situation in the Middle East. The French premier was angry with the Israelis, who he said started the war, and was siding with the Arabs. The French had backed the Israelis in the previous two wars, one in which they fought side by side, but not this time. France also was a primary military supplier of military equipment to Israel.[82]

The next day, the pair met with Chip Bohlen, dean of American diplomats. He was respected because of his service in the Soviet Union at the beginning of the Cold War. Buchanan thought that Bohlen was quite naïve about the Middle East and the Soviets, wondering if perhaps he did not deserve the distinction of being one of the "wise men" of the Cold War. He thought Bohlen overbearing, with a tendency to talk down to people.[83]

Later in the day, they met with Harlan Cleveland, the U.S. Ambassador to NATO. Cleveland agreed with Bohlen and Nixon that the Soviets had goaded the Egyptians into this war. He did not agree with Bohlen's opinion that the Russian run-up to the war was somehow atypical and surprising. Cleveland said that there was too much evidence pointing in the other direction. It was much more in line with Nixon's version of events.[84]

Nixon and Buchanan flew to London, hoping that the war would soon be over and they could salvage their trip. While there, the Egyptians agreed to a cease-fire, but the Jordanians and Syrians had not. The Israelis defeated Jordan in a day and moved into the West Bank. They next moved into the Golan Heights in Syria and defeated the third Arab army in less than a week. After this, the war was over with a resounding Israeli victory and much humiliation in the Arab world. It was also seen as a loss to the Soviet Union, whose chief allies in the Middle East were Egypt and Syria. As the war was ending, the Nixon tour was being hastily re-scheduled. In London, they met with former Foreign Secretary and Prime Minister Sir Alec Douglas-Home, with whom Nixon had met in March. As it turned out, the tour resumed the next day when the pair flew to Frankfurt on the way to Ethiopia.[85] The new tour would now include eight countries in Africa, one in Europe (Greece), and one in the Middle East (Israel).

The treatment Nixon received in Africa was similar to his treatment in other countries. He was often treated as if he were the president, or at least the secretary of state representing the United States. The countries of Africa that had once been European or Asian colonies were going through a period of significant change, much like the rest of the world. Some of these changes had been incremental and peaceful, while others had been revolutionary and destructive. Also, a few of the countries had experienced civil war after gaining independence.[86]

Nixon first toured Ethiopia, in the Horn of Africa. Emperor Hailee Selassie, one of the world's longest-serving rulers, had been in power for 50 years. The U.S. had had good relations with the African country since liberating it from the Italians in 1944. Ethiopia was on the side of the Americans in the Cold War, and the two countries enjoyed a mutual security agreement. What most concerned Selassie was tribalism as it applied to Africa and Somalia. The longtime emperor was worried that Somalia would break up into tribal warfare, and Ethiopia would need American help. The Johnson administration resisted calls for additional military spending but hoped that Nixon could help them with that.[87]

They next visited Kenya, which had gained its independence in 1964. Joseph Palmer, State Department expert on Africa, said that Kenya was one of the few countries on the continent with "real stability." Palmer traced that stability to its founding father and current president, Jomo Kenyatta.[88] Nixon did not meet with Kenyatta but met with several other high government officials in Nairobi. The one member of the government that impressed both him and Buchanan was Tom Mboya, the minister of economic development and planning. Buchanan wrote that the most memorable event during the Kenyan visit was the cocktail party with the cabinet ministers and several younger members of the government. He said, "Many seemed no older than I, and while a few were impressive, most seemed men of little substance, accomplishment, or capacity. You need not have been a devotee of Kipling to have wondered if these fellows could run the countries they had inherited as well as the British."[89]

Next was a short stop in Zambia, once part of Rhodesia. There Nixon met with the foreign minister. Zambia had been granted its independence in 1964 and was ruled by Kenneth Kaunda. The civil service still had many hired British bureaucrats. The land was rich in minerals, especially copper. The country was land-locked, and most of its foreign problems were related to getting along with white-ruled Rhodesia to the south.[90]

The Democratic Republic of the Congo was next on the tour. It was formerly a colony of Belgian but was granted its independence in 1960 followed by a bloody civil war. The president, Joseph Mobuto, was the former chief of staff of the military. He had become president of the country after a series of failed governments could not maintain power. Mobuto was quite a character, described by Joseph Palmer as an "interesting and frustrating individual who has emotional and instantaneous reactions."[91] Nixon met with this Congolese strongman, who had a special request for him to relay back to the Johnson administration when he got back home. After exchanging pleasantries, Mobuto leaned closer to ask Nixon for a special favor. He told of the upcoming African summit in Kinshasa that was going to be in his country. He wanted to make sure that all of the heads of government coming in would have the proper vehicles to get around while visiting his country. What he needed were 20 new Chrysler Imperials and 20 Harley-Davidson motorcycles. Nixon listened while Buchanan tried not to laugh.[92] This request certainly gave the two Americans something to talk about long after this journey was over.

The last two African countries included the Ivory Coast and Liberia. They had to fly through Nigeria to get to the Ivory Coast, a former French colony, whose capital was Abidjan. The country had gained its independence in 1960. Many of the French still lived there and held prominent positions in the economy and bureaucracy. The government was pro–American. The president, Felix Houphouet-Boigny, was out of the country, so Nixon met with the acting president. After a luncheon hosted by Arsene Usher Assouan, the foreign minister, Nixon engaged in a lively discussion with his host. After each question from Assouan, Nixon would respond, and the former minister would offer a spirited reply. Each exchange earned resounding cheers from Assouan's fellow countrymen and was followed by another probing question. Outside of Mboya, Nixon considered the foreign minister to be the sharpest person that he had met while in Africa.[93]

The last stop in Africa was in Liberia, a country founded by American slaves. The capital, Monrovia, was named after former president James Monroe. They were there for less than a day. William Tubman, the president of Liberia, was out of the country, so the American pair met with Vice President William R. Tolbert, who hosted a luncheon for the visitors. The lunch was attended by all the members of the cabinet and their wives. Buchanan thought this was the friendliest group they encountered on the African trip.[94]

Out of Africa

Nixon did not visit Greece in April because of the military coup that had occurred. This time, he would get there by way of London for a short visit lasting only a day and a half. Despite the brevity of the stay, it included meetings with the foreign minister, the prime minister, interior minister, and King Constantine. The meeting with General Stylianos Pattakos, one of the colonels who organized the coup, was the most memorable. Pattakos was the interior minister in charge of domestic security. Nixon was prodded by the American ambassador on what to do if the Greek people took to the streets in protest. Buchanan recalled that when Nixon asked him if he was prepared for student demonstrations and disorder, Pattakos responded, "'We have excellent surveillance, and we will arrest them.' He smiled and awaited the next question. I glanced over at Nixon. His face did not change expression. As we left the building, Nixon said to me, 'That, Buchanan, was a fascist.'"[95]

The last stop on the world tour was among the most important for what it portended for the future of American foreign policy in the Middle East. The visit was to Israel, less than two weeks after their great victory in the Six-Day War that expanded the small Jewish state's borders into Syria, Jordan, and Egypt. The Americans met with all the heroes of the war, including the most prominent generals, Moshe Dayan and Yitzhak Rabin. Both of these men would have promising careers in the future Israeli government. Nixon wrote in his memoirs a decade later:

> I was impressed by the courage and toughness of the Israeli leaders and people. But I was disturbed by the fact that their swift and overwhelming victory over the Arabs had created a feeling of overconfidence about their ability to win any war in the future and an attitude of total intransigence on negotiating any peace agreement that would involve any return of the territories they had occupied.... It left a residue of hatred among their neighbors that I felt could only result in another war, particularly if the Russians were to step up military aid to their Arab clients.[96]

As the world tour was ending, Nixon had a lot to ponder, given what he had learned in the past three months. He wanted to spend some time assimilating these thoughts into a narrative that characterized his view of the world.

8

It Is Your Destiny

Richard Nixon had hardly ended a four-month tour around the world before he was sharing with others what he found. His political moratorium over, he would be talking about policy issues, primarily foreign, without campaigning for president. He was, however, working toward that goal, with his team gathering the support of convention delegates. Nixon had learned a lot during his travels and soon would craft a narrative that reflected his worldview in which America played the lead role in promoting freedom and democracy. The international stage was not a static one and was constantly evolving with the world environment. The purpose of his trip had been to discern what changes had developed, to sharpen his perspective of those changes, and to determine how the United States should respond. Even before these trips, Nixon was known as a world statesman of sorts despite his lack of elective office. However, not everyone in the American political scene was convinced. James Reston of the *New York Times*, for instance, was one of them. Reston, who had never been a big Nixon fan, wrote halfway through the tour: "There is absolutely no evidence that travel has given him any new or deeper visions of America's problems in the world.... We are good, he says, and the Communists are bad."[1] The country would soon find out if Reston were right, and this was the same old Nixon, or instead his views were much more nuanced.

Less than 72 hours after landing at LaGuardia, Nixon was in Washington, sharing what he had learned on his 38-country tour. He took part in three significant events in the next two days. The first was a luncheon for the Zionists Organization of America, where Nixon discussed some of the things that he had learned, especially during the nearly three days he spent in Israel two weeks after their great victory. Had Reston been present, he might have been amazed at what he heard. After a brief introduction, Nixon stated, "The great conflicts that are taking place in Asia—Vietnam—the great split between the Soviet Union and China which overrides all these issues—enthusiastic admiration in the West for the arms that had been demonstrated by Israeli forces. This was true among those who have not been on the Israeli side publicly or privately."[2]

A more casual reception followed the luncheon at the Capitol Hill Club that night. At this talk, Nixon laced his trip stories with humor for the Republicans gathered to select him as "Republican of the Year, 1967." Pat and both of his daughters accompanied Nixon. Tricia also received a warm welcome as an upcoming summer intern in Senator George Murphy's office. The former vice president poked fun at himself and others in Washington: "It's good to win an election again, even if in this case it means edging out my good friend Senator Dirksen by a seven-vote margin."[3] Afterward, Nixon received a safety razor as a gag gift. He was all smiles when he won the award, quipping, "Never again will I lose by a whisker."[4]

115

The next day, he addressed a luncheon hosted by *Reader's Digest*. The magazine was one of the significant contributors to the trip, and Nixon had promised to write several articles later in the year detailing his findings and recommendations for the next president.[5] He spent three days in his office the following week before leaving for a short family vacation in Florida over the July 4 holiday.

Updates on the Three R's

While most of the national press's focus on the Nixon campaign explored George Romney as his primary opponent, this focus was starting to change. Ronald Reagan was emerging as a bona fide contender for the presidency. Reagan's name had been appearing everywhere in the national press over the past several months. He attended the Gridiron Dinner in March in Washington, followed two months later by a national television appearance with Robert F. Kennedy in the "Town Meeting of the World." On this, the California governor made national headlines as he outdebated the New York senator. The two politicians took questions from students in London, England, while Reagan remained in California and Kennedy in New York. This setup was made possible by the successful launch of the Telstar satellite. It was the first time television had used a satellite hookup to broadcast a program. The result culminated in a May 22 cover story in *Newsweek* titled "Ronald Reagan: Rising Star in the West?"[6]

Reagan was again the talk of a significant gathering of Republicans, this time in Omaha at the meeting of the Young Republicans National Federation. The California governor was the closing speaker at the three-day conference. The theme of his speech was unity, something lacking in the 1964 election. Reagan said, "You must pledge before you leave here your unified and complete support of the party and the candidates of the party once the primaries are over." During the half-hour talk, Reagan was interrupted six times by standing ovations.[7] In a straw poll conducted during the conference, Reagan emerged as the winner with 152 votes and 46 percent over Nixon's 100 votes and 30 percent. Rockefeller received 36 votes, followed by Percy and Romney at 21 votes each. None of Nixon's associates attended the meeting, nor did Governor Romney, who sent his wife instead to talk to the young delegates.[8]

Barry Goldwater had spoken earlier at the event, stressing the same themes. He knew first-hand what could happen to a candidate whose party is not entirely unified behind its nominee. Goldwater told the delegates, "If we indulge ourselves in another round of 1964 masochism, we're going to go down the tube again." The former Arizona senator made his preference clear. He reiterated his support for Nixon and stated that if Reagan became an active candidate, supporters of both should "sit down and talk because they are pretty much out of the same box."[9]

Back in the New York office of Richard Nixon, the mention of Reagan was starting to create a stir. Neal Freeman and Tom Charles Huston assured Pat Buchanan that Clifton White was still staying neutral in the political process and had not signed on with any Republican candidate for president.[10] That could soon change. David Broder, one of the most creditable Washington political reporters, wrote that White was not neutral. In the June 27 issue of the *Washington Post*, Broder explained that White was organizing the Draft Reagan Committee, which mostly made the California governor a presidential candidate.[11]

Buchanan wrote a memo to Nixon that pointed to Neal Freeman, who had said none of the ideological conservatives were currently committed to Reagan. He thought, "Nixon could still abort the Reagan thing by moving decisively to the right." In the same memo, he wrote that Freeman had not found anyone impressed with the Parkinson/Walker operation in Washington. Freeman was "surprised that a guy with RN's savvy would have a greenhorn running his operation."[12] It was not the first time that Buchanan and others in the Nixon office in New York had heard these complaints.

At the Western Governors Conference at the end of June in West Yellowstone, Montana, Reagan was the star of the event. Even Tom McCall, the governor of Oregon and the most liberal of all the Republican governors, agreed. McCall, who earlier in the year pleaded for Nelson Rockefeller to enter the race, called Reagan "the hottest political property" in America. He later went on to say, "[Reagan] has more going for him than any political figure in the country. He's probably the best drawing card either party has today."[13] Eleven of the 13 governors from the region were Republican.

Ronald Reagan continued to build momentum within the conservative base of the party by appearing on William Buckley's *Firing Line* the first weekend of July. Buckley's show, syndicated by WOR in New York, was watched with near-religious fervor by conservatives. The host was highly complimentary of Reagan and called him a "premier governor in the United States" and "one who saw no conflict between conservatism and progressivism." In the opening of the program, Buckley assured his West Coast guest that he would shy away from any speculation of the governor as a candidate for president. However, with the mention of the possibility, the wily Buckley was asking his viewers to consider whether it could be true.[14]

The next day, the National Convention of Republican Governors was held 100 miles away in Jackson Hole, Wyoming. At this conference, there was a strong movement on behalf of Romney backers to convince the moderate Republican governors to endorse their candidate. The strategy was based on a consensus of moderate governors agreeing on one candidate to freeze out other moderate candidates and give them additional leverage in nominating the candidate. They were not successful. Nelson Rockefeller and John Chafee, the governor of Rhode Island, were heading the effort to get behind a moderate candidate in next year's presidential contest against Lyndon Johnson.[15]

Spiro Agnew was another moderate governor making a lot of noise in Wyoming. He had previously tried to talk Rockefeller into running and would not endorse Romney even though he thought him an attractive candidate he could support. One of Rocky's aides, in response to Agnew's continued calls for the New York governor to get into the race, said Agnew was "smoking opium" if he thought his boss was going to run for president in 1968.[16] Despite what many saw on the surface, Evans and Novak understood the state of the Republican race differently as the so-called candidates headed into the July 4 holiday. The veteran columnists wrote that Romney was still the Republican frontrunner and that almost no one was talking about Nixon. They also said that the most significant clamor in Republican ranks was about Rockefeller and Reagan.[17]

Over the July 4 holiday, Pat Buchanan went home to Washington for a couple of days. While visiting his family, he also had a good meeting with John Sears, working side by side with Bob Ellsworth in the D.C. office. In this meeting, the two pertinent issues were the Clif White/Reagan connection and problems associated with the Gaylord Parkinson operation. Sears also believed that White was not tied up with

Reagan yet, as Huston, Freeman, and others in the conservative community had been. Sears thought that Parkinson and Walker were not disloyal in any way but that they were "just stupid."[18] In a July 5 memo to Nixon, Buchanan wrote that what Sears had relayed to him in their meeting was a call for a national director "who can really move in the next four months."[19]

Bohemian Grove Pow-Wow

Nixon had a lot to think about as he returned from his Florida holiday. He had heard of many operational issues associated with the Washington office, but his immediate concern was in California. He had been asked to give the keynote address at the annual meeting of the Bohemian Grove Society in the Redwoods, eighty miles north of San Francisco. The speech was given outdoors without many modern conveniences, like a Boy Scout camping trip for men. This annual event was comprised of successful California business and community leaders. President Herbert Hoover, a long-time member of the club, had given many such speeches before his death in 1964. Nixon considered this invitation a great honor and had been preparing since his Florida vacation. Nixon would later write about his preparation for this famous speech in a memorandum to Jonathan Aitken nearly a quarter of a century later: "I took a week off before that appearance, rented a room in a motel, and with John Davies who was my volunteer aide bringing me in Kentucky Fried Chicken for dinner every night."[20]

Nixon had another reason for attending the annual meeting. He wanted to confront Ronald Reagan about his intentions concerning the next year's presidential race. The governor of California also would be giving a speech on the same weekend. A week before the event, David Broder wrote a front-page story in the *Washington Post*, saying Nixon had arranged a meeting with Reagan at the upcoming Bohemian Grove gathering. Broder said Nixon's goal was to make sure Reagan would not discourage Nixon's supporters in the primary states. Reagan had continued to deny he was running for the Republican nomination, claiming he was only a California favorite son candidate. It became less clear given his appearances at numerous national events. Conversely, while Nixon had not yet formally announced his candidacy, his intentions were clear.[21]

Nixon had arranged a meeting with Reagan through George Murphy, a senator from California. Murphy, like Reagan, had been a former Hollywood actor and was friends with both men. Murphy had been president of the Screen Actors Guild before Reagan and had encouraged him for years to think seriously about politics.[22] The California senator was a member of the Bohemian Club and had invited Reagan to be his guest for the annual retreat, as Reagan was not yet a formal member of the private club. While there are no first-hand accounts of what transpired at the luncheon, Thomas Reed discussed the events with Reagan two weeks later on August 8. Reed, who had been running Reagan's unofficial campaign, was a meticulous note-taker. He believed that Taft Schreiber, Reagan's agent, arranged the luncheon meeting through Murphy. Schreiber, clearly a Reagan man, had been a big Nixon backer in the past. Nixon let Reagan know what his plans were but that he was not going to announce until the end of the year. Both Murphy and the former vice president tried to convince Reagan to endorse Nixon, but the California governor just smiled one of his "cheerfully ambiguous responses."[23]

While Nixon did not write an account of the meeting with Reagan, he certainly remembered the speech that he gave at Bohemian Grove which he claimed gave him "the most pleasure and satisfaction of his political career."[24] It was not a simple recounting of his recent world tour but a speech discussing where he thought the country was and where it should be going. While the talk mentioned some of Nixon's trip observations, it was much more reflective of America's role in the world with a tribute that really should have hit home with the members present in the redwoods of northern California. After his talk, Nixon said, "As we enter this last third of the twentieth century, the hopes of the world rest with America. Whether peace and freedom survive in the world depends upon American leadership."[25] The national press briefly recounted the meeting. The Associated Press simply wrote that Reagan and Nixon agreed the party must nominate a candidate who could win.[26]

> Appearance - Bohemian Grove
> July 21--24, 1967

```
7/18/67

RN

Arrangements for this weekend at Bohemian Grove - I think we need to

do something - set up some arrangements.  Governor and RN should get

together.  I think it would be very nice if RN were to ask the Governor

to have lunch with us at Cave Man Camp.  RN is a full-fledged member and

Reagan is just a guest.

We would have it at 12:30 or 1:00 -- RN should call and ask Ron Reagan.

---

Does he have transportation -- 3:00 PM each Sunday our company plane runs

from there to Los Angeles.  We have a bus from the Grove to Santa Rosa

and it comes into Lockheed Airport at Burbank.  Call my secretary -

Miss Ranson - Code 213  624 4014 - let her know.  I know I can call

someone on Saturday where they know what the schedules will be.

My home number -- which is private -- is Code 213  682 1502.

Pasadena -- either Mrs. Hoover will be meeting me or I will have a car

there and we will be glad to take RN wherever he would like to go.

Re the luncheon - we will go ahead and set up those arrangements -

anyone else he would like to have or anyone in the governor's entourage

-- we waxxx won't make arrangements to get anyone in the lunch other

than people from our own camp other than the ones he would like to have.

Let us know.
```

Memorandum from unknown author to Nixon. It is not totally certain who wrote this, but it could have been Rose Mary Woods and was based on calls she was getting on Nixon's trip/speech at Bohemian Grove in July 1967 (Richard M. Nixon Library).

Blowback from Bohemian Grove?

The Evans and Novak syndicated column had been in existence since 1963, reporting behind-the-scenes news that rarely hit the newspapers or other media outlets. What they wrote in their Monday column after the Nixon-Reagan meeting in Bohemian Grove dramatically affected both camps. Their headline of July 24 in the *Washington Post* was "Let Ronnie Have the Kooks," while the headline the next day in the *Los Angeles Times* read "New Nixon Strategy Begins to Show: Shun Far Right."[27] The story introduced a New York Republican delegate named Vince Leibell, who had bucked the state delegation that was sworn to vote for Rockefeller in 1964 but instead switched to Goldwater during the convention. Leibell, still a New York delegate, signaled a few weeks ago that he would back Nixon in 1968. Richard Nixon had no comment, but Evans and Novak said that Charlie McWhorter told them the Nixon campaign was not fostering any raids on state party delegations. The writers went on to say this was not limited to New York but included all of the country. Evans and Novak wrote the shift of "kooks" to Reagan made Nixon all the more acceptable to mainstream Republicans.[28]

As is often the case, the reality was much different. The Nixon people were livid and wondered who talked to Evans and Novak. Buchanan was putting out fires everywhere as a result of this grossly inaccurate column. The campaign wanted to get all Republicans united, unlike 1964. Buchanan's outreach was primarily to the conservatives in the party and was ongoing. The young aide collaborated with Nixon on a series of letters to Governor Reagan, denying the column and promising to fire the leaker. In an August 4 letter, the former vice president emphatically wrote, "This one is fabricated from whole cloth. Neither I nor my personal staff have anything to do with the brace of them for the past two years." Also included was a transcript from *Firing Line* where Rowland Evans admitted that neither he nor Bob Novak ever missed an opportunity to embarrass Nixon.[29]

Buchanan convinced Nixon to include a recent column by John Chamberlain, a syndicated columnist, in the package sent to Governor Reagan.[30] In the opinion piece, Chamberlain thought it was nonsensical to imagine Nixon trying to alienate conservatives and make additional outreach to the liberals in the party. Chamberlain wrote, "What bothers these people is the way which pro–Rockefeller commentators subtly twist some quite neutral facts to make it seem that Nixon is consciously out to repel the Republican conservatives to ingratiate himself with the more extreme liberals who will probably vote for Romney or Rockefeller anyway." He later stated, "The so-called new strategy of divisiveness and rejection attributed to Nixon would be nicely calculated to provoke a migration of Republican conservatives to the Ronald Reagan camp, but it would not have any compensating virtue of luring Romney or Rockefeller supporters into the Nixon ranks."[31]

Ronald Reagan, recovering from recent prostate surgery, wrote a friendly letter back to Nixon. He certainly seemed to agree. Reagan compared some of the political chatter with Hollywood gossip. The California governor wrote that it "is very important that all of us on our side keep reminding ourselves and each other that we shouldn't believe any quotes unless we hear them firsthand. I'm always reminded of the Hollywood days, and how the people in our business would read the gossip columns and your first reaction was always how dishonest they were about yourself, but two paragraphs later you're believing every word when they talk about someone else."[32]

While the Nixon camp was uncertain if there would be any continued negative repercussions from the Reagan meeting at Bohemian Grove, they were confident that there had been another leak from their camp. There also had been continued problems associated with the Washington office that supposedly was in charge of the unofficial Nixon for President campaign. The Nixon staffers in his New York office did not think that the leaks came from New York. Buchanan speculated that they issued from the D.C. office. Something had to give, for the campaign was entering a more substantive phase that would lead up to the New Hampshire primary. As it turned out, outside forces decided for Nixon whether to replace his campaign head in Washington.

Gaylord Parkinson's wife was very ill and receiving treatment in California. Parkinson resigned so that he could join her in California. He also would be taking top aide Robert Walker with him. While there would be some blowback from Parkinson's departure, it was better to do it a year out from the convention than to change staff after the campaign was underway. The question was, who would head up the campaign in Washington?[33]

Nixon talked to Peter Flanigan, who told him that they needed a replacement as soon as possible. Flanigan called Henry Bellmon, a former governor from Oklahoma, who agreed to the job on one condition: that he only serve for a few months because he planned to announce he was running for the Senate seat in his home state. Flanigan and Nixon agreed. Bob Ellsworth would assist Bellmon, bringing him up to date on the inner workings of the operation. Ellsworth would perform this full-time job while on leave from his law office.[34]

At the same time as the retreat at Bohemian Grove, several days of race riots in Detroit stunned the nation with 43 deaths, over a hundred injured, and several million dollars in damage.[35] It occurred after another race-based riot in Newark a couple of weeks earlier. In Michigan, George Romney called in the National Guard and asked for help from President Johnson to quell the disturbances. There was a lot of finger-pointing and backbiting associated with the supporters of a Democratic president and a prominent Republican governor who was essentially preparing to run against him. Both Johnson and Romney got a great deal of negative publicity from the event. President Johnson had sent large sums of money to the urban poor as part of his "great society," and this was what he was getting in return. Governor Romney was supposed to be the leading Republican light on urban problems and domestic peace. A Harris Poll in the second week of August hit LBJ harder: his favorability dropped below 40 percent for the first time in his presidency at 39 percent, a 19-point drop from late June. Only 32 percent said that he "inspired confidence as President." The same poll had not shown a similar impact on Romney. In a two-way race, Johnson still defeated Romney 52–48, while he led Nixon 55–45.[36] The problem with Romney was that fewer and fewer Republicans supported him going into September.

In another development directly related to the Bohemian Grove retreat, the *New York Times* reported a month after the event that Ronald Reagan had talked to Senator John Tower and Florida Governor Claude Kirk about not making any commitments to their respective states' delegates to Nixon during next year's Republican convention. Reagan insisted again that he was not running. Both Tower and Kirk had been strongly considering runs as favorite son candidates. Richard Nixon was working hard to nail down the entire South as part of his core support. If Florida and Texas dropped him, this could unravel the whole region, given the size and importance of the two state delegations.[37] Despite Ronald Reagan's public stance and private ambivalence, Nixon knew he was running for president while also trying to divide Nixon's conservative base.

A September to Remember

A few important items on Nixon's September agenda would pay major dividends in his political future. One was a foreign policy speech at the National Industrial Conference Board, attended by over a thousand people and covered extensively by the news. Next was an off the record meeting at the Harvard Club of New York followed by a guest appearance on Bill Buckley's *Firing Line.* Finally, a significant finance dinner was scheduled for the last week of the month. But before any of these events, one of his political competitors made big news that could help Nixon. On August 31, George Romney taped an appearance on Detroit's *Lou Gordon Show* that was broadcast five days later. After Gordon informed the major national news media of Romney's comments, a near feeding frenzy ensued. The Michigan governor had wavered on his Vietnam stance for months. Romney replied to a question on Vietnam with, "I just had the greatest brainwashing that anybody can get when you go over to Vietnam.... I no longer believe that it was necessary for us to get involved in South Vietnam to stop Communist aggression."[38] While this position might have been acceptable in a college classroom, in the major leagues of American politics, it was not. Many saw Romney's lack of depth and decision-making. While Nixon did not address this issue personally, his new campaign director immediately held a news conference at a meeting of Republican state chairs and committee officials. Former Governor Bellmon was the perfect person for the job because he had been one of the ten governors that toured South Vietnam with Romney. Bellmon adamantly rejected the "brainwashing" charge, saying that they were fully informed of the history and current situation of the war. He criticized Romney's "weaknesses" in handling major foreign policy issues attendant to the presidency. Several other Republicans went on the record, echoing Bellmon's criticism. Another major announcement was made at the press conference involving next year's Nebraska primary. The Nixon camp decided to support delegates pledged to Senator Roman L. Hruska, a long-time friend and Nixon supporter, rather than filing delegates to Nixon himself. Nixon and Hruska reached the decision with the assurance that Nebraska would release Hruska's delegates to the winner of the primary, assuming they were still in contention at the Republican convention.[39]

Nixon was the keynote speaker at the National Industrial Conference Board on September 12 at the Waldorf Astoria. The Board consisted of several prominent trade associations across the business community. Most of the major newspaper and television networks covered the 45-minute speech. After a summary of his world tour observations, he criticized the Johnson administration for allowing the "awesome power" of the United States' international leadership to "succumb to creeping obsolescence." The three-day conference dealt with several issues relevant to the American corporate community. One Nixon addressed involved the lack of food and influence in the developing world. Nixon said that America could not turn its back on the world and that the private sector should lead the way to help those countries most in need. Nixon insisted the United States must exercise leadership because "we cannot safely let the world look elsewhere for that leadership" in the Cold War.[40]

The next night Nixon engaged in a question and answer session at the Harvard Club of New York, attended by 600 or so members representing a sufficient part of the East Coast establishment. For this first of three meetings in 1967, the club wanted Nixon to kick-off the opening session. While the meeting was off the record, the Nixon camp leaked that he had been invited, taken on all comers, and impressed them all.[41]

The following night Nixon attended a taping of Buckley's *Firing Line*. The title of the show was "The Future of the GOP." Buckley acknowledged in his introduction that Nixon was the most prominent Republican running in the race. Buckley addressed several major issues surrounding the future of the Republican Party and queried Nixon on these. He tried to get Nixon to agree that the party should not nominate someone who did not back the ticket in the previous election. Buckley was referring to Rockefeller and Romney but did not mention them by name. Nixon did not take the bait, saying he was a lifelong Republican and would back the party's candidate. His point was unity and not division in 1968. The host then pointed out that Ronald Reagan had won the governor's election in California by a resounding margin while Nixon had lost it four years earlier. Should Reagan be the Republican nominee? Nixon replied that the two races in California had been different and that he had a good relationship with the governor.[42]

Buckley raised the question of whether the party could survive another Nixon defeat. Nixon thought that it would be difficult, but the host thought otherwise, saying that the party should stand on principles whether they win or lose elections. Finally, Buckley mentioned conflicts between Young Republicans (YR) and the Republican Party. Nixon agreed with Buckley that Ray Bliss was listening to the group and knew that they were the future of the party. Buckley also raised the impact George Wallace might have on the upcoming race. Nixon, smiling back at the host, joked that he knew a lot about how well third parties typically did in elections, noting that Buckley ran on the Conservative Party ticket for mayor of New York in 1965 and lost. Nixon acknowledged that Wallace had a lot of support across the country, especially in the Deep South, but did not think that his running would affect the race one way or another. Many of his supporters, Nixon explained, would, in the end, return to Democrats and Republicans in the general election. Nixon handled Buckley's probing questions and made his points about where the party should be heading in the future.[43]

A significant finance dinner attended by heavy hitters took place on September 27. Most attendees were from the East Coast, along with a few Californians who had backed Nixon in prior elections. All of the members of the *Birdwatchers* of 1966 were present. Maurice Stans and Peter Flanigan headed up the event. Al Cole from *Reader's Digest* put together the schedule, if which Nixon would make some specific remarks and take questions. Don Kendall and Elmer Bobst were among the most vocal supporters in these meetings. Bobst recommended the prospective presidential candidate outline what he planned to say when traveling around the country and consider feedback. He told Nixon he should "make his views clear to people and tell the truth."[44] There would be some specific monetary targets, for if at least 25 of the backers could commit monthly, the campaign would stay on sound financial footing at least through the primaries.[45] Once Nixon announced he was formally running, there would be a more focused financial effort.

Richard Nixon would never forget the last day of September 1967. While in a conference with a client, he was interrupted by Rose Mary Woods to tell him that his brother Don was on the phone. Nixon said to her that he would call her back after his meeting. Woods would not take no for an answer. She told him, as she broke down in tears, that he needed to talk to him right now because their mother had just died. While the news hit Nixon hard, he composed himself as he assembled his family for a trip back to California. The last time that he had talked to his mother before the stroke, he had told her not to give up. Even though Hannah Nixon was very weak after an operation that had taken place the day before, she had pulled herself up and told him, "Richard, don't you give up. Don't let anybody tell you you are through." Nixon felt guilty for placing his mother in a home, but she could not get the regular care she needed if she stayed with him or his brother Don.[46]

The next day, Nixon stopped by his office to meet briefly with Woods. She came out of the office and told Pat Buchanan that Nixon wanted to see him. Buchanan wrote in *The Greatest Comeback* a poignant remembrance about what occurred next: "I went in, and though we spoke at length we did not talk at all of his mother and I sensed he did not wish to because, a deeply emotional man, he knew he might break down. So I did almost all the talking, responding to his questions, talking on one subject after another—issues, news, the campaign, until word came that the car was downstairs to take him to the airport."[47]

The funeral was held at the church where he worshiped as a child, Friends Church in East Whittier. Billy Graham and the local minister conducted the funeral service. Memories cascaded through Nixon's mind as he sat with old friends and family. He recounted the scene a decade later with a final tribute to his mother: "At the end of the service, the family was first to leave the church and walk by the open casket. My mother was not pretty, but she was beautiful, and she looked beautiful in death as she had in life."[48]

As the Nixon family was leaving the funeral service, Richard shook hands with both ministers and thanked them. Billy Graham described over thirty years later, what happened next: "Richard Nixon had tears streaming down his face.... The people had filed by the closed casket for the last time and left. The casket was then reopened, and his wife, Pat, and daughters, Julie and Tricia, gathered around. I stretched my arms around their shoulders while the son tearfully expressed his tribute to his mother and loss he felt after her death. Then I offered a prayer for their comfort."[49]

After the burial, the Nixons returned home to New York. For Richard, it had to have been the most emotionally painful event of his life, more so than the losing two of his brothers while growing up and the loss of his father eleven years earlier. Nixon was down for the count now, but he would not be down long. He knew how to get up off the mat and fight back. Nixon learned this lesson many years ago while a member of the football team at Whittier College. Even though he rarely played in any games, his enthusiasm and drive impressed his head coach, Wallace "Chief" Newman. Newman was a full-blooded American Indian who also coached the baseball and track teams at the college. Nixon later said that he admired and learned more from the "Chief" than any other man besides his father: "He inspired in us the idea that if you worked hard enough and played hard enough, we could beat anybody. He used to say, 'Show me a good loser, and I'll show you a loser.' ... He drilled in a competitive spirit and the determination to come back after you have been knocked down or after you lose."[50]

Hannah Nixon had played a significant role in her son's life. She saw her devotion to sons, husband, and God, for she was a woman with great compassion and purpose in life. It instilled in him a determination and a drive to never quit and always move forward. Perhaps one who had always pulled it together in difficult times, Nixon took an inventory of where he was, where he had been, and where he was going. The next few days and weeks would be tough, but he would get through it. If it was one thing that Nixon could count on in times like this, it was his enormous self-discipline. After a period of mourning, he was determined to move forward.

In the next three months, Nixon would publicly decide whether he would be running for president. On October 1, while he was still in California, the *New York Times* published an article that compared the last two months of polling by Harris and Gallup. These two polls took into account the rioting in Newark and Detroit, along with George Romney's brainwashing comment on Vietnam. Both of these polls had good news for the former vice president. In a hypothetical match-up, the Harris Poll showed Romney losing six points (48 to 42) while Nixon gained one (45 to 46). While both of these estimates were within the margin of error of plus or minus three, that did not make a significant difference. In the Gallup poll, which looked at Republican voters for their preference for the nomination, Nixon gained five points (35 to 40) while Romney lost ten points (24 to 14).[51]

Over the next week, Nixon made appearances, particularly in the primary states of New Hampshire, Wisconsin, Nebraska, and Oregon. He also targeted groups of business executives who could help finance his campaign. Nixon's watching the competition for the presidency can be compared to an athletic team getting ready for the season-opening game. While Nixon was in good shape given his world travels and preparations for the upcoming battle, he continued to fine-tune himself and his campaign by staying in the public eye without overexposing himself. Nixon was still experimenting with new ways to communicate with the public. He did this by listening to the people on the road as well as by bringing new people aboard with fresh ideas. All the while, he moved toward his goal. Also, there would be a few strategically timed appearances on national television that reached a much broader audience. After that, he met with his family and officially decided to run or not. That occurred after the first of the year.

The first week back in New York, he split time between work and family back in New York. Perhaps he was still reeling from his mother's death. Nixon canceled two events previously scheduled out west, one in Oregon at Associated Oregon Industries[52] and another at the Hoover Institute in Stanford, California.[53] On October 3, James A. Skidmore, Jr., was named to head a National Citizens for Nixon Committee. Skidmore was an assistant to the president of the Pepsi Company. The committee was an affiliate of the Nixon for President Committee based in Washington.[54] Four days later, a 28-state campaign committee for Nixon was announced with some familiar Republican names who had worked in other campaigns. One of the more critical committees was in Nebraska, the third primary state of next year's presidential campaign. It was a state where Nixon previously enjoyed a lot of support. The two most prominent Republican politicians in the state, Governor Norbert T. Tiemann and Senator Roman L. Hruska, had both said uncommitted delegates, not bound by the results of the May 14 primary, would "bear a moral obligation to back the winner of the primary." Also, John E. Everroad, the state's lieutenant governor, had already announced plans to file for at-large delegates as a pledged Nixon man.[55]

New Faces on the Nixon team

At the same time in Nixon's New York law office, several new faces appeared. Among these were Martin "Marty" Anderson, a professor of economics at Columbia University with a Ph.D. from the Massachusetts Institute of Technology (MIT), and Richard J. Whalen, author of the bestseller *The Founding Father*, a biography of Joseph Kennedy. Whalen was a resident scholar at the Georgetown Center in Washington. Anderson was an expert on urban issues, while Whalen had solid foreign policy credentials. Both were under 35 years of age. Neither man was working full-time yet for the campaign but advised on issues and policy.[56]

Yet another addition, William "Bill" F. Gavin, had a master's degree from the University of Pennsylvania. He was a teacher at a prominent high school in Philadelphia who had written an inspiring letter to Nixon earlier in the summer. The letter earned him an invitation to New York for a meeting with Len Garment to discuss upcoming opportunities that might be available to him during the campaign. Both men had grown up in urban areas of the Northeast, where Democratic machine politics ruled the day. Garment grew up in Brooklyn, while Gavin hailed from across the river in Jersey City. Garment was very impressed with the Philadelphia teacher despite the ideological divide; Garment was a "Kennedy liberal" and Gavin a "Buckley conservative" raised on the *National Review*.[57] In this letter, Gavin wrote:

> Dear Mr. Nixon:
>
> May I offer two suggestions concerning your plans for 1968? Run, You can win. Nothing can happen to you, politically speaking, that is worse than what has happened to you. Ortega y Gasset says in "Revolt of the Masses"; ... "these are only genuine ideas; the ideas of the shipwrecked. All the rest is rhetoric, posturing, face. He who does not really feel himself lost, is lost without remission...." You, in effect, are lost. That is why you are the only political figure with the vision to see things the way they are and not as leftist or rightist kooks would have them. Run. You will win.[58]

Garment recruited all of these men and was the unofficial talent man for the Nixon team. It was just the beginning of the new faces he would bring aboard soon. Nixon had grown close to Garment during his time at the law firm and would often sound him out on things before he moved ahead.[59]

Unofficial Campaign Advances

After spending the last week and a half in his office, Nixon attended two political events over the weekend. He headlined a Republican Key Man dinner in Greenwich, Connecticut, hosted by Al Cole. The Key Man committee provided the financial backing for Republicans in Connecticut. Greenwich was the suburban home for many prominent Republicans who worked in New York.[60]

The popular magazine *Reader's Digest* had a considerable circulation in the United States and was published around the world in at least 30 languages. They had underwritten a good portion of Nixon's previous four trips around the world and had been supportive of Nixon in earlier campaigns. In October, they published an article written by Nixon (with help from Pat Buchanan) entitled "What Has Happened to America?" In this piece, Nixon expanded on some of the domestic themes from his Bohemian Grove speech about the recent breakdown of law and order in places like Newark and Detroit:

> In a civilized nation no one can excuse his crime against the person or property or another by claiming that he, too, has been a victim of injustice. To tolerate that is to invite anarchy.... To heal the wounds that have torn the nation asunder, to re-establish respect for law and the principles that have been the source of American growth and greatness will require the example of leaders in every walk of American life. More important than that, it will require the wisdom, the patience and the personal commitment of every American.[61]

The second mid–October event entailed a Saturday trip to Washington to honor the laying of the cornerstone of the new National Presbyterian Church that Dwight Eisenhower attended while he was president. The old church had been demolished because of an urban renewal program and was being relocated. The church leadership invited Ike for the ceremony and a luncheon at the Mayflower Hotel honoring the general with a tribute to celebrate his 77th birthday. Hubert Humphrey and Charles Percy were the other notable politicians attending. Two members of Ike's cabinet, Arthur Summerfield and Arthur Fleming, also paid tribute to the former president.[62]

Four days later, Nixon returned to Washington for a series of meetings with Republican leaders. He first went to the House of Representatives, where he had a good meeting with old friend and Minority Whip Les Arends. A meeting in the Senate with Minority Leader Everett Dirksen followed. Nixon met briefly with a few other Republican senators before talking to reporters outside Congress. He was in good spirits and said that the Republicans would be much more united in 1968 than they had been four years earlier. When asked whether he or any other candidate could beat President Johnson, Nixon responded, "I'm convinced by the man who survives the primaries and wins the convention."[63]

Magazines, Covers and Contenders

At the same time, Nixon's article titled "Asia After Viet Nam" was in *Foreign Affairs,* published by the Council of Foreign Relations. It was a highly prestigious quarterly journal read by academics and practitioners. An article in *Foreign Affairs* gets the attention of those interested in foreign policy. An editor from the journal had approached Nixon two months earlier, after a luncheon engagement with several highly influential members of the foreign policy media in New York. They had been highly impressed with his lecture on his travels around the world, mainly as it applied to Asia.[64]

Nixon was the perfect politician to write about this subject. He grew up in California, which was much closer to Asia than the rest of the country. Nixon went to school with Asian kids. He served in the Pacific during his tenure in World War II. As a member of Congress, both in the House and the Senate, Nixon often spoke on issues involving Asia. While vice president, he went on a ten-week, goodwill tour to the Far East in 1953. Since joining Mudge Rose in 1963, he had made a number of business-related trips to Asia, often once or twice a year. In this 15-page, single-spaced article, Nixon wrote of the challenges facing the United States once the Vietnam War was over. He wrote that any discussion of the future of Asia must begin with a conversation with the four giants in the Pacific and their interests: India, Japan, China, and the United States. The United States had enormous interests and a stake in the region, politically, economically, and militarily. The last three major wars the U.S. had been involved in were in Asia: Japan in World War II, the Korean War, and the current war in Vietnam. Nixon certainly had great expertise in the region but acknowledged that American foreign policy must take into account Communist "Red" China to foster peace or stability in that part of the world. He was not advocating immediate diplomatic recognition of China but suggesting a different attitude and outlook.[65] Nixon wrote, "Any American policy toward Asia must come urgently to grips with the reality of China. This does not mean ... rushing to grant recognition of Peking, to admit it to the United Nations and to ply it with offers of trade—all of which would serve to confirm its rulers in their present course.... Taking the long view, we cannot afford to leave China forever outside the family of nations."[66]

The next big item for the Nixon team in October was the annual National Governors Conference. While Nixon did not attend the event, surrogates Bob Ellsworth and Henry Bellmon did.[67] Every year, the conference was hosted by a different governor. The selection of the 1967 fall conference had been awarded to the state of New York and Governor Nelson Rockefeller. The wealthy governor decided the best place to host this conference was on an eight-day cruise that traveled from the Big Apple to the Virgin Islands and back. Boasting 42 of the country's governors along with wives, family, and other government officials, the conference was sure to gather a lot of publicity. It was especially true when at least three of the governors were continually mentioned as presidential candidates, one of whom had been traveling the country since the first of the year discussing the major national issues of the day. *Time* magazine ran their October 20 cover story on the event with Rockefeller as president and Reagan as vice president pictured as the winning ticket for the 1968 presidential sweepstakes. The latest Gallup poll had paired the team against the LBJ-Humphrey team in a hypothetical matchup, with the Republican pair winning by a 57 percent to 43 percent.[68] Rockefeller continued to deny interest in the 1968 presidential campaign adamantly stating, "I am not a candidate. I do not intend to be a candidate. I do not want to be a candidate." Spiro Agnew, one of his enthusiastic backers among the governors present on the cruise, was not giving up hope. Agnew did not think that he would turn down a draft saying, "But if he is drafted, it would take a pretty emphatic individual to turn it down. Indeed, I can't conceive of it."[69]

George Romney, the one Republican governor running, had been crisscrossing the country for most of the year. His numbers had dropped following the flip-flop on Vietnam. One of the entourage on the cruise, a Republican state treasurer from Indiana named John Snyder, dubbed Romney "dead." Snyder went on to say, "The 'brainwash' remark didn't make all that much difference ... people were already looking for a reason to turn away."[70]

Ronald Reagan was the other Republican governor most likely running despite his continual denials. Most of the recent national news surrounding Reagan had been positive, especially in Republican circles, as he headlined party fundraisers in South Carolina and Wisconsin along with a coming home party at his Illinois alma mater, Eureka College.[71] He had been the star of the previous governors conference earlier in the year, and this one was no exception. However, the most prominent political news coming out of this conference centered on an episode involving one of his aides, his press secretary, Lyn Nofziger. Nofziger recounted the incident a quarter of a century later in his memoirs. One of Reagan's aides picked up mail marked for the California governor. As it turned out, the letter was written to Texas Governor Price Daniel from the president to get him to line up support for his policy on Vietnam. The media wanted to know where Nofziger got it, and he "finally admitted it had been delivered to Reagan by mistake.... The press didn't believe it. It made a better story if we're perceived to have stolen it."[72] The mix-up with the mail made some political watchers think that Nofziger had stolen Johnson's letter. It reflected poorly on the California governor, but the press secretary vigorously denied any theft. On the other hand, others would argue that LBJ was trying to strong-arm the governors, particularly the Republican ones, from criticizing his Vietnam policy, which the president knew was going to be a big issue in the 1968 presidential race. More than anything, this made clear that the experienced politician was undoubtedly worried about his political future.

Another significant occurrence on the governors' cruise as it applied to the 1968 presidential campaign happened at a private meeting between Rockefeller, Romney, and their wives. This occasion was not publicized. The issue of the presidential nomination was the subject of the meeting. Romney wanted to know for sure that Rockefeller was not interested in running because several rumors suggested otherwise. Romney told him that he would gladly bow out of the race if the New York governor changed his mind. Nelson's wife Happy was quite adamant when she told the Romneys, "We'll never go down that road again." George Romney wanted to make sure because he was close to officially announcing his candidacy.[73]

The end of October saw Nixon making trips to New Hampshire, Chicago, and Wisconsin. These were done to make sure he had the right people aboard strategically placed for the primaries. In New Hampshire, he spoke to the Greater Laconia Chamber of Commerce on what he termed a non-political trip, talking about things of local interest and, at times, poking fun at himself. Nixon had referenced the upcoming Dartmouth-Harvard football game and commented that given he was in Dartmouth territory, he should root for the home team. However, he continued, "Remembering what happened to me the last time that I ran against a Harvard man, I don't think I will." That quip got one of the most enormous laughs of the night.[74] Nixon believed that he would be in good shape in this state as at least two former governors had already come out for him, and the state's largest newspaper, the *Manchester Union Leader*, previously had been a strong supporter. The paper's publisher, William Loeb, hinted at filing a lawsuit against George Romney, challenging his credentials for the presidency. Article II of the United States Constitution requires that a president must be a natural-born citizen. Romney was born in Chihuahua, Mexico, as the son of American parents who had fled the U.S. with fellow Mormons to escape prosecution for polygamy. Loeb had referred to Romney as "Chihuahua George" several times in his paper.[75]

Nixon followed his New Hampshire trip with one to the "Windy City," where he headlined an Executives' Club of Chicago luncheon at the Conrad Hilton. There to a crowd of 1500, he gave what one writer from the *New York Times* called his "most thorough presentation of his views on Vietnam."[76] Two weeks before the event, Nixon received a newspaper clipping from the *Chicago Sun-Times* from Timothy F. Sheehan, the chairman of the Cook County Republican Central Committee, quoting Sheehan on his preference for the nomination: Nixon, Reagan, Percy. Sheehan wrote, "Richard Nixon undoubtedly is the most qualified Republican candidate. His experience in the House, Senate and as vice president for eight years has given him a background in government that no other candidate can match." He went onto say that he considered Romney and Rockefeller as "heresy" to the Republican Party, and he believed they should not be regarded as legitimate candidates given their failure to support the Goldwater campaign.[77]

The next stop for the unofficial tour had Nixon speaking at the Glenn Davis Dinner in Waukesha, Wisconsin. Davis and Nixon were old friends and colleagues from their days in the House. Waukesha County was the fastest-growing county in the state, and the state's political primary was three weeks after New Hampshire. Wisconsin was also a state where George Romney should do well given its proximity to Michigan and its strong progressive history. Romney's old company, American Motors, had a large automobile plant in Kenosha, an hour's drive from both Waukesha and Milwaukee. Nixon returned to the state three weeks later.[78]

Wisconsin was also a state in which Parkinson had worked a great deal while he was heading the Nixon campaign. The former campaign manager lined up associates from the former governor, Warren Knowles, to head up the Nixon team there. He took John Mitchell from the law firm with him to the Badger state on a couple of occasions, while the two disagreed as to how best to organize the state. Mitchell did not have the political experience that Parkinson did; Mitchell did have many contacts throughout local government with his expertise in the bond business. He knew vital people who made decisions on how state and local governments financed their current operations outside of the tax revenue that the states brought in. Mitchell believed that the best way to run their campaign was to align his business clients in local government along with their political allies in state government.[79]

A crowd of 900 attended the Glenn Davis Dinner, where Nixon spoke highly of his old friend and what he meant to the people of Wisconsin. He made several references to local issues that Davis's district was facing and said it was up to the people who lived there, not those in Washington, to make those decisions. One of his colorful comments mentioned his surprise about the robust state leader turnout when the University of Wisconsin was playing a home game earlier in the afternoon. One of the leaders present asked Nixon if he had seen their football team play. Their record was 0–5–1 so far during the 1967 season. Nixon responded, "I know how the Badgers feel." On a more serious note, he said a successful conclusion from the Vietnam war was necessary to avoid a wider war. Nixon elaborated, "If a group of ragged guerrillas can defeat the most powerful nation in the world in Vietnam, isn't that the way they will try reach their goal? In the event aggressions succeeds here, the chances increase that it will happen elsewhere in the world."[80]

Nixon did a brief interview with Chet Huntley two days later on *The Huntley-Brinkley Report*. They were a strong competitor to CBS News and Walter Cronkite.

The program always ended with Brinkley saying to Huntley, "Good night, Chet, from Washington," which was followed by "Good night, David, from New York."[81]

On Halloween, a mini-news frenzy with future ramifications erupted from a column written by Drew Pearson and his muckraking sidekick, Jack Anderson, titled "Scandal in Sacramento." Pearson was a close friend and confidante to Lyndon Johnson. His "Washington Merry-Go-Round" rumormongering columns had appeared in newspapers across the country since the 1930s. In this column, the two writers asserted that a homosexual ring was operating inside the administration of Governor Ronald Reagan and that the governor had known of it for at least six months before taking any action. Two of the homosexuals who were identified were fired as a result. On the governor's cruise earlier in the month, reporters were told this by Lyn Nofziger.[82] At a news conference the same day, Reagan angrily denied the story and said, "Three presidents of both parties, publicly, have called Drew Pearson a liar." Reagan told the reporters that they could ask Nofziger, who was standing near to the governor if it were true. They did, and Nofziger agreed with his boss.[83] The result of this denial was that a significant part of the news media covering Reagan was now more skeptical of him and his pronouncements. Nixon, when told of the contents of the column, directed Rose Mary Woods to tell Nofziger that he had given specific instructions to Pat Buchanan on his response to the Pearson column. It emphatically stated, "Mr. Nixon never dignifies a Pearson column with comment."[84]

November started with a couple of fundraisers. The first, a luncheon in New York hosted by Dan W. Lufkin and Bunny Lasker, was for a small group with deep pockets. The event raised over 40,000 dollars.[85] Two days later, Nixon traveled back to Chicago for a testimonial dinner for Joseph "Joe" I. Woods, the sheriff of Cook County. Woods was a reliable Republican who had Nixon roots. His sister was Rose Mary Woods, Nixon's long-time secretary. Woods controlled about 2,000 jobs in the greater Chicago area and was a staunch Republican counter to Richard Daley's Democratic machine. Senate Minority Leader Everett Dirksen also spoke at the well-attended dinner.[86]

At the same time, the results of the new Harris Poll published in the *New York Post* were good news to Republicans. With the election one year away, the survey showed that all significant Republican contenders would defeat President Johnson if the election were held that day. It showed Rockefeller with the most significant margin of victory over LBJ, 52 percent to 35 percent, with Romney favored by a nine-point margin, 46 percent to 37 percent. Nixon also did quite well, winning by seven points, 48 to 41, followed by Reagan winning by five points, 46 to 41.[87]

A week later, Nixon headlined a luncheon in Cleveland for leading members of the business community. H. Chapman "Chappy" Rose and Thomas F. Patton co-hosted the event. Rose served as an undersecretary in the Treasury Department in the Eisenhower administration and was one of the partners in the Jones, Day law firm. Patton was the president of Republic Steel, the country's third-largest steel producer whose headquarters were based in Cleveland.[88] There was an interesting side note to this event found in the files associated with it. It involved a phone call that Rose Mary Woods received a week before the event from Charles M. White, a former president of Republic Steel. White related to the Nixon aide that he would be attending but wanted to know whether something had happened in the past with her boss and George Humphrey, the former secretary of the Treasury in Ike's first term. White said Humphrey was ranting about the article in *Foreign Affairs*, saying Nixon "is just as bad as a world firster and keep America in all these things and never come home from fighting, etc. I asked him who he was for? I said if you are not for Dick, who are you going to back?" He said, "I don't know."[89] Humphrey and John Foster Dulles had been the most influential members of Eisenhower's cabinet during that period.

The next day, Richard Nixon received much better reports from news from a Los Angeles news conference by William Buckley, Jr. The titular head of the conservative movement declared his support Nixon. Buckley added that if Ronald Reagan were nominated, he would back him as well, but he favored Nixon over Reagan because of his experience and reliability.[90]

The weekend before Thanksgiving, Nixon returned to Wisconsin, this time in Madison, to speak to a group of law students where he got a much better reception than Romney had a few weeks before when the Michigan governor was interrupted several times. During the question-and-answer session, Nixon said he could see the day when the draft should be abolished and replaced with an all-volunteer army. He said, "A change in the Selective Service System at this time is not likely and would probably not be wise. It would be a stop-gap and the wrong kind of change in a system that needs a complete reappraisal." He added an entirely new approach to recruitment was needed after the war ended.[91]

The next day George Romney made his long-awaited announcement formally declaring his candidacy. At a news conference in Detroit, the Michigan governor explained why he was running in a prepared statement with strong moral overtones: "I am concerned about America. The size and complexity of our national problems have bred a widespread sense of personal futility. We've begun to see acceptance of irresponsibility as a way of life."[92]

More Television and Final 1967 Thoughts

Thanksgiving Week 1967 was a short one as it applied to the politics of Richard Nixon. He participated in two television events designed to reach different audiences. The first was a November 20 taped interview with Paul Niven on National Educational Television (NET) in New York. Niven was one of the old "Murrow boys" who worked for CBS during their heyday in the 1940s and 1950s. Niven left the Tiffany news network the past year for NET. The show aired the week after Thanksgiving in prime time. It was a somewhat freewheeling interview hitting on critical political subjects going into the election year of 1968. The show targeted the political establishment. It was titled "A Conversation with Richard Nixon on the Science of Politics."[93] The second television event aimed at a much broader television audience on the popular *Tonight Show* starring Johnny Carson. It showed a more human side of Nixon, much like its predecessor, the *Jack Parr Show*. Even though Carson asked pertinent questions of his guests, he also used a lot of humor and jokes to complement the more serious aspects of the show.

Barbara Delatiner of *Newsday* reviewed the Niven interview and gave it near-rave reviews. She wrote that Nixon projected a "colorful image" to the viewers and thought it could only be viewed as positive by those who wanted him to run for president in 1968. Delatiner went on to write, "Self-assured, articulate, displaying a note of sincerity that had to make even his detractors pause to wonder, Nixon was a personal pundit.... Here Nixon observed that 'politics is the art of the possible.' ... All Nixon watchers should take note of the performance."[94]

On the *Tonight Show*, shown on the night before Thanksgiving, Richard Nixon acknowledged that his bad makeup during his 1960 debates with John F. Kennedy was a factor in losing the election. There was a news item being circulated the day of the program that if Nixon did indeed make a run for the presidency in 1968, that the makeup director on the show would join his staff. Roy Voege, an 18-year NBC staffer, was quoted saying, "Nothing's completely settled yet. I've worked with Nixon on some of his filmings, and we get along fine. Now we have to wait for the formal announcement."[95]

Richard Whalen wrote a critical memo to Nixon on his assessments of the two television appearances in what he called "Reactions to the Tube." He complimented the Carson interview, noting it "went off very well." Whalen had quite a different response to the Niven event. Most of it was technical, some of which Nixon could not control. Whalen dubbed it as "godawful" and "bush-league" with Nixon ill-prepared. He also thought the color was substandard.[96] Nixon's written response was, "NET noted his critique of the technical set up. The NET show was good on content."[97] Nixon knew that there were some technical things that he needed to work on, but he was satisfied with what he was saying.

The last Nixon event for November took place in Oregon, the site of his fourth major primary. He had intended to make this trip on October 1, but the death of his mother changed his plans. Ronald Reagan could make a big difference in this state, given its proximity to California. It was also a state where the Nixon team was extremely well organized. It was accomplished despite the governor, Tom McCall, who had worked on Rockefeller's 1964 campaign. The Nixon campaign manager in Oregon was Howell Appling, Jr. Nixon assured Appling in the spring that he would have to campaign in Oregon if he wanted grassroots support. Appling had headed up Goldwater's team in 1964 when the Arizona senator failed to campaign there for the primary, and Appling was disgusted by this. He had also managed Mark Hatfield's successful run for governor. Appling supplied Nixon with a detailed assessment of all 30 or more people who would be sitting on the stage with him.[98]

Nixon spent two days in Oregon, one in Eugene, and another in Portland. He spoke to a large crowd of 7,000 students at the University of Oregon and headlined a luncheon meeting at the Jaycees Bosses Conference. At the university event, Nixon was critical of an alliance that was aimed against Communist China. He said, "It is important that we do not divide the world between Asia and the whites." A student asked him about the "civil war" in the streets, referring to recent riots. Nixon responded, "The civil war we have at home is more difficult to solve than Lincoln's Civil War."[99] He also had a 75-minute private meeting with McCall while he was there. The Oregon governor was "terribly impressed" with Nixon's "detailed" grasp of both foreign and domestic issues.[100] In Portland, he responded to a question about Secretary McNamara leaving as Secretary of Defense to head the World Bank. Nixon wanted to know if it was going to change the administration's policy on Vietnam, though he guessed not.[101]

The biggest news to come out of the Nixon visit to Oregon had to do with his family. Nixon was asked by a television reporter in Portland whether his daughter

Julie was becoming more serious about her relationship with David Eisenhower, Ike's grandson. Nixon replied that since Thanksgiving, Julie had been wearing a ring that had once belonged to David's grandmother. He acknowledged that he was not making any official announcement of their engagement, "but David goes to Amherst and she goes to Smith. In their freshman year, they hitchhiked between campuses. I'm told that General Eisenhower blew his stack and urged David to get a car."[102] Two days later, the former president replied to reporters who greeted him when he pulled up into his winter home in Palm Springs, "We're proud of him. We think that he made a wonderful pick."[103]

Most of December found Nixon closer to home in New York. He taped an interview on the *Merv Griffin Show*[104] that was shown a week before Christmas. In the middle of the month, he spoke at a Christmas party honoring a state employees' event in Illinois,[105] went to California to be honored by some old friends there,[106] and spent a day campaigning in Nebraska.[107] In New York, he headlined an executive's conference of Stone and Webster, a major national engineering firm.[108]

The next day he made a major speech at the National Association of Manufacturers (NAM) annual banquet at the Waldorf Astoria that got significant coverage. The address was at least two months in the making, with its genesis from an August speech by Daniel Patrick Moynihan, a Harvard professor, at a conference of the Americans for Democratic Action (ADA). The ADA was a liberal political organization that measured the voting records of members of Congress. In the speech, Moynihan was critical of liberals who seemed to blame white people for any problem associated with Blacks, no matter the circumstances. He also decried the role of the federal government in the breakup of the Black family. Additionally, he blamed the government for raising unrealistic expectations about what it could do to alleviate racial problems and poverty. Len Garment saw the speech and wrote Moynihan to ask for a copy. After receiving it, he gave it to Dick Whalen to look over and make some recommendations for Nixon to consider for a major policy speech. After a good bit of tinkering with many of Nixon's edits, the result was the speech given on December 8.[109]

After some introductory remarks about halting aggression in Vietnam, Nixon segued that this was not the only battle being waged in this country. He continued, "The ultimate testing place of America is America itself. If we are divided, if we default on our promises we have made to ourselves, the foundation on which we are attempting to build a better future will crumble."[110] The speech was interrupted five times by loud applause from the usually reserved and conservative businessmen.[111]

December marked the last governors conference in 1967. This time, the Republicans met for three days in West Palm Beach. Romney sat this one out, but Reagan was there for just one day. Rockefeller attended and was the star of the show. While still maintaining he was not a candidate, he did not rule out a draft. The wily governor stated, "If it actually did happen, I'd have to face it."[112] Even though Rockefeller continued to say no, most likely at least two-thirds of the Republican governors would support him if he came out. Outside of Governor Chafee of Rhode Island who had already committed to Romney, Nixon was favored by the other third of the governors. Bellmon, Sears, Ellsworth, and Evans represented the former vice president even though he was not there himself. What the Nixon team wanted to avoid was any division among these ranks that could come out later in the process as a part of a "stop

Nixon" effort. John Love, the current president of the Republican Governors, agreed with them, even though he was a known Rockefeller supporter. Another Rockefeller supporter, David Cargo of New Mexico, took a different view. He thought that the moderate governors should call a meeting after the New Hampshire primary "to see if Romney can go on and if he can't afford what we should do about it. Either that or we should sit down with Nixon right now and develop some rapport with him."[113] It looked like the first couple of primaries would be the "put up or shut up moment" for any moderate candidate to challenge Nixon if he won the early two primaries. Still, it now looked like the Republican governors would have to be happy without one of their own.

There was one more trip before the end of the year to Nebraska, where Nixon had a lot of support. While in Omaha, reporters asked if he were running for president. Nixon replied that he "would throw in his hat if he had to decide today."[114] He did not have to decide that particular day but would do so formally in the next few weeks.

By 1968, Richard Nixon had been working toward running for president for five years. For at least half of that time, he was not sure if he would have the opportunity. As he headed into the Christmas holiday season, Nixon listed the pros and cons of the final step of formally entering the hunt. Early on the morning of December 23, Nixon wrote to himself, "Had I come all this way to avoid the clash? I did want to run. Every instinct said yes. But now, on the brink of that decision, I was surprised to find myself procrastinating." Two days later, on Christmas day, he had a lengthy discussion with Pat and his daughters. He knew that his wife would support him even though she did not want him to run, but he wanted confirmation from his girls. Julie told him, "You have to do it for the country," while Tricia put it in much more personal terms: "If you do not run, Daddy, you will have nothing to live for."[115]

Three days later, Nixon went to Key Biscayne to visit Bebe Rebozo to decide. He invited Billy Graham to join them to offer spiritual guidance. Even though Graham was still reeling from a flu bug, he felt like he owed it to his "Quaker friend" to provide any type of counsel that he could muster.[116] They had engaged in several conversations on the subject, but Graham had not advised Nixon on the matter, although he had known Nixon for almost twenty years. Nixon pressed him, as he was getting ready to return to North Carolina. In his memoirs ten years later, Nixon recalled the conversation between the two of them: "'What should I do?' Billy closed his suitcase and turned toward me. 'Dick. I think you should run,' he said. 'If you don't you will always wonder whether you should have run and whether you could have won or not. You are the best-prepared man in the United States to be President.... I think it is your destiny to be President,' he said."[117]

Before leaving to go back to New York, Nixon received a letter from David Eisenhower, who was engaged to his daughter Julie. Eisenhower told him in this letter how troubled he was to hear that his soon-to-be father-in-law might not run for president. Even though he knew he was too young and too new to the family to say so, Ike's grandson felt compelled to tell Nixon this in his supposed hour of indecision: "Everything I say must be a tremendous understatement since I have never endured a political campaign or political life in its most taxing form. Politics is a sacrifice, in terms of one's family, privacy, and other countless aspects of a man's life.... Only you can determine whether to run is worth the effort and the hardships or not."[118]

As if this were not enough, there was one more meeting with the family to finalize this critical decision. For this January 15 dinner event, Nixon also invited Rose
Mary Woods. After dinner, he told the assembled group, "Politics was not just an
alternative occupation for me. It was my life.... I have decided to go; I have decided to
run again." Manola and Fina Sanchez were also present for the announcement. They
were personal valets for the Nixons, having immigrated to the United States from
communist Cuba, and had lived with them since 1962. Nixon, considering them part
of the family, wanted them present for this celebration. Fina told everyone assembled that Mr. Nixon was "the man to lead the country! This was determined before
you were born."[119] It was only a few days now before he headed to New Hampshire for
the formal announcement and participation in the nation's first presidential primary.

9

This Is Not My Last
Press Conference

Earlier in the week before the decision dinner, Nixon had flown to Philadelphia to tape a segment on the *Mike Douglas Show*. The highly popular daytime variety show had originated in Cleveland and moved to its current destination. Nixon had planned for a late November show but had decided to postpone it until after the first of the year. The taped show would be shown on January 23, a week before the official announcement in New Hampshire. Dwight Chapin accompanied him for the shuttle to Philadelphia. The two met with the producer an hour before taping to get the ground rules, questions, and topics. The producer was a young man from the Cleveland area named Roger Ailes. He was the same age, 27, as Dwight. After going over the basics, Ailes told Nixon he needed a "media adviser" and stressed the importance of a successful image for any presidential candidate. Nixon initially scoffed at the phoniness of television but listened attentively to what Ailes said. The young producer told Nixon that if he were not interested in having a media adviser, it would probably be best that he did not run for president because Nixon would not win if he was indifferent to how he looked on television.[1] It was even more so because of the advent of color television, which was quickly replacing black and white. After the show, Chapin and Nixon went to a luncheon that the former vice president headlined, attended by some prominent Philadelphia businessmen. On the flight back to New York, Nixon seemed interested in Ailes's idea in his conversation with Chapin. A few days later, Ailes got a call to meet with Len Garment and Ray Price about some employment opportunities coming up with the campaign. As it turned out, all of the parties clicked, and Ailes joined them part-time in February to work on television events.[2]

Only a few events were scheduled in January for several reasons. Nixon wanted to be rested when he went to New Hampshire, he was accounting for the chance of bad weather, and he generally wanted to be more flexible before the actual campaign got underway. Most of these events were close to home. He went to Richmond, Virginia, and Washington and Lee University,[3] a young executives' luncheon in Washington,[4] as well as another luncheon in New York with some of his major campaign players.[5] One notable exception was a trip to Texas on January 19 and 20 with stops in San Antonio and Dallas. Nixon met with Texas Republican Party Chairman Peter O'Donnell, Senator John Tower, and other notable Texas political players. He did so to make sure that state was united behind its favorite son candidate, Tower, who was close to Nixon as well as the state chairman. Even though the Texas senator had turned down the offer to run Nixon's campaign, it did not diminish his support for him. There had been rumblings late last year in the state of trying to break up the delegation by supporters of Ronald Reagan led by Tom Reeds' uncle Larry Reed, and Jack Porter.[6]

Campaign Coming into Focus

Everything Richard Nixon did politically had a purpose. He had spent the last year doing what he thought necessary to put himself in serious contention. In 1967, he avoided overexposure. Nixon did not want to burn out, and he also did not want the public to be burned out on him. He had made a mistake in the 1960 campaign of trying to do too much, like going to all fifty states and not paying attention to his close advisers on how best to spend his time on and off the campaign trail. What Ailes and others on his staff said about his television appearances in the last half of 1967 had more than convinced Nixon that he needed to look his best and appear fresh all the time. His moratorium from politics while Romney ran all over the country played into this strategy. He knew explicitly that this was one of his mistakes during the 1960 campaign, and it had worn on him physically and emotionally. Nixon would not make the same mistake again, no matter what critics like Evans and Novak were saying, as he prepared to make his official announcement.[7]

In mid–1967, one of Nixon's aides from two previous campaigns, H.R. "Bob" Haldeman, sent him a detailed 14-page letter about how the campaign should be conducted. Haldeman copied the letter to three other people in the law office: Rose Mary Woods, Tom Evans, and Dwight Chapin. Chapin was very close to Haldeman and had transferred to the New York Thompson office two years before. Haldeman was a vice president and manager of the Los Angeles office and had not formally joined the campaign, even though he was included in everything that Nixon did in California. In the letter, Haldeman insisted his ideas were a general guideline, not an exact science, on what Nixon should do in his pre-primary and primary phases of the campaign. He believed a year would allow some experimentation and refinement on what worked best, especially when it came to television events. The earlier critiques that Nixon had sought from Dick Whalen and Bill Safire were good examples of this. Haldeman believed doing things for television, radio, and newspapers conformed to the news cycle. As for the kind of manic campaigning that only wore the candidate out, Haldeman wrote:

> If a candidate actually does six speeches a day, six days a week, for the full eight-week campaign period, he'll make 288 speeches. If he has a spectacular crowd-gathering ability (or staff), he might average 5,000 per speech (but no one ever has).... He has not time to think.... No wonder the almost inevitable campaign dialogue borders so near the idiot level.... You plan a campaign that is designed to cover the important localities, provide excitement and stimulation for your supporters, generate major news every day, generate intensive coverage in depth by commentators and columnists, develop a meaningful dialogue (even if it is one-sided), and still a reasonable chance of the candidate's survival.[8]

Also, though Haldeman technically had not yet joined the campaign, he spoke to the soon-to-be official candidate several times a week.

Two days before the official announcement in New Hampshire, Nixon got more good news from a national Gallup Poll showing him increasing his lead over his only announced opponent, Romney, to a nearly three-to-one advantage, 68 to 26. The only bad news for Nixon was that Rockefeller, who continually insisted he was not a candidate, had gained ten points in the past two months. The New York governor still trailed Nixon by a nearly three-to-two advantage, 55 to 41.[9]

The picture was much different in Washington at the same time for Lyndon Johnson. The U.S.S. *Pueblo*, an intelligence vessel in international waters close to the coast of North Korea, was seized a week earlier. On top of that, the North Vietnamese and Viet Cong guerrillas mounted a full-scale offensive against South Vietnam throughout South Vietnam. It was the most intense fighting of the war, and all of the provincial capitals of South Vietnam were under siege. Nevertheless, the official campaign was about to begin for Richard Nixon.

Pat Buchanan, Ray Price, and Dwight Chapin accompanied Nixon for a flight to New Hampshire, but they were cut short in Boston by a snowstorm. Unable to complete the trip to New Hampshire, they were met at the airport by Nick Ruwe, who drove them to Manchester for the official campaign opening.[10] Nixon opened the press conference with a satirical reference to "his last press conference" statement after losing the 1962 governor's race in California. He said, "Gentlemen, this is not my last press conference." Afterward, he went on to say he was best placed among the Republicans to defeat the incumbent president: "I believe that I am going to win the New Hampshire primary, come out the decisive winner of the primaries, go on to win the nomination, and if I do that, I believe that I can defeat Lyndon Johnson." Nixon

Pat Buchanan and Dwight Chapin in Nixon's office sometime early in 1968 (Richard M. Nixon Foundation).

explained that he would carry his primary campaign into Wisconsin, Nebraska, and Oregon, much as he had stated many times. He also added the primary states of Indiana and South Dakota to the list. Nixon told them that he would stay out of primaries where there were favorite son candidates. Additionally, Nixon said he would not debate Romney, to the chagrin of the Michigan governor who had been challenging him for the past several months to do so. He did not leave out the possibility of others like Reagan and Percy coming into the campaign when he said, "Any realist knows Gov. Rockefeller could become a candidate at a later time."[11]

As he headed to his first event in New Hampshire, 50,000 households in the state were simultaneously receiving mail from the candidate. In the letter, Nixon wrote, "During the past eight years I have had a chance to reflect on the lessons of public office, to measure the nation's tasks and its problems from a fresh perspective. I have sought to apply those lessons to the needs of the present, and to the entire sweep of this final third of the 20th century. And I believe I have found some answers."[12]

His first day in the "Live Free or Die" state was met with criticism from Governor Romney and the media. Romney was mad because Nixon would not debate him, while the media was upset because they were not invited to a closed-door question and answer session with the candidate. The Hillsboro meeting was held in the courtroom of Nixon's New Hampshire campaign manager's father. The candidate met with ten students from local colleges, along with an equal number of area farmers. The

Nixon with his family announcing his candidacy for president in New Hampshire on February 2, 1968 (Richard M. Nixon Foundation).

exchanges were filmed for later use in commercials during the campaign. Nixon aides shot a couple more of these exchanges in the state when they came back a week later. The first nightly event was a $5 a plate dinner attended by 1200 people in Concord. In this address, Nixon challenged the assembly by asking whether the country should continue the same path or whether it was time for a change. He answered his own question with this statement: "When the strongest nation in the world can be tied down for four years in a war in Vietnam, with no end in sight; when the nation with the greatest tradition of respect for the rule of law is plagued by random lawlessness; when the nation that has been a symbol of human liberty is torn apart by racial strife ... then it is time for new American leadership."[13]

Bob Haldeman had accompanied the Nixon team on the first part of the New Hampshire campaign. He officially joined the campaign two months later. Haldeman thought it might be useful if there was a designated press secretary that performed the same function under Nixon in 1960 and 1962. Klein was still a strong Nixon supporter, but he had not yet joined the team. Haldeman thought that Buchanan might be the ideal man given he had worked in the media and held a master's degree from the Columbia School of Journalism. Pat agreed to try. One of the press secretary's tasks involved schmoozing the press, which often meant having a drink with reporters at the end of the working day. After the Hillsboro taping, Buchanan went back to the hotel and met with Pat Ferguson of the *Baltimore Sun* and Bob Novak, the famed columnist who was always giving Nixon a hard time. Buchanan had seen Novak several times but had never met him. He knew enough to consider him an "enemy." Buchanan introduced himself and sat down with the two reporters over a late afternoon beer at the hotel bar. Immediately, Novak started ranting about how Nixon had tricked the press and not allowed them into the taping at Hillsboro. It went on for about ten minutes, and Buchanan was fuming. Buchanan left and told Haldeman later that the press secretary position was not a good fit for him. He wanted to punch Novak out for his intemperate remarks.[14] The experiment with Buchanan as a press secretary did not work out. The Nixon campaign would leave New Hampshire and return five days later.

The next day was spent in Wisconsin, the site of the second presidential primary. Nixon was upbeat in Green Bay at the Elks Club, the Jaycees Dinner, and a Lincoln Day dinner in Fond du Luc. He saluted the Jaycees and John Byrnes, the Republican congressman from the district who was serving in the House when Nixon was elected in 1946, for their public service. Nixon spoke in glowing terms of Byrnes. There is "no man," Nixon said, "Democrat or Republican, who is more intelligent, more courageous, a more fine [sic] representative of his district and his state and his nation." It was a non-political event, so Nixon then saluted the Green Bay Packers, who had just won their second Super Bowl in a row over the Oakland Raiders a month earlier. The quarterback and field general of the Packers, Bart Starr, was sitting in the front table. All-Pro defensive tackle Henry Jordan was also there for a visit. Nixon made fun of his relations with the media and the negative perception of his television image. Nixon also had to admit to the home crowd in "Titletown U.S.A." that he had lost a small bet on them during the Super Bowl. He came back with the adoration of their leader: "Bart Starr is a great quarterback. But it's not because of the way he faces those great hulking linemen when they charge in on him that I admire him. I admire him for the way he faces those TV cameras."[15]

The Rise of the "Heavyweight"

After Wisconsin, Nixon flew to Oklahoma City and Tulsa to kick off Henry Bellmon's senatorial campaign. There, he attended a separate reception with the Republican state delegates. Nixon wanted to make sure he knew where they stood because Reagan had been there a week earlier, and an Oklahoma committee for Reagan had been announced in January. There was no mention of Bellmon continuing to head the Nixon for President campaign, but Nixon knew when Bellmon accepted the job, he would be leaving soon after the first of the year.

There was a seamless connection in media coverage between Wisconsin, Oklahoma, and the following three-day swing into Denver. The connection was a new campaign manager for Nixon. There were newspaper reports during the past month that at least two people had turned down the job, including John Tower and Rogers Morton. While both Tower and Morton still supported Nixon, they decided against running his campaign. What was clear was that Nixon had undoubtedly decided on a person who had accepted the position. There are at least two different accounts of what took place and when. Len Garment writes in his memoirs that he suggested to Nixon sometime towards the end of 1967 that John Mitchell, the new law partner to Nixon/Mudge/Rose, was the ideal candidate. It was well acknowledged that Garment was a major talent scout for Nixon. He was always bringing in new people to the campaign, and he pitched it to Mitchell a few weeks later at a formal black-tie dinner.[16]

Stephen C. Shadegg, who was a Republican political consultant, had a slightly different account of the decision. A secret meeting was held during the third week of January, two weeks before Nixon's official announcement, at the new Nixon for President Headquarters in New York at the old American Bible Society building on 57th and Park Avenue. Shadegg wrote that at least six people besides Nixon were present for the meeting. Both Mitchell and Bellmon were there, along with John Sears, Maurice Stans, Richard Kleindienst, and Bob Ellsworth. Most likely, Peter Flanigan was also there, even though Shadegg did not mention him. All those present were Nixon regulars except for Kleindienst. He was a highly respected Phoenix attorney who had graduated from Harvard Law School. Kleindienst had worked for Nixon in Arizona in the 1960 campaign. He had also managed the western states for Goldwater in 1964. Kleindienst had been brought into the Nixon campaign in the fall of 1967 to manage the western states except for California.[17] At the meeting, there were several alternative scenarios discussed. Finally, Kleindienst chimed in with another suggestion. He thought that it was not necessary to have a big-name Republican head the campaign because Nixon was the biggest name in the party and ultimately made the final decisions anyway. Kleindienst believed John Mitchell was the perfect person for the job even though he had never participated in a national election.[18] Kleindienst does not take credit for this in his memoirs written 18 years later, but he does discuss a meeting in some detail in the fall of 1967, where he met Nixon and Mitchell in New York.[19]

The two accounts mentioned above are not mutually exclusive and could both be mostly right. Indeed, Nixon was close to Garment during this period, and Garment brought in several people to the campaign. Nixon trusted him and acknowledged later that it was his recommendation that convinced him to hire Mitchell. Shadegg could also be right in his book even though he does not cite it with a footnote. Nixon would frequently preside over meetings in which he solicited input from others when, for the most part, he had already he had made up his mind. He was a good listener and did not seek advice from those he thought were "yes men."[20]

William Safire, who had known Nixon since 1959, had often served as a sounding board for Nixon. Sometime in late 1967, Nixon told Safire, "I've found my heavyweight," referring to John Mitchell. Safire had not yet formally joined the campaign but continued to advise Nixon while running his public relations firm. He believed Mitchell was the perfect match for Nixon. Safire considered others who had advised Nixon in the past, but Mitchell was different because, "Unlike most of the men Nixon had been attracting in 1966 and 1967, Mitchell was tough. It was Mitchell whom Nixon went to for answers, he had a way of getting to the nub of the problem and laying out alternative routes to the solution, proposing his recommendation, and then ... picking up the telephone and making something happen."[21]

John Mitchell was one of the managing partners of Caldwell, Trimble, and Mitchell when the firm merged with Nixon, Mudge, Rose, and Guthrie in January 1967. Most of the Caldwell lawyers were from small Catholic law schools like Fordham or St. John's, unlike the Nixon firm, where most of the attorneys were from Ivy League law schools. Francis X. "Joe" Maloney, one of the junior lawyers at the firm, said at the time, "The large white-shoe New York firms like Sullivan and Cromwell did not deal in this area. There were only five or six firms in New York who did." The firm had clients all over the country with the possible exception of California. Nelson Rockefeller had used the firm a great deal in the financing projects throughout the state of New York. Maloney went onto say that Mitchell "was the number one municipal bond lawyer in the country, no question about it. His reputation on Wall Street was unparalleled."[22]

Mitchell claimed he had known Nixon for some years before the merger, but that is not what Nixon remembers. He says that he did not know Mitchell before the two firms merged.[23] Tom Evans thinks that both Mitchell and Nixon's accounts are most likely correct. Evans said, "John Mitchell felt that Richard Nixon included him in people he knew on a first-name basis and Richard Nixon, briefed by an appropriate staff member, was probably in that same position. But one fact is clear: They were not close, underline not close until Mitchell came to the firm."[24]

How the two firms became acquainted was most likely the result of Bob Guthrie, one of the partners who encouraged Nixon to make overtures to Mitchell about merging the firms. Both Tom Evans and Joe Maloney agreed with this. Evans said, "There were some lunches orchestrated through Bob Guthrie, then the senior partner of this firm, to have Richard Nixon try to talk John Mitchell into coming into this practice. So clearly they were on a first-name basis and I think probably waxing nostalgic about the times they had met in the corridors of power in Washington and so on."[25] Maloney readily agreed, commenting, "Guthrie probably orchestrated this and saw this as a terrific marriage. Our firm had such a great reputation in the municipal bond field marrying a firm like theirs with that corporate expertise."[26]

Mitchell had several clients in the state of Wisconsin, the site of the second primary. He had been active in the state, putting together bond deals for at least the previous five years. One of the critical clients was Jerris Leonard, a Republican state senator. Leonard was active in party politics and remembered how Nixon had come to Milwaukee in 1964, campaigning for Goldwater toward the end of the presidential election. Leonard and another Wisconsin politico, Vincent Mercurio, met with

Mitchell in his new office in January or February 1967 to discuss financing for a $50 million bond project. Most of Mitchell's projects in Wisconsin had been with the Wisconsin State Agencies Building Corporation and the Wisconsin University Building Corporation, which built several new buildings with both the state government and the University of Wisconsin. During this conversation, Leonard mentioned Wisconsin politics and the upcoming presidential campaign. He told Mitchell if Nixon was going to win the Republican nomination, he had to win the Wisconsin primary, which was then favorable to George Romney. Leonard said many major politicians in the state were all lined up to go, but Nixon had to get in early and campaign there. Mitchell told Nixon what Leonard said. Nixon replied, "Whatever he says, he speaks for me." A year later, in the middle of February 1968, all of the politicians that Leonard had mentioned to Mitchell were either supporting or leaning toward Nixon, with polls showing him winning at least 2 to 1 over Romney. It looked like Mitchell and Leonard were doing an excellent job in the Badger State.[27]

The working trip to Denver lasted two and a half days without any public political events. It consisted of a meeting of the fourteen western states' chairmen except for California. Richard Kleindienst was the point man in this effort. During the sessions, Nixon received updates on the delegates' hunts in various states. Kleindienst had done the same thing for Goldwater, but unlike his predecessor four years earlier, Nixon was committed to running a long and hard campaign. An encouraged Kleindienst wrote, "[Nixon] inspired his new organization. He was jovial, friendly, upbeat.... It was an ideal PR event on the eve of the New Hampshire Primary and the 1968 national campaign."[28]

While Nixon met with his western aides, George Wallace announced his third-party candidacy for president. Wallace, the former Alabama governor and life-long Democrat, decided to join the race as an independent and "run to win." Wallace made the announcement in a crowded Washington news conference, supplying media with many great quotes on what he would do if he were elected. The colorful governor said, "I would bring all these briefcase-toting bureaucrats in the Department of Health, Education, and Welfare to Washington and throw their briefcases in the river. I would keep the peace if I had to keep 30,000 troops standing on the streets with two-foot-long bayonets ... and defiance of the national security [was being led] by activists, anarchists, revolutionaries and Communists [who should be put in jail]."[29]

Return to the Campaign

Nixon spent the better part of February in New Hampshire. He was squeezing in a day in Boston where much of New Hampshire got their television news before a trip to Wisconsin. But before Nixon arrived, he headlined a state-wide Republican fundraising event in Washington, Indiana. It was a familiar territory where he had been well received in the past. He won the state handily in 1960 and would run in the state's primary in the spring. Washington, Indiana, was only forty miles from the birthplace of Abraham Lincoln and only seventy-five miles from the childhood home of Nixon's mother in Mount Vernon, Indiana. A crowd of 9,000 people overfilled an auditorium with a capacity of only 7,000.[30] The speech Nixon delivered discussed a new direction and the need for new leadership. He said America was losing its military superiority, as Robert McNamara admitted during questioning before Congress about intercontinental ballistic missiles.[31] He also released a statement on the illegal garbage strike in New York that was trying the patience of its citizens while exposing a rift between the Republican governor and its Republican mayor. He wrote, "That strike violated more than the statutes of the state of New York. It violated the code of decency that binds us all together, that lies at the root of a society based on laws."[32]

After stops in Concord and Dover, Nixon traveled to nearby Manchester, where he criticized President Johnson but refused to attack Governor Romney, who was still begging Nixon for a debate. Nixon also was developing a nuanced policy toward the war in Vietnam based on themes in his *Foreign Affairs'* article, "Asia After Vietnam." He thought the United States should continue to fight the war to a successful conclusion but also needed to think about Asia's future. Nixon said, "But we must look beyond Vietnam.... And it makes little sense for a nation with one-tenth of the world's population to be fighting wars all over the world. In the event that another nation is threatened, we should help them with arms—and with men—but the goal should be to help them fight the war and not fight the war for them."[33] It was the root of what later became known as the "Nixon Doctrine."

At Portsmouth, he predicted the Soviet Union would catch up with the United States strategically in two years if national security policy were not reversed. In a live radio interview there, Nixon argued, "I think our whole strategic position must be reconsidered and that the McNamara position on military policy now is suspect ... and must be completely re-evaluated by a new Administration."[34] In La Crosse, Wisconsin, Nixon asked Johnson to explain whether his policy toward military superiority had changed with his new secretary of defense. He said, "It's time for President Johnson to tell the American people whether United States strategic policy has been changed along with the Secretary of Defense." Nixon went onto say that the new secretary, Clark H. Clifford (a long-time Democratic politico), "has implied that he believes the U.S. should maintain nuclear superiority over the Soviet Union. The outgoing Secretary, Mr. Robert McNamara, has long advocated that the United States accept the prospect of nuclear parity with the Soviet Union."[35]

There was other news in Wisconsin that might have ramifications on the April 2 primary. Nelson Rockefeller removed his name from the ballot while Ronald Reagan and Harold Stassen were added to the ballot. Nixon aides guessed Reagan would be on the ballot there and were concerned by his presence, unlike the addition of a perennial candidate like Stassen, who had run in every Republican presidential race since 1944.[36] Much of the political speculation centered on a potential rematch with Romney in the Badger state, given that the former vice president appeared too far ahead of the Michigan governor in New Hampshire. A Manchester *Union Leader* poll released on February 21 showed Nixon with a 6 to 1 lead over Romney.[37] The governor of Michigan should perform much better in the Midwest, given his state's proximity to Wisconsin, along with his progressive political views aligned with voters in the region.

A day later, Gallup showed Nixon even with Johnson, with 16 percent undecided. The president had lost nine points in the past month due to the Tet Offensive by North Vietnam and the administration's handling of the war. It was becoming increasingly clear that the war in Vietnam was going to be the most important issue of the campaign. It should benefit Nixon.[38] In the same poll, Nixon increased his lead over Rockefeller among Republicans 51 percent to 25 percent, a nine-point jump over January numbers. Among independents, Nixon held an eight-point advantage over Rockefeller, 34–26.[39]

Romney Bombshell and the Aftermath

Less than two weeks before the New Hampshire primary, George Romney shocked the political world by announcing his withdrawal from the race. As Nixon was speaking in Milford, Pat Buchanan received the message from an old classmate from Columbia, Don Oliver of *NBC*, who was covering Romney. Buchanan found Dwight Chapin outside the hall while Nixon was speaking and delivered the good news. After his speech, Chapin caught up with Nixon and whisked him off to a men's restroom where Buchanan waited with the news. Nixon was shocked. A wall of reporters met Nixon as the three men walked out. He told them that he had no comment.[40]

The three-term Michigan governor, who had been running since the end of 1966, cited a lack of support as the reason for not continuing. Everyone guessed he would pull out of the race if he lost badly in New Hampshire and Wisconsin, but not before. Romney said that the timing of his departure coincided with the Republican Governors Conference in Washington and hoped the governors would coalesce around one candidate, presumably Rockefeller. He made this statement in the lobby of the Hilton in the nation's capital as the governors conference was about to convene the next day. While Romney did not announce his support for any other Republican, he signaled his loyalties by saying of Rockefeller, "He has asked nothing of me and has given me more than I asked. He has supported me on his own initiative without reservation."[41]

The Nixon campaign, surprised by the news, continued their journey in New Hampshire. Nixon later made a gracious statement complimenting Governor Romney for waging an energetic and vigorous campaign.[42] Reporters following the governor questioned Nixon aides on what all this might mean. Anthony Ripley wrote a story the next day in the *New York Times* based on interviews with Nixon aides, though none spoke on the record. Much of the speculation centered on Rockefeller's entering the race despite his protests. The Romney resignation also improved Reagan's chances. One of the aides said, "Any moves that Governor Rockefeller makes limit his actions and tend to draw in Reagan." Another opined, "We have to live with Rockefeller as a candidate. But this announcement might have the greatest impact on what it has done for Reagan."[43] Nixon was not as gracious with his aides discussing the withdrawal when they got back to the hotel after all the day's events. He told Buchanan that they were cheated out of a victory and referred to Romney as "just like a businessman, no guts."[44]

Both Reagan and Rockefeller commented on the media's "supposed" candidacies. Reagan told Sacramento reporters that Romney's withdrawal "doesn't alter my position at all—I am not a candidate."[45] The California governor gave an airport interview four days later before leaving for an event in San Diego, where he stated Romney's withdrawal could have a "harmful" effect on the campaign because it would not offer any competition for Nixon. Reagan was also agreeable to Romney after the

Michigan governor clarified that his comment about not supporting "that man in California" was only for the pre-convention and primary phase of the campaign. He would back whomever the party nominated. Reagan commented, "He has explained his position. I'm gratified he does believe in party unity."[46] On the other hand, Rockefeller remained as coy as ever at the Republican Governors Conference in Washington, stating he was "ready and willing to serve the American people if called." When specifically asked if he wanted to be president, Rockefeller replied, "If this is what the party would like, and they feel I could do the job, yes."[47]

The day after the withdrawal, Buchanan sent a memo to William Loeb III, publisher of the *Manchester Union Leader,* about how the Nixon team interpreted Romney's departure. Buchanan had been conversing with Loeb for the past year, and the publisher wrote letters to Nixon. A few weeks before the primary, Buchanan went to New Hampshire to spend the night with the Loeb family. Towards the ends of the memo Buchanan sent to Loeb, he wrote a stinging indictment of Nelson Rockefeller and freely offered it to Loeb to publish under his name. The next day Loeb published it on the front page under the title "Nelse the Knife." Buchanan was referring specifically to how the week before Romney pulled out, Rockefeller went to Michigan and said he would be available for a draft after putting "a political knife in his back."[48]

Ten days before the New Hampshire primary, Rockefeller publicly downplayed any appetite for a significant write-in vote, but privately hoped for one. Rockefeller and Romney both thought a large contingent of Republican voters in the state and the country were not tied to Nixon. Former Governor Hugh Gregg was one of the public officials championing a Rockefeller write-in campaign. An unofficial campaign had been in place for two weeks, headed by John A. Beckett, professor at the University of New Hampshire.[49] A large write-in vote in New Hampshire was not unrealistic. Only four years ago, Henry Cabot Lodge got 30 percent as a write-in candidate.

The latest national Gallup Poll on Republican voters released the next day was terrible news for Rockefeller. Only two weeks earlier, Richard Nixon held a two-to-one advantage (51–25) over the New York governor. Amid the fallout from the Romney withdrawal, one might have thought Rockefeller would pick up support, but the opposite happened. Nixon increased his lead by a much larger margin. Sixty-seven percent of Republican voters favored Nixon to only 30 percent for Rockefeller. Just three weeks of campaigning in New Hampshire added 16 points to Nixon's totals but only five for Rockefeller. Another poll by *Time* magazine among Republican voters in New Hampshire showed Nixon far ahead of Rockefeller and Romney with almost a six-to-one advantage over both of the governors. Rockefeller was ahead of Romney even though he was not on the ballot.[50]

Nixon made the only big news before election day at a rally in Hampton's American Legion Hall. He insisted the Vietnam War was the most crucial issue of the campaign, and whoever made the most persuasive case for a successful conclusion was in the best shape to win. Nixon said, "If in November this war is not over, after all of this power has been at their disposal, then I say that the American people will be justified to elect new leadership. And I pledge to you the new leadership will end the war and win the peace in the Pacific."[51]

It took the Johnson Administration only two days to respond to this new challenge from Nixon on the war. Vice President Humphrey took issue with Nixon on the war but refused to call him by name. Humphrey stated, "I think we have a right to ask: 'If you know how to end the war and bring peace to the Pacific, Mr. Candidate, let the American people hear your formula now.'"[52] Nixon answered Humphrey in an interview the next day by freely admitting that it would be irresponsible to state what he would do now when conditions on the ground in the war might be vastly different after the election. He said, "No one with the responsibility which is seeking office should give away any of his bargaining positions in advance. Under no circumstances should a man say what he would do next January. The military situation may change, and we may have to take an entirely different look."[53]

In the end, Richard Nixon won a smashing victory in New Hampshire. That surprised almost no one. The depth of the success surprised virtually everyone, with 80 percent of the vote going to Nixon while Rockefeller garnered 11 percent, and the remaining 9 percent was split between the others. For the national media, the big news was on the Democratic side, where Eugene J. McCarthy, a senator from Minnesota, got 41 percent of the vote compared to Lyndon Johnson's 50 percent. The president had not campaigned there, and his name was not technically on the ballot. McCarthy, on the other hand, had campaigned heavily on the issue of peace in Vietnam.[54]

Pat Buchanan put together an analysis of the Nixon primary victory, demonstrating the magnitude of the win. Nixon's vote total of 80,668 was the largest of any presidential primary in New Hampshire history. His margin over his closest opponent was seven-to-one. Nixon even got five percent of the vote in the Democratic primary. In the same Democratic primary where Nixon and Bobby Kennedy were both write-ins, the former vice president received four times the total of the New York senator. Kennedy was now starting to be discussed as a challenger to the president. Nixon's total vote was more than all the other Democratic, Republican, and write-in candidates combined.[55] Richard Nixon came out of the New Hampshire primary as a force to be reckoned with in the race for the presidency.

10

Time to Get on That Train

With all the talk about Richard Nixon being a two-time loser, there was no way the Republicans would take a chance with him as their nominee. Nevertheless, no one had stepped up to challenge him after the abrupt withdrawal of George Romney. Romney got out of the race, convinced he would have taken a shellacking in New Hampshire. In March, the buzz about Nelson Rockefeller started to pick up as Nixon campaigned in Wisconsin for the April 2 primary. There also was a movement from the Ronald Reagan camp, even though he still maintained he was only a favorite son candidate.[1]

Only Two R's Left?

The weekend before the New Hampshire primary, Nelson Rockefeller huddled with aides and supporters at his New York residence to discuss the possibility of formally entering the race. He was trying to sort out what would be the best course of action if he ran. His immediate focus was the March 22 registration deadline for the Oregon primary on May 28. Oregon was a state he won in 1964, and he still had a lot of support there, including Governor Tom McCall. His wife Happy had given birth to their second child the year before and was against the idea.

On the front page of the *New York Times,* the day after Richard Nixon won the New Hampshire primary, a headline written by R.W. "Johnny" Apple, Jr., stated, "Friends Say Rockefeller Has Decided to Make Bid." In the story, Apple wrote that the New York governor had decided to run but was uncertain the best course for himself. The article listed three different options: wage an all-out campaign in Oregon, allow his name to remain in the campaign while leaving the ground game to the Draft Rockefeller committee, or file an affidavit of withdrawal from the Oregon primary by the March 22 deadline. The article also mentioned Rockefeller continued to meet with "a wide range of advisers and scholars," including Harvard's Henry Kissinger and Herman Kahn, the director of the Hudson Institute.[2]

In the meantime, Nixon campaigned in Wisconsin for three days before going to Oregon and California.[3] A week after Nixon's win in New Hampshire, another front-page story appeared in the *New York Times* with the headline, "Governor to Run; He Will Disclose Plans Thursday." In the story, Richard Reeves wrote drafts for the upcoming announcement being worked through by his principal speechwriter Hugh Morrow. The one area of concern was what to say about Vietnam. In private, Rockefeller had been highly critical of Nixon's position on the war. He noted that

Nixon had made a "major tactical blunder" to suggest ending the war without saying how. Reeves wrote, "When he has been alone with friends, Mr. Rockefeller has scornfully mocked Mr. Nixon by patting his suit pocket and saying he keeps a peace plan there while hundreds of Americans die each week in Vietnam."[4] It would not be the first or last time that one of Nixon's opponents criticized him for his "secret plan." Nixon, to be fair, never said that he had a secret plan to end the war. What he did say a week earlier was that if elected, "I pledge to you the new leadership will win the war and win the peace in the Pacific."[5] Nixon was clear that all options would be on the table for ending the war if he were elected. There was no reason for specifics now because if he were elected in November, the conditions in the war would likely be quite different.

Meanwhile, all that stood in the way of Nelson Rockefeller's bid for the presidency was an actual announcement. On March 21, he held a news conference but not the one that many of his supporters hoped. Rockefeller stunned them with his statement, "I have decided today to reiterate unequivocally that I am not a candidate campaigning directly or indirectly for the Presidency of the United States.... I have said that I stood ready to answer any true and meaningful call from the Republican party to serve it and the nation. I will so stand."[6] This decision left as Nixon the only candidate for the nomination. For someone who was supposed to be a loser, he was looking quite like a winner given the reluctance of anyone to challenge him.

On the other side of the country, Ronald Reagan watched these events closely. What was making him slowly change his mind had nothing to do with Richard Nixon or Nelson Rockefeller. It was the announcement on March 17 that Bobby Kennedy was going to challenge LBJ for the presidency. Reagan believed Kennedy was terrible for the country. Moreover, his antipathy was personal.[7]

When Kennedy was attorney general, Reagan was summoned to appear to a grand jury about activities related to his acting career. Also, Kennedy had a show Reagan hosted, the *General Electric Theater*, canceled. Kennedy told the CEO of General Electric that they would not receive any federal government contracts as long Reagan hosted the show. To say that Bobby Kennedy got under Reagan's skin would be a gross understatement. After Kennedy's announcement, Reagan called a meeting at his home on March 25, attended by Tom Reed, Clifton White, Lyn Nofziger, William French Smith, and Bill Clark, among others, to discuss what would be the best course to run for the presidency. Reagan seemed ready to run. In reality, for much of the past 16 months, Reed and White had been doing just that, but publicly Reagan would not commit himself to run.[8]

There was more speculation in the press on Reagan's non-candidacy when it was announced Robert C. Walker had been hired by the leaders of Reagan's California favorite-son delegation as "chief of operations" at the Republican convention in Miami Beach in August. David Broder wrote a front-page story about this new development in the March 26 *Washington Post*. In the article, Broder noted that veteran political observers could not remember anyone who was not a candidate opening permanent headquarters five months before a convention. Walker had left the Nixon campaign in August when Dr. Parkinson returned to California to be with his wife, who was suffering from cancer. Walker had been Parkinson's assistant and was the executive director of the Nixon for President Committee.[9] The Nixon campaign did not say publicly why Walker left, but he was fired for several things, including some damaging leaks to the press and possibly to other campaigns, including Reagan's.[10]

Back on the Campaign Trail and More Bombshells

Being the ever-self-disciplined warrior, Nixon trudged on in Wisconsin. On March 26, he got more encouraging news as the results of the latest Gallup poll were released. In a hypothetical three-way race between the president, Nixon, and George Wallace, Nixon led LBJ by two points, 41 to 39, with the Alabama governor receiving the final 14 percent. It was the first time in 15 months of national polling that Nixon was shown leading Johnson.[11]

Three days later, Nixon met with Governor Spiro T. Agnew from Maryland, previously a strong Rockefeller supporter. They got together at the apartment of Mary Gore Dean, the sister of Louise Gore, a prominent Republican in Maryland. Dean was entertaining some Republican women who wanted to meet Agnew.[12] The meeting was set up by John Sears and Bob Ellsworth, who thought it would be a good idea to have the two meet, especially after the way the Rockefeller camp had treated Agnew. Sears was in Alaska trying to convince Governor Walter Hickel to endorse Nixon. When he heard the news about Rockefeller, he knew this was a situation the Nixon team could exploit. Sears called Ellsworth in Washington and told him to meet with Governor Agnew as soon as possible and to set up a meeting between him and Nixon.[13] He would not have called the meeting with them if he knew that Rockefeller was not going to run. Agnew was quite upset that he was not notified of the change of heart by Rockefeller. As it turned out, Agnew was on the list to be notified, but his messenger failed to deliver the message. This omission had a lasting negative impact on him.[14]

The two-hour meeting with Nixon was a pleasant surprise for both. Nixon had never met Agnew and was skeptical given his earlier enthusiasm for Rockefeller. While the Maryland governor would not ultimately come out for Nixon, he indicated his perception of the former vice president had changed markedly for the better. Agnew commented, "I am not ready to announce my support of Mr. Nixon at this time. I have high regard for him." Nixon said he had a good meeting and "the Governor had constructive ideas." He went onto say that he was "not meeting with the governors for the purpose of twisting their arms, but rather for getting positions the party can take. The Governor and I met to discuss the issues, particularly the problems of the cities." Nixon had met with Governor Claude Kirk of Florida earlier in the day. He had plans to meet with two more governors the next week: John A. Volpe of Massachusetts and James A. Rhodes of Ohio.[15]

Much of the rest of the week, Nixon focused on a national radio address he was supposed to deliver on Saturday night, March 30. The speech focused on Vietnam and the last couple of months of intense fighting. It was in the context of a presidential election year during which there had been several unexpected political and military events. Meanwhile, Nixon edited several drafts. Speechwriters Whalen, Price, and Buchanan huddled with Nixon at his New York apartment for a final review. A few hours before Nixon was scheduled to tape the speech, he received a call from Frank Shakespeare. Shakespeare, who had been working on their television campaign, received a call from his old friends at CBS saying that President Johnson had asked for time on Sunday night for a major speech on the war. Of course, the networks consented, which threw a wrench into his Republican challenger's radio address scheduled for the same time. Nixon told his aides to postpone the address to take into account what LBJ had to say.[16]

Nixon had a scheduled event on Sunday afternoon in Milwaukee, two days before the Wisconsin primary. He flew back to New York that night. Nixon had Buchanan waiting for him in a limousine on the tarmac at LaGuardia. Buchanan was listening on the radio to Johnson's address in the limo as Nixon's plane made its final approach.[17] At the end of his speech, the president had made a startling announcement: "With America's sons in the fields far away, with America's future under challenge right at home, with our hopes and the world's hopes for peace in the balance every day, I do not believe that I should devote an hour or day of my time to any personal, partisan causes or to any duties other than the awesome duties of this office—the presidency of your country. Accordingly, I shall not seek, and I will not accept, the nomination of my party for another term as your president."[18]

When the plane landed, Buchanan wanted to get to Nixon before the press. He arrived as Nixon was unbuckling his seatbelt. Buchanan told him, "He's not running. Johnson's not running." After a brief back and forth, a stunned Nixon told the press, "This is the year of the dropouts. First, Romney, then Rockefeller, now Johnson." The substance of the radio address would be put on a near-permanent pause while Nixon reflected on what he should say about the war. Nixon told Buchanan he would not be making any speeches on the war until the political and military position of the Johnson administration became clearer. Johnson also offered a partial bombing pause with the hope of bringing North Vietnam to the negotiating table.[19]

The political fallout had significant ramifications for both parties. For the Democrats, the president who won a historic landslide four years earlier and was one of the most celebrated leaders of the Senate had decided not to run for re-election. It shocked almost everyone, including his vice president, who was not told until he was leaving for a trip to Mexico. Sure, the close call in New Hampshire got his attention, but he still had the enormous support of the delegates needed for the Democratic nomination. Whatever burnout Lyndon Johnson was feeling at the time could have been remedied by the announcement of Bobby Kennedy challenging him for the nomination. There was no love lost between the two, and it would have been perfectly reasonable for LBJ to be chomping at the bit for a contest with Kennedy. Johnson did not want RFK to take the nomination. He blamed him for his own loss of the nomination to JFK in 1960. For Eugene McCarthy, the decision opened up a greater possibility, but with the addition of Bobby Kennedy to the race, the anti-war vote among the Democrats was split. That left a political vacuum in the center of the Democratic party. Most likely, Hubert Humphrey would fill that opening. Humphrey was an old political pro in the party who had a good deal of respect from both its moderate and liberal factions. He had the potential to unite a badly divided party. Nixon even predicted this publicly when he asked for comments later that day. Nixon said, "I would be very much surprised if Vice President Humphrey did not become a candidate."[20]

On the Republican side, the story was different. Richard Nixon had prepared for the past year to run against Lyndon Johnson and had focused on defeating him. In the interest of party unity, he had also made it a central part of his campaign not to criticize any Republican challengers. Nelson Rockefeller continued to deny his candidacy despite indications he was gearing up for a battle with Nixon. Johnson's decision probably made little difference for Ronald Reagan. He had been highly critical of the president in both domestic and foreign policy. If Kennedy were the nominee, that would have been another story. Reagan would love to have that challenge. The different ideological spaces of the Republican party would still be present, with Rockefeller on the left, Nixon in the center, and Reagan on the right. The problem for both Rockefeller and Reagan was Nixon already had the support of the party's center and a good deal of the energized right. Besides, he was acceptable to most Republican liberals and, realistically, was the only one that could unite them.

Two days after Johnson's announcement, the results in the Wisconsin primary were predictable. Nixon won the Badger state with 80 percent of the vote. Reagan earned 11 percent, Stassen received 6 percent, and the final 3 percent split between Rockefeller and George Wallace. On the Democratic side, Eugene McCarthy was the predictable winner with nearly 57 percent, while LBJ pulled in 35 percent, and Kennedy found 6 percent as a write-in.[21]

After Nixon's win in the first two primaries and the unwillingness of either Rockefeller or Reagan to challenge him publicly, an assessment of the campaign strategy was in order. The candidate already had embraced a temporary moratorium on criticizing the Johnson administration's Vietnam policy to give the president some time to attempt a diplomatic breakthrough. He explained his position by saying, "This is no time to mix politics with Vietnam. Events would indicate that there are very delicate diplomatic negotiations in progress, and this is no time to stir the diplomatic soup."[22] For the next two weeks, the campaign slowed.

It did not mean that the Nixon team did nothing. In April, they concentrated on racking up commitments from state delegates. Over three hundred delegates would be chosen in the various state conventions during the month. Bob Ellsworth and Richard Kleindienst worked closely with the regional directors throughout this period. John Sears assisted Ellsworth in identifying problems that the team needed to address. Sears had more specific knowledge of the politics of the various congressional districts in all the states with April primaries. He had played a considerable role in this during the '66 congressional campaign when Nixon built up a lot of IOU's now needed in the delegate hunt.[23]

Meanwhile, rumblings continued among the Reagan and Rockefeller faithful that their respective candidates would splash into the race soon. At the National Press Club in Washington, Reagan said he did not think Nixon had a lock on the nomination but still would not commit to openly challenging him. The California governor said, "I think more people are legitimately concerned about the right choice."[24]

Two days later, Rockefeller hired Emmet John Hughes as his chief of staff. Hughes was currently working for *Newsweek* and had worked in the Eisenhower White House as a speechwriter. One of Rockefeller's closest aides said of Hughes' hiring, "It's impossible not to view this [hiring] as a restatement and re-emphasis of his availability.... [Hughes] will be helping him nationally."[25] A week earlier, the Nixon team learned Rockefeller had recruited William E. Miller to participate in talks about a possible presidential bid. Miller was a former member of the House of Representatives who had been Barry Goldwater's running mate in 1964. Miller had never been associated with the Rockefeller team and was a solid conservative. John Mitchell thought this was a significant indication of Rockefeller's intentions. Why else would he recruit a prominent conservative Republican from his state who had never openly supported him unless he was going to run?[26]

Politicking of all sorts stopped on Thursday night, April 4, as the country reeled from the death of civil rights leader Dr. Martin Luther King, Jr. Soon after King's assassination, riots erupted in some major cities across the country. The nation's capital was the hardest hit, and federal troops were called out to calm the city. All the nation's political leaders issued statements of regret and sympathy for the King family, and Richard Nixon was no exception.

Nixon was conflicted about whether or not he would attend the funeral. While Nixon had been on good terms with King during the 1950s, the relationship soured after the 1960 presidential contest. Nixon did not want to be perceived as grandstanding by going to the funeral, but he wanted to do something that showed his concern. He had been much closer to King's father and finally decided to go to Atlanta and pay a private visit to the widow the day before the funeral. Dwight Chapin was with Nixon when they went to the King house. Nixon went in to offer his condolences to Mrs. King. After returning, he told Chapin that he did not want the visit publicized and was not going to the funeral. The two went on to Key Biscayne to visit Bebe Rebozo. While they were there, Nixon changed his mind and told Dwight to get someone to meet them at the airport the next day in Atlanta to drive them to the funeral.[27]

Most of the major political candidates took some time off after the King assassination. Nixon had already indicated after the Johnson withdrawal that he was taking a temporary moratorium on criticizing the war. He now extended that to other public events to re-evaluate the political landscape in response to recent circumstances. He wanted to put together a coherent strategy whether his opponent turned out to be Kennedy, McCarthy, or Humphrey.

The day after the Wisconsin primary, the Nixon team received a memo from Pat Hillings, who was back in California and keeping a close eye on the Reagan campaign. Hillings was upbeat after conversing with George Murphy's people about the governor's intentions. Hillings assessed that the "consensus is that Reagan is surrounded by a bunch of amateurs and they really are not going all out to put him across to the degree that some of our people believe. The Murphy people say that the Senator is not pushing Reagan's candidacy and they apparently have no admiration for the Reagan staff."[28]

The day after the Hillings memo, Nixon sent Ronald Reagan a letter in which he wrote that he "appreciated your using your very enthusiastic supporters who understandably wanted to launch a major campaign in your behalf in those states." Nixon indicated he understood "the necessity of your maintaining your Favorite Son position in California."[29] Reagan wrote back, congratulating him on his wins in New Hampshire and Wisconsin, saying he was "especially happy to know that you understand the touchy situation I'm in at this time maintaining a neutral stand while running as California's favorite son." He concluded his letter expressing his wish "to have a united Republican Party behind our candidate in November."[30]

While Nixon was not explicitly aware of the White and Reed meeting with Reagan after Bobby Kennedy's announcement, he believed his California friend indeed was running. The day after the Reagan letter to Nixon was postmarked, there was a story in the *Los Angeles Times* about a closed-door meeting being held the next day by Clifton White to report his findings among the state delegations concerning presidential preferences. The article contained several quotes by Henry Salvatori, a Los Angeles oilman funding White on behalf of friends of Ronald Reagan. Salvatori, a significant contributor to Nixon in the past, was adamant about wanting Reagan as the Republican nominee and indicated he was not going "to send an army out now to shout down people who are supporting him." Salvatori speculated that if Kennedy were the Democratic nominee, Reagan "would do better against him than anyone else."[31]

The week before the White meeting, Reagan took off for the Easter vacation and went to Arizona to meet with Barry Goldwater. Reagan hoped to convince him to stay neutral in the Republican race. He was not successful with Goldwater, who was a strong Nixon supporter. The former Republican presidential nominee tried to convince Reagan to come out for Nixon instead. Goldwater remained an adamant Nixon supporter. In a letter sent to Tom Reed the week after the Reagan meeting, Goldwater wrote what he thought the California governor should do:

> Frankly, I think this statement [about supporting Nixon] should come out not much later than June 1 because as long as he seems to be a candidate in spite of his saying no, it will give the Rockefeller forces hope. If Ron should come out for Nixon in June it will pull the rug out from under the Rockefeller forces.... By coming out for Dick, Reagan and California could become real powers in the Republican Party.[32]

At a Sacramento news conference three days after the Clifton White meeting, Reagan admitted he might change his mind about a presidential run. Reagan probably was franker than he ever had been on the subject, acknowledging, "Naturally, I was interested in hearing that. I'm not going to run away and pretend it isn't happening. Obviously, I'm going to try and make an assessment.... The job seeks the man."[33]

Moratorium Over

After a short period of reassessment, Nixon ended his moratorium on campaigning focused on domestic policy and the upcoming May primaries in Indiana, Nebraska, and Oregon. Much of the domestic policy focus would be on soliciting input from governors, especially the Republican governors. He already had a number of initiatives to stress over the next few months but wanted additional advice from the leaders in these states. Before his eight-day western swing, Nixon met with the Association Society of Newspaper Editors (ASNE) in Washington and with Governor Romney in Michigan. There had been a great deal of preparation over the past two weeks getting ready for this question–and–answer session with several prominent newspaper editors from across the country. Nixon wanted to separate himself from other potential presidential candidates, especially Nelson Rockefeller, who had given a speech the day before to the editors offering typical big-government solutions to the nation's cities, costing 150 billion dollars over ten years.

Nixon, given the choice of a format, opted for a back and forth between the editors and himself to show he had a good grasp of the issues beyond Rockefeller's canned "presentations." In this session, Nixon observed his moratorium on war-related issues and defended Secretary of State Dean Rusk from his Democratic critics in calling for 8 billion dollars in budget cuts. Nixon was well-rested and easily handled questions, even mixing satirical asides with serious points. When asked about the recent presidential candidates entering and leaving the race, Nixon said he "was surprised when Romney got out, when Bobby Kennedy got in. And I was surprised when Rockefeller got out ... if he did?" In another witty remark about his assessment of the Democratic race, he quipped, "Well, McCarthy will have the intellectuals, Humphrey will have Lyndon. I guess Bobby will have the World Bank." The World Bank comment came after a campaign film from the Kennedy camp showing Bob McNamara, now head of the World Bank, praising Bobby's actions during the Cuban Missile Crisis.[34]

Nixon's performance drew praise from the editors and reporters covering the event. Jules Witcover from the Newhouse Paper group wrote, "The preparations were well worth the effort. Nixon was a smash success. Not only was he loaded with facts with which to turn back all questions; he conducted himself with a good-humored self-assured flare [sic] that awed the editors."[35]

Pat Buchanan, who was one of the aides along with Ray Price and Len Garment, wrote, "It was one of his finest performances.... We walked out elated, everyone on the staff, and the Boss, too knowing that we had won this one."[36] Goldwater was highly complimentary of Nixon's performance and its impact on his closest rival in 1964. He wrote that while "things are going well out here [in Arizona], I think Nixon made an ass out of Rocky at the Editor's meeting and while God had beaten him to this, a little refurbishing never hurts."[37]

Nixon went to Michigan to seek Governor Romney's opinions on the nation's urban problems and to mend any political fences with his former Republican rival. He got an earful from Romney. Nixon said that he would take Romney's thoughts under advisement and get back to him after meeting with many other governors. In Nevada, Nixon met with Governor Paul Laxalt. He got no commitments from Laxalt or the Nevada delegation. While he was in Reno, he met with Bob Finch. That meeting got the most press coverage because of the California/Reagan connection. Nixon said that he made no inquiries about the California delegation committed to Governor Reagan. Finch acknowledged that Nixon would not oppose Reagan in California and had no problem with the favorite son strategy. Finch was asked whether he thought Reagan would campaign actively in Oregon, where the California governor had some people working on the ground for the primary at the end of May. Finch thought Reagan had a lot of support in California's neighboring state and could easily get 35 percent of the vote.[38]

Nixon spent the next two days campaigning in Oregon. To a crowd of 7,500 at Oregon State University, he stressed the theme of fiscal responsibility when dealing with the nation's domestic problems. Nixon told the cheering crowd it was unfair to the poor to promise billions of dollars that are not available because it raised unrealistic expectations. He said the country must get its fiscal house in order before any large-scale federal aid could go to the cities.[39] Nixon continued this theme in a taped, nationwide radio address broadcast by CBS, where he stressed "black capitalism" as the appropriate remedy "to break the cycle of despondency." Nixon said that if elected, he would work to break this cycle by "providing technical assistance and local guarantees, by opening new capital sources, we can help Negroes to start new businesses in the ghetto and to expand existing one."[40]

The eight-day western swing culminated with stops in Idaho and South Dakota, where Nixon campaigned on behalf of George Hansen, who was challenging incumbent Senator Frank Church in November's election. At a news conference in Boise, Nixon sounded confident when he predicted that he "will do reasonably well in Idaho. At the convention, I will be glad to take my chances with the Idaho delegation." In South Dakota, a large crowd met him at the Aberdeen airport with several signs supporting McCarthy for president. Nixon met with Governor Niles A. Boe and later headlined a fundraiser at the Aberdeen Civic Center. He spoke to reporters before leaving, saying he was very positive on what his campaign had accomplished: "I feel that by the time we get to Miami, I will have a substantial block of delegates from the Western states."[41]

Enter HHH and Rockefeller

On April 27, to no one's surprise in the Nixon camp, Hubert Humphrey announced his candidacy to a capacity crowd of 1,700 in the Regency Ballroom at the Shoreham Hotel in Washington. The smiling Humphrey said he would not enter the remaining primaries and that he would take his campaign to the American people. He stressed that his run for the presidency would be based on the "politics of happiness, the politics of purpose, and the politics of joy. And that's the way it's going to be from here on out." Among those present for the announcement were Democratic members of Congress, George Meany of the AFL-CIO, and Clarence Mitchell of the NAACP.[42]

Three days later, Nelson Rockefeller finally decided to enter the presidential race. After saying for the past year and a half that he was not a candidate, Rockefeller subsequently changed his mind. Rockefeller knew he had a lot of fence-mending to do in the party to get rid of bad memories of 1964, when he refused to support or campaign for Barry Goldwater. He wanted to put that behind him and did not believe that the differences between him and others in the party could not be mended. At the end of the press conference on his entrance into the GOP race, Rockefeller contrasted 1968 with the contest four years earlier: "As I said, in '64 the discussion was more importantly related to ideological concepts and the application of those to the realities of problem-solving in our modern society. And I had some different views there on that subject. Today I don't think there is the same ideological conflict."[43]

Nixon watched Rockefeller's announcement from a Holiday Inn in Harrisburg, Pennsylvania, where he was consulting with Governor Raymond P. Shafer on solving domestic problems.[44] Nixon thought it would be more profitable to try to find appropriate solutions from those at the state and local levels instead of having the federal government dictate from Washington as it had for the past seven and a half years. Nixon welcomed Rockefeller to the race and thought it would be good for the Republican Party.

Rockefeller tried to project himself as a man of the people without entering any state primaries, hoping that convention delegates would see him as the biggest vote-getter among the candidates. Nixon's response turned things around: "Were I advising Governor Rockefeller, I would have advised him to enter the primary races to prove a point that he is trying to make—that he is popular with the people, I with the bosses.... Perhaps it would have been meaningful if he had announced earlier and entered the primaries."[45]

Nixon went on with the Indiana primary on May 7 with a campaign swing that included stops in Evansville, Fort Wayne, and Indianapolis. While in Fort Wayne, Nixon criticized the rhetoric revolving around the best way to end the war in Vietnam. His remarks were aimed at Kennedy and McCarthy without mentioning their names: "Put yourself in the position of the enemy. He is negotiating with Lyndon Johnson and Secretary Rusk. And then he reads in the papers that not a Senator, not a Congressman, not an editor but a potential President of the United States will give him a better deal than President Johnson is offering him.... The enemy will wait for the next man."[46]

The Indiana win was Nixon's third in a row. He ran unopposed and collected nearly half a million votes. Nixon exceeded the Indiana primary record he set eight years before by 70,000 votes. The real excitement was on the Democratic side with Bobby Kennedy winning over Governor Roger D. Branigin, the favorite son, and Eugene McCarthy. The Kennedy people hoped for 50 percent of the vote but only gathered 42 percent. Branigin got 31 percent while McCarthy collected 27 percent.[47]

On the day of the Indiana primary, Nixon appeared in Nebraska before enthusiastic crowds in Omaha, Kearney, and Lincoln. That state's primary was only a week away. Robert Semple wrote in the *New York Times* about the significance of who was listening and accompanying Nixon while in the Cornhusker State. Semple wrote, "What was significant today was not the candidate's words but the identity of those who listened to him and greeted him. They included both of Nebraska's Senators, Carl T. Curtis and Roman Hruska, who flew with him from Washington yesterday."[48] That was another example of the strong support accorded Nixon by the Republican hierarchy. He also expected the big turnout that gave him 62 percent of the popular vote in the 1960 presidential contest, the highest percentage of any state in that election.[49]

The weekend before the Indiana primary, Republicans received more good news in Gallup's most recent poll. Both Nixon and Rockefeller won hypothetical matchups against Kennedy, McCarthy, and Humphrey. Perhaps surprisingly, Hubert Humphrey did better than his Democratic cohorts against the Republicans, even though he had not formally announced his candidacy.[50]

Richard Nixon had another runaway primary win in Nebraska, collecting 70 percent of the Republican vote. Reagan won 22 percent while Rockefeller garnered only 5 percent. The Reagan campaign was happy to double their percentage from a week before in the Indiana primary. While Reagan's name was on the ballot, Rockefeller was not and entered as a write-in candidate. Neither Reagan nor Rockefeller actively campaigned in Nebraska, though the Reagan commentary film was shown several times in the week leading up to the primary election date. Nixon more than doubled the number of votes of the three Republican candidates. On the Democratic side, Bobby Kennedy won his second primary in a row over Eugene McCarthy by a 53–31 percent vote. Nixon said that his own Nebraska vote was "pretty good" and gave high compliments to the California governor and his "good showing, just about what we thought he'd do there and what we think that he will do in Oregon."[51]

No matter what his critics now said about Nixon being a loser, his record after the four major primaries demonstrated he was now 4–0 in primary victories. In each instance, he won over 70 percent of the vote. Not bad for a guy who they said could not win.

John Mitchell, designated campaign manager for pre-campaign activities, announced another couple of significant personnel moves out of the Nixon campaign's New York office. The announcement was not surprising given that Mitchell had worked for the past year gathering delegate support. Also, it was announced H.R. "Bob" Haldeman would become Nixon's chief of staff, joining the team at the end of the month when the candidate campaigned in Los Angeles.[52] Another move made a couple of weeks earlier was that Seattle lawyer and Nixon friend John Ehrlichman was joining the campaign in charge of the Republican convention. Ehrlichman, a friend of Haldeman, worked as an advance man during the 1960 campaign.[53]

On May 28, Nixon rolled into Oregon with a lot of momentum for his fifth primary, one for which the team had done a great deal of preparation. Nelson Rockefeller won Oregon's primary in 1964, and even though his name was not on the ballot, his people expected a double-digit write-in. Also, Oregon was a border state for Ronald Reagan, where his campaign would devote a lot of resources to try to double his 22 percent showing in Nebraska, demonstrating that he was a realistic alternative to Nixon.[54] While Reagan continued saying he was only a favorite son candidate, his campaign expenditures suggested otherwise. Tom Reed had been spending a great deal of time in Oregon since mid–March, purchasing fifty billboard spaces in the Portland and Salem areas and eight weeks of spots on the local NBC and CBS affiliates, "buying any time that is available." Additionally, the Reagan team ran an eight-page color advertisement in Sunday's newspapers before the Tuesday primary. At least 450,000 copies were printed.[55] It was all for a person who said that he was not running for president.

There were plenty of expectations and games going on among the Republican hopefuls. The Reagan team's media budget was meant to show there was an alternative to Nixon. While Reed would not publicly say this, they were hoping for a strong showing. After winning the Nebraska primary, Nixon said he fully expected the California governor to get 20 to 30 percent of the vote in Oregon.[56] Nixon's campaign manager in Oregon, Howell Appling, put Reagan's ceiling at 30 percent. Robert Hazen, head of the Reagan team in Oregon, talked about how the Nebraska primary results were building momentum for his candidate, which he said was "the greatest thing that has happened since we began. If he came in here even for two days, we would take this State by storm."[57]

The Rockefeller team played Oregon low key. Governor Tom McCall had been a strong supporter of Rocky in the past and said that he would write in for him this time. Another prominent Rockefeller backer, William Moshofsky, said he welcomed a strong Reagan showing because it might lead to an "open convention."[58] Neither Reagan nor Rockefeller campaigned in Oregon, but both depended on their surrogates for the primary.

Ten days before the primary, an NBC poll showed Richard Nixon with a strong lead. Nixon garnered 55 percent of the vote while Governor Reagan got 20, and Rockefeller came in with 16.[59] On Nixon's first day in Oregon, he was highly critical of how the administration at Columbia University handled its recent weeklong student revolt that closed the school. He declared this was part of a larger pattern of lawlessness and that universities must not allow anarchy and violence.[60]

Some of the Nixon team thought that he had been too harsh in his assessment of the campus revolt at Columbia. A poll conducted a week later in Oregon said otherwise. When asked if the protests "had been handled too harshly, too easily or just about right," two percent had said, "Too harshly," while 80 percent said, "Too easily." It was only a forty to one margin in favor of the Nixon position. In the same poll, participants were asked, "What did Oregon Republicans think should be done with students who seriously interrupt university activities—or use violence—to invade buildings?" Thirty-seven percent said they should be expelled while two percent said they "should be forgiven because they had good reason to protest." The remaining sixty-one percent thought the protestors should be turned over university disciplinary committees.[61]

A week earlier, the Nixon campaign issued a policy position paper on crime in America titled "Toward Freedom from Fear." It addressed the permissiveness in society and the lack of adequate law and order in the country and was highly critical of the Johnson administration's approach to crime, which treated poverty as the primary reason for the significant increases in crime over the past eight years. Nixon said that poverty as a cause of the rise in crime had been grossly exaggerated and that crime had little to do with poverty levels. He called for stronger legislation and blamed the Supreme Court's decisions in the *Miranda* and *Escobedo* cases of "seriously ham-stringing the peace forces." Both of these decisions of the Warren Court made it much easier for criminals to escape punishment with the application of broader procedural restraints by the police. Nixon claimed doubling the conviction rate would do more to eliminate crime than quadrupling funds for the "war on poverty." He concluded, "Crime creates crime—because crime rewards the criminal."[62]

Rockefeller and Ron Colluding?

Nelson Rockefeller had become a serious candidate for the presidency after spending the last month assembling a top-flight team to challenge Nixon. His strategy focused on an open convention and ignoring the primaries was extremely risky. Rockefeller would not come to campaign in Oregon like he did in 1964 but sent New York's Mayor John Lindsay to claim his candidate was "better equipped to deal with the problems of cities and make a better President." He got positive responses from mainly student crowds at the University of Oregon and Oregon State University. That was not what he got from Howell Appling. Nixon's Oregon campaign manager said that the Lindsay visit raised more questions than it answered about its intentions: "I think it's going to raise a lot of questions again about Rocky's coyness. If Mayor Lindsay cares enough to come—why don't we just vote for him?" If that was not enough, Robert B. Haven, Reagan's campaign manager for Oregon, had to fend off rumors that Rockefeller was giving the Reagan campaign half a million dollars to block Nixon.[63] The Nixon campaign team was being blamed for spreading untrue rumors about the discord. The truth was finally discovered in a confidential memo from William Watts, a Rockefeller aide, on a meeting with Governor

Rockefeller at his Pocantico Hills mansion the day after Lindsay campaigned for him. Watts accurately quoted what the governor said about the decision to send the New York mayor as a surrogate to Oregon: "I wouldn't have sent Lindsay to Oregon. He sounded as if he was campaigning for write-ins for himself."[64] So much for the Nixon rumor-mongering.

Rockefeller knew he could not defeat Nixon alone but needed Reagan's help to gain the Republican nomination. He had been openly courting the California governor for the past year, saying good things about Reagan and minimizing their policy differences. On *Issues and Answers* nine days before the Oregon primary, he addressed these issues: "If you get a ticket that reflects both points of view in the Party, then it gives it great strength," noting every party had a broad spectrum of thinking, but the majority was in the center.[65]

A week and a half earlier, Rockefeller called Nixon a "legislator" and a pure executive who makes crucial decisions and not just criticizes others. At a friendly crowd at the University of Minnesota in one of the most progressive states in the country, Rockefeller called for more public-private enterprises to deal with the problematic issues, a theme that he had been extolling his whole career. Indeed, Rockefeller had more financial resources at his disposal than any other governor in the country, personal and otherwise. He mentioned organizations that utilized municipal bonds to include state university dormitories and the Urban Development Corporation as examples of these public-private partnerships. He said, "We're in a new period where government alone cannot meet these problems. What we have to do is create a framework where government and business can work together to solve problems."[66] What the crowd at the Minnesota event did not know was that the person who put together the exact type of framework was John Mitchell, Nixon's law partner, and the de facto campaign manager.

Rockefeller then went south to Georgia, South Carolina, and Louisiana. In Atlanta, he attacked Bobby Kennedy for tailoring his message to his audiences. Rockefeller prided himself on saying the same thing no matter what part of the country he was campaigning. In Atlanta, he talked of his strong commitment to civil rights to a friendly crowd of 1,000 at Emory University, and he continued his praise of Reagan and criticism of Kennedy. While he didn't mention Nixon's name, he was critical of Nixon's comments on poverty's role in the rising crime rate. After that, Rockefeller flew to South Carolina to meet with delegates who were firmly for Nixon and Reagan.[67]

The next big stop for Rockefeller was in New Orleans to meet with Louisiana delegates. What made the biggest news there was not trying to turn Louisiana delegates but an impromptu meeting with Ronald Reagan. Rockefeller's party did not get to their hotel until around midnight. After that, the New York governor summoned his aides to find some of Reagan's people. They found Lyn Nofziger in the bar talking to the traveling press. Rocky told Nofziger he wanted to meet with Reagan for a brief chat. Nofziger put him off and said that they would try to work something out the next day. While Reagan was finishing breakfast in his suite at the hotel, there was a knock on the door. Rockefeller barged in and told the California governor that they were not that far apart ideologically and should join forces. The eight-minute meeting irritated Reagan. Afterward, Rockefeller called a press conference and talked about the nice meeting that he had held with the governor and how their philosophical differences were minor. The Nixon campaign was notified about the meeting the next day by a phone call to Rose Mary Woods from Robert Finch. Finch had the details from Bill Clark, Reagan's administrative assistant.[68]

Art Buchwald wrote a satirical column on the New Orleans meeting titled "Reagan's Rocky Road to Peace and Presidency." There was even a drawing of salt and pepper shakers with the heads of the two candidates. The piece ended with Rockefeller denying he was making a deal with Reagan and added pointers about his movie career. Buchwald wrote:

> "Ronnie, how can you say such a thing. Happy and I are your biggest fans. We have seen 'King's Row' six times on television. We still run 'Knute Rockne' after dinner every night. But I guess 'Brother Rat' is our favorite. I'm not here to make a deal with you.' "Then why did you come?" "You won't believe this Ronnie but Happy asked me to come up here and get your autograph."[69]

The comparisons were beginning to irritate the Reagan team. A week and a half earlier, the California governor issued a statement aggressively denying they were making any "deal" with Rockefeller. This statement was made at the Western Governors Conference in Honolulu, Hawaii. Carl Greenburg of the *Los Angeles Times*, who was traveling on the Reagan plane to the conference, said a written statement was necessary to assure nervous Pro-Reagan conservatives he wasn't "about to become the political bedfellow of the liberal New York governor."[70] When Reagan was in New Orleans, he certainly sounded like a presidential candidate by blasting the Johnson Administration's handling of the Paris peace talks on the war in Vietnam. He argued, "[The United States] should be willing to make some threats of positive action.... We are going to reassess fighting the war on South Vietnam soil and we may give them [North Vietnam] a taste of war." At Tulane University, Reagan echoed what Nixon was saying about the Columbia University protests and criticized "storm trooper tactics by [students and] radical faculty ... for staging areas for revolt and revolution."[71]

Ronald Reagan left Louisiana for North Carolina, Florida, Illinois, and Ohio, giving persuasive speeches about national defense in his fund-raising/non-candidacy tour before the Oregon primary. It was a significant turning point for the Reagan campaign even though the candidate still maintained he was not running for president. Tom Reed wrote about this particular period nearly half a century later: "RR, his communications director, security aide, tour managers, and policy staff joined 40 members of the press corps aboard a chartered 727 jet. There could be no doubt we were seriously pursuing the presidency."[72] If only they would acknowledge it to the rest of the country.

Two days before the Oregon primary, Reagan appeared on *Meet the Press* to deny he was running for president. When asked about having Governor Rockefeller as a running mate on his ticket, Reagan acted confused and denied this vehemently. In his attempt to explain why he was traveling all over the country if he wasn't running for office, he replied, "Well, I don't have a ticket, and so I couldn't be choosing anybody, and I don't know exactly which way you meant that. But if you are speaking about the rumors around that there has been some kind of a deal for me to take second spot on the ticket, there is no such deal, no one has suggested such a thing, and I have no intention of accepting it if anyone should."[73]

Back to Oregon

Collusion or not, back in Oregon where there was a real primary, Nixon campaigned with stops in Portland, Medford, Hillsboro, Pendleton, and McMinnville.[74] It was a state he had won in 1960. It was also the last time that he had the opportunity to show his electoral strength in a primary state. Nixon knew he was well ahead but was taking no risks, knowing his two primary opponents also wanted to make statements here even though they were not campaigning in person. While in Portland, Nixon was feeling good about his race and had already started thinking about his vice presidential pick. He listed five men, all from states with favorite-son delegations. Four of the men Nixon listed were no surprise, but the fifth one was. The initial four were Ronald Reagan (California), Charles Percy (Illinois), James Rhodes (Ohio), and Raymond Shafer (Pennsylvania). The fifth one was Governor Spiro Agnew from Maryland. Nixon had recently met him in March. The announcement of the proposed vice presidential picks warranted a front-page story by David Broder in the *Washington Post*, whose readers were in Agnew's backyard.[75] Nixon got more good news while campaigning in Oregon from the Tennessee delegation headed by Howard H. Baker, Jr. The Tennessee senator announced that he would deliver the state's 28 delegates to the Republican National Convention.[76]

The Sunday night before Tuesday's primary, Nixon held a telethon in Portland where he took questions telephoned live into the television station. The statewide broadcast lasted 90 minutes and proved a big success. The purpose of this was to have Nixon surrounded by the press with a panel of listeners taking questions from the audience. It highlighted his near-encyclopedic knowledge of political issues.[77] The format was based on "The Man in the Arena" concept that Theodore Roosevelt spoke about in 1910. In this famous speech, Roosevelt asserted that the man who should be credited is the man in the arena who "strives valiantly" but comes up short time and again only to keep fighting no matter the odds.[78] Nixon had patterned his campaign and political biography after that model.

The telethon was hosted by Charles W. "Bud" Wilkinson, the incredibly successful University of Oklahoma college football coach who had retired in 1963. Nixon met him when he was vice president at one of the American Football Coaches Association's national meetings. His introduction to politics occurred a year after his retirement. He ran for United States Senator in the state of Oklahoma as a Republican, where he lost a very close race to Fred Harris in the abysmal year for the Republicans. Nixon had campaigned for him in the last week of that race in 1964. After that race, the two stayed in contact.[79] Wilkinson was considered the greatest living college football coach by his colleagues.[80] During the telethon, he read a letter from Governor McCall, a Rockefeller supporter, who praised Nixon and pledged his support for the winner of the Oregon primary.[81]

Richard Nixon won his fifth consecutive primary by garnering over 73 percent of the vote in Oregon. Reagan got 22 percent with Rockefeller trailing badly with 4 percent. Both Reagan and Rockefeller tried to put their best spin on the results, but they were disappointed.[82] Eugene McCarthy stunned Robert Kennedy in the Democratic primary by a six-point margin, 43 to 37. Kennedy had campaigned hard in the state and spent over half a million dollars on his media campaign.[83] Nixon sounded confident of winning the Republican nomination when he said, "The chances of my now being derailed are pretty much eliminated." The victorious candidate said he expected "some phone calls tonight, some from Republicans who believe 'Now is the time to get on the train before it leaves the station.' This big win will help in making some of the fence-sitters move over."[84]

Ronald Reagan acted as if he did somewhat better than anticipated, saying that his 22 percent was "quite a bit better than the polls indicated."[85] That did not reflect the reality of his loss. Nixon's campaign manager in Oregon thought the California governor would get at least 30 percent. Tom Reed on the Reagan team believed they could climb into the forties and point to that momentum when visiting state delegations over the next two months. Reed wrote of the disappointment of that election night that when the results came in: "We turned out the lights, headed for the elevators, and drove to our homes. The stale chips and champagne were left for the janitor."[86]

Is the Republican Race Over?

Richard Nixon left Oregon looking like a winner, having won handily in his fifth straight primary. In his suite in the Benson Hotel in Portland, while watching the primary returns, Nixon said that he had "some of the same sense of satisfaction that I had on election night in 1966. It was far from over, but things were falling into place."[87] After the primary, Nixon was quite reflective about where his campaign had been and where it was headed in an interview with Robert B. Semple, Jr., of the *New York Times*: "We got rid of three things by going down the primary route road. We got rid of the idea that Nixon is bad on television and the idea that Nixon can't get along with the press. And I hope to God we laid to rest the notion that Nixon is a loser."[88]

Now he needed to continue to lock down delegates in the non-primary states where most of the votes would be. After a trip to Phoenix to meet with Goldwater and the Arizona delegation, whose state was solidly behind him, Nixon headed south, where he had spent a great deal of time in the past two years and had strong support. It was also a part of the country where Ronald Reagan had the most potential to grow his "noncandidacy."

The first stop was in Dallas, where John Tower was the favorite son candidate. Peter O'Donnell was the state party chairman. Dallas also had the most delegates among the southern and border states. While Tower and O'Donnell had not formally endorsed Nixon, they were strongly leaning toward his corner. After the results in the Oregon primary, Tower said, "The outcome of these primaries indicates Americans are attracted to a candidate with the experience.... It would seem to me very unlikely that any sort of concerted stop-Nixon movement will develop." O'Donnell chimed in, stating, "Oregon's primary victory established Nixon as the frontrunner." Nixon headlined a $150 a plate dinner in Dallas, where more than 1,000 persons attended the sold-out event. It was now becoming clear that the former vice president was riding a strong wave of momentum.[89]

The next day Nixon flew to Atlanta to meet with the southern leaders. Three of the southern state party chairmen had been working together since the beginning of the year to try to get the region behind one candidate, which would give them more leverage in the convention. They were Harry Dent of South Carolina, Clarke Reed of Mississippi, and William "Bill" Murfin of Florida. The group called themselves the "Greenville Group" for the name of the city in Mississippi where Reed lived and in which the three met on several occasions in early 1968. They devised a plan that invited the three major Republican candidates to New Orleans in late May to meet with the chairman of the 12-state region. The region represented 334 convention delegates, one more than the half needed to get the nomination. Reagan and Rockefeller had met with the group earlier while Nixon campaigned in Oregon. Reagan made strong in-roads with the delegates, while the New Yorker nearly struck out.[90]

It was a very productive two-day meeting for Nixon. The de facto leader of the southern delegation was Strom Thurmond, whom Nixon had been courting since his defection from the Democratic Party in 1964. However, George Wallace had his greatest strength in this region. Nixon made no bones about what he was doing there. Nixon was openly looking for their support and counting delegates. It was paramount that he nail down the support of the South Carolina senator. Thurmond had run as a third-party candidate for president in 1948 on a segregationist and states' rights platform. Thurmond returned to the Democratic Party after this campaign. He changed his party preference in 1964 to back Goldwater. When Nixon campaigned in South Carolina in 1966, he made it clear that he would not campaign for a Bircher or a segregationist. While Nixon's positions on civil rights were different than Thurmond's, they had similar views on national security and the rising crime rate. There was one other issue the South Carolina senator was most concerned about that directly affected his state: national defense. Thurmond was also concerned with textile imports that were hurting South Carolina's position in the industry. Nixon made it clear that he would enforce the law as it applied to integration but would take into account the views of each state affected. If he could get Thurmond on his side, it would block any attempt Reagan made in the South.[91] Nixon later wrote about his meetings with Thurmond and their effect on the Republican race, acknowledging that he had been consulting privately with the South Carolinian for the past several months.[92]

Nixon left Atlanta with an even better feeling than when he came. Four of the state's party chairmen openly endorsed him: Oklahoma, Tennessee, North Carolina, and Virginia.[93] The leader of Georgia's delegation, G. Paul Jones, who had been openly flirting with endorsing Reagan, changed his mind, saying, "For those who have doubts that this man could lead us to the White House, certainly, this man has laid those doubts to rest."[94] As if that was not enough, William Murfin beat back a motion by Florida Governor Claude Kirk to control his delegation, making himself the favorite son candidate. Kirk, while friendly to Nixon, was a Rockefeller supporter. After the political battle was over with the governor, Murfin said that he thought Nixon had the Republican nomination "wrapped up."[95]

After the successful Atlanta meeting, Nixon flew to Key Biscayne for a few days of relaxation and to sort out where the campaign should be going for the next two months heading into the Republican convention. Before his vacation, there was an important strategy meeting led by John Mitchell during the first week of June. Mitchell had surmised that at least 300 of the southern state's delegates were in Nixon's pocket and that he had virtually sewn up the Republican nomination. Instead of letting up, they would start the general election early. Nixon would remain in the public eye but focus on several competitive battleground states before the convention. He would not be talking about Rockefeller or Reagan but only about the election ahead.[96] There was a California primary on Tuesday, but Nixon would not be competing, leaving it to Ronald Reagan.

California Shocker

Coming out of the Oregon primary, a good many political professionals envisioned a general election campaign between Nixon and Humphrey along with the third-party challenge from George Wallace. Two months ago, Vice President Humphrey thought that he would be campaigning with Lyndon Johnson as number two on the ticket. A lot had changed rather quickly. Eugene McCarthy had initially challenged Johnson in New Hampshire before the president decided to drop out of the race. McCarthy's campaign focused primarily on opposition to the war. No other Democrat was running against the incumbent president until McCarthy did reasonably well in the nation's first primary. After that, Bobby Kennedy joined the race, dividing the party's liberals, Both Kennedy and McCarthy had been approached the year before by prominent liberals in the party to challenge; only McCarthy chose to do so while saying that he did not want to divide the party. Then, seeing blood in the water, the New York senator decided to jump in the race. Humphrey had a great deal of support in convention delegates inclined to support Johnson that he inherited when the president pulled out. He did not run in the California primary or any in other, for that matter. Kennedy banked on name recognition and wealth to make him a winner over Humphrey or McCarthy. Oregon changed that. Kennedy would have to win big in California, where all the delegates were bound by the primary winner. He would still have a big uphill climb to compete with Humphrey for the nomination. On the other hand, McCarthy hoped that a California win would provide him the national stage he needed to show that he was a bona fide contender rather than just a spoiler. Nixon and Rockefeller sat on the sidelines, expecting the Golden State's favorite son candidate to win.

There was only a week for McCarthy and Kennedy to slug it out for an opportunity to challenge Humphrey for the nomination. The California loser either would drop out of the race or be a protest candidate. Both McCarthy and Kennedy spent the week crisscrossing the state and even debated each other on the Saturday night before the primary. Late-night returns from Los Angeles County gave the victory to Kennedy by a 46 to 42 percent margin. As he watched the returns from his suite in the Ambassador Hotel, Kennedy boasted he would "chase Hubert's ass all over the country" to win the Democratic nomination.[97] His competitive response showed a different Kennedy from the one depicted by his unity comments earlier in the year when explaining why he was not running for president. Kennedy came down from his suite and gave a gracious speech about pulling the country together and giving his "thanks to all of you, and it's on to Chicago, let's win there."[98] Ironically, these were the last words that he would say about this campaign. Sirhan Sirhan, a Palestinian immigrant, shot Kennedy as he was exiting the kitchen, an exit his security detail had cautioned him against taking. He was rushed to a hospital where, after three hours of surgery, Kennedy died early on Thursday morning.[99]

Richard Nixon was sleeping in his apartment in New York when Pat Buchanan, who had been watching the results on television, phoned with the news.[100] The country had lost another Kennedy. The body of the younger brother of the former president was flown across the country to New York and then placed on a train to Washington to be buried alongside his brother in Arlington Cemetery. All the presidential candidates declared a moratorium for at least the next two weeks. It was a shocking ending to the past ten tumultuous weeks in the United States. In a period of fewer than three months, an incumbent president had decided not to run, a major civil rights leader was murdered igniting riots in several major cities, and Robert Kennedy was assassinated. A nearly broken country needed a break.

11

Tonight, I See a Child

Richard Nixon was well on his way to one of the greatest comebacks in political history. His campaign manager had assured Nixon he had enough first ballots to secure the nomination. He knew that he was ahead, but the clock was still running, and the other two Republican candidates were still in the game. Nixon knew he was not yet across the finish line. Nelson Rockefeller, meanwhile, budgeted five to six million dollars of advertising to big-city newspapers, explaining how he was the only Republican who could win in November. While Nixon ran well in the rural areas and suburbs, only Rockefeller was winning in the cities, per his strategy. Over the next two months, he pointed to polls providing evidence of this difference.[1] On the other hand, Ronald Reagan still would not admit being a real candidate, even though Clif White was lining up speaking engagements among the numerous "uncommitted" state delegations. No matter what Reagan said about his availability as a candidate or about Rockefeller as his vice president, it was becoming more evident that the two campaigns were cooperating.

Several seasoned political observers in and out of the Republican Party predicted an inevitable Nixon nomination. On the day of the California primary, chairman of the House Republican Conference Melvin R. "Mel" Laird urged Nelson Rockefeller to throw in the towel and avoid dividing the party. Laird, the most knowledgeable Republican on military matters, was close to the New York governor. He believed the only chance Rockefeller had was not to appear divisive, and the only way he could win without being divisive was for Nixon to stub his toe. Laird did not think Nixon was going to do that.[2] A week later, one of the favorite son governors who had been an enthusiastic backer of Rockefeller was completely rethinking his position and that of his state delegation. Governor Agnew of Maryland held a news conference to say as much. Reporters who witnessed the news conference knew he was favoring Nixon.[3]

Before the critical Saturday and Sunday strategy meetings, the Nixon family celebrated Tricia's graduation on Friday, June 14, from Finch College. It was a happy day for the Nixons. The former vice president spoke for thirty minutes at the commencement while Pat was presented with an honorary Doctor of Laws degree from the prestigious women's college. Roland R. DeMarco, the college's president, proclaimed her as the "very personification of highest ideals of womanhood."[4]

Mitchell and Haldeman Head June Strategy Meeting

John Mitchell led the two-day closed meetings of 125 prominent Nixon campaign supporters. Although Nixon was not present at these meetings, he spoke to the group by phone. The purpose was devising a strategy for the next seven weeks to secure the Republican nomination. Mitchell, confident of enough first-ballot votes to win, structured the game plan. Nixon would ignore Rockefeller's criticisms because Mitchell felt that if the New Yorker wanted a vigorous debate, he should have entered the primaries. Nixon already had said as much earlier in the campaign. John Mitchell echoed Nixon:

> [Nixon] would not engage in an exchange of charge and countercharge with Rockefeller or in any of the other tactics of the old politics of divisiveness. [It was not reasonable] to ask Nixon supporters to bear the additional cost of matching the Rockefeller campaign. [He pointed out that Nixon nearly begged Rockefeller to get in the primaries but the governor] chose to wait until the primaries were past and then to take the Madison Avenue route. Our information is that some $5 million is budgeted for his post-primaries advertising campaign.[5]

These meetings solidified an initial strategy with a few modifications that had been laid out a year earlier in a Bob Haldeman memo sent to Nixon before he formally joined the campaign. It built upon what Haldeman perceived as mistakes in earlier Nixon campaigns. He understood what it took to mass-market a product and bring it to fruition. Haldeman explained to Teddy White: "Nixon gets irritated by petty annoyances.... He has no time for small talk, or the ordinary kind of bull when sitting down together."[6]

These procedures were detailed in over 30 pages of handwritten notes Bob Haldeman recorded during the sessions. Haldeman, an extremely organized individual, put his managerial fingerprints all over this campaign. He was going to handle the candidate while Mitchell was in charge of the political campaign. His meticulous approach was designed to achieve optimum results. It centered on removing many duplicated tasks that might foster campaign anarchy and the defeat of his candidate. Accordingly, Nixon would visit only seven or eight states before the convention and during the general election, concentrating on these states that would decide the presidency. Haldeman embraced a vertical hierarchy, a chain of command, a strict division of labor, and accountability for all within the organization. Everyone must know his place. Yes, Max Weber, who was considered the "father of bureaucracy," would be proud of what he intended for the Nixon campaign. Haldeman's notes read that he felt Nixon should concentrate on the content of his speeches and statements over the next five months and not concern himself with campaign details and political operations unless necessary. Haldeman wanted the candidate's time to focus on speech preparation, personal appearances, and the like. Full campaign details were left to his managers:

> Appointments and phone calls—Chapin,
> Press statements, queries, meetings—Klein,
> Schedule requests, appearances—Whitaker,
> Political, organizational information or decisions—Mitchell,
> Issue positions or statements—Buchanan/Price,
> Finance contacts or action—Stans,
> Personal matters, security—Rose Woods, [and]
> Citizens—all facets—Rhyne/Evans.[7]

Three days later, Senator Mark Hatfield of Oregon talked with reporters on what had transpired at these crucial meetings. After summarizing some of Haldeman's major points, Hatfield acknowledged the war in Vietnam was the overriding issue and one that only Nixon as president could successfully resolve. Hatfield said that the overwhelming victory in Oregon's state primary was so convincing Nixon did not need to seek additional state delegates because of his strong position. Therefore, Nixon should focus on the seven or eight large industrial states where Democrats and Independents were vital in the general election.[8]

Rocky Hits Hard

While Nixon was laying low, Nelson Rockefeller made the most noise. He was in Reagan's backyard in Los Angeles in the middle of June as a guest of tire mogul Leonard Firestone. Several California delegates attended the cocktail party. While Firestone was committed to Reagan, he thought the delegates were "very impressed" with Rockefeller, and "if it got down to the wire and he looked like a winner, some of these men would vote for him." Henry Salvatori was also at the party and liked Rockefeller's views on the economy. But thinking on issues like Vietnam and civil disorders, "he didn't do too well." Salvatori was one of the principal backers of the Reagan campaign, but if Reagan released the California delegation, he would back Nixon.[9]

Rockefeller was well represented by several aides at the Republican Governors Conference in Tulsa, Oklahoma. He did not attend, nor did Nixon. Only Governor Reagan was there, though Bob Ellsworth and Dick Kleindienst represented Nixon. What the Rockefeller aides were seeking was the support of the favorite son governors and their delegations. The only governor who committed to him was Raymond Shafer from Pennsylvania, who earlier vowed support for his New York counterpart. Other governors, like Rhodes of Ohio, Romney of Michigan, and Love of Colorado, would not budge. Spiro Agnew was highly critical of Rockefeller, said he was "puzzled by his lack of views," and said that Nixon's stand on racial matters and black capitalism addressed black social and economic problems. Agnew said he saw the tremendous movement toward Nixon after the King assassination and the subsequent riots. Although not yet formally endorsing Nixon, Agnew certainly was headed in that direction, hinting to the Maryland GOP he might drop his favorite son status and open the delegates up to Nixon.[10] Haldeman's notes on June 16 indicated Agnew would indeed endorse Nixon after the Maryland convention and wanted to meet with Nixon soon after that.[11]

Stephen Shadegg wrote about a midnight conversation with one of Rockefeller's top aides at the Tulsa conference who admitted that it was all over, and Nixon was a sure winner. Shadegg pressed him on why his candidate would spend that money and time criticizing Nixon when he knew Nixon would win. The aide told Shadegg, "It's just his thing. He has to do it.... He never really wanted to get into it.... It's too bad that the Republicans will never nominate him."[12]

Before flying to Chicago to dine and meet with the editors of the *Chicago Tribune* and the *Chicago Sun-Times*, Nixon met with Spiro Agnew for two hours at his apartment in New York. The meeting had been arranged by Nixon aides at the Tulsa Governors Conference. Much of their conversation dealt with the growing civil disorder and what should be done about it.[13] The two candidates just missed each other while in Chicago when Governor Rockefeller met with the editors for lunch and afterward spoke at a downtown rally at the intersection of Michigan and State streets in the heart of the business district. There he teed off on Nixon by name, criticizing his stance on Vietnam, arguing "blind and headlong pursuit of this kind of victory could cost even more than 25,000 more lives."[14] Rockefeller got personal as he called out the former vice president: "[As head of] the leadership that failed eight years ago…. He carried Illinois until he got to Chicago, and then he lost the state. He carried Pennsylvania until he got to Philadelphia, and then he lost the state. He carried New York until he got to New York City, and then he lost the state."[15] Later in the speech, when someone in the crowd yelled out, "Nixon's the one," Rockefeller quickly responded, "That's right, he's the one who lost it for us in '60."[16]

On *Meet the Press*, the New York governor called George Wallace a "racist." He tried to tie him to the Nixon campaign based on a comment that Bo Callaway, Nixon's southern campaign coordinator, made in Jackson, Mississippi, saying that Wallace should be a Republican.[17] The Rockefeller campaign was alerted to this by Newt Gingrich, a graduate student at Tulane University and their southern regional director.[18] Richard Nixon refused to be duped by the claims of Wallace's support. In an airport interview in New York, he responded: "What he was trying to say was that people who want a change in the United States should not waste their vote on a third-party candidate. I believe that. I believe a vote for Wallace on the right or, shall I say a peace candidate on the left, is a wasted move."[19]

Despite his criticisms, Rockefeller was not making much headway. Spiro Agnew and Mark Hatfield both had all but endorsed Nixon by the end of June. On the first day of July, John Tower dropped his favorite son status and gave Nixon most of his state's 56 delegates. Tower said, "Dick Nixon already has about fifty delegates more than the six hundred sixty-seven he needs for the nomination. He's already over the top, and this is cream on the cake."[20]

More Politics as Usual?

In the last week of June, the chief justice of the Supreme Court, Earl Warren, announced he would be retiring at the end of his term in September. Warren had enjoyed a long career and, after some soul-searching, thought it a good time to retire. Some Republicans thought otherwise, particularly given the president not running for re-election would have a chance to appoint a new chief justice during the heat of a presidential campaign. Ronald Reagan was out front with his criticism of his fellow Californian, saying that Warren was playing "dirty pool" and did not trust the American political system.[21] It was also well known that Warren had long ago left his Republican roots and did not have a lot of good things to say about Richard Nixon. Many speculated Warren knew Nixon had an excellent chance of winning the presidency and did not want him to choose his successor, especially given Nixon's criticisms of the court's handling of criminal procedure questions. Much of Warren's animosity went back to the 1952 Republican Convention when Nixon endorsed Eisenhower rather than the then California governor running as the favorite son presidential candidate. Warren had been on the ticket as Tom Dewey's vice presidential candidate four years earlier in 1948.

Most Republicans were waiting for Lyndon Johnson to announce his choice before making any public comments. It did not take long, for two days later, the president announced his choice for chief justice by picking one of the current members of the court who was also a close friend to LBJ for over thirty years: Abe Fortas. If he moved up to chief justice, then his associate justice position would be open. That gave not one but two new picks on the court in a presidential election year. Johnson chose Texas long-time friend Homer Thornberry, who served on the U.S. Court of Appeals. Thornberry took over Johnson's House seat when LBJ went to the Senate in 1948 before becoming a federal judge. Over half of the Republicans in the Senate announced they would oppose the nomination by filibuster if necessary. Senate Minority Leader Everett Dirksen thought otherwise, saying that Fortas was "a very able lawyer," and Thornberry was "a very solid citizen."[22] On the other hand, Dirksen's son-in-law Howard Baker was dead set against these two choices. Baker contacted Tom Evans and wanted to know how Nixon thought it would be best to proceed. The Tennessee senator said there were swirling Washington rumors that if these two nominees went through, Hugo Black and William Douglas would follow suit and retire from the court. The top new choices would be Abe Goldberg, who had earlier served on the court and now was Johnson's man in the United Nations, and Thomas Kuchel, the Republican California senator who had lost earlier in the year in a primary fight to Max Rafferty. Kuchel was another Californian politician who had mixed and sometimes bad relations with Nixon.[23]

Pat Buchanan talked to Bill Rogers, Eisenhower's second attorney general and an old friend of Nixon, about what their response should be. Rogers told Buchanan that Nixon should stay out of it and let the Senate decide. There was also the issue of Fortas being Jewish. If Nixon were seen leading the fight, he would be perceived as anti–Semitic. Nixon agreed that he should not interfere overtly but still had his doubts. The question for Nixon was what to tell Baker on the subject. There were risks with any response. If the two choices went through and it looked like Nixon was leading the fight against them and lost, then it could hurt the election. If they did nothing, they risked solidifying the liberal wing of the court for another decade or so.[24] John Tower's office called Martin Anderson the next day and asked Nixon to get Dirksen to back off Fortas and Thornberry. Anderson contacted Buchanan, who relayed the message to Nixon, adding that Thornberry was ultra-liberal and had a 16 percent ACU (American Conservative Union) rating. Buchanan was also recommending passing this information to their southern friends to see what they would make of it.[25] He next drafted a statement that would oppose Fortas and put Nixon right in the heart of this fight, basically urging the Senate to withhold confirmation hearings until after the election.[26]

Nixon wanted to be apprised of any change in political winds around the Fortas and Thornberry nominations. The Senate would take up the matter after the July 4 holidays. Even though both nominees had southern roots, there would be a lot of people in that part of the country who would oppose them being on the court.

A Month Before the Convention

Back on the Republican nomination trail, Governor James Rhodes of Ohio said that he would keep his favorite son status and would not endorse Nixon at the July

Midwest Governors Conference. There had been a great deal of speculation as to whether the Ohio governor would follow John Tower's endorsement of the former vice president.[27] While Rhodes was ideologically closer to Rockefeller, he was on reasonably good terms with Nixon. One wonders if he was not waiting for the right deal for him and his state's delegation. Rhodes suggested Nixon pick John Lindsay as his vice presidential candidate. The Ohio governor did not believe that Rockefeller had any chance of overtaking Nixon with Lindsey as his running mate.[28]

Rockefeller was campaigning in Oregon right before the July 4 holiday weekend. While there, a meeting was arranged by Emmet Hughes to go down to Los Angeles to meet with Ronald Reagan on behalf of the New York governor. Rockefeller knew he needed Reagan's help to stop Nixon from clinching a first-ballot nomination. The meeting lasted an hour and a half, and absent a deal, Hughes got Reagan's assurances that he "was in the race for keeps."[29]

Soon after the Hughes/Reagan meeting, Tom Reed and Clif White met with the California governor about his plans for the Republican convention, then only a month away. After Reagan indicated he was still firmly in, they discussed vice presidential possibilities. Ohio Governor Rhodes would be offered the number two spot on the ticket, most likely at the Cincinnati Governors Conference. Reed said the two governors had become close friends over the past two years, and Ohio's delegates would be pivotal to any Reagan nomination and a must for a Republican to win in 1968.[30]

While the secret meeting between Reagan and a Rockefeller surrogate was not widely reported, there was a lot of speculation that Reagan would be announcing his candidacy for president at any time. It would have been easy for the California governor just to come out and say it, but that was not how it happened. The announcement was made known by a message sent from Reagan to Henry A. Bubb of Topeka, Kansas, head of the Citizens for Reagan National Information Center. Bubb told Reagan that he would have to let his name be placed in nomination, and when it was, some delegates from other states would openly come out for him. Clif White knew that his candidate had a good deal of support from the Alabama delegation, which, as the states went in alphabetical order, would be the first to announce their votes at the convention. The Alabama delegates, however, were split between Reagan and Nixon. White believed that he could get the Alabama chairman to yield to California for the first state on the roll call. That would place Reagan's name in nomination followed by Alabama, providing the California governor with about 100 delegates and signaling other southern states that Reagan was in this race to win. With all of that momentum, much of Nixon's support would switch to Reagan. Reagan assured Bubb that he was not making any Shermanesque (referring to a prominent Union general who adamantly said that he was not a candidate for president and would not serve if elected) comment about accepting the nomination. Bubb notified Reagan supporters all over the country that the California governor thought Reagan had a good chance of getting the nomination on the first ballot, and that they did not have to wait for a second or third ballot to come out for him. The Topeka media widely reported Reagan's message.[31]

In the middle of July, Reagan toured the southern states and Indiana. While in Indiana, he attempted to convince delegates to break their first ballot commitments to Nixon. Reagan was warmly received across the South but had to get past the wall that the Greenville Group had erected earlier in the year. Reagan also would contend with Strom Thurmond, who had a lot of credibility for southern conservatives. While Thurmond thought the world of Reagan, as a practical politician, he strongly believed that Richard Nixon was the only Republican who could win the general election. Nixon already had assured Thurmond he would govern conservatively. For Thurmond, a man born at the turn of the 20th century but a man of the previous century, a man's word and honor were still sacred. He had already given Nixon his word and commitment. Thurmond would now have to convince his fellow southern Republicans to do likewise. The Nixon people were starting to worry about their southern flank, which they had thought was quite solid. Only Ronald Reagan could break it.

While Reagan was traveling through the South, Nixon met with General Eisenhower at Walter Reed Hospital in Washington. Eisenhower had suffered a heart attack while playing golf and was back in the hospital. Much of the visit highlighted the former vice president checking up on his former boss and showing concern about his well-being. Two days later, Ike held a brief news conference in his hospital suite with some excellent news for the Nixon team. Ike read his carefully crafted statement to the reporters: "I endorse Richard M. Nixon for the Republican nomination. I do this not only for the appreciation for his great services to the country during the years of my Administration but rather and far more because of his personal qualities."[32] While the endorsement was not a big surprise, Nixon was very grateful for it. Eisenhower had never tried to interfere in intra-party politics in his post-presidency and, in 1964, had only made his feelings known after the Republican convention. But 1968 was different, given the close ties between the two families, and the upcoming marriage of David and Julia coupled with his health situation. Ike felt that it was time to get out front two weeks before the Republican convention.

Nixon got the news as he was traveling to California for the weekend. He had a lot of things on his plate in his native state. On Sunday afternoon, there was a welcome home celebration at the Century Plaza Hotel. The reception, initially by invitation only, was expanded to the general public because of high demand. People got to meet the entire Nixon family, including the soon to be new member, David Eisenhower. Between 12,000 and 15,000 people attended. Robert Semple, covering the event for the *New York Times*, was quite surprised at the turnout and described the scene: "The line of well-wishers started from a raised platform.... It snaked back through the lobby, out a door down Constellation Street for about a half block and around the corner onto a parking lot."[33]

Before the Sunday afternoon event, Nixon held a closed-door meeting on Saturday with many members of the California delegation. The former vice president indicated that he was not trying to raid the delegation that was pledged to Governor Reagan and that the visit was entirely "social." He also held a news conference and talked about the upcoming convention. Nixon said he would make his pick for vice president after winning the nomination. Nixon stated he sought a "very personal relationship" between himself and his choice. He also indicated that he had "been watching a number of people" and listening to several important persons on the subject.[34] Also, while Nixon was in California, it was announced that a film based on the "Man in the Arena" concept would be shown in that state in the next two weeks, with the former vice president answering questions from six Californians. It was filmed earlier in the week in New York. The film was similar to some of the other videos earlier in the campaign, though this one had a purely California flavor.[35] Nixon spent several more days in the Los Angeles area working on his acceptance speech and film-ing some television commercials before going back to New York for the Republican convention.

There was more political news from Nixon's opponents as Reagan and Rockefel-ler tried to get convention delegates to switch allegiances. Much of the national press speculated Nixon was very close to the 667 mark. There was even some talk among unnamed Nixon aides that they doubted that they could win if the convention got past the second ballot.[36] Barry Goldwater, who had been a Nixon supporter since the beginning, had tried several times unsuccessfully to get Reagan to pull out of the race. Goldwater sent out telegrams to the southern states of Alabama, Mississippi, Geor-gia, Louisiana, North Carolina, and Florida trying to get uncommitted delegates to vote for Nixon. An aide to the Arizona politician said this was just the beginning, and more states would be added in the next few days.[37]

With two weeks to go before the Republican convention and on the eve of another governors conference, speculation continued as to whom Nixon would pick as his running mate. A front-page story written by Ward Just in the *Washington Post* on July 21 strongly suggested that he would pick a liberal, like John Lindsay. The arti-cle quoted Governor Rhodes of Ohio, who supported Lindsay, stating he would help in the large industrial states.[38] Both Nixon and Lindsay lived in and were registered to vote in New York. That ticket would be a constitutional violation of the 12th amend-ment, which barred presidential and vice presidential candidates from the same state. Where that idea came from was not exactly clear. Perhaps it was a trial balloon floated by the Nixon campaign to see how it was perceived. It also could have come from Rhodes, who was being portrayed as almost a kingmaker in the party because of his large number of delegate votes in Ohio. Another motivating factor for Rhodes was his offer of the vice presidential slot on a Reagan ticket. He thought it would benefit the California governor in the long run by creating doubt in the South. Reagan and Clif White were running a guerrilla campaign in the South to raid those states' delegates who were mostly committed to Nixon. They did this by claiming that not only was Nixon not conservative enough and could not win, but he could not be trusted. They waved the "Tricky Dick" image in front of them as they traveled.

At the National Governors Conference in Cincinnati, Ronald Reagan jumped on the speculation that Nixon might choose a liberal running mate to balance his ticket and help him by attracting liberal voters. Reagan adamantly held that whoever was chosen should share a "similar viewpoint." Once again, the California governor was the star of this conference, being greeted by 2,700 people at the airport in nearby Covington, Kentucky. Secret Service officials met with him privately when he first arrived, telling Reagan that the FBI had uncovered a plot by a Black militant group that had decreed his execution. It followed on the heels of two young Black men try-ing to firebomb the executive mansion in Sacramento two weeks earlier.[39]

On the first night at the conference, there was a near fistfight between Clif-ton White and Richard Kleindienst at a social gathering. Both had worked together during the Goldwater campaign and were friends. Kleindienst, who always laid his cards on the table very directly, confronted White about actively seeking delegates while saying that Reagan was not a candidate. He would have had no problem with White if the campaign had not been hiding behind the veneer of Reagan's favorite-son status. John Mitchell had to separate the two, telling Kleindienst that he could not

make him the attorney general if he were going to get into fistfights with his opponents. Kleindienst apologized to White the next day, but still resented him, as did
many in the Nixon camp.[40]

At the conference, there was a move by Governor Agnew to try to get Ohio and
Michigan to join with Maryland in a loose coalition of uncommitted favorite son governors. Even though Agnew was supporting Nixon now, he had not come out publicly. James Rhodes reacted strongly against any move that threatened his favorite
son status, even though a large number of his delegation most likely favored Nixon.
There was pressure put upon Rhodes by several of the big money men in Cleveland to
come out and support Nixon, but he would not budge. George Romney said many of
the same things that Rhodes did, but without the same enthusiasm. Evans and Novak
even wrote a column on this saying, "Only a gossamer screen separates Nixon from
the nomination, but the uncommitted delegates in Cincinnati made it clear that the
screen still exists."[41]

Two days later, Charles Percy endorsed Rockefeller for the Republican nomination. He did this despite a vast majority of the Illinois delegates supporting Nixon.
Percy did give the Nixon campaign a heads-up with a call the day before, but still, it
came as a bit of a surprise. Herb Klein told reporters that the Illinois senator must
have been offered the vice president's job by Rockefeller. Still, Percy said it was the
New York governor's position on Vietnam that was the major factor behind his
endorsement. Percy believed that a military victory was not possible, and only a
negotiated settlement among the parties would end the war.[42] William Buckley had
a similar but perhaps more cynical view on why Percy chose to make this announcement at this time. The conservative columnist wrote a column on the subject on the
eve of the convention:

> It isn't as though Percy had been studying the relative qualifications of Richard Nixon and
> Nelson Rockefeller, holed up in the archives, and only yesterday completed his readings of
> the collected works of two men and—the examination finally completed like say, the War-
> ren Commission's—the time comes to issue a report. So what happens? At first, the pundits
> conclude that the decision is based on Percy's discovery that Nixon does not intend to con-
> fer upon him the vice presidential nomination. But don't you see—the second wave comes
> in riding the crest of super-sophistication—don't you see that if Nixon is nominated, he will
> look for means by which to unify the Republican Party. That means he will want to give the
> vice presidency to someone prominently identified as a Rockefeller man. In anticipation of
> this, Percy has neatly situated himself over there, as the most nubile of them all.[43]

It was that issue that summoned Richard Nixon to Washington the next day for
an intelligence briefing on Vietnam with President Johnson. Since LBJ's pullout from
the presidential race, Nixon had maintained his public moratorium on any criticism
of the administration's handling of the war. It was an expansive meeting that lasted
90 minutes and included Dean Rusk and Walt Rostow. Nixon did not make any specific comments on the substantive aspects of the meeting, except to say that it was
"candid and forthright."[44] After the briefing was over, Rusk and Rostow left the room,
with only Nixon and Johnson remaining. It was readily apparent to Nixon that his old
political rival and friend was troubled about the war. Nixon wrote nearly a decade
later what Lyndon Johnson had said to him as he left the meeting: "You know, Dick,
all this talk about me being obsessed with power is just hogwash. I never cared about
having any goddamn power. The only thing that appeals to me about being President

is the opportunity it provides to do some good for the country."[45] Nixon was not sure that he ever bought into the president's bit about seeking or gaining power, but he was moved by what he heard. He later told reporters outside the White House that win or lose, he had accepted an invitation to visit the president's ranch in Texas. It had been a long-standing request going back to the Eisenhower years when Nixon was vice president, and Johnson was the majority leader of the Senate.[46]

A week before the convention, three national polls were released that were guaranteed to impact the uncommitted delegates to the Republican convention. The first two were Gallup while the third came from Harris. Gallup's first inquiry polled GOP voters across the country. It was a resounding victory for Nixon, with respondents preferring him two to one over his two competitors.[47] Two days later, Gallup released a poll that showed Nixon to be the strongest Republican candidate against Humphrey or McCarthy. The survey showed Nixon winning over Humphrey by two percent and McCarthy by five percent. For the Nixon campaign, it was just what the doctor ordered. The effect was just the opposite for the Rockefeller folks. John Mitchell said that the supposed gains by the two Republican governors were "unrealistic" and that he thought that there would be "a desperate surge of gadgeteered polls from other candidates." One of Rockefeller's chief backers, Governor John H. Chafee of Rhode Island, called the news "very discouraging."[48] Finally, Rockefeller got some good news with the Harris Poll, which showed him defeating Humphrey or McCarthy by six points, while Nixon ran behind by five points.[49]

It was then up to the opposing camps to explain which poll mattered most and why. Objectively speaking, Gallup had consistently been more accurate than Harris over time. Harris Polls had tended to overestimate Democrats and underestimate

Nixon conferring with President Johnson on Vietnam on July 30, 1968, in the White House (Lyndon Baines Johnson Library).

Republicans and Independents. Harris had been the pollster for John Kennedy. Nelson Rockefeller had been claiming for four months that he could do better nationally than Richard Nixon, particularly in states with large populations. The day after the Harris Poll was leaked, George Gallup, Jr., acknowledged their poll was conducted a couple of days earlier than the Harris Poll and that Rockefeller "has moved to an open lead" over his two Democratic opponents.[50] As it turned out, Gallup Jr. spoke without clearing it with his father, who disagreed with what his son had just said.[51] Herb Klein talked to reporters, comparing the various polls to their internal delegate counts. Klein dismissed the latest Harris Poll along with the younger Gallup's comments:

> It looks like there's a pollsters' protective society being organized. This doesn't contradict the fact that Nixon is doing very well. He is doing very well and he is going to win. I hope we finally are at the end of the numbers game regarding polls. The results are in. I submit that Governor Rockefeller has failed in history's most expensive two-month campaign.... [After] backing away from a vote of the people in the primary elections, [Rockefeller] declared a new set of ground rules based on the notion of nomination by polls.[52]

Earlier in the day, Len Hall saw things differently and shared what the Gallup polls had meant to him much earlier in the campaign. Hall said, "Mr. Nixon seems to be in a freakish situation, [but] the one sure winner in the fall is a man by the name of Nelson Rockefeller. [It was] further confirmation of the momentum that has been building in recent weeks all over the country for Governor Rockefeller." The veteran political consultant who ran Nixon's campaign in 1960 and had up to March of 1968 been doing the same for George Romney made another comment concerning what he thought of Gallup's polling efforts: "Mr. Gallup almost convinced me a year ago that Mr. Romney would be the nominee."[53] Ultimately the decision would be up to the delegates now as they began to gather in Miami Beach for the Republican Convention. A week from now, the Grand Old Party would have themselves a nominee.

Delegates from all over the country came to Miami Beach, where all three Republican candidates headquartered in different hotels: Nixon's team at the Hilton, Rockefeller's at the Americana, and the Reaganites at the Deauville. State delegations scattered across Miami Beach. On Sunday, the day before the convention, Nelson Rockefeller appeared on *Meet the Press* while Ronald Reagan began to make rounds at the various southern state delegations. Richard Nixon was back in Montauk, New York, on the tip of Long Island, busily preparing his acceptance speech as he had been for the past two weeks, writing and re-writing. There were only a few close aides there like Bob Haldeman, John Mitchell, Pat Buchanan, Ray Price, and Rose Mary Woods. Haldeman and Mitchell flew to Miami Beach over the weekend to join most of the Nixon team.[54]

Going into the convention, two of the three significant television networks and the *New York Times* had Nixon well over the six hundred mark in his delegate count. Still, none had him over the 667 number he needed to clinch the nomination. According to CBS, Nixon had 657 delegates while ABC claimed 623, and the *Times* had him at 619 votes.[55] Privately, Richard Kleindienst, director for operations at the convention, thought Nixon was at 700. At the end of May, he thought that his boss had enough support for the nomination. Nonetheless, over the past two months, all the political talk from Rockefeller and Reagan focused on the erosion of Nixon's delegate strength. The key for Kleindienst and the Nixon team was to hold onto what they had and to convince the few uncommitted delegates to come to their side. Rockefeller and Reagan needed each other to block Nixon. Rocky's strength was in the liberal Northeast and moderate Midwest, while Reagan was most influential in the conservative South.[56]

Was Nixon Stoppable?

Early Monday morning, the convention buzzed about the movements of Ronald Reagan. He had met Sunday with several state delegations, many from the South, trying to convince them an open convention would unify the party. Later that morning, the South Carolina delegation threatened to bolt to Reagan, even though their favorite son, Senator Strom Thurmond, had committed them to Nixon. John Mitchell represented the Nixon team while Robert Walker spoke for Governor Reagan.[57]

There was also a front-page story in the *New York Times* indicating that Nixon had narrowed his choices for the vice president to three liberals: Nelson Rockefeller, John Lindsay, or Charles Percy.[58] It followed a similar front-page story two weeks earlier in the *Washington Post* that claimed that Nixon was indeed seriously considering a liberal for vice president.[59] Who leaked the story was unclear. It could have come from any number of places, including Bob Ellsworth or Richard Whalen from the Nixon side, who were anti-war and favored a withdrawal from Vietnam, or perhaps from the Reagan people who wanted a wedge issue to disrupt Nixon's strong southern lead. There were myriad possibilities. Later, Herb Klein emphatically denied the field had narrowed to three. Klein said that the vice presidential choice might come from any state and mentioned Mark Hatfield as an example.[60] Harry Dent called the meeting for clarification. Mitchell told the South Carolinians that he "talked with Dick Nixon this morning, and it's not his intention to cram down your throat any candidate not fully acceptable." The Nixon campaign manager went on to assure them that the vice presidential nominee would be chosen after consulting with all segments of the party. Walker followed Mitchell, imploring the delegation to remain uncommitted until Reagan met personally with them. Dent joined his other two members of the Greenville Group, Clarke Reed and Bill Murfin, for lunch with Reagan and Alfred Goldwaithe, head of the Alabama delegation and a supporter of the California governor. The threesome tried to talk Reagan out of running, saying that they liked him but were committed to Nixon and that Senator Thurmond had given him his word at the May meeting in Atlanta. Thurmond was not one who took breaking his word easily unless someone double-crossed him.[61]

The same afternoon, Reagan finally announced his candidacy despite the warnings from the Greenville Group. After the announcement, Reagan continued to make the rounds of state delegations trying to convince the uncommitted or wavering he was the real voice of the Republican Party.[62]

Meanwhile, Spiro Agnew publicly committed to Nixon. It was no surprise to the Nixon people. Agnew had indicated in a meeting in June that he was for him but was just waiting for the proper time to come out. At least 16 of the 26 Maryland delegates were pledged to him. It came as a shock to Rockefeller because he thought Agnew would stay uncommitted to give Maryland more leverage. Agnew praised Nixon and said that he "has the courage to make hard decisions, to take positions that may be temporarily unpopular but will be proven right."[63]

Right after Nixon's plane arrived in Miami Beach, he journeyed to the Hilton and was met by over 800 cheering supporters as he entered. It was a "loud and boisterous" multitude that greeted him.[64] Little did he know that there was trouble brewing in the southern delegations. Much of the weekend's political talk was about the erosion in Nixon's support peddled by the Rockefeller and Reagan people. The *Washington Post* reported a shift of 6–8 votes from Nixon to Reagan in the North Carolina delegation. Their source was James C. Gardner, whom Nixon campaigned for in 1966. The former vice president felt that Gardner owed him support, but over the past week, Reagan had held a fundraiser in North Carolina for Gardner, who was running for governor. Of course, Gardner did not mention this as the reason for shifting his allegiance to the California governor but said instead that Nixon's rumored choice of Lindsay for vice president was too much to take. The article also quoted Clarke Reed, one of the original Greenville Group and Mississippi chairman. They said that his delegation of 20 for Nixon was now "loose and it could go either way. If Lindsay is tapped by Nixon, I feel like we've been done shot down."[65]

Later that night, Harry Dent called John Mitchell and said that the threat was real. They needed to meet tonight instead of their scheduled Tuesday morning appointment. Mitchell agreed and scheduled a 10 p.m. meeting in Nixon's suite. Dent was accompanied by the senator and Fred Buzhardt, another prominent Thurmond aide. Bob Haldeman and John Ehrlichman were also present at the meeting. Dent recalled what occurred next nearly a decade later:

> I told Nixon that Reagan's announcement had stirred all conservative delegates and alternates and that some defections were already taking place. I mentioned the Gardner switch, which startled Nixon. Mitchell reacted with strong language, indicating a double cross. Nixon stopped the conversation and barked some orders on the Gardner problem.... Nixon's reaction also permitted me to launch into my spiel about Thurmond tearing his shirt for Nixon. I explained that the senator had faith in the candidate, despite all this "Tricky Dick" talk. I said, "We're with you, and we're going to stick with you." Nixon then asked what he could do to help.... Then Nixon volunteered a rundown on all the key issues. He covered virtually everything, and we were overjoyed with his positions. I responded: "Tell all that directly to the delegates you'll be speaking to tomorrow morning. It'll have much more impact coming from you rather than a conduit, even though Senator Thurmond is the best conduit possible to the southern states' most conservative delegates...." Surprisingly, Nixon, without hesitation, said, "OK, I'll do it."[66]

The next morning, Nixon and Mitchell did just that. They met with two separate groups, repeating their message to the South Carolina trio from the night before. The southern storm had not passed, but it was starting to abate a bit.[67] Besides, Nixon asked Barry Goldwater to stay and talk to the delegates as his surrogate. Goldwater had spoken at the convention the previous night and got a rousing ovation. He was happy to do what he could to help. He told the different delegate groups that Richard Nixon was the only Republican who could win and that he was with him all the way. Goldwater was keeping his pledge to Nixon from soon after he lost the 1964 election to help him should he decide to run for president. His presence before the southern and western delegations did just that.[68]

Throughout the day on Tuesday and Wednesday, there were separate meetings among the states' delegations, the most important among them situated in the southern delegations of South Carolina, Florida, Mississippi, and Alabama. These were the four states from which Reagan was attempting to steal Nixon's widespread support. All of the delegations were present in the morning when Nixon outlined his position on the issues, and now it was Reagan's turn with the four states. Strom Thurmond also got to talk to states other than his own. Alabama was the only state that had substantial Reagan support, as evidenced by its state chairman, Alfred Goldthwaite, but even there, Nixon still held a slight majority of the votes. The other three states were comprised of the leaders of the Greenville Group, which had pledged its support to Nixon at the end of May.

On Tuesday afternoon, Reagan met with the South Carolina delegation. Strom Thurmond followed, saying that he was "a great admirer of Reagan, but our South Carolina delegation is going to Nixon all the way."[69] Bobbie Ames, one of the Alabama delegates who had previously supported Reagan, changed her mind after hearing Thurmond's position. Ames was emphatic in her praise for the South Carolina senator, saying, "Sen. Thurmond's the greatest living man in this country today, and when he said that Nixon satisfied him, you could hear the sighs of relief all over the room."[70]

After two days of meeting with the Reagan and Nixon team, Florida voted. The vote was 19–14–1 in favor of Nixon, though there were still a few undecideds who could change their mind. Most of the female members of the delegation were quite taken with Reagan, more so from his movie-star status than his ideological positions. Several of them changed their minds three times, making it a problematic meeting for Murfin. Ultimately, the Florida delegation was a conservative one. Toward the end of the Nixon presentation, when one of the delegates asked Strom Thurmond if Nixon would name a liberal as vice president, the veteran senator said that he had never asked that a Southerner be put on the ticket but was adamant in putting his reputation on the line for Nixon's "reliability."[71]

Mississippi was the next southern delegation that Ronald Reagan intended to raid, but he would have to get past Clarke Reed, the founder and ringleader of the Greenville Group. Nixon had campaigned for him two years earlier in his unsuccessful gubernatorial run while Reagan would not give him the time of day. Conversely, Reed did provide the California governor time with his state's delegation. After Reagan was through with his speech, the Mississippi chairman told him he would call Reagan later in the day. Clarke Reed did just that. The British authors of *An American Melodrama* wrote an elegant description of Reed's reply: "It was one of those delicious moments that political bosses, particularly Southern bosses, love to savor. Reagan had forgotten about his failure to come to Reed's rescue in the Mississippi gubernatorial race in 1966.... The full sweetness of Reed's revenge was distilled into a final piece of advice before he put down the phone on his petitioner: 'Perhaps you had better try where you have a few favors owing.'"[72]

Rockefeller believed that his messages about Nixon being a "loser" would now, on Wednesday, start to sink in with the Republican delegates, and they would turn to him in November. After all, Rockefeller had won three straight elections in a Democratic state. Romney's strategy had also been based on Nixon being a loser. The actuality was that Rockefeller had almost no support in the South or the West, and that was where Republicans were the most popular. What Rocky did in the general election campaign of 1964 could not be easily forgiven. For that reason and that reason alone, he could not have won the nomination in 1968 without a lot of apologizing and explaining, something that he had not done and was not accustomed to doing. The Reagan team of Clif White and Tom Reed thought that after several deadlocked ballots, Nixon's support would continually erode and or he would throw in the towel and join the California governor against Rockefeller. It isn't clear what Ronald Reagan himself thought. He seemed to agree to whatever Reed and White wanted him to do without really being committed to doing what it took to be a presidential candidate. He may have thought that winning the nomination would be like winning the governorship. Reagan commented to several of the southern state delegations that he just wanted an open convention, and after three or four ballots, "we could all go back and rally around Dick."[73] In the end, he was a reluctant candidate, and currently in his political career, was in over his head. The reality for both Rockefeller and Reagan was that neither one of these candidates could have supported the other, but in the end, one of them would have had to turn to Nixon.

With all the good news on Wednesday about shoring up Nixon's southern support, there was bad news as well. The day before, General Eisenhower had suffered another heart attack while in the hospital at Walter Reed. Ike had addressed the convention just twelve hours earlier on the telephone. It was the former president's third heart attack in the past three and a half months. His condition was listed as "serious." The general's son, John Eisenhower, left the convention to be with his father in Washington.[74]

D-Day in Miami Beach

The process on Wednesday night started at 5:30 with nominating speeches for Ronald Reagan, Nelson Rockefeller, Richard Nixon, and the various favorite sons. Reagan's name was placed in nomination first, as Alabama yielded their place to California. Next came pro forma nominations of the favorite sons: Walter Hickel of Alaska, Winthrop Rockefeller of Arkansas, George Romney of Michigan, Frank Carlson of Kansas, and Hiram Fong of Hawaii. After these preliminaries, Governor Raymond Shafer of Pennsylvania nominated Nelson Rockefeller. Shafer said that his candidate "is the one Republican who can win."[75]

The final nominating speech of the night was by Spiro Agnew for Richard Nixon. Agnew had been chosen by the Nixon team a couple of weeks before to do the honors. He said that Nixon had "the confidence to make hard decisions; the courage to keep cool before one man in Moscow or a mob in Caracas ... and helped lead this party to its greatest victories in the past two decades, and stood by it and its candidates in its darkest hour." Agnew also harkened back to Nixon's contributions by being on the ticket with General Eisenhower and, above all, for standing up for Goldwater in 1964 when several prominent Republicans like Romney and Rockefeller refused to campaign for the Republican nominee.[76]

After all of the nominating speeches were over, the actual roll call balloting of the states began at 1:17 a.m. Thursday. There was a big sigh of relief when Florida gave the former vice president 33 of its 34 votes, just as Murfin and Thurmond said they would. It took almost an hour before Wisconsin gave Nixon the victory. Nixon watched the returns on television with his family and a few chosen aides like Mitchell, Haldeman, Buchanan, Price, and Chapin. After viewing the results, a happy Richard

Nixon turned to them and said, "It is time to get to work."[77] But now there was the issue of choosing a vice presidential candidate. The new nominee wasted no time in addressing that problem.

Who Should Be the Vice President?

Somewhere after 2:15 a.m., when the balloting had ended, several prominent Republicans were invited to the 15th floor of the Hilton to meet with Nixon to discuss the possibilities for vice president. Before the group assembled, Nixon met with 24 men of his team outside the solarium of his suite. It was a forty-five-minute meeting to discuss the standard possibilities. While nothing was settled, the group agreed that the shortlist was made up of liberals, conservatives, and moderates. The liberals were Lindsay, Percy, and Hatfield, while the conservatives centered on Reagan and Howard Baker along with two Texans: John Tower and George H.W. Bush. The moderates were Spiro Agnew and John Volpe. The next meeting included Goldwater, Thurmond, and Rhodes, along with Billy Graham and Herbert Brownell, who had been Eisenhower's first attorney general. The Southerners wanted Reagan, while the Northerners and Rhodes wanted Lindsay. Graham said whoever it was, it should be a man of high moral standing. The distinguished minister had publicly mentioned Hatfield and Bush in the past couple of months as the type of man that he would like to see on the ticket with Nixon.[78] Bush was one of the surprise choices. Surprisingly, he had a lot of support in Texas as well as from big businesses on the East Coast with people like George Champion, the head of Chase Manhattan Bank.[79] Bob Finch told the group that Reagan would not accept the offer of vice president, despite his support for the number two position.[80]

What seemed to come out of this second meeting was that both sides wanted to roll the dice on the vice president. Even though the Southerners were adamant about not having Lindsay on the ticket, he had a lot of support in the Northeast with the hope of challenging the Democrats in the large cities. Thurmond and Goldwater wanted Reagan (as well as Buchanan and Sears), and Finch had told them that Reagan would not accept a running mate offer. Rhodes came back to the two conservatives, saying that Reagan would be a disaster for Ohio and that his state would lose worse than it did in 1964 when Johnson won by over a million votes.[81] Drew Pearson said that powerful lawyer and Democratic fund-raiser Eugene Wyman told him that one of the California delegates had relayed to him that Rhodes encouraged Reagan to come out now. If he did so, Rhodes would stay uncommitted and back Reagan on the third ballot.[82] How ironic, given that he had been offered the number-two position job by Reagan and did not turn down the offer.

Perhaps the only plausible explanation was that politicians sometimes make strange bedfellows. Nixon had let the group know that he was not interested in the "glamour boys," meaning Lindsay and Reagan, and wanted somebody a bit different. He also let them know all of their polling with various vice presidential choices showed that none of the possibilities would help the candidate. He ran better alone. Nixon then stated his thoughts on the matter. He wanted a governor with "some knowledge of the cities." He also mentioned going after the "ethnic vote."[83] While the meeting adjourned with no clear choices, Volpe and Agnew had moved to the top of the list. On the way out, Nixon asked Goldwater if he could live with Agnew as vice president. The Arizona Republican said that of course he could and said that it did not matter if no one knew who he was. It was not atypical to have a vice presidential candidate that was not well known. After that, Nixon retreated to his room for a well-deserved two hours of sleep before getting up for another meeting at 8:30 a.m. on Thursday.[84]

Thirty minutes after waking, Nixon was convening with his third group made up of party leaders, including Everett Dirksen, Gerald Ford, John Tower, and Ray Bliss, among others. Again, there was no consensus, and most of the more conservative members wanted Reagan while the others wanted either Lindsay or Hatfield. Some suggested Nixon should name someone from one of the big states like Texas. Nixon would have none of it, and the meeting ended without a clear consensus.[85]

Then Nixon called a meeting with just six people, three of his people, and three from the previous session. The Nixon staffers were Mitchell, Haldeman, and Ellsworth, while Finch, Morton, and Tower joined from the last group. Nixon asked, "Who should I take?" Spiro Agnew got the nod.[86]

At around 12:40, Nixon held a press conference to announce his choice. He was very upbeat about his decision despite the press asking, "Spiro who?" Nixon described Agnew as having "old-fashioned patriotism" having "come through the fire."[87] Nixon felt that Agnew was like himself, a mostly self-made man who rose to prominence the hard way.

About an hour earlier in the morning, Ronald Reagan had called Nixon and congratulated him on his nomination. Reagan seemed in high spirits and said that he would be in touch when Nixon came to California over the weekend. The California governor watched on television a few minutes later as Nixon introduced his choice of Agnew as his running mate in a short news conference. Reagan thought that it was a good pick. He had a lot of respect for the Maryland governor and commented, "It will be acceptable to the South and all sections of the country. Governor Agnew has a good record for dealing firmly with rioters. I've known him and admired him at Governors' conferences and as a friend. He's a fine choice."[88]

The opposite was the case when it came to supporters of Governor Rockefeller. While the governor was graceful and said nothing about the choice, adding that it was "Mr. Nixon's day," that was not the case with a number of his close supporters. While none would go on the record for the press, it was clear that they were miffed that they had not been consulted about the Agnew choice. They also thought that it might be difficult for a New York Republican to back a centrist or center-right ticket.[89] The reality of the situation was that they had lost, and one of their most vocal past supporters was now on the Nixon ticket. After the 1964 blowout, the party had decided that they were out of touch with the American people and needed to return to their more progressive roots as symbolized by their northeastern politicians. One sure thing that came out of the 1968 convention was that the most motivated Republicans were from the South and the West, and the party was now more conservative.

The Big Night

Before Richard Nixon's acceptance speech, there was some housekeeping to be done. Spiro Agnew still had to be nominated by the delegates assembled in Miami

Beach. There was some pushback from the liberals on this, and they tried to convince John Lindsay to say that he was available to serve on the ticket, but he turned them down. Instead, they turned to George Romney, who, a year earlier, saw himself being where Nixon was right now. In the end, Agnew won the nomination handily, with over 1100 votes and Romney trailing at 178. The Michigan governor gladly accepted his fate and acknowledged Agnew as the vice presidential candidate. John Lindsay made the nominating speech for the Maryland governor.[90]

It was now Richard Nixon's time. After a five-minute ovation, the former vice president began his acceptance speech. He had worked on this speech for the better part of two weeks, re-working and re-writing in typical Nixon style. While the address was written by him, he had a lot of input from Price, Buchanan, and others. Those who had covered him for the past two years had heard parts it before, but certainly not all of it. Nixon started it off with a "report from Mamie Eisenhower," saying that even though her husband was critically ill, there was nothing more that he wanted now than a Republican victory in November. He said, "Let's win this one for Ike." After mentioning Americans dying in foreign fields, he reminded the audience of where they had died before: in Valley Forge, Normandy, and Korea.[91] Nixon got into the heart of his speech by saying that there a lot of voices being raised in America, but the ones that he heard were the great majority who were not the ones making all the noise and demonstrating. They were the "good people" who worked hard and paid their taxes and cared most about this country. He pledged to end the war honorably. Finally, he spoke of seeing "the face of a child ... he is black, or he is white." It did not matter where he came from or the color of his skin. What mattered was "an American child" who may not have everything or maybe very little, but that child could dream and be everything he wanted to be. He had been that child who listened to the train go by and dream where it might take him. Nixon finished with salutes to his mother, father, and all those who had inspired him where he was on that Thursday night. He pledged "to leave the valley of despair and climb the mountain so that we can see the glory of the dawn" of a new and better America.[92]

The speech was warmly received, and Nixon and Agnew were joined onstage by other prominent Republicans for a fitting ending of their national convention. For one Nixon aide, the last part of the speech where he spoke from the heart of the two children—a hypothetical one growing up poor in a crowded city with no hope and the other referring to himself—had a special meaning. Bill Gavin had traveled down over the weekend with the rest of the Nixon team for the convention. When he got there, Gavin found out that he was not staying at the same hotel as the Nixon headquarters but on down the road in another hotel. Gavin attended some of the sessions but felt left out of the loop. He watched the last night of the convention on television with another aide, Jack Caufield, who was a former New York City policeman now working security for the Nixon team. When Nixon got to the end of his speech and started to talk about seeing a child and what followed, Gavin perked up and turned to Caufield, speaking more loudly than usual, saying that was his stuff that Nixon was now using. A smile soon crossed his face because Gavin saw that maybe he was part of the team. After that, both Gavin and Caufield returned to hotel rooms for the night, missing the Nixon parties at hotels nearer the convention. The next morning, Gavin went to the Hilton Hotel, where Nixon got to thank all his people for doing a great job at the convention. After addressing the crowd, Nixon came down and mingled a bit, seeking out Gavin. He found him and pulled him aside, putting his arm around him and thanking him for his contributions to the campaign so far and for his part in the speech. Gavin was dumbfounded that Nixon would take the time to single him out. Nixon told him that he had been looking for him last night but could not find him. It was entirely out of character for Nixon. For the former high school teacher from Philadelphia, it was a heck of an ending to the convention. certainly not the one that he had been expecting when he left his hotel that morning.[93]

The winning of the Republican nomination for president was not the end for Richard Nixon. It was just another part of the process of Nixon reinventing himself since the "last press conference." After losing the 1962 governor's race, the conventional political wisdom was that Nixon was dead. However, it was Nixon who went around the country listening to the American people and putting in all the hard work of campaigning in the 1964 and 1966 elections. Nixon's actions contrasted sharply with two of his closest Republican rivals, Rockefeller and Romney, neither of whom campaigned for Goldwater in 1964. Still, both Rockefeller and Romney were proclaimed big winners by the national media after the 1966 elections. The other major rival and the big winner from the '66 elections was Ronald Reagan. All three of these politicians had stood in the way of Nixon getting the Republican nomination.

Nixon stated several times to close associates in late 1967 and early 1968 that to be successful, he must prove that he could win again and shed the "loser" image widely portrayed in the national media and by his detractors. Nixon had to run in five contested political primaries and win. Not only did he win, but Nixon also won big in gathering 70 percent of the vote in these contests. He started with a resounding victory in New Hampshire with Romney dropping out a week before the election after running for president for the past year. Nixon followed up that with a decisive win in Wisconsin. During this period, Rockefeller held a news conference in the middle of March, announcing that he was not running for president. Six weeks later, he changed his mind and decided to throw his hat into the ring, even though he was not running in any of the party's primaries.

In the two months leading up to the Republican convention, Rockefeller was actively running for president while Reagan was crisscrossing the country, claiming that he was not a candidate. After the big Oregon win in May, Nixon met with the southern delegations in Atlanta, nailing down support from the region of the country that provided half of the votes that a candidate needed to win the Republican nomination. Even though Reagan was the darling of the Southerners and the conservative movement, he had been hesitant. Reagan operated in the shadows as Nixon correctly understood the mood of the Republican voter. After that, he began planning for the general campaign. Simultaneously, both Rockefeller and Reagan tried to collect enough ballots from winning a first-ballot victory. Even though they represented different ideological sides of the Republican coalition, the two governors were essentially colluding against Nixon. They were hoping the convention would deadlock and choose one of them to be the nominee. In the end, neither was successful, and he easily won the nomination on the first ballot. In three months, he might even be president of the United States. Nixon looked forward to the rest of this journey.

12

Now You're Gonna Take My Dog

Before he left Miami Beach, Richard Nixon did some last-minute housekeeping with the Republican Party while also announcing some additional vital appointments for the upcoming campaign. Nixon met with party leaders in a closed-door session of the Republican National Committee (RNC) and promised to work closely with them to add Republican governors, senators, and members of Congress in November. He did this because of the nagging suspicion some party members had held since the 1960 campaign, including running his campaign instead of letting professionals do it. The same charge cropped up earlier in the primaries (principally from his '60 campaign manager Len Hall), and Nixon wanted to allay these fears. Additionally, he said he would not repeat mistakes made in 1960, like pledging to visit all fifty states. Nixon told the party faithful that his campaign would make the most of television, radio, and other media instead of relying on in-person visits. It described Nixon's campaign strategy in the primaries recommended by Bob Haldeman's 1967 summer memorandum. This time, the candidate would only make 1–2 stops a day, unlike eight years earlier.[1]

In making the promise to work closely with the Republican National Committee, Nixon said Richard Kleindienst, who had been working alongside John Mitchell throughout the previous year, would go to Washington to work with the committee. Kleindienst joined as deputy counsel to Ray Bliss, who had been re-elected as chairman of the RNC before the convention. In this position, Kleindienst served as the liaison between the New York headquarters and the RNC in Washington. For the sake of unity, Nixon agreed Bliss should be re-elected, even though he had issues with him from the 1966 congressional campaign. While Nixon certainly would not acknowledge this, probably the real reason Kleindienst (who was on good terms with Bliss) was going to Washington was to be sure they were coordinated with Nixon headquarters in New York. The same oversight had been carried out the year before when Nixon sent John Sears to Washington to work with Gaylord Parkinson and Robert Walker.[2]

Nixon also announced Maurice Stans as the national committee finance chairman, succeeding General Lucius Clay. Stans had been a long-time money-man for Nixon in his political comeback. He served with the "Birdwatchers in '66" and the Nixon for President Committee the past year and a half. The other announcement was the re-election of J. William Middendorf II as the treasurer of the RNC. Middendorf was a prominent Wall Street investment banker who had presided in the same position in the Goldwater campaign four years earlier.[3]

Nixon also told the assembled press President Johnson had invited him to attend a national security briefing at his ranch in Texas on his way to California. Spiro Agnew would accompany him on the cross-country journey on Saturday. It would be Nixon's first trip to the Johnson ranch in rural Texas, and he certainly looked forward to it. The Republican nominee told the newsmen that LBJ said, "Dick, you have my congratulations and my sympathy."[4]

After this, Nixon made a short trip south to Key Biscayne for some rest before heading to Mission Bay, California, the next day. He met again with the press before retiring to a seaside resort near his old friend, Bebe Rebozo. He spent almost the entire 45 minutes in a spirited defense of his vice presidential choice. Nixon said of his running mate, "[Spiro T. Agnew] is one of the most underrated political men in America.... When it comes to carrying the attack and resisting the attack, he's got it. You can look him in the eye, and you know he's got it."[5]

The two Republican running mates left Florida and flew to San Antonio, where they were met by a military aide to take them to the Johnson ranch some seventy miles away via the presidential helicopter. Nixon and Agnew arrived along with four of their aides around noon. After brief introductions, President Johnson gave them a tour around the ranch in a Lincoln convertible. From there, they had lunch with Johnson and Secretary of State Rusk, Cyrus R. Vance, one of the negotiators at the Paris Peace Talks, and Richard Helms, the director of the CIA. The two Republican nominees got a situation briefing on strategic issues from the American perspective of the Johnson administration. As Nixon boarded the presidential helicopter for the trip back to San Antonio, Johnson's dog Yuki moved past him and jumped in the cabin. LBJ then called to Nixon, saying, "Dick, here you've got my helicopter, you're after my job, and now you're gonna take my dog." The former vice president laughed and told

Nixon and Agnew at LBJ ranch with the president and Lady Bird Johnson on August 9, 1968 (Lyndon Baines Johnson Library).

the president that two out of three were enough for him.[6] Nixon talked to the press briefly after returning to San Antonio and said that there were "no significant new developments to report" in the peace talks. He also stated that the president "said that he would make the same information available to me that he would make to the Democratic nominee."[7]

Mission Bay

Nixon spent the next week and a half on what he called a "working vacation" in the Mission Bay section of San Diego, California. Most of his principal staff were there going over final plans for the campaign. The first item addressed dealt with the campaign budget. Stans told the Nixon team they had spent nine million dollars on the primaries and the convention, and they needed to raise another 24 million dollars for the general election. It would be accomplished through a series of $1,000 per plate dinners in 22 cities across the country on September 16. At the events, donors would see Nixon beamed in from New York via closed-circuit television. Stans did not anticipate any money problems, which would offer them a massive advantage over the Democrats. With an eased mind, Nixon phoned leading Republicans to ensure their support for the upcoming campaign to include Romney and Rockefeller. The theme was unity because he knew that the Democrats were indeed divided, and the next convention would show the rest of the country what he and others already knew.[8]

Nixon made another position announcement while in Mission Bay. He named James Keough as director of the writing and research team. Keough had written a biography titled *This Is Nixon* in 1960. Since then, he had been an executive editor of *Time* magazine. Keough had taken a leave of absence from the popular weekly news magazine to serve on Nixon's team.[9]

A week into the working vacation, Nixon had an hour-long meeting with Governor Ronald Reagan. The meeting went well, and Reagan said he would do what he could to help Nixon carry California. However, his campaigning would probably be limited to television appearances due to criticism for time he spent trying to secure the Republican nomination. Any way that you looked at it, having Reagan's support was a significant plus for the Nixon team. The California governor went out of his way to tell reporters they were wrong about Agnew, who had been criticized by Black leaders in Maryland. He reminded the reporters that Agnew had vigorously supported open housing laws there.[10]

Overall, the stay was relaxing for Nixon, and things went generally well except for one incident involving a member of the policy research team. After the mid–June reorganization, the research side of the campaign complained that they had very little time with the candidate. They felt shunted aside by the image-making side of the campaign. Richard Whalen was especially miffed one night when they were told of an upcoming meeting with the nation's mayors to discuss urban problems along with an introduction of Nixon's national security team to the media. Whalen had come to work for Nixon because he believed in his ideas for fixing the country but felt that the campaign was going to be about image and not issues. He voiced his concerns to Mitchell, who was very short in his response. The next morning Whalen left the campaign.[11]

Pat Buchanan later met with Nixon and tried to convince him to let Whalen come back to the campaign. The whole research team knew the value he added to their endeavor. Nixon told Buchanan it was better for him to quit now rather than later in the campaign when the press might focus on it. Buchanan then got a call from Arthur Burns, a prominent business professor at Columbia University, trying to convince Nixon to take Whalen back because of his smart mind. Burns told him that a lot of brilliant people were high strung and sometimes too emotional. The team should take that into account, knowing what they got out of him. Despite all of this, Nixon did not change his mind and felt that it was best to let Whalen go.[12]

Nixon waves from a golf cart a week after the 1968 Republican Convention in Mission Bay, California, on August 12, 1968 (Richard M. Nixon Foundation).

Before he left California, Nixon held a news conference. He stated that he would not be speaking out on issues until after the Democratic Convention, which was scheduled a week later. Nixon said he would be making stops in Illinois, Michigan, Ohio, and Pennsylvania before going to New York. In Illinois, he was meeting with the Republican candidate for governor, Richard Ogilvie. In Michigan, Nixon followed up on an earlier phone call with Governor Romney. In Ohio and Pennsylvania, he would meet with Governors Rhodes and Shafer, who both supported other candidates during the convention. When Nixon got back home, he would meet with Governor Rockefeller, followed by lunches with Senators Edward Brooke and Howard Baker. He also announced that he had transferred four of his aides, including John Sears and Charlie McWhorter, to help Governor Agnew with his campaign. Finally, Nixon made it clear that his campaigning was not going to be on national television. He said, "I will not barricade myself in a television studio and make this an antiseptic campaign." Nixon wanted to make the campaign real by having "a certain chemistry that takes place only when a candidate meets the voters. I want to have it."[13]

Unity Theme Continues

Richard Nixon continued with meeting the core of liberal Republicans on his way back to New York, stressing party unity. The first stop was with his first rival in the primaries at George Romney's office in Lansing. The meeting went well, with Romney telling reporters that he was happy to campaign for the Nixon-Agnew team in Michigan and elsewhere. The Michigan governor was all smiles when asked if he was upset that he was not on the ticket with Nixon as his running mate. Romney said, "What happened in Miami is similar to someone who has a little stomach tension and then gets a good big burp. I think I enabled the delegates down there to have a good big burp and leave Miami united."[14] It was a far cry from Romney's response after the Goldwater nomination four years earlier when he pledged to work for the Republican Party but would not commit to campaigning for Goldwater.

From Michigan, Nixon stopped in the Illinois state capitol for a short meeting with prominent Republican leaders in the state legislature along with the gubernatorial candidate, Richard Ogilvie. He told the Illinois lawmakers to watch closely the proceedings of the Democratic Convention the following week. Nixon said, "Never has a party been more deeply divided.... They're going to split that party at the convention, whichever way they go. Let's get those that they leave behind."[15] Then the divisions in the party would be evident to all, unlike the Republicans. Afterward, he placed a wreath on the tomb of the first Republican president, Abraham Lincoln. He addressed a crowd of over 3,000 in front of the capitol, following up with the same themes discussed earlier with the politicians.[16]

The next day, the Republican presidential candidate visited Ohio and Pennsylvania. In Columbus, Nixon got assurances from Governor Rhodes about his commitment to the Republican ticket. Rhodes agreed to go "wherever needed" as a surrogate for the campaign. There was a near repeat performance as Nixon got guarantees in Pennsylvania from Governor Shafer and former Governor William Scranton. Scranton, who was a presidential contender four years earlier, would serve as a "principal adviser" to Nixon on foreign relations. Shafer told reporters outside his Harrisburg office that he was "wholeheartedly behind his campaign and we are going to carry Pennsylvania on behalf of Dick Nixon and Ted Agnew."[17]

On the flight home, the Nixon campaign got great news with the first post-convention Gallup national presidential preference poll among registered voters. Nixon led both of the Democratic rivals four days before the start of their party's convention. While the survey only indicated a small lead of five percent of Nixon over Eugene McCarthy, the more important news was that his lead over the prospective Democratic nominee Hubert Humphrey had increased by 14 points from the last poll taken before the Republican Convention. Nixon went from a slim 40–38 lead to a 45–29 percent advantage. George Wallace got 18 percent in the latest poll. This poll suggested that 17 percent of the national Democratic vote defected to Nixon while 19 percent had gone to Wallace. Nixon led in the East, Midwest, and West, while he trailed Wallace by only three points, 36–33, in the South.[18] It was not the kind of news that the majority party wanted to hear on the eve of the convention, but it was music to the ears of Nixon supporters.

Back home in New York, the unity tour continued with four separate meetings with John Lindsay, Nelson Rockefeller, Jacob Javits, and Edward Brooke. All four Republican liberals issued positive statements after they appointed Nixon. The Lindsay meeting took place in the mayor's residence at Gracie Mansion. While Nixon already had Lindsay's support, he wanted to call on the most visible Republican mayor in the largest city in the country.

What caught Nixon's attention after the meeting was the overnight invasion of Czechoslovakia by the Soviet Union. The attack came after months of reforms that the Communist government of Alexander Dubcek had instituted in the central European country. President Johnson called him after midnight the night before and discussed the situation with him. Several aides were there with Nixon when the call came through. These included Buchanan, Price, Ellsworth, and Dick Allen. LBJ asked Nixon not to take a strong stand against him. The president hoped that by appealing to Nixon's sense of patriotism and general alignment with him on national security, Vietnam would be enough to convince the Republican presidential nominee to stand down on this one. It worked.[19] Nixon had a statement ready the next morning, and it was issued to the press outside Gracie Mansion concerning the recent events. At the same time, he met with the New York City mayor: "The voices of all who value freedom ought now to demand the removal of [Warsaw Pact] troops. And those who wish for long-term peace must also hope that the Soviets consider this brutal act—not only in sympathy with the Czech and Slovak people but also because it jeopardizes those broader negotiations if peace is to be secured for the balance of this century. It violates the basic tenets of international law; it violates both the letter and the spirit of the United Nations charter, it violates the basic spirit of human decency."[20]

The next three meetings took place at Nixon's 5th Avenue apartment. Governor Rockefeller did not have to go far to visit Nixon, given that he lived in the same building. After a successful session, the two issued a joint communiqué stating, "Toward the end [winning in November] the Governor will assume personal direction of the campaign in New York State, and also will appear in support of the Republican ticket in a number of other states." After a brief meeting with Nixon, Senator Javits announced the Soviet invasion of Czechoslovakia, making it vital to have a man of Nixon's experience in the White House. Senator Brooke, who was the only Black member of the United States Senate, followed Javits for a meeting with the Republican presidential candidate at Nixon's abode. Brooke issued a statement supporting Agnew: "I know Ted Agnew very well. He had problems handling the disturbances in Baltimore, but Ted Agnew is certainly not a racist. In my view, he's a progressive. The so-called hard line he took in Baltimore does not indicate at all he's a racist."[21]

The Democratic Convention, or the Wacky Chicago Adventures of Pat and Bill

After the New York meetings, Nixon flew to Key Biscayne for a week of relaxation while monitoring the news around the campaign. He would not make any more public comments until after the Democratic Convention. What he did do was to send Pat Buchanan and Bill Safire, who had officially joined the campaign in June, to Chicago to monitor the Democrats. They got a suite on the 19th floor at the Conrad Hilton, the same hotel where the Humphrey and McCarthy campaigns resided.[22]

The hotel was located on Michigan Avenue right across Grant Park and near the stockyards on Halsted Street. The Democrats had their 1952 and 1956 conventions here, as did the Republicans in 1960. The site was chosen the year before, after lobbying by Mayor Richard J. Daley. He sweetened the deal by offering three-quarters of a million dollars in subsidies along with $150,000 in city services to the Democratic National Committee (DNC). Daley also promised the president that he would get over 65 percent of the vote in Cook County when he ran for re-election. Johnson made the deal. It was supposed to be the beginning of his re-election campaign. All of the significant people controlling the convention were Johnson's people, headed by Marvin Watson, who was then the postmaster general of the United States. The convention had extremely tight security, requiring credentials to even get within the parameters of the stockyards.

About a month before the convention, Hubert Humphrey approached Johnson and wanted to change the location of the convention to Miami Beach. The president refused. Humphrey had received information that several radical groups, including the Students for a Democratic Society (SDS), the Weatherman, and others, were interested in making trouble for the majority party's convention. Besides, the vice president was concerned about planned strikes from electrical workers and bus drivers that would make it difficult for the convention to function appropriately. Daley had promised the president that he would be ready for any eventuality. He placed his nearly 12,000 strong police force on twelve-hour shifts and called up 5,600 National Guardsman to help with security. He also had in reserve 7,500 army troops in Texas that Johnson had guaranteed him if things got out of hand. Many of the protestors were setting up shop in or around Grant Park nearly a week before the convention.[23]

Traditionally in American politics, when one party was putting on a national convention, the other had a presence of some sort. In this case, Nixon sent two top speechwriters, along with John Love and Donald Rumsfeld. Love was the governor of Colorado, while Rumsfeld was a member of the House of Representatives in suburban Chicago. Bill Timmons, who was the chief aide to Congressman William Brock of Tennessee, was also there. The Republican listening post was a hospitality suite that served drinks and snacks to select media. Those selected were anyone the group decided to invite. Meanwhile, Buchanan and Safire wandered around, observing the comings and goings of conventioneers.

On the first night, Buchanan walked through the lobby of what he called the "Comrade Hilton" and crossed the police line into Grant Park. Dressed neatly in coat and tie, he walked past demonstrators who assumed he was a cop or a member of the "f.... FBI." He had experienced such a crowd the previous year at one of the demonstrations outside the Pentagon. Buchanan described most of the protestors as "in their twenties, and their vocabulary was as filthy as they could make it, women as well as men." Most of the pointed barbs were pointed toward the president, assorted politicians, and the police. Buchanan thought that police would like to have responded more forcefully to the protestors, but at this point, they exercised restraint.[24]

The second day started with stink bombs thrown by protestors as Buchanan and Safire made their way down to the lobby.[25] A couple of blocks outside the hotel, Buchanan caught a whiff of tear gas. He walked back to the hotel; it got worse. Gasping for air, Buchanan went straight to the men's restroom to wash out his eyes. Right beside him, doing the same thing, was Tom Wicker of the *New York Times*.[26] While Buchanan fought tear gas, Safire drove to the airport to pick up Governor Love who was arriving from Colorado. When the two returned to the hotel, they were greeted by signs that said, "Make Love, Not War." The governor thought this a positive expression of his entrance, and Love complimented Safire that they had done an excellent advance job. Safire did not correct him.[27] Later that night, after observing loud protestors on the street below, the two made their way to their rooms to sleep. After midnight, Buchanan was awakened by a phone call from Nixon, who wanted to know what was going on. Buchanan walked the phone to the window to let Nixon listen for himself. The mob below was chanting "Dump the Hump" and "F...you Daley."[28]

As the convention continued, the Johnson (and ultimately Humphrey) forces won the major platform fights. A lot was going below the surface that concerned Hubert Humphrey, who feared Johnson might run again. Governor John B. Connally of Texas, a protégé of Johnson for more than twenty years, was running interference for the president throughout the convention. Johnson had asked him to query the southern delegations to see if they favored a re-nomination draft. He did and got a resounding no from southern colleagues, who staunchly backed Humphrey.[29] Additionally, Humphrey feared Edward "Teddy" Kennedy might emerge as a nomination draft. Senator Kennedy had met with Eugene McCarthy, who agreed to drop out of the race if Kennedy wanted to jump into the race at the last moment. During their conversation, Stephen Smith (Kennedy's brother-in-law) got angry when McCarthy told him that he would do it for Teddy, but that he could have never done it for Bobby. Given the history between McCarthy and Bobby Kennedy, it is easy to see McCarthy's perspective after their hotly contested California primary in June. As it turned out, the younger Kennedy decided to stay on the sidelines.[30]

On the third day of the convention, there was a big fight over the Vietnam platform. The peace forces (perhaps at any cost) were led by Senator George McGovern of South Dakota, and McCarthy, who wanted the plank to stop the bombing of North Vietnam entirely. The Humphrey/Johnson team would not go along with that, arguing that a total bombing halt would be detrimental to American and South Vietnamese troops. Humphrey ran the precise language by Rusk and Rostow, who had no objections, but the president did. Johnson wanted the statement to say precisely, "Stop the bombing of North Vietnam when this action would not endanger the lives of our troops." Humphrey wanted to go with the earlier "taking into account" language, but Johnson would have none of it. Johnson maintained the North Vietnamese were not serious about the peace talks and told Humphrey that. Ultimately, the Johnson/Humphrey position passed the platform committee by a 62 to 35 vote with a 500-vote margin by the 2600 plus Democratic delegates.[31]

That in place, an orderly nomination process should have occurred on Wednesday night. That was not to be. Earlier that day, the National Mobilization Committee to End the War (the Mobe) held a scheduled demonstration in Grant Park. When the demonstrators heard the news of the anti-war plank failing, they became more restless, and their leader, David Dellinger, led them out of the park to march on the amphitheater some five miles south. They were met by police when they arrived at the intersection of Michigan and Balbo Avenues. The police, wearing gas masks and riot gear, tossed tear gas grenades into the crowd and then rushed to push them back with billy clubs and mace. With the rioting underway, the Democratic Convention began the nomination speech of George McGovern by fellow Senator Abraham Ribicoff of Connecticut. Ribicoff told the assembled crowd at the amphitheater, "with George McGovern as president, we wouldn't have to have Gestapo tactics in the streets of Chicago." With that, the television cameras switched to Mayor Daley in the audience, who yelled an expletive at Ribicoff. The Connecticut senator stared back and said,

"How hard it is to accept the truth, how hard it is." It was riveting television to the millions of viewers throughout the country, and yes, they saw the Democratic Party tear themselves apart.[32]

Buchanan was back at the suite on the 19th floor by himself when Norman Mailer walked in with former lightweight champion Jose Torres, looking to imbibe. With drinks in hand, the three turned to look out the window at all the commotion below. Buchanan described what they saw:

> The protestors in Grant Park were continuing their stream of insults in front of the Hilton. But to our left at the corner of Michigan and Balboa, a parade of marchers heading south for the convention had been halted. The mule train of the Reverend Abernathy's Poor People March had been allowed to pass. The rest were blocked. Now up Balboa came a column of cops that halted briefly. Stand-off. Then the cops pulled out their clubs, broke ranks, and tore into the protestors and radicals who scattered and ran into the park. The cops did not stop. They chased and clubbed them to vans. On and on it went. Mailer was silent, transfixed, as was I. Torres, watching each takedown, was cursing the cops in heavily accented English, "Sons of bitches! Sons of bitches!"[33]

Later that night, sometime after midnight, Hubert Humphrey won the nomination over Eugene McCarthy and George McGovern. The television cameras alternated between the convention and anarchy in the street. It was not what the Democratic nominee had hoped for, but he would try to make the best of it. After Pennsylvania put Humphrey over the top, Nixon called him and congratulated him. Nixon empathized with the victorious nominee, having now walked this path twice, once years before and again three weeks ago. The two exchanged further pleasantries and ended their conversation.[34] After that, sometime in the wee hours of Thursday morning, Humphrey decided on a vice presidential choice: Edmund Muskie, the Senator from Maine.

At the Nixon observation post on the 19th floor, Safire got the word from Key Biscayne that they should lay low and refuse to celebrate. On the last night of the convention, Humphrey made his acceptance speech with thanks to his party's competitors, McCarthy and McGovern. He then recounted the wonderful things that the new Democratic pantheon from Franklin Roosevelt to Lyndon Johnson had done for the American people. Humphrey promised to keep it up. After the speech, Buchanan and Safire dragged the phone into the bathroom, out of their noisy suite that was buzzing with late-night drinking. Nixon wanted to talk to one of them about the speech. Nixon critiqued the speech both in substance and style. He thought it went too long and had too many clichés. The one thing that annoyed him was Humphrey's jabs about him going after the attorney general and the judges. Nixon had been critical, as had much of the country, at Ramsey Clark's approach to law and order and the liberal inclinations of the Warren Court. Nixon believed that the country was on their side and let Safire know it: "We're going to crack that Attorney General issue. We got to him. He's taking us on in an area that is bad for him, and that's a mistake."[35]

It was after midnight when Buchanan and Safire took one more stroll into Grant Park. They heard many speeches disparaging LBJ, Daley, the police, and the whole American political and economic establishment. Later, an assortment of garbage was thrown on the police from one of the upper floors of the Hilton. The police, after pointing fingers upward, rushed into the hotel to find the offenders. The two Nixon observers headed back to their rooms on the 19th floor but mistakenly got off on the 15th floor, to witness a bunch of bloodied heads among the young McCarthy supporters and police hauling them off. When they got back to their rooms, Safire told Buchanan that he could not believe the police would have invaded the political headquarters of one of the candidates. He considered it a "sanctuary."[36] The police took the "kids" down to the bottom of the hotel for additional questioning. On their way down, they passed Richard Goodwin, one of McCarthy's campaign managers, and asked him for help. Goodwin called both McCarthy and Humphrey's suite to vouch for the young Democratic supporters. McCarthy agreed to come down, but one of Humphrey's aides told Goodwin that the vice president was asleep and could not be disturbed. When McCarthy got down to the lobby, the police let the supposed offenders go back to their room.[37]

A Week Before the Big Dance

Immediately out of the convention, Nixon had a commanding lead over Hubert Humphrey. He knew that the next two months were going to be the most important of his political life despite his current leading position. The good news out of the last poll was that nearly two-thirds of the country did not want Humphrey as their president. The bad news was that only 27 percent of the country identified as Republicans, while 42 percent did so as Democrats and 28 percent called themselves Independents.[38] Nixon's challenge was to hold onto the 26 states that he carried in 1960 and come up with some combination of 41 electoral votes from the other states.

Six weeks earlier, John Sears had prepared a detailed 43-page confidential memorandum of the campaign detailing which states could be carried and how. He had spent the past two years researching every state and congressional district. Sears had also talked with and met nearly all of the key Republicans around the country, getting a sense of what worked in each state or district. Additionally, Sears had attended every governors' conference and developed good relationships with most, if not all, of the Republican governors.[39] Sears had observed there would most likely be problems of overlap between the "citizens' movement" and regular Republican campaigns in some states. There was also no need for citizen groups in states that they had no chance of winning or in states that were already solidly Republican. There, they could depend on regular Republican campaigns to get out the vote. Many of the Republican governors had voiced concern that this kind of duplication would cause internal problems in their various state campaigns. It should be made clear which organization had priority in a particular state. In addition, in the key "swing states," there needed to be a "Nixon man from outside the state to keep a close watch on the day to day activities of the organizations." Before his state by state evaluations, Sears expressed the paramount importance for a Nixon supporter to sit in on joint meetings with the regular Republican chairman, the citizens' chairman, and the other campaign chairmen to ensure the proper coordination. It would save time and clear up the confusion that might bog down a campaign at an inopportune time. The only Sears recommendation that Nixon disagreed with centered on the role of surrogate speakers. Sears believed that the best use of surrogates was in their states, while Nixon thought that they could be used more widely. In some states, such as Texas, there were rival Republican factions that backed either Tower or Bush. It would probably work better if the more prominent person stayed in the state and sent the other speaker to areas of the country where they could be most useful.[40]

The Sears memorandum, coupled with the mid–June strategy meeting headed by John Mitchell and Bob Haldeman, laid the groundwork for the clear lines of command within the organization chart of the upcoming general election campaign. The table was divided into four coordinated divisions, with Mitchell in charge of the campaign and Haldeman in charge of the candidate. The financial division was headed by Maurice Stans, who led all the fund-raising within the campaign. The campaign division headed by Mitchell put together the priorities, decided where the resources were to be directed, and liaised with regional and state chairs. They were physically located in a building on Park Avenue. The internal polling was done there under Mitchell and supported by prominent Indiana University political scientist David Derge. They used focus groups from key battleground areas and measured how their preferences varied within the political environment. The third division, called the creative staff, housed the researchers, speechwriters, and communications team. They were located in the old Bible Institute building across the street from the campaign division. Haldeman headed the fourth and final division, the traveling group. Ron Ziegler traveled with the candidate while the speechwriters alternated trips.[41]

Nixon took Sears' advice and concentrated on the "big state" strategy. He would spend over 75 percent of his time over the next two months in seven big states with 210 electoral votes: New York (43), California (40), Pennsylvania (29), Illinois (26), Ohio (26), Texas (25), and Michigan (21), focusing on major metropolitan areas. All of these states except New York, despite the public comments by the Nixon campaign, were realistic probabilities for Nixon. Of the seven, he had won only California and Ohio eight years earlier, and he had lost Texas, Michigan, and Pennsylvania by two percent. Also, Nixon lost Illinois, Missouri, and New Jersey by less than one percent. Missouri and New Jersey contained 29 electoral votes. If he could hang on to his winning states and add the three "almost won" states, Nixon would win the presidency with 274 electoral votes no matter how he did anywhere else. Of course, winning all seven states was not a given.

The candidacy of George Wallace presented another challenge. His base was all of the eleven former Confederate states. While Nixon had only won Virginia, Florida, and Tennessee eight years earlier, the Alabama governor was in striking distance in all of the southern states Nixon carried in 1960. Also, in 1964, Goldwater carried the five Deep South states of Louisiana, Mississippi, Alabama, Georgia, and South Carolina. Nixon should now be strong in these states, but Wallace was blocking him there. The only realistic possibility was in South Carolina, where Strom Thurmond should help blunt the Wallace vote. The others, with the possible exception of Georgia, were hopeless.

On the other hand, North Carolina and Texas were real possibilities. He had only lost these by less than two percent in 1960. If Wallace were not in the race, Nixon believed that he could sweep the South, which had never been done by a Republican. This region of the country was the most ideologically conservative and should have leaned toward Nixon, absent Wallace, who was in the race to stay. Ironically, the Nixon camp feared Humphrey would play to his Democratic base in the South, despite being behind in all the states. The entire southern delegation in the

Democratic Convention had backed Humphrey. The current vice president could conceivably collude with Wallace, who was a Democrat even though he was running as a third-party candidate. In doing this, the two might block Nixon out of the region.

Before the Democratic Convention, Nixon had predicted the country would see how fractured the majority party was, and he was right. The convention had been a disaster viewed on national television. One close Nixon associate said, "We intend to hang the Administration around Humphrey's neck, and the fact that so many Democrats seem willing to do the same thing makes our job much easier."[42] Further evidence of the country's dissatisfaction with Lyndon Johnson appeared as his approval rating dropped to the lowest point in his five-year presidency, 35 percent, according to a Gallup Poll released the day after Labor Day.[43] Vice President Humphrey, whether he liked it or not, was tied to the president's policies. Nixon would not let the American people forget this, despite his moratorium on criticizing the president on the war. Nixon would not interfere in the peace process, but he questioned privately how it ever got to this point in the war.

Bob Haldeman sent a confidential memo to Peter Flanigan, John Mitchell's chief deputy in the New York office, that summarized Nixon's thoughts on the eve of the campaign. The note was sent after a meeting that Haldeman had with Nixon. The candidate and the surrogates needed to take the initiative and keep it. The points that were emphasized by all the state and county Republican chairmen along with other connected politicos were as follows:

Nixon with H.R. Haldeman on campaign in fall 1968 (Richard M. Nixon Foundation).

1. *The Come-back Theme:* This has immense appeal and RN does not believe it has adequately been covered in columns or the press....

2. *The Calibre of the Nixon team:* This gives us the opportunity to point the superb RN pre–Convention organization, that it has high intellectual quality, great morale and great loyalty....

3. *The Youth of the RN Organization:* Emphasizing the number of men under 30, under 40....

4. *The Immense Effect of the RN Acceptance Speech:* Key on best elements of the acceptance speech....

5. *RN as Party Unifier:* Even several of the less favorable press men pointed out that the week when we were at Mission Bay plus the swing of the major states was probably one of the major political stories of our time and would have been covered as such had the Czech Revolution not occurred in the same period....

6. *RN, "the man for the times":* Perhaps most important of all—there should be an emphasis on RN, as a "man of the times." In spite of losing two political races, the country needed him in a period of Crisis similar to when Churchill came back on the political scene at the beginning of World War II.[44]

The two most significant issues of the upcoming campaign were the war in Vietnam and the breakdown in law and order. Nixon had been talking about both a great deal for the past four years. He had told President Johnson that he would not directly criticize him on the war or interfere in the peace process. Nixon avoided specifics on how he would prosecute the war, but he was well situated between the hawks, who wanted a more aggressive strategy, and the doves, who wanted to pull out as soon as possible. Nixon believed winning the war was nearly impossible and that the best he could do was withdraw with South Vietnam intact as the essence for an "honorable peace." On the issue of crime, Nixon clearly stated he believed the complete breakdown of law and order was caused primarily by the Democratic administration and a series of rulings by the liberal Warren court empowering the criminal elements along with preventing the police from doing their job. Nixon specified Attorney General Ramsey Clark as epitomizing the Democrats' approach to crime. Nixon promised a more assertive attorney general and Supreme Court picks who respected the Constitution. He would now take these issues, and more, to the American people as the Labor Day holiday was over, and the real fight for the presidency began.

General Campaign Begins

There would be only two events per day and much more concentrated use of television. The first week of the campaign would be in the large battleground states of Illinois, California, and Texas. The choice for the beginning of the general election campaign would be precisely where Democrats had blundered in Chicago. The Nixon team believed this would show straight on their opponent's turf, a solidly Democratic city headed by the irrepressible Mayor Daley, who had taken a lot of heat from the national press on the actions of his police department during the convention. Buchanan wrote a memo a week before the Chicago visit cautioning Nixon that bad-mouthing the cops would get him "absolutely zero in support" and would ultimately hurt him if he was too critical of their actions. Reasonable people like the "forgotten Americans" that Nixon had spoken so eloquently about a few weeks earlier in his acceptance speech thought the protestors got what they deserved.[45] Buchanan acknowledged that while some of the police might have overstepped their bounds, the vast majority of them acted promptly and professionally.[46]

In Chicago, the Republican candidate was greeted by a ticker-tape parade that he called the "greatest" reception that he had ever received. Nixon was joined in the open car motorcade by his wife, two daughters, and David Eisenhower. The size of the crowd differed in each account, but the most reliable number was 400,000 as they wound through 19 blocks in the heart of the Windy City. This contrasted with the Democratic Convention held a week before in having no incidents or protests, no fights between police and protestors. After winding through the city, Nixon went to the Sheraton-Blackstone hotel for a short lunch and meeting with his aides. Nixon waved to the crowd assembled outside the hotel but did not speak to them. However, he did have Edmund Brooke and Nelson Rockefeller make brief comments on his behalf. Later in the afternoon, he went to a nearby television studio to tape a telecast shown that night across Illinois, Missouri, and parts of Indiana. It was the standard "man in the arena" concept with six panelists that included two members of the press along with a studio audience chosen by the campaign. Nixon's first public comments on the riots and demonstrations from the Democratic Convention were diplomatic and statesmanlike. He said that there had been several reports of "a great deal of activity on the part of the demonstrators that irritated the police, which was certainly provocative in nature and it would be easy to lob a lot of criticism at Democratic leaders." Without directly disparaging the opposition party, Nixon noted a bipartisan commission headed by Milton Eisenhower was looking into the causes of violence and how it could be prevented.[47]

The following day Nixon received a similar reception during another ticker-tape parade through the San Francisco financial district and into Chinatown, with an estimated crowd of 300,000 lining the streets of this ordinarily Democratic city. He was accompanied by Thruston Morton and Ed Brooke, both former Rockefeller supporters. Nixon was greeted at the airport by Governor Reagan and Bob Finch, giving further evidence of the unified nature of the Republican Party. Reagan encouraged "a warm welcome for our fellow Californians, and we have made up our mind that they are going to live 3,000 miles away from California for the next few years." Finch accompanied the Nixon team downtown and to a rally in neighboring Santa Clara to an overflowing crowd of 25,000 at Buck Shaw Field, which only seated about 7,000 people. Nixon continued his theme outlined in his acceptance speech, predicting "forgotten Americans," who have had enough of the lawlessness and disorder on the domestic front along with the war in Asia, would come together in 1968 to work for "peaceful change" in the leadership of this country.[48]

Nixon capped off the first week in Houston with a crowd of 30,000 in Miller Memorial Amphitheater, where he criticized Humphrey by linking him to Warren Court decisions expanding the rights of accused criminals. This message was well-received in conservative Houston, which was the home of one of Nixon's surrogates, George H.W. Bush.[49] Texas was also the home to some of the country's deepest pockets that had propelled Lyndon Johnson to the White House. Conservative John Connally and liberal Ralph Yarborough split the Democratic vote.

Connally was the state's most powerful politician and a long-time protégé of President Johnson. Connally had been contacted by Nixon and offered the secretary of defense position in his cabinet if he could do three things for him. The first involved not being seen with Humphrey when he came to Texas. The second was helping Nixon raise money by making available his wealthy contacts throughout the state. The last was making sure that Nixon got a fair vote count in the state, particularly in the southern part of Texas that was notorious for irregularities in 1960. Connally had not yet been seen with Humphrey, and Nixon had been able to raise a fair amount of money from the business community that usually reserved their funds for Democrats.[50] The weekend concluded with a short stop in Oklahoma, home of Bud Wilkinson. The first week of the Nixon campaign offered great visuals to the American television audience of large and enthusiastic crowds in three of its largest cities. The Nixon Team controlled the message in the media cycle in their favor starting out of the blocks, but they knew that it would be more difficult as they got closer to November.

The Second Week

After a couple of days resting and strategizing in Key Biscayne, Richard Nixon returned to the campaign trail with events in Charlotte and Indianapolis before going west for a five-day trip to California. He got more good news from the early September Gallup Poll, showing him still leading Humphrey and Wallace by 43–31–19, with eight percent undecided. He led in three of the four regions of the country and trailed Wallace in the South by seven points. The Alabama governor led 38 to 31, with only 25 percent of the region saying that they would vote for Hubert Humphrey for president. Nixon also led the relevant independent category with 39 percent. Wallace gathered 33, and Humphrey earned only 20.[51]

On his California swing, Nixon held a news conference outside the Disneyland Hotel to respond to Humphrey's campaign manager's charges on *Meet the Press* that Nixon was appealing to "racist" Wallace supporters in the South. Nixon made it clear that he was not racist and that the backers between southern Democrats and Wallace's third party were conspiring against him with the hopes of throwing the election into the House of Representatives, where the Democrats held a substantial majority. Nixon called on Humphrey to repudiate this error and said that he would not participate in any debates that gave more credence to the Alabama governor. Nixon said, "I would hope that Vice President Humphrey would show the same degree of statesmanship in perhaps getting Mr. [Lawrence] O'Brien and some of his real henchmen to be perhaps a little more responsible in their statements."[52] Later that night, Nixon spoke to an overflow crowd of over 10,000 at the Anaheim Convention Center. Earlier in the day, he had visited Yorba Linda and the house in which he was born. The current inhabitant of the house was a gardener employed by the Yorba Linda school. The crowd assembled outside the school numbered more than 3,000 while Nixon stood on a car to make some brief comments. It brought back memories of his earlier congressional campaigns when he often stood on the bumper of a car with a microphone in hand. Nixon poked fun at his father's failed business foray in the lemon business, saying that "this used to be the site where my father's 9-acre lemon grove, but it didn't grow very good lemons. I'm glad to see now that it's growing a better crop—children."[53]

During the California trip, Nixon made a cameo appearance on the off-the-wall, satirical television show *Laugh-In*, entering its second season as the number one rated show on television. He was on the show for only five seconds and said, "Sock it to me!" Nixon agreed to be on the show hosted by Dan Rowan and Dick Martin because their lead writer was Paul Keyes, who had met Nixon over five years earlier when he wrote for the *Jack Paar Show*. The two clicked, and Keyes provided Nixon with several funny lines over the past five years. Dwight Chapin recalled that the most he had ever seen Nixon laugh was while the aide was riding along with the two in a car during the 1964 Republican Convention.[54] Keyes thought a guest appearance would help with Nixon's image among young people, who were the biggest fans of the show. Humphrey had also been asked to be on the show but declined.

Nixon then headed across the country and campaigned in Illinois before heading to a fundraiser in New York, shown closed-circuit to 19 other cities across the country. It raised five million dollars. Earlier in the day, Nixon drew a more massive crowd than Humphrey in Philadelphia, which was a Pennsylvania Democratic stronghold. A crowd estimated between 200,000 and 250,000 witnessed the ticker-tape parade through the country's fourth-largest city. Pennsylvania was one of the battleground states that Nixon was focusing on and Philadelphia, in particular, because it was the reason he lost the state in 1960. Kennedy carried Philly by over 300,000 votes as Nixon won in the rest of Pennsylvania by 200,000. Nixon filmed a television question and answered session shown on local television the same night as the fund-raiser in the typical man-in-the arena format. Nixon also did interviews with local television personalities that often irritated the national press following him. The reporters felt that they should be getting access to the candidate as opposed to their local and regional rivals in the media.[55]

Last Week in September

The campaign seemed to be churning like a well-oiled machine going into the last week of September. It was a dramatic contrast to that of Hubert Humphrey, who was speaking to much smaller crowds and trailed Nixon by a significant amount in fund-raising. Humphrey ran into hecklers that disrupted his speaking. It became woefully apparent that his campaign had done very little planning past getting the Democratic nomination. By not having adequate cash on hand, the vice president did very little television or radio advertising in September. Wealthy Democratic donors had been sitting on the sidelines waiting to see if Humphrey's poll numbers were going to go up.[56] A CBS state-by-state survey released on Monday did not give Humphrey any better news. It showed Nixon winning in a landslide with 333 electoral votes and 31 states, followed by Wallace with 39 electoral votes, and Humphrey bringing up the rear with 39 electoral votes.[57] The Gallup Poll released six days later showed Nixon leading Humphrey by 15 points, 43–28. Humphrey had lost two points, and Wallace had gained two points to 21 from the previous survey two weeks earlier.[58]

Despite the good news on the election front, the Nixon campaign started to show problems with their vice presidential candidate. Spiro Agnew had said some things that riled up the national media, arguing that Humphrey was "soft on communism" and that a Japanese-American reporter was a "fat Jap." The media focused on the Maryland governor's gaffes while ignoring similar screw-ups by Edmund Muskie; the Maine senator received glowing praise while the media daily lampooned Agnew. To combat this, Stephen Hess was dispatched to travel with Agnew to help him in his speeches. While the Nixon team hoped that this was done discreetly, Evans and Novak found out about it and wrote a column.[59] John Sears had a direct line to Nixon and talked to him several times a week about what was happening with Agnew. Nixon wanted to make sure that he had someone talking to him directly from the ground.[60] With just over five weeks to go in the campaign, Richard Nixon was upbeat, but knowing the hills and valleys involved in this endeavor, he had to be prepared for anything.

13

Nut-Cutting Time

Sometimes in a presidential campaign, political events outside the campaign necessitate a candidate's response. In this case, with five weeks to go, one of these issues came front and center to the campaign: President Johnson's July nominations of Abe Fortas to be chief justice and Homer Thornberry as an associate justice to the Supreme Court. We must go back a few months to understand why this was still an issue in September. For three days in the middle of July, Fortas had agreed to go before the Senate Judiciary Committee to answer questions about his pending nomination as chief justice. No sitting associate justice nominated as chief justice had ever been turned down by the Senate in American history. Besides, no associate justice had ever agreed this early in the process to testify on his own behalf, as Fortas did. Conversely, 10 out of 17 nominees to the court have failed to be confirmed in the president's final year of office. Justice Fortas thought that he could do better than those odds. During his three days of testimony, Fortas was intensely questioned about his numerous meetings with Johnson while a member of the court. It was widely known in Washington that Fortas had been LBJ's fixer for several years and that the president relied heavily upon his advice on a wide range of matters, political or otherwise. It also did not help that Fortas had represented a Soviet sympathizer and Communist scholar during the 1950s.[1] According to presidential scholar Michael Nelson, senators grilled him about his alleged reluctance to advise President Johnson on issues like legislation, executive actions, and the war in Vietnam. Fortas denied many of these activities. He even outright lied about the over 100 meetings that he had with the president while on the court. Fortas also discussed a railroad merger case with Johnson before writing the majority opinion in the case.[2]

Later in the testimony, Fortas was confronted by Strom Thurmond, who asked a series of questions on why Fortas voted with the majority on several cases involving the rights of the accused, pornography, and obscenity. Over 50 times, Fortas refused to answer the senator, citing separation of powers issues. As it turned out, the Judiciary Committee postponed its report to the entire Senate as Congress was adjourned for their summer recess. In September, when the hearings picked back up, Thurmond found out Fortas had received a $15,000 fee to teach a class one night a week for nine weeks at American University. The stipend was funded by a group of wealthy businessmen solicited by Fortas's former law partner Paul Porter. The dollar amount was over seven times what someone would be paid to teach such a class. It amounted to over a third of his salary as an associate justice on the court. While it was not unnatural for a prominent judge to teach a class in a law school and be handsomely paid, the compensation package from some of the most prominent business people in the country was questionable. The financers also had both personal and commercial interests regulated by the federal government. It was later learned that Fortas was being paid $20,000 a year for life by the Wolfson Family Foundation. It had been set up by Louis Wolfson, a Florida financier who had earlier been represented by Fortas and still was by his former firm. Fortas's wife, Carolyn, was also a lawyer at the firm. It was at a time when Wolfson had a pending federal case before the court. After the committee voted 11–6 to recommend Fortas, Senator Robert Griffin of Michigan launched a filibuster. It took 60 votes to invoke cloture to shut off debate. President Johnson was not sure he had 60 votes, but he was confident that he had close to it. On October 2, the cloture vote failed, and the associate justice asked the president to withdraw his name. It was not necessary to bring up Thornberry's nomination since the Fortas nomination was withdrawn.[3]

Earlier that month, Humphrey had blamed Nixon for Fortas's confirmation problems. He said that Nixon "made a deal with Strom Thurmond to undermine Fortas. He could have Mr. Fortas confirmed in a week if he'd say the word because it's his troops in the Senate, his supporters that blocked the nomination." Nixon refused to be drawn into the discussion, saying that he did not oppose the nominee but did oppose a filibuster.[4] It had been less than two years earlier when Fortas voted for Nixon's side in the *Time v. Hill* privacy case, but that favor was light-years away in a political campaign. Johnson considered Nixon would not make that public to thwart what would have become of the first Jewish Chief Justice. Privately, he thought the next president should appoint any qualified justice to the court.

HHH Rolls the Dice

Hubert Humphrey suffered a bad first month after receiving the Democratic presidential nomination in August. His campaign experienced a myriad of problems, including inadequate fund-raising, poor management, lack of a business plan, a Gallup poll showing them 15 points behind, and serving a president whose public approval ratings were in the low 40s. Humphrey had gotten Larry O'Brien, an experienced political operative, to run his campaign. He had been joined in the last week by George Ball, a former member of the Johnson administration and ambassador to the United Nations. Ball detested Nixon and did not think he had the intestinal fortitude to be president. Ball also had been a critic of the president's policy in Vietnam from the beginning. The flip side of this problem was that Humphrey was the nominee of the political party in the country which controlled both houses of Congress, as well as a majority of governorships and state legislatures. The trouble with the Democratic Party, which had primarily been in power in the United States for over 35 years going back to the initial election of Franklin Roosevelt, had to do with party divisions. The party on the right split during the 1948 presidential cycle when several of the southern states walked out of the convention over the civil rights plank in the platform and nominated Strom Thurmond as their candidate. The party split on the left when former Vice President Henry Wallace ran as an independent. After the Democrats reunited, they split again in the mid-sixties after the passage of the Civil Rights and Voting Rights Acts. This time, the split was more extensive, and a Democratic governor, now running as a third-party candidate, was polling over twenty percent of the national vote and leading in seven states. Humphrey's principal rival for the presidential nomination, Eugene McCarthy, had not endorsed him in the final five weeks of the campaign. If Hubert Humphrey were going to get back into the race and make it competitive, he would have to roll the dice. If the vice president were successful, a lot of his former problems would take care of themselves.

Humphrey had made up his mind that if he was going to lose this race, he was going to do so on his terms. He felt that President Johnson had been his boss too long. Johnson had refused to give his vice president his list of donors in September and had been adamant that his policy on the war in Vietnam did not undercut him. As the vice president, it was Humphrey's duty to back the president, but now he was running for president. From the beginning of the Vietnam conflict, Humphrey's convictions had been much closer to Ball's, but being the good soldier, he had backed his boss. As Humphrey was preparing for a major speech in Salt Lake City on September 30, the vice president decided that he would change his policy on the war and separate himself from Lyndon Johnson. He was up nearly all night preparing for the speech and soliciting advice from his advisers. Finally, Humphrey had enough and told them, "Everybody has their own point of view, everything that we talked about, somebody said that will irritate the President, or that will irritate Teddy Kennedy, or that will irritate the McCarthy people, until I said to them, 'I don't care who it pleases, I'm going to write this speech the way that I want it, and if people don't like the speech, that's the way it's going to be.'"[5]

Pat Buchanan notified Nixon that Humphrey had just broken with Johnson on the war issue when he heard about the upcoming Salt Lake City speech from Phil Potter, head of the Washington bureau of the *Baltimore Sun*. Potter, who was politically liberal but supported the war, felt like a cynical Humphrey had betrayed the president.[6] Humphrey was now saying, "As President I would stop the bombing of the North as an acceptable risk for peace because I believe that it could lead to success in the negotiations and thereby shorten the war."[7]

Buchanan urged Nixon to ask how the bombing pause would affect those troops on the DMZ.[8] Bombing the North would not have worked. A bombing shift to the Ho Chi Minh trail in Laos would have worked better but was not considered. The speech had been taped earlier in the day before it was broadcast nationally that night. Humphrey only notified Johnson of the statement 15 minutes before airtime. The president was not happy but knew his vice president would give the speech anyway. Humphrey did not know Nixon had talked to Johnson 45 minutes earlier.[9] Nixon, in his hotel suite in Detroit, summoned Dwight Chapin to get the president on the phone. He thought Rose Mary Woods might know and asked her how to contact President Johnson. Woods told him the number, and Chapin called it. Chapin then told the White House operators he was calling for former Vice President Nixon and wanted to talk to the president. The operators told him to get Nixon on the line so that they could verify his identity. Chapin was amazed to hear Nixon conversing with the operator, asking about her family and how all the White House staff was doing. The operators then transferred the call to the president. In the end, Nixon said he was still with Johnson on the war. The president seemed appreciative of his support. As they were leaving for the airport the next day for Pennsylvania, Johnson's motorcade passed Nixon's on the way to the speech later that day in Detroit.

Nixon called the president in his car and told him that he warmed up the crowd for him, and they also were with him.[10]

In the speech later that night, Nixon asked Humphrey to clarify what he meant by "an acceptable risk for peace" in the absence of meaningful concessions by Hanoi. He did not go as far as Buchanan wanted but did say that Humphrey's comments could undercut ongoing peace negotiations. Nixon refrained from saying anything that might endanger negotiations as he thought his Democratic challenger had done.[11]

Nixon understood that Humphrey's gambit might shore up the anti-war portion of the Democratic base, which remained ambivalent. If the left of his party got aboard the Humphrey train, this could also help fund-raising. With five weeks left in the campaign, they were unlikely to change their minds absent a big difference in Humphrey's poll numbers since big money people are reluctant to support a sore loser. If the latest polls were accurate, Nixon might want to be more critical of Wallace instead of Humphrey. So far, Nixon had not called the Alabama governor by name. That soon changed.

What About George Wallace?

Toward the end of September, *Newsweek* published a poll showing George Wallace winning nine southern states with a total of 87 electoral votes.[12] If that was the case, Nixon needed to win nearly all of the battleground states. At this point, Nixon was ahead in all of these, but he knew that New York was not probable, no matter what John Mitchell said. While he was ahead in Michigan and Pennsylvania, it was not unrealistic for a big Democratic push, particularly in Detroit and Philadelphia, to affect the outcome by motivating large Black and union constituencies. Nixon had lost both states in 1960 by two percent. On October 3, George Wallace was campaigning in Pittsburgh when he introduced General Curtis E. LeMay as his vice presidential running mate. LeMay was a highly decorated general who had served as head of the Strategic Air Command (SAC) and Air Force Chief of Staff. At the press conference, Wallace asked LeMay to make a few comments to the assembled news media. When asked what he would do to end the Vietnam conflict, LeMay answered, "If I thought it was necessary in the Vietnam War, I would use anything we could dream up, including nuclear weapons if necessary." Although LeMay stated that he did not think it was necessary, the press went on a feeding frenzy.[13]

Meanwhile, Nixon's motorcade rolled through downtown Atlanta through a crowd of 150,000 in the heart of Wallace country. A week earlier in Seattle, Nixon had discussed with his speechwriters how he should take on Wallace. Nixon said, "I am willing to take the Wallace thing on. But not like a knee-jerk liberal. That will only help him."[14]

Nixon did just that at a post-speech press conference calling Wallace "irresponsible" and "disagree[ing] completely" with LeMay's possibility of using nuclear weapons if needed in Vietnam. It placed Nixon right in the middle of Wallace and Humphrey on the issue of Vietnam and much closer to President Johnson. Also, he spelled out differences between himself and the Alabama governor, stating, "He's against a lot of things Americans are frustrated about.... The difference is I'm for a lot of things.... We need a policy that will give us new leadership in foreign policy that will re-establish the great alliance with Europe that will get at these trouble spots and future wars."[15]

Nixon also did not question Wallace's motives or intentions. Nixon reasoned while maybe half of Wallace supporters were racists, the rest were regular people fed up with what was going on in the country. Humphrey called Wallace "the apostle of hate and racism."[16] He knew he had to take on Wallace delicately in the Alabama governor's backyard, the irony being for Humphrey that without Wallace in the race, he did not stand a chance. Nixon felt a lot of people in states like Tennessee, Kentucky, Virginia, North Carolina, and Missouri were not racists but were moderates and conservatives. Nixon also knew Wallace had the deep southern states that Goldwater carried in 1964, except for South Carolina. The only state in this region in which Humphrey had a chance was Texas, where both Wallace and Nixon were strong.

That Wallace showed strength among blue-collar workers in the Midwest surprised the national media but not Nixon. In a poll conducted among 16,000 workers at the Buick plant in Flint, Michigan, Wallace's lead over Humphrey increased by 10 points the day after the LeMay announcement. He had earlier won endorsements at other local unions in the United Auto Workers (UAW), but these were smaller plants with small voter turnouts. Over 8,000 people voted in the Flint local union. While the leaders of the UAW and other large labor unions were staunchly Democratic, there appeared to be dissent among the rank and file. The AFL-CIO had formally endorsed Humphrey back in September.[17] Four days later, Princeton Opinion Surveys released

Nixon with cheerleaders in Norfolk, Virginia, on October 2, 1968 (Richard M. Nixon Foundation).

Sign in the crowd dedicated to General Eisenhower who was in the hospital. This photograph was taken when Nixon visited Nashville, Tennessee, on October 2, 1968 (Richard M. Nixon Foundation).

the results of a national poll of union members. These numbers were much closer than the auto workers' surveys, with Humphrey favored with 34 percent, Nixon with 32 percent, and Wallace at 25 percent, with nine percent undecided.[18]

Four More Weeks

With four weeks in the campaign, Nixon thought Wallace had peaked, and that a lot of the Democrats who were sitting on the sidelines would begin gravitating toward Humphrey. Their private polls predicted this, and they wanted to be ready when the gains started showing up in the national polls. At the same time, it looked as if Lyndon Johnson was coming off the sidelines to help his vice president down the home stretch. In an October 7 phone call to Richard Daley, Johnson complained about how the Humphrey people did not seem to want him involved. Daley readily agreed with the president. Daley had told Humphrey that he needed to quit talking about all the problems associated with their administration and, instead, tell the American people about all the good things Democrats accomplished in the past four years. Daley had also told the vice president that he could not win without Johnson's support and had better quit talking about how unpopular the president was. Hearing this was music to Johnson's ears. The president told his Chicago friend he was giving a radio speech the next day at the behest of the International Ladies Garment Workers Union and how he hoped it could help Humphrey.[19]

Indeed, the president was highly complimentary of Humphrey, calling him one of the "few men that I have ever known who understand our urgent national needs." Conversely, LBJ pointed out Nixon's opposition to Medicare and other progressive legislation.[20] It was a clear signal that that Johnson was rallying to help his vice president down the final stretch.

Another way LBJ could assist Humphrey was to announce a breakthrough in the Paris peace talks. In September, Henry Kissinger, a Harvard professor who had been advising the Rockefeller campaign, contacted Dick Allen, Nixon's primary foreign policy adviser. Kissinger, who provided some national security advice to the Johnson administration, told Allen something big was about to occur in the peace talks. Kissinger called Allen four times during September, with updates on the negotiations. He appeared to make these calls on his own, and not at the behest of the president or the Humphrey campaign.[21]

Two days later, at the midpoint of the campaign, the new Gallup Poll showed Nixon still retained a strong lead over both Humphrey and Wallace. The significant increase in Humphrey's numbers that the Nixon camp fearfully anticipated had not yet occurred. The poll still showed Nixon with a 15-point lead over Humphrey, with Wallace trailing with 20 percent. This poll was conducted during the last weekend of September. Humphrey's Salt Lake City speech and General LeMay's comments on the use of nuclear weapons did not show up in this poll. Gallup pointed out in his explanations of the survey that some people sympathetic to the Humphrey campaign were comparing this election to Harry Truman's comeback win in 1948. The veteran pollster cautioned against this comparison because Truman gained steadily throughout September up to the day of the vote. In this election, Humphrey had not shown any gains in September that would indicate a growing momentum.[22] At this same time, Wallace was getting enormous pushback from the media to LeMay's blunder on Vietnam. The former Alabama governor sent him on a "fact-finding" trip to Vietnam.[23]

Going into the last three weeks, Nixon knew the polls were tightening, and he needed to step up his game. He also knew what to do. During a three-day rest and preparation period in Key Biscayne, Nixon had instructed his researchers to double their production of policy papers because he was going to launch a radio series of recommendations on a wide variety of issues. It responded to complaints from the press and charges from the other two candidates that Nixon only talked in generalities. Bob Haldeman told the speechwriters, "He is going to give 'em substance until it runs out of their ears."[24] Nixon himself said that he was preparing "the strongest finish in American political history."[25]

In addition to the politicking his two primary opponents would be doing over the duration, finding a place in the news cycle would be difficult because some other newsworthy events were competitive. There was the Apollo VII mission, the first manned spaceflight in 20 months since the fire that killed three astronauts in January of 1967. The mission would last for eleven days. The month-long teachers' strike in New York City showed no sign of ending. The last two games of the World Series between the St. Louis Cardinals and the Detroit Tigers were being played. And finally, the biggest television event of the year, the Summer Olympics from Mexico City, aired nightly on ABC from October 12 through the 24th. Nixon himself had earlier scheduled a trip to the Olympics during the middle of the month but later decided against it. As if that was not enough, the story that dominated the news cycle the last three weeks of the 1968 campaign was the Paris Peace Talks over the war in Vietnam. For the political campaign, it was the classic elephant in the room.

More Rumors and More Polls

On October 12, the Nixon campaign got another secret message from Henry Kissinger on the status of the talks. Kissinger told them that a breakthrough in the negotiations was going to occur before October 23 and that Nixon should avoid criticisms of Humphrey on this issue. Nixon was perplexed as to why Kissinger would make such a recommendation. Over the next few days, rumors flew in all directions. On October 16, Nixon was campaigning in Kansas City when he was told that President Johnson had a conference call waiting for him and the two other candidates. Nixon was downtown at Union Station, where he was about to address a massive rally, when he was told to find a phone. In short, Johnson reported there was no Paris breakthrough.[26]

Later that day, Nixon traveled to New York for the annual Al Smith Dinner, which LBJ and Humphrey would also be attending. He spoke with the president there and received assurances on his three points. Johnson urged him not to make any significant statements or criticisms about the talks. Nixon agreed.[27] However, he did get in some funny lines at the dinner before yielding to the other speakers. Nixon said of Humphrey and himself, "Regardless of what others may call us, he's the son of a druggist, and I'm a son of a grocer." James A. "Jim" Farley, the former postmaster general and Roosevelt adviser, was the headlining speaker of the annual event. Still, President Johnson stole the show with his satiric criticisms of both Nixon and Humphrey, among the other presidential contenders. He told the sold-out event of 2,500, "Pretty soon you won't have Lyndon Johnson to kick around anymore," in an apparent barb toward Nixon and his 1962 meltdown after the California gubernatorial election. About a large number of Republicans in the audience, Johnson compared himself to George Armstrong Custer who was killed at Little Big Horn: "I don't think any veteran could appreciate my feelings on this night, except General Custer, and I don't know of any chief—executive or otherwise—who has ever been surrounded by so many Indians." Johnson went on, saying that he was "the resident prisoner of a big white jailhouse and looking toward Humphrey or Nixon as a fellow convict." His final "secret thoughts" included several jabs at some other candidates. He said that Nixon was hoping for "a resurrection" and Humphrey was looking for a "little miracle" in his search for campaign funds. Johnson then quipped, "They almost got

[Rockefeller] to the church on time," while John Lindsay thought that they would "get me to the church next time." Finally, LBJ ended his comedic routine by saying that Senator McCarthy "has refused to come to church—he has chosen to go off in the desert and fast."[28] At the same time as the Al Smith dinner, Tommie Smith and John Carlos won the gold and bronze medals in the 200-meter run and raised their fists adorned with black gloves during the playing of the national anthem, an act typifying the unrest of the times.[29]

While Nixon was reassured that there was no breakthrough in the peace talks, he remained wary. After all, he did not get to this point by being naïve. Furthermore, Henry Kissinger's sources at the talks were telling him something different. But Nixon stuck to his pledge while campaigning in Johnstown, Pennsylvania, and backed President Johnson. He also held to the three points that he had earlier outlined to LBJ when he said, "If a bombing halt can save lives in Vietnam ... one which will not endanger American lives, and one which will increase the chances of bringing a peaceful and honorable solution to the war, then we are for it." Nixon ended his comment on the subject by saying the "one man who can make that determination is the President of the United States" and pledging his support for him.[30]

The next day, on October 18, a new Harris Poll that showed the race tightening. Over the weekend, Humphrey gained four points in the poll, but with Nixon still leading 40–35–18. Nixon had won a point since the last survey done a month earlier, but Wallace had lost three points. Even though Nixon did not have as much confidence in the Harris Poll, he believed Humphrey was doing better, as he also anticipated. The last Gallup Poll was done at the end of September.[31] At the same time, there was news coming out of Texas that did not please the Nixon campaign. Governor John Connally called a news conference to announce he would travel with Humphrey while he campaigned in Texas. At the time, Nixon had a small lead in the battleground state where Connally had helped him raise money; when Humphrey campaigned in Texas a month earlier, Connally was nowhere to be seen. Nixon hoped that would continue but realized Johnson must be pressing Connally to help Humphrey in the president's home state. Also, Connally made it clear he would welcome Senator Ralph Yarborough if he wanted to join the tour. Connally and Yarborough were long-time political rivals who rarely spoke, much less campaigned together.[32]

Over the weekend, Nixon got good news when *Life* magazine endorsed him. It stated, "What is needed, in our judgment, is a government that can reassert the workability of our political institutions and thereby calm our nerves, restore a measure of national self-confidence and encourage Americans to start trusting each other again." At the same time, a large number of other newspapers including the *Los Angeles Herald-Examiner, Kansas City Star, Omaha World-Herald, Pine Bluff Commercial,* and the *Charlotte Observer,* also endorsed him as well.[33] (The *Los Angeles Times* had earlier done so.)

On Monday, Nixon stayed in New York and taped several radio addresses that would play over the final two weeks of the campaign. Gallup released their latest poll the same day, showing Nixon with a strong lead, but acknowledging Humphrey was gaining on him. Gallup showed the race at 43–31–20. This poll was conducted over October 3–12 but showed different results from the previous Harris Poll. Nixon had led by 15 points in Gallup's last survey at the end of September. Wallace remained at 20 percent of the popular vote. The president of the Gallup Poll Organization, Paul

K. Perry, stated in the latest poll that they had followed procedures developed and used successfully since 1952.[34] Despite the differing numbers, after considering the polling rule of plus or minus three percent, Gallup and Harris were saying the same thing ninety-five percent of the time. If you subtract three percent from Nixon and add three percent to Humphrey in the Gallup survey, you would have a 40–34 lead, which would be almost identical to the Harris one. On another related polling front, CBS stated their most recent survey on the presidential race. It had Nixon winning 28 states and 256 electoral votes, Wallace with six states and 58 electoral votes, and Humphrey ahead in only three states and the District of Columbia, with only 25 electoral votes. The news organization said that 13 states were too close to call.[35]

On weekdays throughout October, ABC's nightly news telecast ran an opinion piece by a journalist about what constituted an "ideal president." On October 21, Stewart Alsop, the younger brother of Joseph, both political insiders writing since the 1930s, said that the ideal president would be one who had Robert McNamara's brains, John Gardner's looks, Clark Clifford's ability to deal with people, Richard Nixon's political astuteness, Hubert Humphrey's goodness of heart, and George Wallace's charisma.[36] Given Alsop's background and view of the world, it is not unusual that he might come up with something like this. All of the above would be considered Washington political insiders except Wallace.

With the race tightening, Haldeman summoned Pat Buchanan from the Agnew campaign to travel with Nixon during the final two weeks. Nixon wanted Buchanan to work up some strong themes on law and order to hammer away at Humphrey.[37] On October 22, Nixon conducted a 247-mile, twelve-hour whistle-stop campaign through Ohio, starting at Cincinnati and finishing in Toledo. He had campaigned on the same route eight years earlier in his race for the presidency. At each stop along the tracks, Nixon made a specific comment about the place in response to an earlier statement that Humphrey had made. In Columbus, Nixon appeared on the platform with Woody Hayes, the coach of the Ohio State Buckeyes football team, who had defeated number one ranked Purdue the week before. Comparing his campaign with the Buckeye football squad, Nixon said, "They play rock-em, sock-em football and that's just what we're going to do the rest of the campaign. From now on we're going to sock it to 'em with everything we've got." Earlier in Middletown, he called HHH the "most expensive senator in American history—a man who gives no indication he believes that there's a bottom to the well of the United States Treasury." In Marion, he told his audience that they could choose between "Nixon with money in your pocket or Humphrey with his hand in your pocket." In London, he said that Humphrey "acts like we're in church," when he referred to the actions of the Supreme Court. Nixon hit harder when he pointed out, "Perhaps Mr. Humphrey's respectful silence on these far-reaching matters may stem from the fact that he has spent four years in an obedience school. The Supreme Court is not infallible."[38] Throughout the day, Nixon made strong comments on law and order, with the Deshler stop lowering the boom: "In the 45 minutes it took to ride from Lima (last stop) to Deshler, this is what happened in America—there have been one murder, two rapes, 45 major crimes of violence, and countless robberies and auto thefts. If you want your President to continue the do-nothing policy of crime in the past four years, vote for Humphrey. If on the other hand, you want to fight crime, vote for Nixon."[39]

On the same day as the whistle-stop campaign, Nixon had to compete for top billing on the three television networks because Apollo VII had just ended its successful 11-day journey with a splashdown in the Atlantic Ocean. Hubert Humphrey also campaigned in Texas with Connally and Yarborough at his side. It was clear that Lyndon Johnson's hand had to be in this. Even Lady Bird got into the act, appearing unexpectedly at Love Field in Dallas and hugging the vice president after his stop for brief comments. On ABC's nightly telecast, Ted Koppel described the love fest in Texas with the Democrats finally coming together by saying, "Custer got along better with Sitting Bull than Connally does with Yarborough. It took Larry O'Brien one week to put this together."[40]

In the days following Nixon's train ride, he was heavily criticized by numerous liberals in the media of returning to the "old Nixon" with his criticisms of Humphrey. They were saying that with the race tightening, Nixon was returning to his old form of partisan politics and making outlandish claims about his opponents. An editorial entitled "Who's Taking the Low Road Now?" in the *Los Angeles Times* gave a much more balanced perspective of the presidential race as it was heading into the home stretch:

> In the closing days of his campaign for the Presidency, Hubert H. Humphrey has seen fit to call Richard Nixon a liar, a coward and a servant of the "special interests" to cite a few examples from his speeches. This being the case, it plainly isn't so much the "old Nixon" who is indulging in dubious campaign tactics as it is the "new Humphrey." .... In one speech, Humphrey accused Nixon of voicing a "bald-faced lie." On other occasions, he called him "Richard the chicken-hearted." It has even been suggested that Nixon is an ally of George Wallace on racism.... Since then, Nixon has held his temper, but the same restraint is not visible in the Democratic camp. Addressing a Negro audience in Watts this week, Humphrey actually said, "You will all lose your jobs if there's a Republican administration." This is reckless as well as ridiculous talk, when it is considered what an emotionally charged issue employment is in the poverty areas. Whatever the qualities of the next President should be, a talent for vituperation and intemperance is not among them. We have enough disunity already.[41]

Later that night, after the journey through Ohio, Nixon got a memorandum from Bryce Harlow, claiming that a source inside the Johnson administration had given him some startling news on the status of the Paris peace talks. Harlow was an aide to President Eisenhower and had been working in Washington since World War II. He was known to have great sources, not only Republicans but Democrats as well. Harlow also had established a good relationship with Lyndon Johnson over the years. Nixon knew better than to question the integrity of Harlow. However, he still wondered about the substance of all of this. The more times that Nixon read the memorandum, the angrier he got. Nixon felt that he had been had by the president on the conditions for negotiations. Nixon wrote in his memoirs: "The President is driving exceedingly hard for a deal with North Vietnam. The expectation is that he is becoming almost pathologically eager for an excuse to order a bombing halt and will accept almost any arrangement.... White Housers still think they can pull the election out for HHH with this ploy; that's what is being attempted."[42] After that, he asked John Mitchell to check with Henry Kissinger on what Nixon had just read. Kissinger told Mitchell that he had not heard anything. Nixon next phoned Everett Dirksen and told him to confront Johnson with this news and see how he responded. Dirksen did just that, and Johnson angrily denied it. While Johnson and Dirksen were from different parties and had separate constituencies, they had a relationship that went back nearly twenty years from the president's days in the Senate.[43]

With this in mind, Nixon campaigned the next day across Michigan with criticisms of Humphrey on both foreign and domestic issues. In Saginaw, he said that the vice president had the "fastest, loosest tongue in American politics." Nixon then accused Humphrey of being two-faced on the issue of the bombing halt: "On this great issue of war and peace, on the great issue particularly of whether or not we should have a bombing pause, he's been for it unconditionally, and then he said that we need to have conditions." Nixon believed Humphrey's statement provided mixed messages, not only to the American soldiers in Vietnam, but also to the Vietcong and North Vietnamese. He stressed that in a Nixon presidency, citizens would have "strong men who see that America is strong, men who are firm and consistent." Later in Battle Creek, with baseball stars Al Kaline and Jim Northrup from the World Champion Detroit Tigers at his side, Nixon hit broadly at Humphrey's outdated domestic policies. He stated, "The bankruptcy of Mr. Humphrey's philosophy is written not only in the cities of America; it is visible in the candidacy and campaign of Hubert Humphrey this fall. He is a man lost in memories of days gone by. He brings to this campaign no new roadmap with which to guide America's future."[44]

On October 24, Gallup released its latest poll, which was much closer to the last Harris Poll. Their survey showed Nixon still ahead with 43 percent of the popular vote, but Humphrey had gained seven points with 38 percent, and Wallace trailed at 13 percent, a seven-point decline. James K. Kilpatrick, the veteran conservative columnist, gave his assessment of the "ideal president" on ABC's nightly news telecast. Kilpatrick said he had looked "in all dimensions of time, past, present and future ... but the nation can survive with Richard Nixon or Hubert Humphrey. If we had a perfect president, all of us critics would be out of a job." Perhaps this quote summed up the state of American journalism in 1968.[45]

On the same day, Nixon got another message from Harlow that the Johnson administration had reached an agreement with the North Vietnamese the day before and that it would be announced in the next few days. While Nixon was initially skeptical, Harlow assured him that his source was extremely credible. It presented Nixon with a dilemma. While he had promised the president that he would not undercut him on his policy in the war, and particularly the peace negotiations, Nixon felt that Johnson was playing politics with his war policy to win the presidency for Hubert Humphrey.[46]

Furthermore, Nixon believed the only way to counter this was to go public on the next bombing halt. In doing this, he could blame his close political advisers and not the president himself. Nixon knew better than to anger LBJ ten days before the election. Two days later on October 26, he made a statement on the peace talks: "In the last thirty-six hours, I have been advised of a flurry of meetings in the White House and elsewhere on Vietnam. I am told that top officials in the administration have been driving very hard for an agreement on a bombing halt, accompanied possibly by a cease-fire, in the immediate future.... In every conversation I have had with him he has made it clear that he will not play politics with this war."[47]

At a luncheon at the Waldorf over the weekend, President Johnson put all his restraint away and went after Nixon hard. He went through a laundry list of reasons why the Republican candidate should not be elected president. Johnson said that he was a man who "distorts history" to his advantage and focused on the "Tricky Dick" image that Democrats had used against Nixon his entire political career. Johnson resented what Nixon had implied about his recent moves at the Paris peace talks. He also used a variation of the "give me a week" comment by Ike to consider how Nixon could have been nominated for president again by his party after losing races in 1960 and 1962. Despite this, Johnson nearly broke down when he stated, "There's not a man in all this world that wants progress [in Paris] as much as I do and there's not anybody that's doing more about it either."[48]

Nixon gave a nationally broadcast radio speech on CBS on Sunday. He said that any hints of a coalition government in South Vietnam would be a "disguised surrender." Nixon said, "To the Communist side, a coalition government is not an exercise in cooperation but a sanctuary for subversion.... Far from ending the war, it would only ensure the resumption under conditions that would guarantee Communist victory." The former vice president acknowledged that peace talks were entering a crucial phase and that he would not do anything to interfere with that process. He went on to say "never in four years" had Humphrey disagreed with anything that the administration had done on the war, and only in the last month had he turned away from his vice presidential duties. On Sunday night, the former vice president appeared on a special edition of *Face the Nation* on CBS television. It was his first appearance on a national news show in nearly two years. Nixon was asked two days earlier why he was changing up the pattern of his campaign so late in the game. "I never turn down 10 million people," Nixon replied. When asked about Johnson's comments that Nixon had made "ugly and unfair charges" about his recent peace moves, he replied, "President Johnson has been consistent. Mr. Humphrey ought to get in line, agree with his President for a change."[49]

Furthermore, on the program, Nixon was asked about the charges that the *New York Times* had made earlier in the week, saying that Agnew was guilty of impropriety. At the same time, he was governor as well as serving as director of the Bank of Towson. By performing the role of governor, he could not ensure the banking regulations of the state without having a conflict of interest. It had to do with the purchase of land in connection with the construction of a parallel span of the Chesapeake Bay Bridge and bank ownership. Much of this was old news that had surfaced in Agnew's gubernatorial campaign in 1966. As if this were not enough, the paper on Saturday said, "Mr. Agnew has demonstrated that he is not fit to stand one step away from the presidency." Nixon responded to the editorial, saying that this was "the lowest form of gutter politics that a great newspaper could engage in and a retraction will be demanded of the *Times* legally tomorrow."[50] There was a meeting the next day, October 28, between the newspaper's vice president and Everett I. Willis, a partner in Dewey, Ballantine, Bushby, Palmer, and Wood. According to the *Times*, Willis criticized a sentence that said, "In response to public criticism, Governor Agnew later sold the land." Later in the week, the paper acknowledged some inaccuracies in their editorial but refused to retract it.[51]

One More Week

With a week to go and the recent polls suggesting a tightening in the race between Nixon and Humphrey, CBS had Nixon winning 28 states with 270 electoral votes in their latest survey.[52] The next day, ABC ran a segment on their nightly telecast with odds-maker Jimmy "The Greek" Snyder from his office in Las Vegas. Snyder predicted that Nixon would win next week's election with 330 electoral votes and at least 42 percent of the popular vote. He said that there was a one in five possibility of an upset, but he did not anticipate it. Snyder told the interviewer that he had picked every presidential election correctly in the last 20 years, including the 1948 one with Truman upsetting Dewey.[53]

On October 29, Eugene McCarthy finally decided to endorse Humphrey. McCarthy had earlier refused to do so at the convention. After the convention, McCarthy went off to Europe on a trip. He spent the first two weeks of October covering the World Series for *Life* magazine. On October 9, McCarthy laid down three conditions that had to be satisfied if he was to be on board publicly for the Democratic candidate: Humphrey's commitment to a new government in South Vietnam, fundamental changes in the military draft, and reforms in the procedures in the Democratic Party. While individually, Humphrey had not done all of those per se, he felt that he had moved in that direction. It was enough for McCarthy, even though his endorsement was not enthusiastic. He said that Humphrey's positions had fallen "far short" but that he had "shown a better understanding of our domestic needs and a stronger will to act than has been shown by Richard Nixon." The Minnesota senator went on to say that he would not be running for re-election as a Democrat in 1970, nor would he seek the presidency in 1972 as a member of that political party. Finally, McCarthy let it be known in this "endorsement" that he was not happy with the Democratic Party and that he had "not forgotten or condoned the things that happened both before Chicago and at Chicago."[54] Despite all of this, Humphrey would have most likely appreciated his endorsement earlier in the campaign, instead of now when he was closing the gap.

On October 30, the *Christian Science Monitor* predicted that if the election happened that day, Nixon would win 34 states and 333 electoral votes. The paper said that Humphrey would win six states and possibly 17 others. Wallace would win five states and 45 electoral votes. They also suggested that Humphrey might get enough electoral votes to throw the election into the House of Representatives.[55]

On October 31 at 8:00 p.m. Eastern time, President Johnson announced that he was halting the bombing of North Vietnam for 12 hours until 8:00 a.m.:

> I have reached this decision by the developments in the Paris talks. And I have reached it in the belief that this action can lead to progress of a peaceful settlement of the Vietnamese war.... We have reached the stage where productive talks can begin. We have made it clear to the other side that such talks cannot continue if they take military advantage of them. We cannot have productive talks in an atmosphere where the cities are being shelled and where the demilitarized zone is being abused.... But it should be clear to all of us that the new phase of negotiations which opens November 6th does not—repeat, does not—mean a stable peace has yet to come in Southeast Asia. There may well be very hard fighting ahead. Certainly, there is going to be some very hard negotiating, because many difficult and critically important issues are still facing these negotiators. But I hope and I believe that with goodwill we can solve them. We know that negotiations can move swiftly if the common intent of the negotiators is peace in the world.[56]

That same night after the presidential address, Nixon held a massive rally at Madison Square Garden that drew over 19,000 people. An hour of it was telecast on ABC across the nation on 247 stations. On the platform appearing with Nixon and Agnew were several important Republican governors that included Nelson

Rockefeller, George Romney, Raymond Shafer, John Volpe, and James Rhodes. Four of the five governors were from large battleground states: New York, Michigan, Pennsylvania, and Ohio. Buchanan and Sears urged Nixon to take a more proactive position on winning the war in Vietnam during October, but given the tenuous nature of the peace talks, Nixon refused to do so. He talked with Johnson over the phone before the address was shown. Nixon said, "As a presidential candidate—and my vice-presidential running mate joins me in this—neither he or I will say anything that might destroy the chance for peace. We want peace.... The subject [the Paris peace talks] is off limits, let us make sure that we do not overlook the necessity to have a new foreign policy, to make sure that we are not involved in another Vietnam." Also, Nixon did promise to help "defuse trouble spots" around the world whenever possible. Earlier in the day, the Nixon family all voted absentee in New York. They did so because their campaign schedule would not put them back in the city until early Tuesday night on Election Day.[57]

The day after the Johnson announcement, President Thieu of South Vietnam said that his government would not be participating in the peace talks. After all, it was Thieu's country, and allowing the NLF into the negotiating process probably looked like suicide to him. It was all about national survival for Thieu. On the threshold of the presidential election, LBJ appeared to have made a hasty decision on the bombing halt. Johnson's people were saying that they had assurances from the South Vietnamese government but somehow must have forgotten the president of the country. Nixon pounced on this during a campaign swing through Texas when he said, "In view of the early reports that we've had this morning, the prospects for peace are not as bright as they looked only a few days ago." Additionally, he had Bob Finch make a statement to the press. The California lieutenant governor explained, "We had the impression that all the diplomatic ducks were in position. I think this will boomerang. It was hastily contrived." When Johnson read the papers the next morning, he almost lost his marbles. Bryce Harlow called Nixon and told him that he needed to call the president and calm him down. Nixon did just that. Johnson was initially livid and kept asking who this guy "Fink" was and why he was saying this. Nixon corrected him, but he kept on calling Finch "Fink." Nixon furthermore pointed out to the president that he had not done anything to embarrass or undercut the president's authority. Eventually, Johnson calmed down and said that he was glad that Nixon had called to get this straightened out.[58]

On the final weekend of the campaign, Nixon spent the second day in Texas while Humphrey was in New York barnstorming through the nation's most populous city. Nixon stuck to his word to Johnson and made no specific reference to the bombing pause. He did criticize his Democratic opponent for having outdated notions on the origins of crime. Nixon said that he would appoint a more aggressive attorney general who would stand up for the "abused in our society [that] deserve as much protection as the accused." Nixon said that his attorney general pick would be analogous to Lincoln's appointing Ulysses S. Grant as his supreme Union commander in the Civil War, reversing the course of the war into ultimate victory.[59] Nixon also went on *Meet the Press* on Sunday and reiterated that he would not stand in the way of peace, offering again to do anything to help President Johnson in this endeavor.[60]

On Sunday, Gallup and Harris released their final polls of the 1968 presidential campaign. Nixon stayed where he had been for the past six weeks in the Gallup

Nixon on *Meet the Press* on November 2, 1968. Lawrence Spivak was hosting with panelists which include Robert ("the enemy") Novak, third from left (Richard M. Nixon Foundation).

survey with 42 percent of the vote, while Humphrey had moved up four points to 40 percent, and Wallace trailed behind with 14 percent. Only 4 percent considered themselves undecided. On the other hand, Humphrey moved into the lead in the Harris Poll 43–40 over Nixon, with Wallace at 13 percent. John Mitchell jumped on the differences in the polls, stating it was apparent that Harris had oversampled Democrats as they had done in the past, and thus, the survey was not credible. Looking closer at the details of the survey did not back up Mitchell's claim, but what was readily apparent was the number of likely voters the two pollsters called. Gallup screened their calls from 4,455 total to 2,800 likely voters, while Harris drew on fewer than half, 1,206 likely voters of 2,455 total.[61] At the White House, Fred Panzer, Johnson's private pollster, said that Harris was "certain Humphrey will win the popular vote but not sure if he can win the electoral college."[62]

On the eve of the election, both the Nixon and Humphrey camps ended their political journey in California with national telethons. Muskie appeared on stage with Humphrey, but Agnew stayed back on the East Coast to campaign there.[63] Before that, Nixon appeared in a buoyant mood in Long Beach when he said, "We started in California and we finished in California. This is our home; it will always be our home in our hearts, and we will be here many times."[64] Also, on Monday, Ike issued a late appeal to voters to ignore the last week's political maneuverings around the Paris peace talks and vote for Nixon. The former president stated from Walter Reed Hospital that he had "an urgent obligation" to speak on behalf of his trusted vice president for eight years. Ike said, "Nixon deserves the plaudits of the American people for his extraordinary responsible conduct of his campaign respecting Vietnam."[65]

Nixon held a nationally televised four-hour telethon out of Burbank. The first two hours of the event were primarily for the East Coast, and the last two were for the West Coast. Bud Wilkinson was hosting the national telecast, taking questions that were called in by viewers all over the country. The format was right up Nixon's alley. Nixon was the ultimate test taker. He was always prepared. Not only had Nixon been using this format throughout his campaign, but Nixon was also ready for a national audience in this final push to the presidency. He did an excellent job throughout the four hours except for one late comment about "getting down to the nut-cutting" that most of the country missed. On the plane ride back to New York the next day, Buchanan told his boss, "That nut-cutting remark of yours last night on TV nearly killed us all." Nixon laughed it off, giving an account of how in a campaign nearly twenty years ago in Missouri, he was helping a fellow Republican out in an election and had "lamb fries." He even told his assistant that when the election was over, they would all go out and have some.[66]

Judgment Day

It took five hours for the *Tricia* to carry the Nixon team from California to New York. The candidate had a long talk with the family on the plane ride back about what was going to occur on this election day. All but David Eisenhower had heard it eight years earlier, but it had a much more significant meaning to the Nixon daughters who were now 22 and 20. Nixon told them that it was going to be a close race, but that he thought that they were going to win. However, he also wanted to prepare them in case they lost the election. On the ride back, he also had short one-on-one meetings with the staff. Reporters questioned Nixon on the plane about the Harris Poll that showed him three points down. He pointed out that he believed that the Gallup Poll was much more accurate. Nixon then got a bit more philosophical when he said, "Even though it will be extremely close, we can win. I think we probably will. If we don't win, we'll simply go on to other projects, which, from a personal viewpoint, may give us more satisfaction. And we won't have the spotlight of the world on us and on every movement that we make."[67] The plane landed at the Newark airport a little after 6:00 p.m. EST. The team was shuttled off to the Waldorf Astoria, where they would watch the returns that night.

Nixon led in the popular and electoral vote most of the night, with Humphrey pulling even in the popular vote a little after 10:00 p.m. EST. At around midnight, Humphrey had a slight lead in the national election, even though Nixon had over 230 electoral votes. An hour earlier, Nixon had found out that there were some problems with the voting in Dallas, and that all of the state's votes would not be counted until Wednesday. It certainly sparked flashbacks for Nixon to what had happened there eight years when he lost to Kennedy. It looked like the race was going to boil down to the same five states that had decided the 1960 election: Illinois, California, Ohio, Missouri, and Texas. Nixon felt confident sometime in the early morning hours of Wednesday that he had indeed nailed down California and Ohio, even though the networks had not called them yet, and was leading in Illinois. Could it happen again that Illinois and Texas would decide Nixon's fate? Nixon had Bryce Harlow call Larry O'Brien to tell Mayor Daley to release his election figures. In 1960, he had held them

Herb Klein and John Mitchell stand near president-elect Nixon, who holds an embroidered Presidential Seal made by his daughter, Julie. Morning election return figures are seen broadcasting on the television in New York on November 6, 1968 (Richard M. Nixon Foundation).

back. This time, Nixon had high confidence he had won Illinois no matter what games Daley was playing. At around three in the morning, Nixon felt sure that he had won the presidency, but the networks were not calling Illinois yet. He phoned Agnew and Rockefeller and told them that he was confident that they had won. Nixon later met with the senior staff to inform them of the good news. He then retired for what would be a short nap for the night.[68]

Finally, right before eight in the morning, the networks said that Ohio and California were in the Nixon column. Thirty minutes later, Dwight Chapin burst into the Nixon suite with the excellent news that ABC had just called the election for Nixon.[69] Two hours, CBS and NBC followed suit. An hour later, Vice President Humphrey called Nixon to congratulate him and offer his full support to the newly elected president. Nixon then gathered his family, and they went down to the ballroom at the Waldorf to make some brief comments about the election and thank all of his supporters across the nation. Nixon smiled when he told the reporters that he knew how Humphrey felt because he had experienced it eight years earlier in 1960. Winning was a better feeling. Nixon showed off an embroidered piece of artwork that Julie had created during the campaign with the Great Seal of the United States. The president-elect finished off his comments with something he observed on the train tour through Ohio two weeks earlier and what he hoped it portended for the nation's future:

> I saw many signs in the campaign. Some of them were not friendly, and some were very friendly. But the one that touched me the most was the one that I saw in Deshler, Ohio, at the end of a long day of whistle-stopping. A little town, I suppose five times the population

Nixon's family the day after the election in New York on November 6, 1968. Pictured from left to right: David Eisenhower, Julie Nixon Eisenhower, Tricia Nixon, Richard Nixon, Patricia Nixon (Richard M. Nixon Foundation).

was there in the dusk, almost impossible to see—but a teenager held up a sign, "Bring Us Together." And that will be the great objective of this administration at the outset, to bring the American people together.[70]

Many things were going through Richard Nixon's mind as he made his way back to his apartment in New York the day after the election. There had indeed been peaks and valleys in his two-decade political life since his election to the House in 1946, but none were as satisfying as this one. The last six years had been trying ones, but now it was all worth it. There would be no more circling the political arena because he was right in the middle of it. He had invested a lot of blood, dust, and sweat into this pursuit. In two months, he would officially become the 37th president of the United States. Nixon was, without a doubt, ready for the task before him. With both houses of Congress in the Democrats' hands, he was facing a steep road ahead. No president since 1848 had been elected with both houses represented by the opposite party. Richard Milhous Nixon had faced tough political situations in the past and had learned from them. This time would be no different.

14

Finale

When Walter Cronkite reported overnight on August 8, 1974, the dramatic and stunning news of Richard Nixon's resignation as president of the United States, the only such occurrence in American history, the switchboards at the White House lit up. Over 500 calls an hour began flooding in, virtually all in support of the beleaguered Nixon, imploring him not to resign.[1] In his resignation speech, Nixon himself pointed to the loss of congressional support as his reason ultimately to give up the political fight to save his presidency. However, he also chose to emphasize the many positive accomplishments of his time in office. Given the immediate and spontaneous reaction of myriad Americans, though, it seemed that Nixon had not entirely lost his entire base of support, nor had these citizens forgotten his achievements.[2]

Nor was this unprecedented. The same thing had occurred over two decades earlier, on the night of September 23, 1952, when Nixon, faced with a brewing scandal over campaign finance improprieties, went on national television and radio to save his spot on the Republican ticket. In the famous "Checkers" speech, Nixon showed great courage in this political firestorm after the Republican candidate for president, Dwight Eisenhower, had essentially left him fighting for his place on the ticket. A few minutes after Nixon ended his address to the nation, coincidentally enough, Eisenhower was moving to the podium to give a speech of his own in Cleveland, Ohio. Before he could take the stage, large segments of the audience began chanting, "We want Nixon."[3] Faced with such a genuine, grass-roots response, it did not take the famous general long to decide that Nixon would remain his vice presidential running mate. Even though Ike was probably the most popular public figure in the country at the time, the "Checkers" speech demonstrated that Nixon had a constituency of his own, totally separate from Eisenhower's. Both it and his later political successes showed that Nixon had a real feel for what the American people wanted out of their public figures and knew how to communicate it.

Watergate and Nixon's resignation have obscured the many accomplishments of his administration. Interestingly, Nixon succeeded in yet another comeback in the two decades after he left office, transforming himself from political outcast to author and elder statesman before his death in April 1994. Today, a quarter of a century later, a reexamination of the process by which Nixon reinvented himself during the dark days of the 1960s amid a changing America is in order. After losing the presidency in 1960 and the governor's election in California two years later, Nixon realized there needed to be a significant reassessment of himself if he wanted any political future. The period between 1962 and 1968 served as a laboratory for his rebirth. In a real sense, it mirrored his initial meteoric rise to prominence between 1946 and 1952, when he had gone from an obscure congressman to being elected vice president on the ticket with Dwight Eisenhower. Then, as in the later period, his rise had been fueled by a series of sharp political assessments and crucial decisions. Nixon's emergence after 1962 was a dynamic two-way process, reflecting both what he perceived and how he came to be viewed by others, and that dynamism was one key to his political evolution. He realized some important things along the way: how to bridge the gap between Goldwater conservatives and moderate Republicans; how the temper, mood, and tenor of large sections of the American public were moving against the Democrats; and how one presidential candidate could take advantage of this shift. It is the unknown Nixon, a far more human Nixon than the Herblock caricature of a shady political figure who would do anything to win. The real Nixon is more complex, insightful, and multi-faceted than the generally understood caricature.

The initial process of Nixon's political comeback can be traced to an event outside his control and perhaps even his imagination. Less than a week after he lost the California gubernatorial election in 1962, ABC released a documentary titled *The Political Obituary of Richard Nixon*, hosted by legendary political journalist Howard K. Smith. The program had convicted perjurer Alger Hiss as one of the featured contributors. The rising furor in the country created by the Hiss appearance was shown in the hundreds of letters criticizing him and offering support for Nixon. Before the program aired, two primary sponsors of the program tried to pull their advertising. Somewhere between 60,000 and 80,000 letters came into the show, nearly all in favor of Nixon and accusing Smith of beating a man when he was down. Most of the criticism revolved around having convicted perjurer Alger Hiss as one of the guests. Even a significant number of newspapers that had no love for Nixon were highly critical of the program.[4] Although this all transpired without any prompting by Nixon, the Smith documentary and the reaction to it effectively birthed the groundswell of support that Nixon later would term the "silent majority." Also, of crucial importance, of course, was Nixon's recognition of and understanding of how this mood could be exploited politically.

As part of his reinvention process, Nixon had several opportunities outside politics during his wilderness period. As a well-known and prominent sports fan, he might have become Commissioner of Baseball, for example, since he could boast support from some owners.[5] Indeed, during this period it was Nixon who was consulted by the Baseball Players Association in their search for a strong candidate to lead their fledgling union. His suggestion of Marvin Miller as the best applicant proved prescient and paved the way for the big money contracts that baseball players enjoy today.[6] As well, Nixon was offered the job of CEO of Chrysler Corporation.[7] Again, though, of fundamental importance for the future was his decision to move from California for a job as a partner in a law firm in New York City. It not only offered Nixon the chance to prove himself in the "Big League" of legal firms, but it also allowed him to remain on the margins of the political arena, something these other jobs would not so clearly have permitted. Whether a conscious consideration or not, it also placed Nixon smack in the middle of the regional political base of one of his biggest political rivals, Nelson Rockefeller. Once settled in New York and the Mudge Rose law firm, Nixon proved a magnet for new business. He managed several large accounts, including Pepsi. The soft drink manufacturer was well positioned in Asia at the time, and this allowed Nixon to travel there at least once a year, and sometimes more often, while a partner at Mudge Rose. In these many travels to Asia to service these accounts, Nixon also met with many heads of state and influential political figures. These meetings provided Nixon with a continued presence in national news reporting and kept his name recognition alive, although he had no immediate political plans at the time.

Nixon also proved adept at responding to unexpected political circumstances,

CHARLES K. HOOD ASSOCIATES
INSURANCE CONSULTANTS

CHARLES K. HOOD
ROBIN E. ROBERTS

December 16, 1965

501 SWEDE STREET
NORRISTOWN, PENNA. 19401
215/272-3210

Mr. Richard Nixon
20 Broad Street
New York City, N.Y.

Dear Mr. Nixon:

    Jim and I would like to thank you for the opportunity of speaking with you on Wednesday. We, also, are of the opinion that having a law firm as our Counsel seems to be the correct approach.

    We will be in touch with you in the very near future.

              Sincerely yours,

              Robin E. Roberts

RER/mc

Letter written by Robin Roberts to Nixon after meeting him in December 1965. Roberts and Jim Bunning were getting advice from Nixon on the selection of a player's representative. They, along with Harvey Kuehn, submitted several candidates to Nixon the next month, then the players chose Marvin Miller as their best representative. The rest is history in terms of baseball players' salaries (Richard M. Nixon Library).

such as the assassination of President Kennedy in November 1963 and the subsequent turmoil this created in the 1964 presidential campaign. Although initially urged to write an ongoing analysis of the campaign like Theodore White's best-selling book chronicling the 1960 election, after Kennedy's death, Nixon tossed these plans aside and decided to observe the upcoming battle on a more personal basis. He believed strongly that, given the situation, no one could defeat Lyndon Johnson. Still, Nixon briefly considered running himself, only to reject the idea, even though several prospective Republican candidates, including George Romney and William Scranton, consulted him about taking on the conservative Barry Goldwater, who had emerged as the likely Republican nominee. In further evidence of his political insight, Nixon thought it best to work behind the scenes and not in the glare of the national press. He made a persuasive speech at the San Francisco convention on behalf of Goldwater. He worked tirelessly during the campaign for the candidate even though Nixon knew the Arizona senator had little chance of winning the election. Many people observing the campaign thought Nixon worked harder than the actual Republican candidate. Rockefeller and Romney sat out the election, refusing to endorse Goldwater publicly. As expected, Johnson won in a landslide, but Nixon had secured valuable political IOUs, at little cost, in the event he chose to run for president in 1968. He had also done much to bridge the gap between conservatives and moderates in the Republican party. It was another positive harbinger for the future.

The election debacle of November 1964, though, left the Republican Party in shambles and without a national leader Given his tireless efforts during the previous campaign, and the political debt owed him by Goldwater and his supporters—something Goldwater acknowledged and vowed to redeem—Nixon, almost by default, assumed the role of de facto party leader. More importantly, even though they had lost the election badly, Nixon perceived that the real energy among Republicans resided in the party's conservative base. It was a critical insight that is mostly overlooked today, at a time when the centrist Nixon is generally regarded erroneously as having always been a conservative. In the 1960 campaign, though, he had drawn support from a not insignificant number of Democrats and Independents, with the conservative wing of the Republican Party, which regarded him as a moderate, more reluctant in its support. Now, with the party badly split and in need of repair, Nixon again set to work, helping the party rebuild its brand. Although still active in his role at the Mudge Rose law firm, Nixon toiled in the shadows, at the height of LBJ's popularity as he set about building the Great Society, to repair the damage to the Republican Party. As an indicator of the success of his efforts, Americans felt so strongly about Nixon that nearly every private organization or association outside the Democratic Party wanted Richard Nixon to speak to its group. Most of these groups were not even political. For every speech he gave during the mid-sixties, Nixon turned down fifteen or twenty opportunities. Many people today forget how popular he was during this period, despite the "loser" label. In the fifty years from 1948 to 1998, Nixon made the top-ten list of most admired Americans twenty times. Only Billy Graham, Eisenhower, and Reagan surpassed him.[8] A good bit of this popularity, in turn, was the result of his interactions with average Americans. While on the campaign trail, for example, Nixon made it a point to talk with the "little" people at the many hotels in which they stayed—the maids, clerks, restaurant personnel—to ask them about their concerns, their families, their hopes, all of which made them feel that some-one prominent had cared, even for a moment, about them.[9]

Any assessment of Nixon at this point, in the mid–1960s, must acknowledge the transformational insights gained during his many speeches and travels throughout the country. Many of the talks were not necessarily of a political nature but just commenting on the issues of the day and listening to his audiences. Nixon was already a moderate on civil rights and he listened to those voices in the South who wanted an alternative to a segregationist like Wallace but were frustrated with the president. At the same time, Nixon was evolving politically. While he supported President Johnson generally on the war, he was carving out alternatives to the top-down nature of the Johnson domestic initiatives. Nixon could sense that the elites in Washington thought they had everything figured out on civil rights, Vietnam, student protests, and the like, but the country was not agreeing with them. He sensed a widespread dissatisfaction with political elites among those who perceived themselves as hard-working, tax-paying, law-abiding, decent people who were playing by the rules, and being ignored. Nixon was positioning himself as an alternative to Johnson as well as the Rockefellers, Scrantons, and Romneys of his party. He understood the conservatives and had a realistic possibility of attracting moderate voters and thus winning a presidential election. At the same time, he was viewing the Democrats starting to implode on the war and starting to turn on the president.

In addition to the insights he gathered on the mood of the nation, Nixon knew that if Republicans were going to have any chance of winning back the White House in 1968, they had to do much better in the 1966 mid-term elections. At the beginning of that year, Nixon hired his first full-time political aide, Pat Buchanan, to work beside him in his law office. Buchanan took the job to help on the '66 campaign as a one-year sabbatical from his position as editor of the *St. Louis Globe-Democrat*. If the Republicans did not do well, then Buchanan would go back to his day job, and Nixon would return to work for his law firm. As it turned out, the two worked tirelessly during the year. Emphasizing to the party faithful that he would campaign for any Republican no matter their ideology—except for John Birchers or segregationists—he was instrumental in rebuilding the Republican Party. Nixon's efforts were particularly important in the South, where he—and not Ronald Reagan, as some observers have asserted—laid the groundwork for the Republicans to be the majority party. Without Nixon's groundbreaking efforts, it is arguable that Reagan would have been effective in gathering southern support in 1980. Harry Dent also played a prominent role in building the party in the South from the 1960s until he died in 2007. In an interview nearly twenty years after Nixon's resignation, Dent testified to Nixon's impact by noting that everywhere he went in the South, people told him how strongly they felt about the former president. Having worked for Nixon provided Dent with almost instant credibility.[10] As a result of the efforts of Nixon, Buchanan, and others, the Republican party did quite well in the 1966 midterm elections, much better than the political prognosticators generally realized. Throughout the year, Nixon continually commented on the new strength of the Republicans. Still, as in many moments of his career, his vision reached farther than the opinions of the national media.

Following the success of his strenuous efforts in 1966, Nixon again displayed his acute political instincts when he decided at the end of the year that he would take a hiatus from the political stage in the first half of 1967. He believed strongly that the Republican front-runner, George Romney, would not be ready for the national stage, no matter what the pundits were saying. Nixon also thought it was essential to stay in the background and not be politically overexposed. It did not mean he would shy away from politics, but instead, he would focus on updating his knowledge of international affairs. Nixon did this by making a series of foreign trips that covered Europe, Asia, Africa, the Middle East, and Latin America. On each of the four visits, he took a different aide with him. Two of the four (Ellsworth and Rebozo) had either expertise and experience in that part of the world, in this case, in Europe and Latin America. On the other two trips to Asia and the Middle East/Africa, Nixon took two novices, Price and Buchanan, with him.

In mid-summer, right after the race riots in Detroit, Nixon gave a private speech to a gathering at Bohemian Grove in northern California that garnered considerable positive publicity despite its "private" audience. Much of the rhetoric centered on his recent travels around the world. He told the gathering that he was not going to dwell on the current wars in Vietnam or the Middle East but focus on how the world had changed since the end of World War II. He acknowledged the two largest countries in landmass had communist governments but did not see much enthusiasm for that type of government in the future. Nixon pointed to non-communist Asia, saying, "[It] is the area which has experienced the most hopeful change.... Japan, Korea, Taiwan, Singapore, Malaysia, and Thailand are all dramatic economic success stories." He also asserted that American military superiority was being threatened by the Soviet Union but stressed that he was willing "diplomatically" to have discussions with the Soviets "where bilateral agreements would reduce tensions." In both examples, he was signaling what he would do in foreign policy when he won the presidency, as well as establishing his credentials as a thoughtful, restrained observer of the international situation.[11] It was a much more nuanced approach to foreign policy than he exhibited during the 1960 campaign. At the retreat, he had also had a short meeting with Ronald Reagan, trying to ascertain what the California governor's presidential intentions were.

Then, in late summer, Nixon met in New York with a group of prominent academic and policy elites on international affairs and discussed his recent travels around the world. They encouraged him to write an article on his findings for their quarterly journal, *Foreign Affairs*. He did just that and titled it, intriguingly, given the recent intensification of the Vietnam conflict, "Asia After Vietnam." It provided a hint of Nixon's profoundly revisionist thinking on Vietnam—that the war should be conducted differently: that communism was not necessarily the wave of the future in Southeast Asia and that it might be possible to triangulate the relationship between the United States, China, and the Soviet Union to American advantage. It proved a most opportune time. At precisely the moment Nixon's image as a thoughtful statesman was being enhanced, his primary rival for the GOP nomination, George Romney, was being barraged with negative publicity for his handling of the domestic race riots as well as his "brainwashing" comment on Vietnam. Besides, following the summer riots, President Johnson's approval rating dropped below 40 percent for the first time in his presidency.

Given a promising opening, Nixon spent the last quarter of 1967 testing and fine-tuning his message for the upcoming campaign, the theme of which would appeal to GOP conservatives and moderates alike. One of those themes had to do with the breakdown of law and order in the country. In a widely read piece in *Reader's Digest*, Nixon blamed many of the nation's leaders for these problems. While acknowledging with a sense of pride that our legal system affords the accused more safeguards than any other on earth, "The first responsibility of government ... [is to ensure its citizens] the right to be protected from domestic violence." He went on to write, "In recent years our system has failed dismally in that responsibility—and it cannot redeem itself by pointing to the conscientious manner in which it treats suspected criminals." Finally, Nixon wrote, "In a civilized nation no man can excuse his crime against the person or property of another by claiming that he, too, has been a victim of injustice. To tolerate that is to invite anarchy."[12] The conventional wisdom at the time was that Romney or perhaps Rockefeller would be his main competitor for the nomination. Still, Nixon, again displaying his political acuity, demonstrated in his emphasis on the "law and order" theme a concern with Reagan. John Sears, who oversaw the delegate count for the Republican nomination, said Nixon did not think that the party would nominate Rockefeller or Romney because of their actions in 1964 but felt that the real threat would come from Reagan.[13] Throughout 1967, the California governor had generated considerable positive publicity as he traveled around the country maintaining—despite all appearances—that he was not a candidate for president.

Once he officially announced his candidacy on February 1, 1968, in a snowstorm in New Hampshire, declaring that the problems facing the country were "beyond politics," Nixon's first goal was to get rid of the "loser" tag that his detractors used against him. He thought the best way—although one not without risk—to accomplish this was to openly compete in the five major primaries that did not have a favorite son slate and to win these convincingly. Starting in New Hampshire and ending in Oregon, Nixon did precisely that, in large part because his approach to campaigning had adapted considerably since 1960. In place of the stiff, uncomfortable Nixon of popular media caricature, there now appeared a relaxed Nixon who spoke more spontaneously—and effectively. He also benefited from external circumstances. As Nixon had anticipated in 1967, George Romney proved unequal to the rigor and scrutiny of a national campaign and, dogged by his "brainwashing" comment the previous year, the Michigan governor suddenly exited the primary in New Hampshire a week before the vote. In Wisconsin, none of the other "contenders" chose to campaign in the state. After Wisconsin, Rockefeller announced that he was not a candidate. By Oregon, Rockefeller had become a candidate, while Reagan had not openly committed but was spending quite a bit of advertising money.

Against the backdrop of Romney's exit from the campaign and the ambivalence of both Rockefeller and Reagan, Nixon's bold move to compete in these five significant primaries now appeared a stroke of genius. In each of the five primaries, Nixon won close to 70 percent or more of the vote, burying the loser's tag. In May, all the candidates went to Atlanta and met with the leaders of the southern delegations. The liberal Rockefeller got nowhere, while the conservative candidate, Reagan, made a lot of noise but received no commitments. Only Nixon got the critical commitment from the influential South Carolina Senator Strom Thurmond and the Greenville Group. In the two months before the convention, to head off the Nixon steamroller, Rockefeller spent over five million dollars trying to drum up support, and Reagan crisscrossed the country, asserting that the Republicans needed an open convention. Neither Rockefeller nor Reagan could win the nomination outright, but they hoped to deny Nixon the 670 votes required for the nomination. Essentially, the leaders of the liberal and conservative wings of the Republican Party were colluding against Nixon. The reality was that neither could ever have been acceptable nominees to the bulk of the party in 1968. Only Nixon could unite the ideological wings of the GOP.

By the time the convention in Miami Beach rolled around in early August, the two governors had tried one more time to block Nixon from the nomination. Rockefeller could count on a plurality of northeastern delegates, and Reagan, having finally entered the race, made a strong effort to split the southern delegations. After a flurry of activity in the first three days of the convention, during which he coolly deflected attempts to detach southern delegates from his camp, Nixon won the nomination on the first ballot. Now he had to select a vice president to run with him. Much of the liberal wing of the party was pushing John Lindsay while the conservative wing was behind Ronald Reagan. In making his choice, Nixon let it be known to his closest advisers that he did not want to choose either of the "glamour boys." That removed Lindsay and Reagan from the list. He ended up choosing Spiro Agnew, the governor of Maryland. Nixon cued in on Agnew, a former Rockefeller supporter and leader of the nascent "draft Rockefeller" movement. He did this primarily because he was seen as someone who, as a governor from a border state, could be a "bridge between North and South," had an excellent civil rights record, and spoke clearly on the issue of law and order. Agnew had defeated a segregationist Democrat in Maryland for governor and talked tough to Black leaders after riots broke out in Baltimore.[14] Whatever legal troubles that Agnew would incur later, forcing him to resign from the vice presidency, were not known to Nixon at the time. In any case, the campaign's internal polling results indicated that the vice president was irrelevant to Nixon's success in the general election. The people would vote for Nixon alone. He made a persuasive acceptance speech at the convention and got a good bump in the national polls.

In the three weeks before the Democratic Convention, Nixon rested and considered what final touches the campaign needed before the general election. Since 1964, Nixon's theme had been unity among the Republicans. He met individually with critical officeholders all over the country to make sure everyone remained on the same page. He wanted to take the same theme of unity into the general election to appeal to a deeply divided country. Nixon did no campaigning until after the Democratic convention in Chicago. After the Democrats imploded in the Windy City, Nixon had a commanding lead in the polls going into September. He began the campaign in Chicago, with a motorcade crowd of nearly a half a million. Nixon's enthusiastic reception stood in stark contrast to the images of conflict the Democrats had provided. Much of the rest of the month went smoothly as Humphrey campaigned to much smaller crowds, finding difficulties raising money. At the same time, the independent candidate George Wallace was saying that there was not a "dime's worth of difference between the two parties" as he carried his third-party message across America. At the end of the month, despite Democrats holding a commanding fifteen-point lead in party identification, polls showed Nixon leading Humphrey and Wallace at 43–28–21. September was a big month for Nixon.

The next month would be much different. Humphrey broke with the president on the war in September with a speech in Salt Lake City. A week later, Wallace began his downward fall in the polls after General Curtis LeMay, his running mate, made disturbing comments about nuclear weapons. Concurrently, Agnew was being criticized heavily by the national press with several "gaffes." Also, President Johnson, who had been silent during September, came out strong for his vice president in the last four weeks of the campaign. By the middle of the month, the race was tightening, as Nixon always knew it would. He had been criticized for not taking definitive stands on numerous issues but rectified that with a compiled list of his positions and several targeted speeches on the issues. A few in the Nixon campaign even thought that their candidate had been too cautious, allowing Humphrey to not only rebound nicely but come within shouting distance of overtaking the lead. Kevin Phillips (who was writing a book on changing voting patterns in 1968) believed the general campaign was "a catastrophe—millions of dollars spent by Madison Avenue lightweights who converted certain victory into near defeat. The soap salesmen drained all the issues out of the campaign."[15] Buchanan termed the last four weeks of the campaign "dreadful," as he thought they had blown the election.[16] Entering the final weekend, though, Nixon had a healthy lead in the electoral race. The popular vote was essentially tied between Nixon and Humphrey, with Wallace getting about thirteen percent of the vote. There was also Lyndon Johnson's "October Surprise" peace initiative and Nixon's reaction to it. Nixon had anticipated that Johnson might pull some political surprise at the end of the campaign to put Humphrey over the top. As it turned out, that is precisely what happened with a bombing halt and an announcement that negotiations with North Vietnam would soon follow. The problem was the South Vietnam government had not bought into the United States peace gambit before the president announced it. Johnson accused Nixon of sabotaging the arrangement by telling President Thieu not to accept it. The president had bugged the South Vietnam embassy as well as one of the Nixon campaign planes. The wiretaps had Anna Chennault, who was loosely connected to the Nixon campaign, talking to the South Vietnamese ambassador, telling him not to accept the United States proposal and saying that they would get a better deal under Nixon. The reality was that Thieu did not need Nixon, Anna Chennault, or anyone else telling him what was in the strategic interest of South Vietnam.

The last weekend entailed a frenzy of campaigning from all the candidates. Nixon did a four-hour live telethon from Los Angeles on CBS, with half of the time shown on the East Coast and the final two hours shown on the West Coast. Humphrey did a similar live telethon from New York on ABC for two hours. When the dust finally cleared on the morning after the election, Nixon was declared the winner in Illinois. That put him over the 270 electoral vote threshold needed for victory. Some might call it ironic, or even poetic justice, that one of the two states that cost him the 1960 election provided him with the winning margin eight years later. He carried 32 states versus Humphrey's 13 states and Wallace's 5. Nixon won the popular vote by a little over 600,000 votes, but he won the electoral vote by a 301–191–46 count. Of the eight percent Wallace lost in the final five weeks, Nixon got sixty percent of the defecting votes to Humphrey's forty percent. Teddy White, in his post-election analysis, termed it a "negative landslide," since Nixon's and Wallace's combined vote totaled nearly 57 percent, contrasted with Johnson's 61

Nixon alumni 50 years later at the National Archives on September 21, 2018. Pictured from left to right: Dwight Chapin, Pat Buchanan, Annelise Anderson, Ken Khachigan, and Geoff Shepard (Richard M. Nixon Foundation).

percent winning total four years earlier.[17] LBJ's vice president thus received almost 18 percentage points less than the Democratic Party garnered in the previous presidential election, a decline comparable to Herbert Hoover's 1932 loss of 17 percentage points in the popular vote.

What in November 1962 had seemed highly unlikely, if not impossible, had come to pass. Mostly because of his sharp political instincts and successful reinvention, Richard Nixon had been elected president. Having spied an opportunity, Nixon took the steps necessary to not only circle the arena but plunk himself down right in the middle of it. It would not be the last surprise of this remarkable politician, but it was undoubtedly the most extraordinary.

Chapter Notes

Prologue

1. Richard M. Nixon. *The Memoirs of Richard Nixon*. New York: Grossett and Dunlap, 1978, 8.

2. Mazo, Earl. 23 November 1971, Oral History Research Project: Eisenhower Administration, Columbia University. 5–6.

3. Retrieved from https://www.latimes.com/archives/la-xpm-1994-04-27-mn-51035-story.html.

4. Dwight Chapin, interview with the author, Washington, D.C., August 9, 2012.

5. Stephen Hess, interview with the author, Washington, D.C., August 14, 2012.

6. Garment, Leonard. *Crazy Rhythm: My Journey from Brooklyn, Jazz, and Wall Street to Nixon's White House, Watergate, and Beyond*. New York: Times Books, 1997, 70–74.

7. Whitaker, John C. (Editor). "Vernon C. Coffey." *What Richard Nixon Was Really Like: As Told by Those Who Really Knew Him*. John C. Whitaker personal collection. 74–75.

8. Small, Melvin (Editor). *A Companion to Richard M. Nixon*. Malden, Massachusetts: Wiley-Blackwell, 2011.

9. Nixon, 65–71.

10. Aitken, Jonathan. *Nixon: A Life*. Washington, D.C.: Regnery Publishing, 1993, 218–220.

11. Wicker, Tom. New York: Random House, 1991.

Chapter 1

1. Ambrose, Stephen E. *Nixon: Volume 2—The Triumph of a Politician, 1962–1972*. New York: Simon and Schuster, 1989. 13–14.

2. Dwight Chapin, interview with the author, Washington, D.C., August 9, 2012.

3. *Ibid.*

4. Smith, Howard K. *Events Leading Up to My Death: The Life of a Twentieth Century Reporter*. New York: St. Martin's Press, 1996. 3.

5. *Ibid.*, 22–36.

6. *Ibid.*, 143–145.

7. *Ibid.*, 268–275.

8. *Ibid.*

9. Kates, James. "Kicking Nixon: Howard K. Smith and the Commentator's Imperative." Liverpool, England: American Studies Resources at LJMU, May 23, 2013. 7.

10. Smith, 290.

11. Smith, 291.

12. *Ibid.*

13. Howard K. Smith papers (Hereafter referred to as the Smith papers). Madison, Wisconsin: Wisconsin Historical Society. Associated Press (AP). "Eisenhower Says Hiss TV Role Amazed Him," *Los Angeles Times*, November 14 1962, 1, 16, clipping in Box 52.

14. Smith papers. "Fullerton Firm Drops ABC for Hiss Interview," *Los Angeles Times*, December 1, 1962, 14, clipping in Box 52.

15. Smith, 291.

16. Smith papers. "Say Ike Didn't Try To Get Hiss Off Air," *New York Mirror*, November 14, 1962, 4, clipping in Box 52.

17. Smith papers. "Howard K. Smith News and Comment, Sunday, November 11, 1962," transcript pp. 1–2 in Box 43.

18. *Ibid.*, 2–3.

19. *Ibid.*, 4.

20. *Ibid.*

21. *Ibid.*, 5–6.

22. *Ibid.*, 6–7.

23. *Ibid.*, 7.

24. *Ibid.*, 8.

25. Smith papers. "Nixon Ex-Aide Assails ABC 'Equal Time' Offer," *The Evening Star*, November 13, 1962, A-2, clipping in Box 52.

26. *Ibid.*

27. Smith papers. "Witch Burning," *Los Angeles Herald Examiner*, November 13, 1962, Editorial page, clipping in Box 52.

28. Smith papers. "Broadcasting Hiss' Hate," *Chicago American*, November 13, 1962, Editorial page, clipping in Box 52.

29. Smith papers. "Weekly 'Traitors' Hour," *Omaha World Herald*, November 13, 1962, Editorial page, clipping in Box 52.

30. Smith papers. "Hiss Remarks Are in Bad Form," *Nashville Tennessean*, November 13, 1962, Editorial page, clipping in Box 52.

31. Smith papers, "Nixon Ex-Aide...," clipping in Box 52.

32. Smith papers, "Hagerty Defends Hiss'

Appearance," UPI, *New York Daily News,* November 19, 1962, 27, clipping in Box 52.

33. Smith, 291.

34. Nixon, 246.

35. Smith papers, "Attitudes toward The Howard K. Smith Show and Its Sponsor." New York: ARB Surveys, January 1963, Box 51.

36. Smith papers, "Parr Is Planning a Show on Nixon," *New York Times,* November 24, 1962, clipping in Box 52.

37. Nixon, 247.

38. Witcover, Jules. *The Resurrection of Richard Nixon.* New York: G. P. Putnam's Sons, 1970. 40.

39. Richard M Nixon papers. Wilderness Years: Series V: Appearance Files 1962–1968: (PPS) "Sports Reception at House." PPS 214, Box 1, Folder 8.

40. *Ibid.*, Box 1, Folder 9.

41. "New York Trip/Florida Trip." PPS 214. Box 1, Folder 10.

42. "Jack Parr Show—New York City." PPS 214 Box 1, Folder 13.

43. *Ibid.*, 7.

44. *Ibid.*, 11

45. *Ibid.*, 15–16.

46. *Ibid.*, Box 1, Folder 14.

47. John S. Whitaker, interview with the author, Chevy Chase, MD, March 23, 2013.

48. "American Society of Newspaper Editors." PPS 214, Box 3, Folder 1.

49. Bobst, Elmer H. *Bobst: The Autobiography of a Pharmaceutical Pioneer.* New York: David McKay Company, 1973, 326.

50. *Ibid.*, 327

51. Li, Victor. *Nixon in New York: How Wall Street Helped Richard Nixon Win the White House.* Lanham, Maryland: Rowman and Littlefield, 2018, 23–24.

52. Ambrose, 1989, 21–23

53. Eisenhower, Julie Nixon. *Pat Nixon: The Untold Story.* New York: Simon and Schuster, 1986, 216.

54. *Ibid.*, 217.

55. "Grocery Manufacturers of America: New York City." PPS 214, Box 4, Folder 4.

56. Nixon, 250.

57. "New York City." PPS 214, Box 3, Folder 10.

58. Garment, Leonard. *Crazy Rhythm: My Journey from Brooklyn, Jazz, and Wall Street to Nixon's White House, Watergate, and Beyond.* New York: Times Books, 1997, 59–60.

59. *Ibid.*, 60–61.

60. "New York City." PPS 214, Box 3, Folder 10.

61. Witcover, 50–51.

62. "Grocery Manufacturers of America: New York City." PPS 214 Box 4, Folder 4.

63. "Reception: Firm Partners: 810 Fifth Avenue, New York City." PPS 214, Box 3, Folder 21.

64. *Ibid.*

65. White, Theodore H. *The Making of the President 1964.* New York: Atheneum House, 1965, 75.

66. "Reception: Firm Partners: 810 Fifth Avenue, New York City." PPS 214, Box 3, Folder 21.

67. Garment, 65.

68. *Ibid.*, 68–69.

69. *Ibid.*

70. Aitken, 210–211.

71. Nixon, 252.

72. Stephen Hess, interview with the author, Washington D.C., August 14, 2012.

73. Nixon, 252.

74. *Ibid.*, 253.

75. *Ibid.*

76. *Ibid.*, 254–255.

77. "Minneapolis, Minn." PPS 214, Box 6, Folder 1.

Chapter 2

1. Witcover, 66.

2. *Ibid.*, 67.

3. *Ibid.*

4. Associated Press (AP), "No Retreat, Says Nixon on Canal." *Washington Post*, January 18, 1964, 1.

5. Broder, David S. "Nixon Sounds More Like an Aspirant." *The Evening Star*, January 31, 1964, 31.

6. "William Safire to Richard M. Nixon letter." January 30, 1964, PPS, Box 5, Folder 1.

7. United Press International (UPI), "Responsible Civil Rights Leaders Needed-Nixon." *Columbus Citizen Journal*, February 13, 1964, 1.

8. Baker, Russell, "Nixon Asks Speed on V-P." *New York Times,* March 6, 1964, 1, 15.

9. *Ibid.*

10. Baker, Russell. "Nixon, in Capitol, Essays Two Roles." *New York Times*, March 6, 1964, 15.

11. Witcover, 73–74.

12. Ambrose, 40.

13. Smith, Jean Edward. *Eisenhower in War and Peace.* New York: Random House, 2012, 506–510.

14. Luke A. Nichter (historian), email conversation with the author, May 11, 2020. Nichter is one of the most accomplished authors on Nixon in the field. Nichter is also a leading authority on Henry Cabot Lodge, Jr. His book *The Last Brahmin: Henry Cabot Lodge Jr. and the Making of the Cold War* was published in 2020.

15. "Notebook 1964 Far East Schedule," Wilderness Series II, Trip Files, PPS 347, Box 4, Folder 1.

16. "Richard Nixon handwritten Notes," PPS 347, Box 4, Folder 6.

17. Nixon, 256.

18. *Ibid.*, 257.

19. *Ibid.*, 257–258.

20. Nichter email conversation.

21. Nixon, 258.

22. *Ibid.*

23. Witcover, 77.

24. *Ibid.*, 78.

25. Kihss, Peter. "GOP Nomination Still Wide Open, Publishers Feel," *New York Times*, April 20, 1964, 1.

26. Witcover, 79–80.

27. "National Conference of Christians and Jews." PPS 214, Box 7, Folder 14.

28. Black, 436–464.

29. Perlstein, Rick. *Before the Storm.* New York: Simon and Schuster, 2001, 351–355.

30. "Sherman Unger letter to Nixon on Republican Governor's Conference," 1–2. PPS 214, Box 9, Folder 8.

31. *Ibid.*, 2–3.

32. *Ibid.*, 3–4.

33. Pearlstein, 358–359.

34. Witcover, 93–94.

35. *Ibid.*, 95.

36. *Ibid.*, 98–99.

37. *Ibid.*, 100–101.

38. *Ibid.*, 100.

39. Pearlstein, 398–400.

40. "Nixon letter to Cy Laughter." PPS 214, Box 10, Folder 16.

41. "Nixon Acts to Cast 1st N.Y. Vote," Clipping from PPS 214, Box 11, Folder 1.

42. Jones, David R. "Nixon Asks Unity in Ranks of GOP," *New York Times*, September 20, 1964, 74.

43. "New Release: 1964 Campaign Schedule of Richard Nixon," PPS 249, Box 1, Folder 1.

44. *Ibid.*

45. Ambrose, 56–57.

46. Lee Huebner, interview with the author, Washington D.C. May 5, 2014.

47. "1964 Campaign," PPS 132, Box 5.

48. Brennan, 97–98.

49. Patrick J. Buchanan, interview with the author, McLean, VA. August 14, 2012.

50. Nixon, 263.

Chapter 3

1. Nixon, 263.

2. Mazo, Earl, "Nixon Terms Rockefeller 'Divider' As G.O.P. Quarrels." *New York Times*, November 6, 1964.

3. "Taiwan." PPS 347, Box 6, Folder 9.

4. "Tokyo, Japan." PPS 347, Box 6, Folder 7.

5. Brennan, 104–105.

6. *Ibid.*

7. "Barry Goldwater letter to George Romney." George Romney Papers (GRP—University of Michigan) RA 45, Goldwater, Barry. December 6, 1964.

8. "George Romney letter to Barry Goldwater." GRP, RA 45, Goldwater, Barry. December 21, 1964.

9. "George Romney letter to Dwight D. Eisenhower," December 28, 1964. Dwight D. Eisenhower Presidential Library, Museum, and Boyhood Home (DDE), Abilene Kansas. Post-Presidential Papers: Special Names Series, George Romney, Box 17.

10. Brennan, 106.

11. "Sherman Unger Summary of Nixon Meeting with Romney at Republican Governor's Convention." PPS 214, Box 11, Folder 19.

12. NA. "Elected Chairman." *New York Times*, December 1, 1964, 19.

13. NA. "Nixon Gets Role in Pulp Project." *New York Times*, April 12, 1965, 52, 55.

14. Tanner, Henry. "Nixon Back in Moscow, Debates Again." *New York Times*, April 11, 1965, 1, 13.

15. *Ibid.*

16. *Ibid.*

17. *Ibid.*

18. Donovan, Robert J. "Over-Nominated, Under-Elected, Still a Promising Candidate." *New York Times*, April 25, 1965, Section 6, pp. 14, 15, 90, 92, 94, and 96.

19. NA, "Nixon Backing LBJ on Troop Actions." *Nashville Banner*, May 3, 1965, 1, 12.

20. *Ibid.*

21. *Ibid.*

22. Hemphill, John. "Nixon Backs Island Action." *Nashville Tennessean*, May 3, 1965, 1, 19.

23. *Ibid.*

24. "A Salute to Ray Bliss." PPS 214, Box 12, Folders 12, 13.

25. "Nixon letter to James A. Rhodes." PPS 214, Box 12, Folder 13.

26. Van Dyke, Laurie. "Need '66 Gain, Nixon Says." *Milwaukee Sentinel*, May 12, 1965, 1, 12.

27. NA (Editorial). "Nixon Realistic." *Milwaukee Sentinel*, May 12, 1965.

28. Paul S. Smith. February 9, 1977, Richard M. Nixon Oral History Project. California State University, Fullerton (COPH) OH, 814, 16.

29. Shepard, Geoff. Interview with the author, Alexandria, VA, June 10, 2013.

30. "American Foundation of Religion and Psychiatry." PPS 214, Box 13, Folder 5.

31. "Fundraising Dinner for Senator Mundt." PPS 214, Box 13, Folder 8.

32. NA. "Nixon Attacks 2 Democrats' Vietnam Views." *Los Angeles Times,* July 11, 1965, 4.

33. "Anne Volz letter to Paul Keyes." PPS 214, Box 13, Folder 14.

34. NA. "Nixon Speech Hits 1-Party Congress." *Washington Post*, August 1, 1965, A23.

35. Evans, Rowland and Robert Novak. "Inside Report: The Nixon Bandwagon." *Washington Post*, August 11, 1965.

36. *Ibid.*

37. "Nixon Speech in Congressional Record." PPS 214, Box 14, Folder 10."

38. "Itineraries and Correspondence." PPS 347, Box 7, Folder 2.

39. Black, 474–475.

40. Hillings, 99–102.

41. Broder, David S. "Nixon Urges Warning to Peking to Keep 'Hands Off' Fighting." *New York Times*, September 13, 1965, 10.

42. "Earl Mazo letter to Nixon." PPS 214, Box 14, Folder 14.

43. Stans, Maurice H. *The Terrors of Justice: The Untold Side of Watergate.* New York: Everest House Publishers. 1978, 128–129.

44. *Ibid.*, 129.

45. Editorial. "Nixon 'Speaks Up' for Minority Party as City Plays Host to Bow." *The Alliance Review,* September 23, 1965, 4.

46. Kaye, Peter. "Party Unity Vital, Nixon Warns GOP." *San Diego Union,* September 24, 1965, 1.

47. Latimer, James. "Nixon Speaks to About 8,000, Flies 1,100 Miles Over State." *Richmond Times Dispatch,* October 6, 1965, 1.

48. Sullivan, Ronald. "Dumont Attacks Rutgers Teach-In." *New York Times,* October 19, 1965, 30.

49. AP. "Nixon Claims Rutgers Should Fire Professor." *The State,* October 25, 1965, 1.

50. "Arthur Krock letter to Nixon." PPS 214, Box 16, Folder 10.

51. Nixon, Richard M. "Nixon Explains Stand on Ousting Genovese." Letter to the *New York Times,* October 29, 1965, 42.

52. "Dwight D. Eisenhower letter to Nixon." PPS 214, Box 16, Folder 10.

53. Anderson, Raymond N. "Nixon Views Vietnam War as a Major Issue in '68 Vote." *New York Times,* November 22, 1965, 1, 6.

54. Witcover, 120.

55. "Program on Chicago Boy's Club 'Night of Inspiration.'" PPS 214, Box 17, Folder 3.

56. Gray, Douglas W. "Nixon Warns U.S. Faces Inflation." *New York Times,* December 4, 1965, B1.

57. *Ibid.*

58. Buchanan interview.

59. *Ibid.*

60. Buchanan, Patrick J. *The Greatest Comeback: How Richard Nixon Rose from Defeat to Create the New Majority.* New York: Crown Forum Books. 2014, 27.

61. Witcover, 123.

Chapter 4

1. Beale, Betty. "Party for Dirksen Draws Nixon." *The Evening Star,* January 12, 1966, C1.

2. "Von's Grocery Company Dinner: The Links, New York City." PPS 214, Box 19, Folder 4.

3. "The Alfalfa Club Dinner: Washington D.C." PPS 214, Box 19, Folder 5.

4. "National Institute of Rug Cleaners." PPS 214, Box 19, Folder 7.

5. "Issues and Answer-ABC." PPS 214, Box 19, Folder 9.

6. *Ibid.*

7. *Ibid.*

8. *Ibid.*

9. *Ibid.*

10. Hess interview.

11. Whitaker interview.

12. "Nashville: Tennessee." PPS 214, Box 19, Folders 15, 16.

13. "Whitaker Comments." PPS 214, Box 19, Folder 17.

14. "Lincoln Day Appearance: Seattle, Washington." PPS 214, Box 19, Folder 18.

15. Broder, David S. "Nixon Campaigns at a Tiring Pace for Republican Candidates." *New York Times,* February 10, 1966, 24.

16. "Lincoln Day Appearance: Seattle: Washington." PPS 214, Box 19, Box 19, Folder 18.

17. "Atlanta: Georgia." PPS 214, Box 20, Folder 2.

18. "Lincoln Day Appearance." PPS 214, Box 20, Folder 5.

19. Trohan, Walter. "Washington Scrapbook." *Chicago Tribune,* March 13, 1966, 5.

20. NA, "Gridiron Club Tuneful, Digs Poke Fun at Many." *Chicago Tribune,* March 13, 1966, 5.

21. Nixon, 272–273.

22. *Ibid.*

23. "Gridiron Dinner: Washington D.C." PPS 214, Box 20, Folder 10.

24. "Buchanan Memo." PPS 214, Box 20, Folder 13.

25. NA, "Answer Please, Mr. Nixon." *National Review,* March 8, 1966, 196.

26. Cato. "Focus on Washington." *National Review,* October 19, 1965, 407.

27. Buchanan, Patrick A. "To the Editor: Nixon and the Buckleyites." *National Review,* April 5, 1966, 294.

28. Cato. "Mr. Nixon's Reply." *National Review,* April 5, 1966, 304.

29. Roberts, Steven V. "The Best Republican for '68." *Esquire,* March 1966, 84.

30. *Ibid.*

31. *Ibid.,* 85.

32. Rushton, Bill. "Race Issue Dead-Nixon." *The Tulane Hullabaloo,* April 21, 1966, 1.

33. Kolb, Carolyn. "Just Here for Fun, No Politics, Says Pat Nixon." *Times-Picayune,* April 17, 1966, 20.

34. "Tribute to Dean Justin Miller." PPS 214, Box 21, Folder 6.

35. Garment, 79–83.

36. Witcover, 128–129.

37. NA. "True Crime Inspires Tense Play." *Life,* February 28, 1955, 75–78.

38. Garment, 84.

39. *Ibid.*

40. Murphy, Bruce Allen. *Fortas: The Rise and Ruin of a Supreme Court Justice.* New York: William Morrow and Company, 1988.

41. Garment, 87–89.

42. O'Neil, Frank. "This NH Group, GOP Can Win, Dems Divided." *Manchester Union-Leader,* May 3, 1966, 1, 14.

43. "Ford Press Releases—Birch Society/Extremists 1965." Ford Congressional Papers. Press Secretary and Speeches File, Gerald R. Ford Presidential Library (GRFL). Box D6.

44. *Ibid.*

45. "Buchanan Memo to RN." PPS 214, Box 21, Folder 13.

46. Whitaker interview.

47. Mansell, Walter. "Nixon Would Gut Spending for Space." *Houston Chronicle,* May 3, 1966, 1, 12.

48. "Boys Club Dinner Program." PPS 214, Box 21, Folder 15.

49. "Notes from Phone Conversation from Agnes Waldron." PPS 214, Box 22, Folder 1.

50. "Millsaps Speech." PPS 214, Box 22, Folder 2.

51. *Ibid.*

52. *Ibid.*

53. "Clarke Reed Letter to Nixon." PPS 214, Box 22, Folder 3.

54. *New York Times* Service. "Nixon Builds Support in South for Possible 1968 Race." *The Plain Dealer*, May 8, 1966.

55. *Ibid.*

56. "Schedule of Richard M. Nixon and Robert H. Finch." PPS 214, Box 22, Folder 4.

57. NA, "Nixon Arrives Monday for 2- Day Visit," *San Diego Union*, May 6, 1966, 1.

58. "Pillars of Freedom Speech, S- D Kiwanis." PPS 214, Box 22, Folder 6.

59. Stone, Joe. "Win Vietnam War Soon, Nixon Urges." *San Diego Union*, May 11, 1966, 1.

60. Edson, Arthur. "Nixon Girds for Party—and—Personal—Comeback." *Kansas City Times*, March 14, 1966, 36.

61. "Buchanan Memo to RN, Re: Visit to Decatur." PPS 214, Box 23, Folder 1.

62. Keith, Allan H. "Nixon Rakes Viet War Policy." *Decatur Herald & Review*, May 16, 1966, 1.

63. NA, "I Do Not Believe We Will Have a War, Nixon Says." *The Plain Dealer*, May 17, 1966, 1.

64. *Ibid.*

65. "Program Cover of 'Republican—a—Go—Go.'" PPS 214, Box 23, Folder 11.

66. NA, "Nixon and the Go—Go GOP." *New York Post*, May 20, 1966, 7.

67. "Address by Richard M. Nixon presented at the National War College." PPS 214, Box 23, Folder 1.

68. "Fundraising Dinner (Goodell)." PPS 214, Box 24, Folder 2.

69. "'Clipping' from Fundraising Dinner (Goodell)." PPS 214, Box 24, Folder 2.

70. "Westchester County Association Annual Dinner." PPS 214, Box 24, Folder 4.

71. Safire, 22–26.

72. NA, "UR Students to Vote on Degree for Nixon." *Rochester Democrat and Chronicle*. April 15, 1966, 11A.

73. "Rhyne Letter to New York Times in Commencement Address at University of Rochester." PPS 214, Box 24, Folder 6.

74. "Commencement Address: University of Rochester." PPS, Box 24, Folder 6.

75. *Ibid.*

76. "Congressional Gala: Washington D.C." PPS 214, Box 24, Folder 11.

77. "General Federation of Women's Clubs: Chicago, Illinois." PPS 214, Box 24, Folder 12.

78. "Republican Fundraising Dinner: Indianapolis, Indiana." PPS 214, Box 24, Folder 13.

79. "Fundraising Dinner (Laxalt): Reno, Nevada." PPS 214, Box 25, Folder 4.

80. "Fundraising Dinner: Los Angeles, CA." PPS 214, Box 25, Folder 5.

81. *Ibid.*

82. "Nixon Letter to Reagan." PPS 214, Box 25, Folder 6.

83. Ambrose, 83–84.

84. Witcover, 134.

85. Witcover, 148–153.

Chapter 5

1. "Itineraries." PPS 347, Box 8, Folder 1.

2. *Ibid.*

3. "Richard Nixon Interviews." Walter J. Brown Media Archives (WBM), University of Georgia Libraries. Transcript from Day 9, 25–26.

4. "Paris, France; Rome, Italy; Tel Aviv, Israel; and Karachi, Pakistan." PPS 347, Box 8, Folders 4–9.

5. "Itineraries from Saigon, Vietnam." PPS 347, Box 8, Folder 14.

6. "Background from Philippines Trip." PPS 347, Box 8, Folder 14.

7. *Ibid.*

8. "Tokyo, Japan and Seoul, Korea." PPS 347, Box 9, Folders 1–2.

9. *Ibid.*

10. "Honolulu, Hawaii." PPS 347, Box 9, Folders 3–4.

11. "VFW Distinguished Guests Banquet." PPS 214, Box 26, Folder 14.

12. "Memo to RN from Buchanan: VFW Convention." PPS 214, Box 26, Folder 14.

13. "RN's Schedule." PPS 214, Box 26, Folder.

14. Evans, Rowland and Robert Novak. "Inside Report: Nixon's Shoreham Meeting." *Washington Post*, September 7, 1966, A25.

15. "Memo to RN from Buchanan: William Rusher." Patrick J. Buchanan Personal Collection (PJB), August 5, 1966.

16. Cato. "Focus on Washington." *National Review*, September 6, 1966, 871.

17. "List of Acceptances for Dinner/Links Club." PPS 214, Box 26, Folder 17.

18. NA. "Nixon Says the War Can Be Shortened." *New York Times*, August 27, 1966, 2.

19. "Rusk Letter to Nixon." PPS 214, Box 26, Folder 21.

20. "Nixon Letter to Rusk." PPS 214, Box 26, Folder 21.

21. "Appearance File by Rose Mary Woods." PPS 138, Box 1, Folder 1.

22. Nixon, Richard M. "Too Little, Too Late, Says of Johnson." *Los Angeles Times*, September 11, 1966, 2.

23. AP. "Nixon Warns of a Peril to Two-Party System." *New York Times*, September 15, 1966, 24.

24. AP. "Nixon in Iowa." *New York Times*, September 16, 1966, 27.

25. AP. "Politics Played on Prosperity, Nixon Charges." *San Diego Union* September 16, 1966, A2.

26. NA. "Nixon Would Curb Shipping to Hanoi." *New York Times*, September 17, 1966, 4.

27. NA. "GOP Leaders Give Nixon An Edge for 1968." *New York Times*, September 16, 1966, 27.

28. AP. "Nixon Mum on Poll." *San Diego Union*. September 17, 1966, A6.

29. Bergholz, Richard. "Nixon Presses Victory Theme at GOP Dinner." *Los Angeles Times*, September 17, 1966, 2.

30. *Ibid.*

31. Chapman, William. "Nixon Rebuff to Bircher Jolts Alaskan Alliance." *Washington Post*, September 19, 1966, 1.

32. Buchanan, 58.

33. Frankel, Max. "Johnson Reacts to Polls." New York Times, September 20, 1966, 31.

34. Buchanan interview.

35. Herbers, John. "Nixon Campaigns in North Dakota." *New York Times,* September 22, 1966, 46.

36. Herbers, John. "Johnson Becomes Top Nixon Target." *New York Times*, September 24, 1966, 9.

37. Herbers, John. "Farm Policy and Daylight Time are Targets of Nixon in Iowa." *New York Times*, September 24, 1966, 51.

38. NA. "Nixon in Tarrytown, Says Johnson is Losing Support." *New York Times*, September 27, 1966, 14.

39. Parish, John. "Nixon Promotes GOP and Himself." *Jackson Sun,* September 28, 1966, 1.

40. *Ibid.*

41. Semple, Robert B., Jr. "Nixon Criticizes U.S. Peace Steps." *New York Times*, September 28, 1966, 13.

42. Hope, Paul. "Carolina 'Had Enuff?' GOP Asking Voters." *The Evening Star*, September 29, 1966, A1.

43. Semple, Robert B., Jr. "Nixon on the Stump—An Old Timer at 53." *New York Times*, October 2, 1966, 207.

44. Buchanan, 70–71.

45. Semple, Jr., Robert B. "Nixon Asks GOP to Unite in South." *New York Times,* September 30, 1966, 37.

46. Semple, Robert B., Jr. "Nixon on the Stump—An Old Timer at 53." *New York Times*, October 2, 1966, 207.

47. AP. "Johnson Peace Motives Doubted Nixon Says." *Los Angeles Times*. October 2, 1966.

48. UPI. "Humphrey, Nixon View Johnson Election Role." *Los Angeles Times*. October 10, 1966, 18.

49. Broder, David S. "GOP Gains Are Expected to Be Modest." *Washington Post*, October 9, 1966, 1.

50. Glass, Andrew. "Nixon Praises JFK at Al Smith Dinner." *Washington Post*, October 14, 966, A4.

51. NA. "Nixon Bids Johnson Apologize to GOP for Vicious Attack." *New York Times*, October 15, 1966, 1.

52. Nixon, Richard M. "Quest for Peace or Quest for Votes?" *Los Angeles Times*, October 16, 1966, 3.

53. NA. "Nixon Bids Johnson Apologize to GOP for Vicious Attack." *New York Times*, October 15, 1966, 1.

54. Mackenzie, John P. "Nixon Charges Life with Lie about Clients." *Washington Post*, October 19, 1966, A2.

55. Garment, 90–91.

56. NA. "It's the Party of Nixon Now." *The Sunday Star*, October 23, 1966, A2.

57. Broder, David S. "It's the TR Thing that Prods Nixon." *Washington Post*, October 23, 1966, 1.

58. Broder, David S. "Administration Challenged by Nixon to Repudiate Racists Seeking Office." *Washington Post*, October 19, 1966, 1.

59. NA. "Nixon Sees 400,000 Vote Edge for Reagan." *Los Angeles Times*, October 21, 1966, 21.

60. Buchanan, 62.

61. Broder, David S. "Political Parade Campaigning Through California." *Washington Post*, October 25, 1966, 19.

62. *Ibid.*

63. Buckley, Thomas. "Nixon Forecasts GOP Comeback." *New York Times*, October 24, 1966, 1.

64. Harris, Louis. "Heavy Ticket Splitting Seen Reducing GOP Gains in Congressional Races." *Washington Post*, October 24, 1966, 1.

65. Kallina, 203.

66. Gallup, George, Jr., and John Davies III. "3 Out of 4 Are Worried By Viet War." *Washington Post*, October 24, 1966, A2.

67. White, William S. "Going for Broke: Nixon Has Most to Win or Lose." *Washington Post*, October 25, 1966, 19.

68. Dejonge, Maury. "Nixon Raps 'Lap-Dog' Congress." *Grand Rapids Press*, October 26, 1966, 15.

69. Broder, David S. "Nixon Accuses Kennedy of Undercutting Absent President." *Washington Post*, October 26, 1966, 1, 8.

70. *Ibid.*

71. Wicker, Tom. "Nixon Says A 'Johnson Blitz' Threatens Great Republican Tide." *New York Times*, October 28, 1966, 28.

72. Buchanan, 66–67.

73. UPI. "Nixon Hits 'Scoreless' Congress." *Los Angeles Times*, October 29, 1966, C6.

74. Janson, Donald. "Nixon Proposes Tax Deductions on Savings to Counter Inflation." *New York Times*, October 29, 1966, 68.

75. Buchanan interview.

76. Evans, Rowland, and Robert Novak. "Inside Report...Romney's Coattails." *Washington Post*, October 28, 1966, 21.

77. Nixon, Richard M. "Democrats on Racism in South." *Los Angeles Times*, October 30, 1966, 12.

78. *Ibid.*

79. Blair, William H. "Nixon Says Vote Perils Humphrey." *New York Times*, November 2, 1966, 26.

80. The Papers of William Safire (WS). Library of Congress. Box 8, Folder 2.

81. *Ibid.*

82. Buchanan interview.

83. NA. "'Economic Front' To Help End War is Urged by Nixon." *New York Times,* November 3 1966, 29.

84. *Ibid.*

85. Jennings, Bill. "Baker Victory Seen by Nixon." *Johnson City Press,* November 4, 1966 1–2.

86. *Ibid.*

87. Herbers, John. "Nixon Criticizes Manilla Result." *New York Times,* November 4, 1966, 1.

88. Buchanan interview.

89. Transcript of the President's News Conference on Foreign and Domestic Matters. *New York Times,* November 5, 1966, 10.

90. *Ibid.*

91. Horner, Garrett S. "Nixon Attack a Johnson First." *The Evening Star.* November 5, 1966, 1.

92. Witcover, 164–166.

93. Horner, op cit.

94. Buchanan interview.

95. Phelps, Robert H. "Nixon Sees Break in Bipartisan Line." *New York Times,* November 5 1966, 1.

96. *Ibid.*

97. Gal, Harold. "Nixon Defended by Eisenhower After Criticism by the President." *New York Times,* November 6, 1966, 68.

98. *Ibid.*

99. Sibley, John. "Nixon Denounces McNamara's Data." *New York Times,* November 7, 1966, 33.

100. *Ibid.*

101. Witcover, 167–168.

102. Buchanan, 92–93.

103. McGrory, Mary. "Nixon in Catbird's Seat Pardons Self." *The Evening Star,* November 7 1966, A1, A6.

104. Janson, Donald. "Nixon In Indiana For A Final Plea." *New York Times,* November 8, 1966 35.

105. Safire, 32–33.

106. Buchanan, 95–96.

107. Multiple authors. "Elections: A Party for All." *Time,* November 18, 1966, 23.

108. Witcover, 169–170.

109. NA. "Mr. Nixon's View of the Election." *New York Times,* November 13, 1966, 227.

110. Buchanan, 97.

Chapter 6

1. Buchanan interview.

2. Schumach, Murray. "Nixon Finds Vote a Johnson Rebuke." *New York Times,* November 10 1966, 29.

3. Weaver, Warren Jr. "Nixon Bats .686 for 1966 Season." *New York Times,* November 13 1966, 54.

4. "Republican Resurgence." *Time,* November 18, 1966; "The New GOP Galaxy." *Newsweek,* November 21, 1966.

5. Buchanan, Patrick J. "Nixon: GOP's Big Winner In '66." No Date, PJB.

6. Buchanan interview.

7. *Ibid.*

8. Witkin, Richard. "Rockefeller Again Asserts He Won't Seek Presidency." *New York Times,* November 10, 1966, 1.

9. Sheehan, Neil. "Romney Says Republican Gains Assure Party's Victory in 1968." *New York Times,* November 14, 1966, 30.

10. *Ibid.*

11. *Ibid.*

12. Turner, Wallace. "Reagan Cautions Romney on 1968." *New York Times,* November 21, 1966, 24.

13. Thomas C. Reed. *The Reagan Enigma: 1964–1980.* Los Angeles, California: Figueroa Press, 2014, 57–62.

14. "Buchanan Memo to RN, November 10, 1966." PJB.

15. Herbers, John. "Romney Attacks Rockefeller Plan on 1968 Strategy." *New York Times,* November 21, 1966, 1.

16. Herbers, John. "Romney Endorses G.O.P. Consensus As a Principle." *New York Times,* November 22, 1966, 1.

17. Weaver, Warren Jr. "Four Hearties of the Good Ship G.O.P." *New York Times,* November 27, 1966, Section 6.

18. NA. "Nixon Shuns Politics at Hoover Memorial Dedication." *New York Times,* November 29, 1966, 32.

19. Buchanan, 98.

20. "Luncheon for Bob Finch: Links Club, New York." PPS 214, Box 27, Folder 13.

21. "American Farm Bureau Federation: Las Vegas, NV." PPS 214, Box 27, Folder 14.

22. "California State Chamber of Commerce: 39th Annual Meeting." PPS 214, Box 27, Folder 15.

23. Witcover, 180–181.

24. Herbers, John. "Romney Attacked Goldwater Race As Keyed To South." *New York Times,* November 29, 1966, 1.

25. Hess, Stephen and David S. Broder. *The Republican Establishment.* New York: Harper & Row, 1967, 120–121.

26. Evans, Rowland and Robert Novak. "Inside Report: Behind Romney—Goldwater Feud." *Deseret News,* December 16, 1966. 10A.

27. Herbers, John. "Romney Attacked Goldwater Race As Keyed to South." *New York Times,* November 29, 1966, 1.

28. Herbers, John. "Romney's Charge Called Baloney." *New York Times,* December 1, 1966, 39.

29. Personal and Political Papers of Senator Barry M. Goldwater (BG) 1880s—2008. FM MSS 1, Box 94, Folders 27–29.

30. Buckley, William F., Jr. "Romney's Reasons for Taking His Walk Out in Open Now." *Los Angeles Times,* December 7, 1966, B5.

31. Evans, Rowland, and Robert Novak. "Inside Report: Behind Romney—Goldwater Feud." *Deseret News*, December 16, 1966, 10A.

32. Witkin, Richard. "A Romney Parley Held at Waldorf." *New York Times*, December 29, 1966, 17.

33. NA. "57 Debutantes of 12 Nations Make Ball." *New York Times*, December 30, 1966, 28.

34. Francis X. Maloney, interview with the author. New York, October 16, 2015.

35. Thomas W. Evans, interview with James Rosen. James Rosen Collection (JR). Box 50, Folders 18–19. Northwestern University: Evanston, Illinois, April 22, 1992.

36. Shelley Scarney Buchanan, interview with the author. McLean, VA, June 11, 2016.

37. Rugaber, Walter F. "Wallace Disturbs G.O.P. South." *New York Times*, January 4, 1967, 60.

38. Safire, 42–44.

39. *Ibid.*, 44.

40. *Ibid.*

41. "Buchanan Memo to RN." January 4, 1967." PJB.

42. Safire, 45.

43. "RN Trip to DC." PPS 214, Box 27, Folder 20.

44. "Boys Club Benefit: Minneapolis Minnesota." PPS 214, Box 27, Folder 22.

45. "Boys Club: Broward Co: Fort Lauderdale." PPS 214, Box 27, Folder 24.

46. "University of Florida: Gainesville, Fl." PPS 214, Box 27, Folder 23.

47. Broder, David S. "Romney-Nixon Wis. Test Seen." *Washington Post*, January 22, 1967, A5.

48. Buchanan, 102–103.

49. Broder, David S. "Nixon Begins Building Up Staff for '68." *Washington Post*, January 27, 1967, A1.

50. NA. "Romney Defeating Nixon or Is It Vice-Versa." *Washington Post*, February 14, 1967, 1.

51. Witcover, 184–185.

52. Evans, Rowland, and Robert Novak. "Inside Report: The Romney Disorganization." *Washington Post*, February 13, 1967, A17.

53. Witcover, 188.

54. "Memo to RN." February 20, 1967, PJB.

55. Buchanan interview.

56. Raymond Price, Interview with the author, New York, August 11, 2012.

57. *Ibid.*

58. *Ibid.*

59. Chapin interview. Chapin told the author that during the 1964 Republican Convention, Nixon had a meeting with the delegates of the 1960 Republican Convention. The meeting lasted several hours as he and his wife greeted every one of the delegates and thanked them. Chapin was surprised at how friendly, patient, and humble he was. It was a characteristic that he noticed time and time again during the 1968 campaign.

60. "An Oral History Interview with Robert F. Ellsworth." January 30, 2008. Richard Nixon Oral History Project. Richard Nixon Presidential Library and Museum: Yorba Linda, California.

61. "Europe Trip." PPS 347, Box 9, Folder 10.

Chapter 7

1. "Europe Trip." PPS 347, Box 9, Folder 11.

2. "Statement of Richard M. Nixon." PPS 347, Box 9, Folder 11.

3. Nixon, 280–281.

4. "Ellsworth Letter to Parker." PPS 347, Box 9, Folder 9.

5. Pope, Philip H. Unpublished Dissertation: *Foundations of Nixonian Foreign Policy" The Pre-Presidential Years of Richard M. Nixon, 1946–1968.* University of Southern California, August 1988. 510–511.

6. "Europe." PPS 347, Box 9, Folder 10.

7. Nixon, 280–281.

8. Black, 495.

9. Nixon, 280–281.

10. "Conversation between Richard M. Nixon and Soviet Engineer Vladmir Panov." PPS 347, Box 9, Folder 19.

11. "AmEmbassy Bucharest: Visit to Romania by Former Vice President Richard M. Nixon." PPS 347, Box 9, Folder 20.

12. "Memorandum of Conversation," 1–3. PPS 347, Box 9, Folder 20.

13. *Ibid.*, 4.

14. *Ibid.*, 5–7.

15. *Ibid.*, 7–10.

16. *Ibid.*, 10–11.

17. "Prague." PPS 347, Box 347, Box 10, Folder 1.

18. *Ibid.*

19. Aitken, 328.

20. Gallup, George. "Nixon Gains Clear Lead Over Romney." *Washington Post*, March 19, 1967, A2.

21. Buchanan interview.

22. "Buchanan Memo to RN." March 28, 1967.

23. Broder, David S. "Nixon Wary on Europe Pullout." *Washington Post.* April 2, 1967, A9.

24. "Far East Trip (Itineraries and News Releases). PPS 347, Box 10, Folder 3.

25. *Ibid.*

26. Price, 20–21.

27. Price interview.

28. Price, 21.

29. "Ranking of the World's Richest Economies by GDP (1967)." er.classora.com/reports/+24369/ranking-of-the-worlds-richest-countries-by-GDP? editions-1967.

30. Price, 21.

31. "Tokyo, Japan." PPS 347, Box 10, Folder 6.

32. NA. "Nixon Says Asians Back U.S. On War." *New York Times,* April 8, 1967, 3.

33. "Hong Kong." PPS 347, Box 10, Folder 7.

34. "Tapei, Taiwan." PPS 347, Box 10, Folder 8.

35. Price, 21–22.

36. "Bangkok, Thailand." PPS 347, Box 10, Folder 10.

37. Buckley, Tom. "Nixon Urges Halt to War Criticism." *New York Times,* April 15, 1967, 2.

38. "South Vietnam." PPS 347, Box 11, Folder 1.

39. *Ibid.*

40. "South Vietnam." PPS 347, Box 11, Folder 2.

41. Buckley, Tom. 'Nixon Indicates He Seeks Step-Up in War Efforts." *New York Times,* April 18, 1967, 2.

42. "Djakarta, Indonesia." PPS 347, Box 11, Folder 3.

43. NA. "Nixon Sees Singapore Chief." *New York Times,* April 19, 1967, 3.

44. "Singapore." PPS 347, Box 11, Folder 4.

45. Price, 27.

46. "Pakistan." PPS 347, Box 11, Folder 6.

47. Price interview. Price told the author that he was amazed at Nixon's patience and generosity to everyone on this trip and that included all the regular or little people with whom he came in contact. It included waiters, cab drivers, hotel clerks, secretaries, etc. It was a side of Nixon that most of the American people never saw.

48. "Iran." PPS 347, Box 11. Folder 7.

49. NA. "Nixon Is Doubtful Raids Will Bring Peking Into War." *New York Times,* April 25, 1967, 12.

50. *Ibid.*

51. Gallup, George. "Nixon First Choice of GOP County Chairmen for '68" *Washington Post,* April 16, 1967, F4.

52. Broder, David S. "Rockefeller Writes I'm Out for 1968." *Washington Post,* April 20, 1967, A8.

53. Weaver, Warren, Jr. "Virginia Republicans Term Visit by Romney a Major Success." *New York Times,* April 17, 1967, 18.

54. Evans, Rowland and Robert Novak. "Inside Report: Romney's Gain." *Washington Post,* May 5, 1967, A25.

55. Eisen, Jack. "Agnew Loses Bid to Get Rockefeller to Run." *Washington Post.* May 5, 1967, A25.

56. "Boy's Club Convention: Pittsburgh, PA." PPs 214, Box 28, Folder 5.

57. Gellman, Irwin F. *The President and the Apprentice.* New Haven, Connecticut: Yale University Press, 2015, 499–513.

58. Gellman, 2015, 510.

59. Gellman, 2015, 500–501.

60. "Peru." PPS 347, Box 12, Folder 4.

61. "Chile." PPS 347, Box 12, Folder 8.

62. "Argentina." PPS 347, Box 12, Folder 12.

63. "Brazil." PPS 347, Box 12, Folders 13–14.

64. Montgomery, Paul. "Nixon and Rio Slum Dwellers Discuss Their Economic Needs." *New York Times.* May 14, 1967, 28.

65. "Brazil." PPS 347, Box 12, Folder 14.

66. AP. "Nixon to Compete in Primary Races If He is Candidate." *New York Times,* May 16, 1967, 24.

67. NA. "Special to the New York Times." *New York Times.* May 17, 1967, 34.

68. NA. "Survey Finds Nixon Leads in 28 State GOP Units." *New York Times,* May 15, 1967, 27.

69. Harris, Louis. "Romney Loses Momentum: Nixon Leading in GOP Favor." *Washington Post,* May 17, 1967, A2.

70. Gallup, George. "Nixon Increases Lead Over Romney; Becomes Independents' First Choice." *Washington Post,* May 21, 1967, A2.

71. "American Feed Manufactures Association: Chicago, Illinois." PPS 214, Box 28, Folder 8.

72. "Empire Club: Toronto, Canada." PPS 214, Box 28, Folder 10.

73. Witcover, 202.

74. *Ibid.,* 201–202.

75. "Nixon Day Banquet: Bowling Green, Ohio." PPS 214, Box 28, Folder 11.

76. "World Affairs Council Luncheon: Philadelphia, Pa." PPS 214, Box 28, Folder 13.

77. "Bobst Institute Hahnemann Medical College; Philadelphia, Pa." PPS 214 Box 28, Folder 14.

78. Buchanan, 162–163.

79. Gellman, 2015, 465–482.

80. Buchanan, 164.

81. *Ibid.,* 164–165.

82. *Ibid.*

83. *Ibid.,* 167.

84. *Ibid.*

85. *Ibid.,* 167–172.

86. "Background Notes." PPS 347, Box 13, Folder 4.

87. Buchanan, 172–173.

88. "Background Notes." PPS 347, Box 13, Folder 4.

89. Buchanan, 173–174.

90. "Background Notes." PPS 347, Box 13, Folder 4.

91. *Ibid.*

92. Buchanan, 175–176.

93. *Ibid.,* 177–178.

94. *Ibid.,* 178.

95. *Ibid.,* 180–181.

96. Nixon, 283.

Chapter 8

1. Reston, James. "Washington: Richard Nixon's Campaign." *New York Times,* May 7, 1967, 228.

2. "Zionist Luncheon." PPS 214, Box 29, Folder 2.

3. "Capitol Hill Club Reception: Washington D.C." PPS 214, Box 29, Folder 3.

4. *Ibid.*

5. "Reader's Digest Luncheon: N.Y. City." PPS 214, Box 29, Folder 4.

6. Reed, 88–94.

7. Weaver, Warren, Jr. "Young GOP Unity Urged by Reagan." *New York Times,* June 24, 1967, 12.

8. Weaver, Warren, Jr. "Young Republicans Color Them Conservative." *New York Times,* June 25, 1967, E3.

9. Weaver, Warren, Jr. "Young Republicans Near a Party Split." *New York Times*, June 22, 1967, 8.

10. "Buchanan Memo to RN." June 30, 1967, PJB.

11. Broder, David S. "Political Parade: Stirrings on the Right." *Washington Post*, June 27, 1967, A17.

12. "Buchanan Memo to RN." July 5, 1967, PJB.

13. Broder, David S. "Reagan Bandwagon Already Rolling, Ore. Governor Says." *Washington Post*, 27 June 1967, A5.

14. Evans, Rowland and Robert Novak. "Inside Report: Romney Downbeat." *Washington Post*, July 3, 1967, A17.

15. Broder, David S. "GOP Governors Support Unpledged Delegates in '68." *Washington Post*, July 1, 1967, A2.

16. Evans, Rowland and Robert Novak. "Inside Report: Romney Downbeat." *Washington Post*, July 3, 1967, A17.

17. *Ibid.*

18. "Buchanan Memo to RN." July 5, 1967. PJB.

19. *Ibid.*

20. Nixon, 284.

21. Broder, David S. "Nixon Plans to Meet Reagan." *Washington Post*, July 16, 1967, A1.

22. King, Larry L. "Under the Big Dome with Senator Murphy." *Los Angeles Times*, August 13, 1967, A8.

23. Reed, 97.

24. Nixon, 284.

25. "Transcript Speech Given by RN at Bohemian Grove." White House Special Files Collection (WHSF), Box 1, Folder 5.

26. AP. "No Dealing, Both Nixon, Reagan Say." *Washington Post*, July 25, 1967, A8.

27. Evans, Rowland and Robert Novak. "Inside Report: Let Ronnie Have the Kooks." *Washington Post*, July 24, 1967, 24.

28. Evans, Rowland and Robert Novak. "New Nixon Strategy Begins to Show: 'Shun Far Right.'" *Los Angeles Times*, July 25, 1967, A5.

29. "Nixon Letter to Reagan." August 4, 1967, PPS 501, Box 1, Folder 1.

30. Buchanan, 123.

31. Chamberlain, John. "1968 Sweepstakes." No date, King Features Syndicate. PPS 501, Box 1, Folder 1.

32. "Reagan Letter to Nixon." August 16, 1967, PPS 501, Box 1, Folder 1.

33. Buchanan, 123.

34. "An Oral History Interview with Peter Flanigan." April 23, 2007, New York. Richard Nixon Oral History Project, Richard Nixon Presidential Library and Museum: Yorba Linda, California.

35. Kabaservice, Geoffrey. *Rule and Ruin: The Downfall of Moderation and the Destruction of the Republican Party from Eisenhower to the Tea Party.* Oxford University Press: New York, 2012, 214.

36. Harris, Louis. "Harris Survey: 19 Point Drop." *Washington Post*, August 12, 1967, A1.

37. Weaver, Warren, Jr "Reagan Asks Delay in Support of Nixon." *New York Times*, August 22, 1967, 1.

38. Witcover, 213.

39. Broder, David S. "Nixon Aide Scores Romney." *Washington Post*, September 8, 1967, A8.

40. de Onis, Juan. "Nixon Says U.S. Leadership Declines Under Johnson Policies." *New York Times*, September 13, 1967, 29.

41. "Ray Price Memo to Rose Woods." June 27, 1967. PPS 214, Box 29, Folder 11.

42. "Dwight Chapin Letter to Agatha Schmidt." September 5, 1967. PPS 214, Box 214, Folder 12.

43. Author Observations from *Firing Line,* September 14, 1967.

44. "Rose Mary Woods to Nixon." September 12, 1967. PPS 214, Box 29, Folder 16.

45. "Nixon to Rose Mary Woods." September 14, 1967. PPS 214, Box 29, Folder 16.

46. Nixon, 287–288.

47. Buchanan, 119.

48. Nixon, 288.

49. Graham, Billy. *Just As I Am.* New York: Harper and Row, Revised Edition, 2001, 440.

50. Nixon, 19–20.

51. Weaver, Warren, Jr. "Polls Are Crowding Out the Primaries." *New York Times,* October 1, 1967, 183.

52. "Associated Oregon Industries." PPS 214, Box 30, Folder 1.

53. "Hoover Institute: Stanford, California." PPS 214, Box 30, Folders 2–4.

54. AP. "National Citizens for Nixon Gets Businessman as Head." *New York Times.* October 4, 1967, 25.

55. NA. "Nebraska Group for Nixon Named." *New York Times.* October 7, 1967, 59.

56. Whalen, Richard J. *Catch the Falling Flag: A Republican's Challenge to His Party.* Houghton Mifflin: Boston, Massachusetts, 1972, 22–23.

57. William F. Gavin. Interview with the author. McLean, VA. August 2, 2013.

58. Gavin, William F. *Speechwright: An Insider's Take on Political Rhetoric.* East Lansing, Michigan: Michigan State University, 2012, 34.

59. Whalen, 22–23.

60. NA. "Nixon Will Address GOP Dinner October 13." *Greenwich Time*, September 28, 1967, 1.

61. Nixon, Richard M. "What Has Happened to America?" *Reader's Digest*, October 1967, 49–54.

62. "Eisenhower's Birthday Luncheon: Washington D.C." PPS 214, Box 30, Folder 7.

63. UPI. "Nixon Optimistic on Visit to Capital." *The Evening Star*, October 19, 1967, A-8.

64. Price interview.

65. Nixon, Richard M. "Asia After Vietnam." *Foreign Affairs.* Council of Foreign Relations: New York, October 1967, 111–125.

66. *Ibid.*, 121.

67. Witcover, 221–222.

68. NA. "Republicans: Anchors Aweigh." *Time,* October 20, 1967, 17–21.

69. Weaver, Warren, Jr. "Rockefeller Denies

Wanting Presidency." *New York Times*, October 18, 1967, 1.

70. NA. "Republicans: Anchors Aweigh." *Time*, October 20, 1967, 17.

71. Reed, 119.

72. Notziger, Lyn. *Notziger*. Regnery Gateway: Washington, D.C., 1992, 86.

73. Shadegg, Stephen C. *Winning's a Lot More Fun*. The Macmillan Company: London, 1970. 102.

74. Semple, Robert B., Jr. "New Nixon Stomping Old Trail." *New York Times*, October 30, 1967, 17.

75. Weaver, Warren, Jr. "Romney Foes or Friends: Expected to File Court Test of His Citizenship." *New York Times*, November 1, 1967, 28.

76. Semple, Robert B., Jr. "Nixon Sees Need for Vietnam Role." *New York Times*. October 28, 1967. 10.

77. "Executives Club: Chicago, Illinois." PPS 214, Box 30, Folder 11.

78. "Waukesha: Wisconsin." PPS 214, Box 30 Folder 13.

79. Shadegg, 109.

80. Bartelt, James. "Can't Risk New Conflict for Viet Solution—Nixon." *Green Bay Gazette*, October 29, 1967, 1.

81. "Huntley TV Show." PPS 214, Box 30 Folder 16.

82. Pearson, Drew and Jack Anderson. "Scandal in Sacramento." *New York Post*, October 31 1967, 46.

83. Reed, 124.

84. "Memo from RMN to Buchanan." November 1, 1967. PJB.

85. "The Lufkin/Lasker Luncheon." PPS 214 Box 31, Folder 2.

86. "Testimonial for Joe Woods." PPS 214, Box 31, Folder 2.

87. NA. "6 in GOP Top Johnson in Poll: Rockefeller Strongest, 52 to 38." *New York Times* November 7, 1967, 35.

88. "Ohio." PPS 214, Box 31, Folder 3.

89. "Ohio." PPS 214, Box 31, Folder 4.

90. AP. "Buckley Backs Nixon in '68." *New York Times*, November 11, 1967, 37.

91. Semple, Robert B., Jr. "Nixon Backs Eventual End to Draft." *New York Times*, November 18 1967, 21.

92. Ripley, Anthony. "Romney Declares He Is in '68 Race, Predicts Victory." *New York Times* November 19, 1967, 1.

93. "NET-TV-Paul Niven." PPS 214, Box 31 Folder 11.

94. Delatiner, Barbara. "Nixon Protects Colorful Image." *Newsday*, November 29, 1967, 2A.

95. NA. "Nixon Calls Makeup on TV a Big Factor in His 1960 Defeat." *New York Times*, November 29, 1967, 28.

96. "NET-TV-Paul Niven." PPS 214, Box 31 Folder 16.

97. *Ibid.*

98. Shadagg, 107–108.

99. Hughes, Harold. "UO Audience Hears

Criticize Proposed Alliance Against Red China." *The Oregonian*, November 30, 1967, 1.

100. Semple, Robert B., Jr. "Nixon Cool to Eisenhower View on Strategy of U.S. to Vietnam." *New York Times*, November 30, 1967, 21.

101. NA. "Nixon Expects No Changes in Viet Policies." *The Oregonian*, November 30, 1967, 29.

102. NA. "Eisenhower Grandson to Marry a Nixon Daughter." *New York Times*, December 1, 1967, 1.

103. NA. "Eisenhower is on Coast: Proud of His Grandson." *New York Times*, November 30, 1967, 38.

104. "Merv Griffin TV Show: New York City, NY." PPS 214, Box 32, Folder 7.

105. "Ray Page's Christmas Party for State Employees: Springfield, Illinois." PPS 214, Box 32, Folder 13.

106. "AB England's Party in Honor of Pat and Dick Nixon: Los Angeles, California." PPS 214, Box 32, Folder 14.

107. "Nebraska." PPS 214, Box 32, Folder 17.

108. "Stone and Webster Executive Conference." PPS 214, Box 32, Folder 8.

109. Garment, 121–122.

110. "NAM Annual Banquet." PPS 214, Box 32, Folder 10.

111. Burnham, David. "Nixon Puts Rights Ahead of Vietnam." *New York Times*, December 9, 1967, 1.

112. "Rockefeller Refuses to Rule Out His Acceptance of a Draft in '68." *New York Times*, December 9, 1967, 1.

113. *Ibid.*

114. Door, Robert. "Nixon Would Throw in Hat if He Had to Today." *Omaha Times-Herald*, December 15, 1967, 1.

115. Nixon, 291–293.

116. Graham, 444.

117. Nixon, 292–293.

118. *Ibid.*, 293.

119. *Ibid.*, 294.

Chapter 9

1. Sherman, Gabriel. *The Loudest Voice in the Room: How the Brilliant, Bombastic Roger Ailes Built Fox News—And Divided the Country*. Random House: New York, 2014, 32–33.

2. Chapin Interview.

3. "Washington and Lee: Richmond, Va." PPS 214, Box 33, Folder 3.

4. "YPO 'Smoker'—Georgetown." PPS 214, Box 33, Folder 9.

5. "Links Club Appearance: New York City, NY." PPS 214, Box 33, Box 10.

6. Evans, Rowland and Robert Novak. "Reagan Drive for Texas Delegates Running Out of Steam Before Start." *Washington Post*, January 3, 1968, A17.

7. Evans, Rowland and Robert Novak. "Nixon's Absence from N.H. Scene Stressed need for

His Guidance." *Washington Post,* January 22, 1968, A15.

8. "To Nixon from Haldeman: Re Campaigning and Implementation." White House Special Files (WHSF), Richard Nixon Library, Box 33, Folder 12.

9. Gallup, George. "Nixon Gains on Romney, Lead Over Rocky is Cut." *Washington Post,* January 31, 1968, A2.

10. Chapin Interview.

11. Broder, David S. "Nixon Bars Romney Debate, Predicts Nomination Victory." *Washington Post,* February 3, 1968, A1.

12. Witcover, 232.

13. Broder, David S. "Nixon Warns About 'Crisis of the Spirit'" *Washington Post,* February 9, 1968, A1.

14. Buchanan, 205–206.

15. "Jaycees Dinner: Green Bay Wisconsin." PPS 214, Box 33, Folder 19.

16. Garment, 119–120.

17. Shadegg, 128–129.

18. Kleindienst, Richard G. *Justice: The Memoirs of an Attorney General.* Jameson Books: Ottawa, Illinois, 1985, 37–38.

19. Shadegg, 128–129.

20. Buchanan interview.

21. Safire, 263–264.

22. Maloney interview.

23. Thomas W. Evans interview with James Rosen. April 23, 1992. James Rosen Collection (JR): Box 50, Folders 18–19. Northwestern University, Evanston, Illinois.

24. *Ibid.*

25. *Ibid.*

26. Maloney interview.

27. Jerris Leonard Interview with James Rosen. JR, October 14, 1999. Box 55, Folders 8–9. Northwestern University, Evanston, Illinois.

28. Kleindienst, 45.

29. Franklin, Ben A. "Wallace in Race; Will Run to Win." *New York Times,* February 9, 1968, 1.

30. "Washington, Indiana." PPS 214, Box 34, Folder 3.

31. Mooney, Robert B. "Nixon Warns Hoosier: 'We Can't Afford LBJ." *Indianapolis Star,* February 11, 1968, 1.

32. "Washington, Indiana." PPS 214, Box 34, Folder 3.

33. Semple, Robert B., Jr. "Nixon Developing a Vietnam Stand." *New York Times,* February 14, 1968, 29.

34. UPI. "Nixon Campaigning, Cites Soviet Power." *New York Times,* February 24, 1968, 36.

35. AP. "Nixon Queries Stand on Missile Parity." *New York Times,* February 22, 1968, 26.

36. Weaver, Warren, Jr. "Wisconsin Awaits Nixon and Romney." *New York Times,* February 18, 1968, 49.

37. NA. "Johnson and Nixon Lead Poll." *New York Times,* February 22, 1968, 34.

38. NA. "Nixon Catches Up to Johnson in Poll." *New York Times,* February 25, 1968, 1.

39. George Gallup. "Nixon Gains As Rocky Slips." *Washington Post,* February 21, 1968, 1.

40. Buchanan, 212–213.

41. Weaver, Warren, Jr. "Romney Suddenly Quits: Rockefeller Affirms Availability to a Draft." *New York Times,* February 29, 1968, 1.

42. Ripley, Anthony. "Nixon Surprised by Romney News." *New York Times,* February 29, 1968, 22.

43. *Ibid.*

44. Buchanan, 212–213.

45. NA. "Reagan Says Position is Same: Not a Candidate." *Los Angeles Times,* February 29, 1968, 21.

46. UPI. "Reagan Sees Harm in Romney's Action." *Los Angeles Times,* 5 March 1968, 35.

47. Weaver, Warren, Jr. "Rockefeller Says that He Will Run if Asked by G.O.P." *New York Times,* March 2, 1968, 1.

48. "Memo from Pat Buchanan to Mr. Loeb." February 29, 1968. PJB.

49. Fenton, John H. "Primary Pot Boils in New Hampshire." *New York Times,* March 3, 1968, 37.

50. NA. "Poll Shows Nixon Leads Rockefeller." *New York Times,* March 4, 1968, 18.

51. Semple, Robert B., Jr. "Nixon Vows to End War with A New Leadership." *New York Times,* March 6, 1968, 11.

52. NA. "Nixon's War Policy Asked by Humphrey." *New York Times,* March 9, 1968, 16.

53. Semple, Robert B., Jr. "Nixon Withholds His Peace Ideas." *New York Times,* March 11, 1968, 1.

54. Weaver, Warren, Jr. "McCarthy Gets About 40%, Johnson and Nixon on Top in New Hampshire Voting." *New York Times,* March 13, 1968, 1.

55. "PJB Analysis of N.H." No Date. PJB.

Chapter 10

1. Kopelson, Gene. *Reagan's 1968 Dress Rehearsal: Reagan's Emergence as a World Statesman.* Figueroa Press: Los Angeles, California, 2016, 247–249.

2. Apple, R. W. "Friends Say Rockefeller Has Decided to Make Bid." *New York Times,* March 13, 1968, 1.

3. "Chicago, Illinois; Stevens Port, Wis.; Beloit College Rally, Wis.: Marshfield and Wisconsin Rapids, Wis." PPS 214, Box 35, Folder 5.

4. Reeves, Richard. "Governor to Run: He Will Disclose Plans Thursday." *New York Times,* March 19, 1964, 1.

5. Semple, Robert B., Jr. "Nixon Vows to End War with a New Leadership." *New York Times,* March 6, 1968, 11.

6. Apple, R.W., Jr. "Rockefeller Not to Run, But Would Accept Draft." *New York Times,* March 22, 1968, 1.

7. Reed, 141–142.

8. *Ibid.*

9. Broder, David S. "Miami Beach to Be Set Up for Reagan." *Washington Post,* March 26, 1968, 1.

10. Buchanan interview.

11. Gallup, George. "Poll Finds Nixon Leads President." *New York Times*, March 27, 1968, 32.

12. Chapin Interview.

13. Witcover, 267–268.

14. Smith, Richard Norton. *On His Own Terms: A Life of Nelson Rockefeller*. Random House: New York, 2014, 516–517.

15. Arnold, Martin. "Nixon Consults with Agnew." *New York Times*, March 30, 1968, 17.

16. Whalen, 134–142.

17. Buchanan, 232.

18. Wicker, Tom. "Johnson Says He Won't Run." *New York Times*, April 1, 1968, 1.

19. Buchanan, 232–233.

20. Spiegel, Irving. "Nixon Expecting Humphrey Race." *New York Times*, April 1, 1968, 27.

21. NA. "Primary Results in Wisconsin." *Washington Post*, April 4, 1968, 2.

22. Semple, Robert B. "Nixon's Strategy under Study; He May Cut Pace of Campaign." *New York Times*, April 4, 1968, 20.

23. Shadegg, 164–166.

24. NA. "Reagan is Doubtful on Nixon's Future." *New York Times*, April 6, 1968, 36.

25. Clarity, James F. "Rockefeller Hires Campaign Chief." *New York Times*, April 10, 1968, 1.

26. Shadegg, 141–142.

27. Chapin Interview.

28. "Hillings Memo to Nixon." April 3, 1968, PPS 501, Box 1.

29. "Nixon Letter to Reagan." April 4, 1968, PPS 501, Box 1.

30. "Reagan Letter to Nixon." April 10, 1968, PPS 501, Box 1.

31. Greenburg, Carl. "Reagan's Favorite Son Slate Will Get Strategist's Report." *Los Angeles Times*, April 12, 1968, 3.

32. "Goldwater Letter to Tom Reed." BG, FM MSS1, Box 18, Folder 7.

33. Gillam, Jerry. "Reagan Reassessing Chances in View of Increasing Support." *Los Angeles Times*, April 17, 1968, 1.

34. Just, Ward. "Nixon Urges Halt to Talks Criticism." *Washington Post*, April 20, 1968, A1.

35. Witcover, 288–289.

36. Buchanan, 245.

37. "Goldwater Letter to Kleindienst." BG, FM MSS1, Box 18, Folder 7.

38. Irwin, Don. "Nixon, Finch, Hold Nevada Conference." *Los Angeles Times*, April 24, 1968, 3.

39. Just, Ward. "Nixon Urges Program to Aid Black Capitalism." *Washington Post*, April 26, 1968, A1.

40. *Ibid.*

41. Irwin, Don. "Nixon Feels 'Very Up' After Western Swing." *Los Angeles Times*, April 27, 1968, 4.

42. Weaver, Warren, Jr. "Humphrey Joins Presidency Race; Calls for Unity." *New York Times*, April 28, 1968, 1.

43. NA. "Transcript of Governor Rockefeller's News Conference on Entering G.O.P. Race." *New York Times*, May 1, 1968, 36.

44. Witcover, 292.

45. NA. "Nixon Welcomes Rockefeller Entry." *New York Times*, May 1, 1968, 31.

46. Semple, Robert B., Jr. "Nixon Sees Peril in War Discussion." *New York Times*, May 4, 1968, 11.

47. Weaver, Warren, Jr. "Kennedy Wins in Indiana; Branigin Leads McCarthy; Nixon Draws Strong Vote." *New York Times*, May 8, 1968, 1.

48. Semple, Robert B., Jr. "Nebraska G.O.P. Applauds Nixon." *New York Times*, May 8, 1968, 27.

49. White, Theodore H. *The Making of the President 1960*. Giant Cardinal Edition, 5th Printing. Atheneum House: New York, 1962, 461.

50. NA. "Poll finds Rockefeller and Nixon Lead All Top Democratic Rivals." *New York Times*, May 12, 1968, 58.

51. Weaver, Warren, Jr. "Nebraska Gives 53% to Kennedy." *New York Times*, May 15, 1968, 1.

52. Irwin, Don. "Nixon Names Haldeman, L.A. Executive to Campaign Post." *Los Angeles Times*, May 19, 1968, 2B.

53. Kleindienst, 48.

54. Reed, 147.

55. "Untitled Memorandum, No Date." PPS 501, Box 1.

56. Weaver, Warren, Jr. "Nixon Only Primary Hurdle is Reagan in Oregon." *New York Times*, May 20, 1968, 38.

57. Broder, David S. "McCarthy, Reagan—Vital Test in Oregon." *Washington Post*, May 16, 1968, A1.

58. Weaver, Warren, Jr. "Nixon Only Primary Hurdle is Reagan in Oregon." *New York Times*, May 20, 1968, 38.

59. *Ibid.*

60. Janson, Donald. "Nixon Bids Columbia Oust 'Anarchic Students.'" *New York Times*, May 16, 1968, 38.

61. Buchanan, 256.

62. Roberts, Chalmer M. "Nixon Hits Rise in Crime." *Washington Post*, May 9, 1968, A1.

63. Fedderman, Stan. "Lindsey in Oregon for Rocky." *Washington Post*, May 25, 1968, A1.

64. "Bill Watts Memo to Emmet Hughes and Bob Douglas," May 27, 1968. Graham Molitor Papers, Nelson Rockefeller Archives (NR): Tarrytown, New York, Box 29.

65. Maffre, John. "Rocky Sees Strong Slate with Reagan." *Washington Post*, May 20, 1968, A1.

66. Apple, R.W., Jr. "Rockefeller Terms Nixon 'Legislator.'" *New York Times*, May 9, 1968, 32.

67. Aarons, Leroy F. "Rocky Sails into RFK and Nixon in Atlanta." *Washington Post*, May 25, 1968, A1.

68. "Reagan Memo to RN." May 20, 1968, PPS 501, Box 1.

69. Buchwald, Art. "Reagan's Rocky Road to

Peace and Presidency." *Los Angeles Times*, May 26, 1968, K7.

70. Greenburg, Carl. "Rumor of 'Deal' with Rockefeller Hurting Reagan." *Los Angeles Times*, May 13, 1968, 3.

71. Greenburg, Carl. "Reagan Says U.S. Should Threaten to Invade N. Vietnam." *Los Angeles Times*, May 20, 1968, 1.

72. Reed, 154.

73. "Excerpt from Ronald W. Reagan: Meet the Press," May 26, 1968. George Hinman Files, NR, Box 29, Folder 1711.

74. Janson, Donald. "Nixon: Still in Front." *New York Times*, May 19, 1968, 1.

75. Broder, David S. "Nixon Eyes Agnew as Running Mate." *Washington Post*, May 17, 1968, A1.

76. AP. "Nixon Victory in Tennessee." *New York Times*, May 26, 1968, 53.

77. Nixon, 303–304.

78. Roosevelt, Theodore. "The Man in the Arena." *Almanac of Theodore Roosevelt*. http://www.theodore-roosevelt.com/trsorbonnespeech.html.

79. Wilkinson, Jay with Gretchen Hirsch. *Bud Wilkinson: An Intimate Portrait of an American Legend.* Sagamore Publishing: Champaign, Illinois, 1994, 170.

80. Siler, Tom. "Rockne Crowned King of Coaches." *The Sporting News*, September 13, 1969, 51–52.

81. Irwin, Don. "Nixon Presses Oregon Drive with Telethon." *Los Angeles Times*, 27 May 1968, 9.

82. Davies, Lawrence E. "Nixon is a Strong Winner." *New York Times*, May 29, 1968, 1.

83. Weaver, Warren, Jr. "McCarthy Beats Kennedy in Oregon Primary Upset." *New York Times*, May 29, 1968, 1.

84. Davies, Lawrence E. "Nixon is a Strong Winner." *New York Times,* May 29, 1968, 1.

85. *Ibid.*

86. Reed, 159–160.

87. Nixon, 303.

88. Semple, Robert B., Jr. "Nixon's the Happy One." *New York Times*, June 2, 1968, E3.

89. Chriss, Nicholas. "Reagan's Texas Support Cut by Oregon Primary Showing." *Los Angeles Times*, May 31, 1968, 3.

90. Crespino, Joseph. *Strom Thurmond's America*. Hill and Wang: New York, 2012, 210–211.

91. Dent, Harry S. *The Prodigal South Returns to Power*. John Wiley & Sons: New York, 1978, 80–81.

92. Nixon, 305.

93. AP. "Nixon Backers Win Fla. GOP Control." *Washington Post*, June 2, 1968, A4.

94. Semple, Robert B., Jr. "Nixon Building Up Support in South." *New York Times*, June 2, 1968, 27.

95. AP. "Nixon Backers Win Fla. GOP Control." *Washington Post*, June 2, 1968, A4.

96. Witcover, 313.

97. Chester, Hodgsen, and Page, 351.

98. *Ibid.* 353.

99. Hill, Gladwin. "Kennedy is Dead, Victim of Assassin." *New York Times*, June 6, 1968, 1.

100. Buchanan interview.

Chapter 11

1. Buchanan interview.

2. UPI. *New York Times,* June 5, 1968, 32.

3. Herbers, John. "Gov. Agnew Hints a Swing to Nixon." *New York Times*, June 12, 1968, 29.

4. Kaufman, Michael T. "Nixons Take Over at Finch: B.A., LL.D. and a Speech." *New York Times*, June 15, 1968, 37.

5. AP. "Nixon is Bypassing Rockefeller Drive, Aims at November." *New York Times*, June 17, 1968, 29.

6. White, Theodore H. *The Making of the President 1968*. Pocket Books: New York, 1970, 176–177.

7. "H. R. Haldeman's Handwritten Notes on Topics Including but Not Limited to: RN, campaign/political operations, etc., No Date. WHSF Collection, Box 34, Folder 3.

8. Semple, Robert B., Jr. "Nixon Preparing to Court 7 or 8 Industrial States." *New York Times*, June 21, 1968, 20.

9. NA. "Reagan Delegation Not Dented by Rockefeller, Salvatori Says." *Los Angeles Times*, June 14, 1968, 3.

10. Staff Writer. "Agnew Raps Rocky on Lack of Views." *Washington Post*, June 14, 1968, A1.

11. Semple, Robert B., Jr. "12,000 See Nixon at Coast Meeting." New York Times, July 22, 1968, 29.

12. Shadegg, 191–192.

13. Jay, Peter A. "Agnew Meets Nixon in N.Y., Then Blasts March of Poor." *Washington Post*, June 21, 1968, B1.

14. Apple, R.W., Jr. "Rockefeller Scores Nixon on Vietnam." *New York Times*, June 21, 1968, 30.

15. Witcover, 319.

16. *Ibid.*

17. Apple, R.W., Jr. "Rockefeller Calls Wallace a 'Racist' and Taunts Nixon." *New York Times*, June 23, 1968, 1.

18. "Racism." Graham T. Molitor Papers, RA, Box 21, Folder 613.

19. Witcover, 320.

20. *Ibid.*, 321.

21. Wicker, Tom. "Reagan Questions Motive for Warren's Retirement." *New York Times*, June 24, 1968, 1.

22. Graham, Fred P. "Johnson Appoints Fortas to Head Supreme Court; Thornberry to Justice." *New York Times*, June 27, 1968, 1.

23. "Memo to RN." June 25, 1968, PJB.

24. *Ibid.*

25. *Ibid.*

26. *Ibid.*

27. *Ibid.*

28. Janson, Donald. "Rhodes Will Keep Delegation Open." *New York Times*, July 1, 1968, 24.

29. Witcover, 321.

30. Reed, 167–168.

31. Greenburg, Carl. "Reagan's Name May Be Placed in Nomination before Nixon's." *Los Angeles Times*, July 5, 1968, 3.

32. Semple, Robert B., Jr. "Eisenhower Backs Nixon, Praising His Experience." *New York Times*, July 19, 1968, 1.

33. Semple, Robert B., Jr. "12,000 See Nixon at Coast Meeting." *New York Times*, July 22, 1968, 29.

34. Bergholt, Richard. "Nixon in L.A., Says He Will Select His Own Running Mate." *Los Angeles Times*, July 21, 1968, E23.

35. NA. "Nixon Makes TV Film." *New York Times*, July 21, 1968, 38.

36. Semple, Robert B., Jr. "12,000 See Nixon at Coast Meeting." *New York Times*, July 22, 1968, 29.

37. AP. "Goldwater Opens Drive for Nixon." *New York Times*, July 25, 1968, 21.

38. Just, Ward. "Nixon Expected to Choose Liberal Running Mate." *Washington Post*, July 21, 1968, 1.

39. Greenburg, Carl. "Reagan Says GOP Nominees Should Have Similar Views." *Los Angeles Times*, July 22, 1968, 1.

40. Shadegg, 196.

41. Evans, Rowland and Robert Novak. "'Gossamer Screen' Still Separates Nixon from First Ballot Nomination." *Washington Post*, July 24, 1968, A17.

42. Weaver, Warren, Jr. "Percy Endorses Rockefeller Bid for President." *New York Times*, July 26, 1968, 1.

43. Buckley, William F., Jr. "Now for a Vice President..." *Los Angeles Times*, July 31, 1968, A5.

44. Semple, Robert B., Jr. "President Gives Briefings to Nixon and Wallace." *New York Times*, July 27, 1968, 10.

45. Nixon, 308.

46. Semple, Robert B., Jr. "President Gives Briefings to Nixon and Wallace." *New York Times*, July 27, 1968, 10.

47. NA. "Nixon Polls 60% With G.O.P. Voters." July 28, 1968, 49.

48. Broder, David S. "Poll Jolts Stop-Nixon Drive; Rocky Camp Glum." *Washington Post*, July 30, 1968, A1.

49. Apple, R.W., Jr. "Harris Poll Gives Rockefeller a Lift." *New York Times*, August 1, 1968, 1.

50. Witcover, 331.

51. Clarity, James F. "G.O.P. Rivals Note 'Incredible' Polls." *New York Times*, August 1, 1968, 16.

52. *Ibid.*

53. *Ibid.*

54. Buchanan interview.

55. White, 278.

56. Kleindienst, 53.

57. Dent, 92–93.

58. Weaver, Warren, Jr. "Nixon Said to Want Rockefeller, Lindsay, or Percy for 2d Place." *New York Times*, August 4, 1968, 1.

59. Just, Ward. "Nixon Expected to Choose Liberal Running Mate." *Washington Post*, July 21, 1968, 1.

60. Roberts, Chalmer. "Reagan Declares Candidacy, Nixon is Endorsed by Agnew." *Washington Post*, August 6, 1968, A1.

61. Dent, 92–93.

62. Hill, Gladwin. "Reagan Officially in Race; Acts to Bar Nixon Sweep." *New York Times*, August 6, 1968, 1.

63. Homan, Richard. "Agnew Gives Nixon 16 Backers." *Washington Post*, August 6, 1968, A1.

64. Semple, Robert B., Jr. "Nixon Makes New Gain as Republicans Convene." *New York Times*, August 6, 1968, 1.

65. Roberts, Chalmer. "Reagan Declares Candidacy, Nixon is Endorsed by Agnew." *Washington Post*, August 6, 1968, A1.

66. Dent, 96–97.

67. *Ibid.*, 97–98.

68. Shadegg, 205–206.

69. Chapman, William. "2 Rivals Press Fight." *Washington Post*, August 7, 1968, A1.

70. Nelson, Jack. "Thurmond Stops Reagan, Holds South for Nixon." *Los Angeles Times*, August 7, 1968, O1.

71. Evans, Rowland and Robert Novak. "Thurmond Helps Nixon Forces Prevent Fla. Bolt." *Washington Post*, August 9, 1968, A21.

72. Chester, Hodgson, and Page, 466.

73. *Ibid.*, 457.

74. Auerbach, Stuart. "Ike's Condition 'Serious' After Heart Attack." *Washington Post*, August 7, 1968, A1.

75. Wicker, Tom. "Nixon is Nominated on the First Ballot." *New York Times*, August 8, 1968, 1.

76. *Ibid.*

77. Theodore H. White. Video of *The Making of the President 1968*.

78. White, 291–295.

79. "Congressional Files, 1963–1971: Subseries: Congressional File, Box 1. George H.W. Bush Presidential Library (GHWB).

80. White, 293.

81. Chester, Hodgson, and Page, 487.

82. Pearson, Drew. *Washington Merry Go Round: The Drew Pearson Diaries, 1960–1969*. University of Nebraska Press: Lincoln, Nebraska, 2015, 600.

83. Chester, Hodgson, and Page, 487.

84. Witcover, 354.

85. Chester, Hodgson, and Page, 488–489.

86. Witcover, 354–355.

87. *Ibid.*

88. Hill, Gladwin. "Reagan Cheerful Despite Setback." *New York Times*, August 9, 1968, 18.

89. Apple, R.W., Jr. "Rockefeller Aides Bitter over Agnew." *New York Times*, August 9, 1968, 19.

90. Wicker, Tom. "Rebels Put Down." *New York Times*, August 9, 1968, 1.

91. Nixon, Richard M. "Address Accepting the Presidential Nomination at the Republican National Convention in Miami Beach, Florida." August 8, 1968.

92. *Ibid.*

93. Gavin interview.

Chapter 12

1. Weaver, Warren, Jr. "Johnson to Brief Nixon and Agnew on Talks in Paris." *New York Times*, August 10, 1968, 1.

2. Phone interview with John Sears by the author, November 2, 2017.

3. Weaver, Warren, Jr. "Johnson to Brief Nixon and Agnew on Talks in Paris." *New York Times*, August 10, 1968, 1.

4. *Ibid.*

5. Semple, Robert B., Jr. "Nixon Defends His Choice." *New York Times*, August 10, 1968, 1.

6. "Memorandum for the President from Bob Fleming." August 19, 1968. White House Famous Names, Service Set. Lyndon Baines Johnson Presidential Library and Museum (LBJ): Austin, Texas, Box 8. Nordliner, Stephen F. "President Briefs Nixon and Agnew." *Baltimore Sun*, August 11, 1968, 1.

7. Jones, David R. "Nixon and Agnew Meet President for War Briefing." *New York Times*, August 11, 1968, 1.

8. Ambrose, 179.

9. Semple, Robert B., Jr. "Politics: 5 Million Workers Sought." *New York Times*, August 13, 1968, 27.

10. Irwin, Don. "Reagan to Help Nixon Campaign in California." *Los Angeles Times*, August 17, 1968, 3.

11. Whalen, 211–212.

12. "Buchanan Memo," August 15, 1968. PJB.

13. Irwin, Don. "Nixon Ends Visit to Southland on Optimistic Note." *Los Angeles Times*, August 19, 1968, 3.

14. Hoffman, David. "Romney to Stump for Nixon-Agnew." *Washington Post*, August 20, 1968, A1.

15. Witcover, 370.

16. *Ibid.*

17. Shafer and Scranton to Aid Nixon." *Washington Post*, August 21, 1968, A7.

18. Gallup, George. "Nixon Leads Democratic Rivals in First Test Since G.O.P Convention." *Washington Post*, August 21, 1968, A21.

19. Buchanan, 320–321.

20. NA. "Soviet Invasion Scored by Nixon." *New York Times*, August 22, 1968, 20.

21. Hoffman, David. "Rocky, Lindsay and Brooke to Aid Nixon." *Washington Post*, August 22, 1968, A2.

22. Safire, 60.

23. Michael Nelson. *Resilient America: Electing Nixon in 1968, Channeling Dissent, and Dividing Government*. University of Kansas Press: Lawrence, Kansas, 2014, 161–162.

24. Buchanan, 323–324.

25. Safire, 60.

26. Buchanan, 325.

27. Safire, 60.

28. Buchanan, 324.

29. Connally, John with Mickey Herskowitz. *In History's Shadow: An American Odyssey*. Hyperion: New York, 1991, 203.

30. Nelson, 166–167.

31. *Ibid.*, 170–171.

32. Chester, Hodgson, and Page, 585–586.

33. Buchanan, 327.

34. White, 1968, 398–399.

35. Safire, 61–62.

36. *Ibid.*, 62.

37. White, 1968, 386–387.

38. "Trends in Party Identification, 1939–2014." Pew Research Center. http://www.people-press-org/interactives/party-id-trend/.

39. Sears interview.

40. "To RN from John Sears," July 19, 1968. WHSF, Box 33, Folder 12.

41. Klein, Herbert G. *Making It Perfectly Clear*. New York: Doubleday & Company, 1980, 17–18.

42. Semple, Robert B., Jr. "Associates of Nixon Delighted by Rifts in Democratic Parley." *New York Times*, August 29, 1968, 27.

43. NA. "Johnson Rating Reaches New Low in Gallup Poll." *New York Times*, September 11, 1968, 30.

44. "Rose Mary Woods Memorandum from Bob Haldeman," September 6, 1968. WHSF, Box 35, Folder 11.

45. Buchanan Memo, August 1968, PJB Personal Collection.

46. *Ibid.*

47. Irwin, Don. "Nixon Receives Big Chicago Welcome." *Los Angeles Times*, September 5, 1968, 1.

48. Irwin, Don. "25,000 Applaud Nixon's Speech in Santa Clara." *Los Angeles Times*, September 6, 1968, 3.

49. NA. "Nixon Denounces Humphrey Views." *New York Times*, September 7, 1968, 1.

50. Sears interview.

51. NA. Republican Runs Ahead in Gallup Poll, 43–31, a Slight Decline." *New York Times*, September 15, 1968, 1.

52. Semple, Robert B., Jr. "Nixon Sees Plot by Rivals in South." New York Times, September 18, 1968, 1.

53. Seelye, Howard. "More Than 3,000 Greet Nixon on His Return to Birthplace." *Los Angeles Times*, September 17, 1968, F1.

54. Chapin Interview.

55. NA. "Nixon Promises to Head Dissent in Making Policy." *New York Times*, September 20, 1968, 1.

56. Nelson, 180.

57. NA. "Survey Finds Nixon Landslide

Winner." *New York Times*, September 24, 1968, 35.

58. NA. "Nixon 43%, Humphrey 28, Wallace 21." *Washington Post*, September 27, 1968, A1.

59. Evans, Rowland and Novak, Robert. "Concerned Nixon Assigns Adviser to Oversee Agnew's Campaigning." *Washington Post*, September 19, 1968, 25.

60. Sears Interview.

Chapter 13

1. Longley, Kyle. *LBJ's 1968: Power, Politics, and the Presidency in America's Year of Upheaval.* Cambridge University Press: New York, 2018, 165.

2. Nelson, 201.

3. Bass, Jack and Marilyn W. Thompson. *Ol' Strom: An Unauthorized Biography of Strom Thurmond.* Longstreet Press: Marietta, Georgia, 1998, 213–216.

4. Nelson, 202.

5. White, 1968, 413.

6. Buchanan interview.

7. Shadegg, 254–255.

8. Buchanan interview.

9. "Lyndon Johnson and Hubert H. Humphrey on 30 September 1968." Johnson Administration, Conversation WH6809-04-13435, Miller Center, University of Virginia.

10. Chapin interview.

11. Shadegg, 256.

12. *Ibid.*

13. Rugaber, Walter. "Gen. LeMay Joins Wallace's Ticket as Running Mate." *New York Times*, October 4, 1968, 1.

14. *Ibid.*, 75.

15. Witcover, 408–409.

16. Kenworthy, E. W. "Nixon Strategy in South: Humphrey Attack on Wallace Causes G.O.P. Nominee to Shift His Tactics." *New York Times*, October 5, 1968, 20.

17. Flint, Jerry. "Wallace Wins Over Humphrey in Auto Union Poll, 49% to 32%." *New York Times*, October 6, 1968, 75.

18. Millones, Peter. "Humphrey Leads in Labor Poll, 34–32." New York Times, October 9, 1968, 1.

19. "Conversation with Lyndon Johnson and Richard Daley, Telephone Operator and Office Secretary." October 7, 1968. Number 13518, Miller Center, University of Virginia.

20. Sheehan, Neil. "Present Says G.O.P. Threaten Domestic Gains." *New York Times*, October 11, 1968, 1.

21. Black, 548.

22. NA. "Gallup Poll Finds Nixon Maintaining Large Lead." *New York Times*, October 10, 1968, 51.

23. ABC News, October 10, 1968. "Wallace-LeMay Trip," Vanderbilt News Archives, Vanderbilt Libraries, https://tvnews.vanderbilt.edu/broadcasts/28.

24. Safire, 76.

25. Oberdorfer, Don. "Nixon is Preparing Three-Week Blitz." *Washington Post*, October 15, 1968, A1.

26. Nixon, 325.

27. *Ibid.*

28. Fox, Sylvan. "Johnson Shares Dais Here with Nixon and Humphrey." *New York Times*, October 17, 1968, 1.

29. NA. "2 Accept Medals Wearing Black Gloves." *New York Times*, October 17, 1968, 59.

30. Witcover, 420.

31. Phalon, Richard. "Humphrey Gains in Harris Poll." *New York Times*, October 19, 1968, 11.

32. NA. "Texas Governor Announces Plans for Campaigning with Humphrey." *Washington Post*, October 19, 1968, A3.

33. NA. "Life Magazine Endorses Nixon; Warns of Peril in Wallace Vote." *New York Times*, October 20, 1968, 75.

34. NA. "Gallup Polls Shows a Humphrey Gain; Nixon Leads 43–31." *New York Times*, October 22, 1968, 1.

35. CBS News, October 21, 1968. "CBS Poll," Vanderbilt News Archives, Vanderbilt University Libraries, https://tvnews.vanderbilt.edu/broadcasts/198036.

36. ABC Evening News, October 21, 1968. "Commentary (Ideal President)," Vanderbilt News Archives, Vanderbilt University Libraries, https://tvnews.Vanderbilt.edu/broadcasts/190.

37. Buchanan interview.

38. Apple, R.W., Jr. "Nixon Intensifies Blows of Humphrey on Ohio Train Tour." *New York Times*, October 23, 1968, 1.

39. *Ibid.*

40. ABC Evening News, October 23, 1968. "Humphrey Texas Story," Vanderbilt News Archives, Vanderbilt University Libraries, https://tvnews.vanderbilt.edu/broadcasts/219.

41. NA. "Who's Taking the Low Road Now?" *Los Angeles Times*, October 25, 1968, C6.

42. Nixon, 326.

43. *Ibid.*

44. Semple, Robert B., Jr. "Nixon Asserts Humphrey Confuses Vietnam Talks." *New York Times*, October 24, 1968, 1.

45. ABC Evening News, October 24, 1968. "Commentary (Ideal President)," Vanderbilt News Archives, Vanderbilt University Libraries, https://tvnews.vanderbilt.edu/broadcasts/28.

46. Black, 553.

47. Nixon, 327–328.

48. Sheehan, Neil. "Johnson Calls Nixon 'Unfair' in Implying Cynical Peace." *New York Times*, October 28, 1968, 1.

49. Apple, R.W., Jr. "Nixon Would Bar Forced Coalition in South Vietnam." *New York Times*, October 28, 1968, 1.

50. NA. "Nixon Assails the Times for Editorial on Agnew." *New York Times*, October 28, 1968, 39.

51. NA. "Times Replies to Nixon Charge on the

Sale of Land by Agnew." New York Times, October 29, 1968, 34.

52. CBS News, October 28, 1968. "CBS Poll," Vanderbilt News Archives, Vanderbilt University Libraries, https://tvnews.vanderbilt.edu/broadcasts/198137.

53. ABC Evening News, October 29, 1968. "Election/Jimmy Snyder," Vanderbilt News Archives, Vanderbilt University Libraries, https://tvnews.vanderbilt.edu/broadcasts/296.

54. Herbers, John. "McCarthy Backs Humphrey Race; His Plans Vague." New York Times, October 30, 1968, 1.

55. AP. "Christian Science Monitor Says Nixon Wins in Survey." New York Times, October 31, 1968, 30.

56. Public Papers of the Presidents of the U.S: Lyndon B. Johnson, 1968–69. Volume II, Entry 572, pp. 1049–1103. Washington D.C.: Government Printing Office, 1970.

57. Semple, Robert B., Jr. "Nixon Hopes Johnson's Step Will Aid the Talks in Paris." New York Times, November 1, 1968, 1.

58. "Phone Call from Lyndon Johnson to Richard Nixon." November 3, 1968. Transcript for Foreign Relations of the United States, 1964–1968 Volume VII, Vietnam, September 1968 to January 1969, Document 187.

59. Kenworthy, E.W. "Nixon in Texas, Sharpens His Attack." New York Times, November 3, 1968, 1.

60. Ibid.

61. ABC Evening News, November 4, 1968, "Election/Polls," Vanderbilt News Archives, Vanderbilt University Libraries, https://tvnews.vanderbilt.edu/broadcasts/738.

62. "Fred Panzer to Jim Jones." November 4, 1968. White House Famous Names, Service Set, LBJ, Box 8.

63. Wicker, Tom. "Nation Will Vote Today; Close Presidential Race Predicted in Late Polls." New York Times, November 5, 1968, 1.

64. Greenburg, Carl. "Nixon, Humphrey Will End Campaigns in L.A." Los Angeles Times, November 2, 1968, A1.

65. AP. "Eisenhower Issues New Nixon Appeal." New York Times, November 5, 1968, 29.

66. Safire, 93.

67. Nixon, 330–331.

68. Ibid., 333.

69. Chapin interview.

70. Nixon, 335.

Chapter 14

1. Walter Cronkite. "CBS News Special Report: August 9, 1974.

2. "President Nixon Resignation Address." August 8, 1974. C-Span Video Library. Washington, D.C.

3. Ambrose, 1987, 290.

4. Smith, 290–293.

5. Ambrose, 1989, 16.

6. Wilderness Years: Series VI: Legal Papers: 1963–1967: PPS 253, Box 1. The general counsel to the players was pitched to Nixon by Robin Roberts. See pages 222–223 of Roberts' memoir entitled Throwing Hard Easy: Reflections on a Life in Baseball.

7. Ambrose, 1989, 16.

8. Newport, Frank, David Moore, and Lydia Saad. "Most Admired Men and Women: 1948–1998. Gallup News Service. http://news.gallup.com/poll/3415/most-admired-men-women-1948-1998.

9. Chapin interview.

10. Harry Dent interview with James Rosen. March 2, 1992. (JR), Box 50, Folder 11. Northwestern University, Evanston, Illinois.

11. "Transcript Speech Given by RN at Bohemian Grove. (WHSF) Box 1, Folder 5.

12. Nixon, Richard. "What Has Happened to America?" Readers Digest, October 1967, 49–54.

13. Sears interview.

14. Aitken, 356.

15. Boyd, James. "Nixon's Southern Strategy." New York Times, May 17, 1970, 215.

16. Buchanan interview.

17. White, 1969, 493.

Bibliography

Archival Material

Barry Goldwater collection at Arizona State University, Tempe, Arizona.

Center for Oral History (Eisenhower Collection) at Columbia University, New York.

Dwight D. Eisenhower Library in Abilene, Kansas.

George H. W. Bush Presidential Library in College Station, Texas.

George Romney collection at the University of Michigan, Ann Arbor, Michigan.

Gerald R. Ford Presidential Library in Ann Arbor, Michigan.

Harry S. Truman Library in Independence, Missouri.

Herbert Klein collection at the University of Southern California, Los Angeles, California.

Howard K. Smith collection at Wisconsin Archives, Madison, Wisconsin.

James Rosen collection at Northwestern University, Evanston, Illinois.

Lyndon B. Johnson Presidential Library in Austin, Texas.

Nixon Alumni Oral Histories compiled by John Whitaker, Chevy Chase, Maryland.

The Nixon/Gannon Interviews at the University of Georgia, Athens, Georgia.

Patrick J. Buchanan personal collection of memos from 1966–1968, McLean, Virginia.

Richard Nixon Oral Histories at California State Fullerton, Fullerton, California.

Richard Nixon Presidential Library in Yorba Linda, California.

Rockefeller Center Archives in Tarrytown, New York.

Vanderbilt Television News Archive in Nashville, Tennessee.

William Safire collection at the Library of Congress, Washington, D.C.

Interviews

Aram Bakshian, Jr.
Patrick J. Buchanan
Shelley Scarney Buchanan
Steve Bull
Dwight Chapin
Neal Freeman
William Gavin
Stephen Hess
Lee Huebner
Tom Charles Huston
Kenneth Khachigan
Bobbie Kilberg
Francis X. Maloney
Ed Nixon
Robert Odle
Raymond Price
Sandy Quinn
John Sears
Geoff Shepard
Craig Shirley
John Whitaker

Books

Aitken, Jonathan. *Nixon: A Life*. Washington, D.C.: Regnery Publishing, 1993.

Ambrose, Stephen E. *Nixon: Volume 1—The Education of a Politician, 1913–1962*. New York: Simon & Schuster, 1987.

Ambrose, Stephen E. *Nixon: Volume 2—The Triumph of a Politician, 1962–1972*. New York: Simon & Schuster, 1989.

Bass, Jack, and Thompson, Marilyn W. *Ol' Strom: An Unauthorized Biography of Strom Thurmond*. Marietta, Georgia: Longstreet Press, 1998.

Black, Conrad. *Richard M. Nixon*. New York: Public Affairs, 2007.

Bobst, Elmer H. *Bobst: The Autobiography of a Pharmaceutical Pioneer*. New York: David McKay Company, 1973.

Buchanan, Patrick J. *The Greatest Comeback: How Richard Nixon Rose from Defeat to Create the New Majority*. New York: Crown Forum Books. 2014.

Buchanan, Patrick J. *Nixon White House Wars: The Battles That Made and Broke a President and Divided America Forever*. New York: Crown Forum Books, 2017.

Califano, Joseph A. *The Triumph and Tragedy of Lyndon Johnson: The White House Years*. New York: Touchstone, 2015.

Caro, Robert A. *The Years of Lyndon Johnson: The Path to Power.* New York: Random House, 1981.

Chester, Lewis, Godfrey Hodgson, and Bruce Page. *An American Melodrama: The Presidential Campaign of 1968.* New York: Viking Press, 1969.

Connally, John, with Mickey Herskowitz. *In History's Shadow: An American Odyssey.* New York: Hyperion, 1991.

Crespino, Joseph. *Strom Thurmond's America.* New York: Hill and Wang, 2012.

Dent, Harry S. *The Prodigal South Returns to Power.* New York: John Wiley & Sons, 1978.

Eisenhower, Julie Nixon. *Pat Nixon: The Untold Story.* New York: Simon & Schuster, 1986.

Evans, M. Stanton, and Herbert Romerstein. *Stalin's Secret Agents: The Subversion of Roosevelt's Government.* New York: Threshold Edition, Simon & Schuster, 2012.

Frank, Jeffrey. *Ike and Dick: Portrait of a Strange Political Marriage.* New York: Simon & Schuster, 2013.

Garment, Leonard. *Crazy Rhythm: My Journey from Brooklyn, Jazz, and Wall Street to Nixon's White House, Watergate, and Beyond.* New York: Times Books, 1997.

Gavin, William F. *Speechwright: An Insider's Take on Political Rhetoric.* East Lansing, Michigan: Michigan State University Press, 2012.

Gellman, Irwin F. *The Contender: Richard Nixon, The Congress Years 1946–1952.* New York: The Free Press, 1999.

Gellman, Irwin F. *The President and the Apprentice: Eisenhower and Nixon, 1952–1961.* New Haven, Connecticut: Yale University Press, 2015.

Graham, Billy. *Just As I Am.* New York: Harper and Row, Revised Edition, 2001.

Hess, Stephen, and David S. Broder. *The Republican Establishment.* New York: Harper & Row, 1967.

Hillings, Patrick J., with Howard Seelye. *The Irrepressible Irishman: A Republican Insider.* Harold D. Dean, Publisher, 1994.

Kabaservice, Geoffrey. *Rule and Ruin: The Downfall of Moderation and the Destruction of the Republican Party from Eisenhower to the Tea Party.* New York: Oxford University Press, 2012.

Kallina, Edmund F., Jr. *Kennedy v. Nixon: The Presidential Election of 1960.* Gainesville, Florida: University of Florida Press, 2010.

Klein, Herbert G. *Making It Perfectly Clear.* New York: Doubleday & Company, 1980.

Kleindienst, Richard G. *Justice: The Memoirs of an Attorney General.* Ottawa, Illinois: Jameson Books, 1985.

Kopelson, Gene. *Reagan's 1968 Dress Rehearsal: Reagan's Emergence as a World Statesman.* Los Angeles, California: Figueroa Press, 2016.

Kornitzer, Bela. *The Real Nixon: An Intimate Biography.* New York: Rand McNally and Company, 1960.

Li, Victor. *Nixon in New York: How Wall Street Helped Richard Nixon Win the White House.* Lanham, Maryland: Rowman and Littlefield, 2018.

Longley, Kyle. *LBJ's 1968: Power, Politics, and the Presidency in America's Year of Upheaval.* New York: Cambridge University Press, 2018.

Miller, Marvin. *A Whole Different Ball Game: The Inside Story of the Baseball Revolution.* Chicago, Illinois: Ivan R. Dee Publishing, 2004.

Murphy, Bruce Allen. *Fortas: The Rise and Ruin of a Supreme Court Justice.* New York: William Morrow and Company, 1988.

Nelson, Michael. *Resilient America: Electing Nixon in 1968, Channeling Dissent, and Dividing Government.* Lawrence, Kansas: University of Kansas Press, 2014.

Nixon, Richard M. *The Memoirs of Richard Nixon.* New York: Grosset and Dunlap, 1978.

Nofziger, Lyn. *Nofziger.* Regnery Gateway: Washington, D.C., 1992.

Parmet, Herbert S. *Richard Nixon and His America.* New York: Konecky & Konecky, 1990.

Pearson, Drew. *Washington Merry Go Round: The Drew Pearson Diaries, 1960–1969.* Lincoln, Nebraska: University of Nebraska Press, 2015.

Perlstein, Rick. *Before the Storm.* New York: Simon & Schuster, 2001.

Pope, Philip H. Unpublished Dissertation: *"Foundations of Nixonian Foreign Policy": The Pre-Presidential Years of Richard M. Nixon, 1946–1968.* University of Southern California, August 1988.

Reed, Thomas C. *The Reagan Enigma: 1964–1980.* Los Angeles, California: Figueroa Press, 2014.

Roberts, Robin, with C. Paul Rogers III. *Throwing Hard Easy: Reflections on a Life in Baseball.* Lincoln, Nebraska: University of Nebraska Press, 2003.

Rosen, James. *The Strong Man: John Mitchell and the Secrets of Watergate.* New York: Doubleday, 2008.

Rusher, William A. *The Rise of the Right.* New York: National Review, 1993.

Safire, William. *Before the Fall: An Inside View of the Pre-Watergate White House.* New York: Tower Publications, 1975.

Schoen, Douglas E. *The Nixon Effect: How the Nixon Presidency Fundamentally Changed American Politics.* New York: Encounter Books, 2016.

Shadegg, Stephen C. *Winning's a Lot More Fun.* London: The Macmillan Company, 1970.

Sherman, Gabriel. *The Loudest Voice in the Room: How the Brilliant, Bombastic Roger Ailes Built Fox News—And Divided the Country.* New York: Random House, 2014.

Smith, Howard K. *Events Leading Up to My Death: The Life of a Twentieth Century Reporter.* New York: St. Martin's Press, 1996.

Smith, Jean Edward. *Eisenhower in War and Peace.* New York: Random House, 2012.

Smith, Richard Norton. *On His Own Terms: A Life of Nelson Rockefeller.* New York: Random House, 2014.

Stans, Maurice H. *The Terrors of Justice: The Untold Side of Watergate.* New York: Everest House Publishers. 1978.

Whalen, Richard J. *Catch the Falling Flag: A Republican's Challenge to His Party.* New York: Houghton-Mifflin, 1972.

White, Theodore H. *The Making of the President 1960.* New York: Atheneum House, 1961.

White, Theodore H. *The Making of the President 1960.* Giant Cardinal Edition, 5th Printing. New York: Atheneum House, 1962.

White, Theodore H. *The Making of the President 1964.* New York: Atheneum House, 1965.

White, Theodore H. *The Making of the President 1968.* New York: Pocket Books, 1970.

Wilkinson, Jay, with Gretchen Hirsch. *Bud Wilkinson: An Intimate Portrait of an American Legend.* Champaign, Illinois: Sagamore Publishing, 1994.

Wilson, James Q., and John J. DiIluio. *American Government: Institutions & Policies, The Essentials.* Stamford, Connecticut: Cengage Learning, 2004.

Witcover, Jules. *The Resurrection of Richard Nixon.* New York: G. P. Putnam's Sons, 1970.

Witcover, Jules. *Very Strange Bedfellows: The Short and Unhappy Marriage of Richard Nixon and Spiro Agnew.* New York: Public Affairs, 2007.

Index

www.ingramcontent.com/pod-product-compliance
Lightning Source LLC
Chambersburg PA
CBHW081737270326
41932CB00020B/3302